Sew beside the Sea

Mollie Winters
mollie.winters@hotmail.co.uk

YINKA SHONIBARE MBE

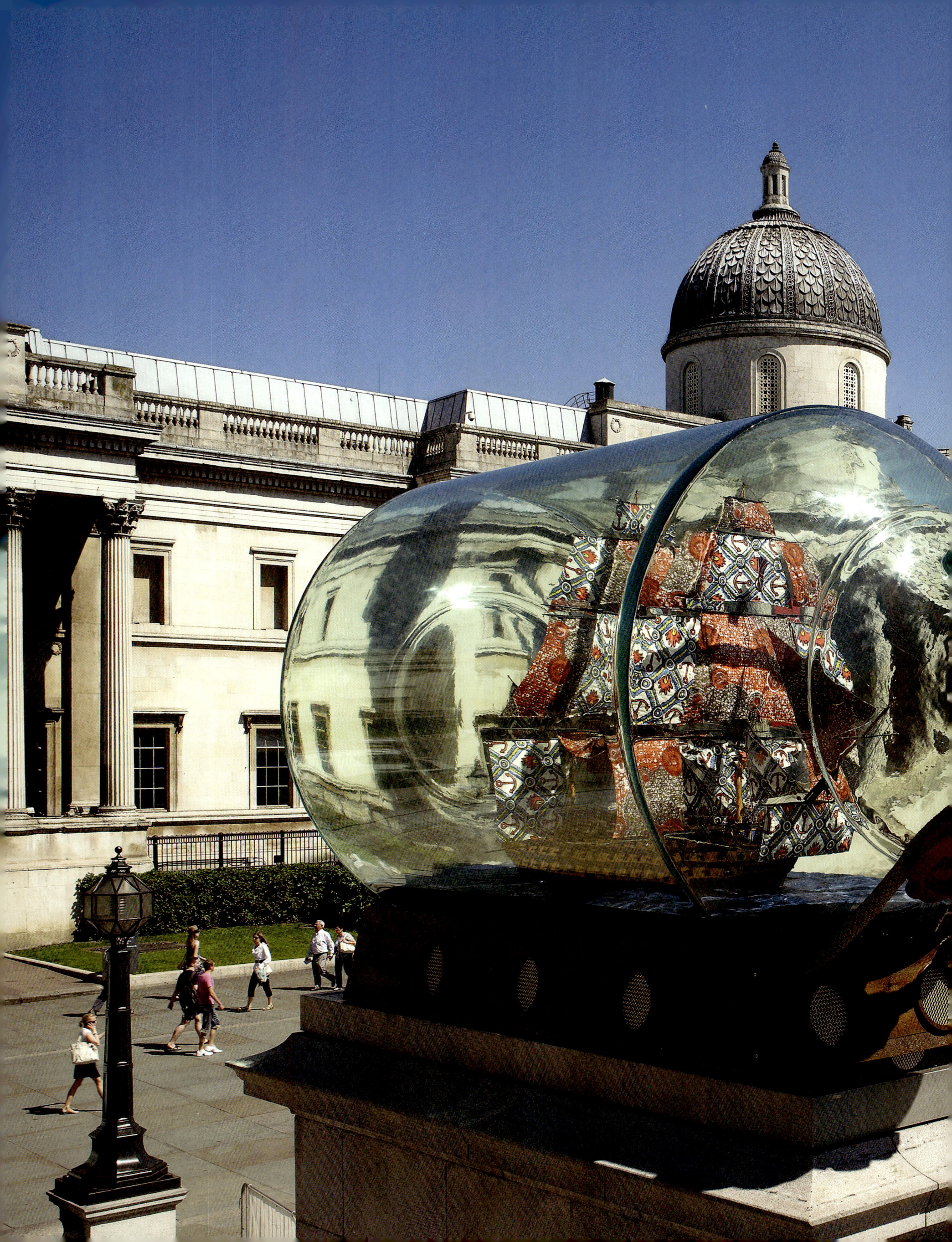

YINKA SHONIBARE MBE

Edited by Rachel Kent

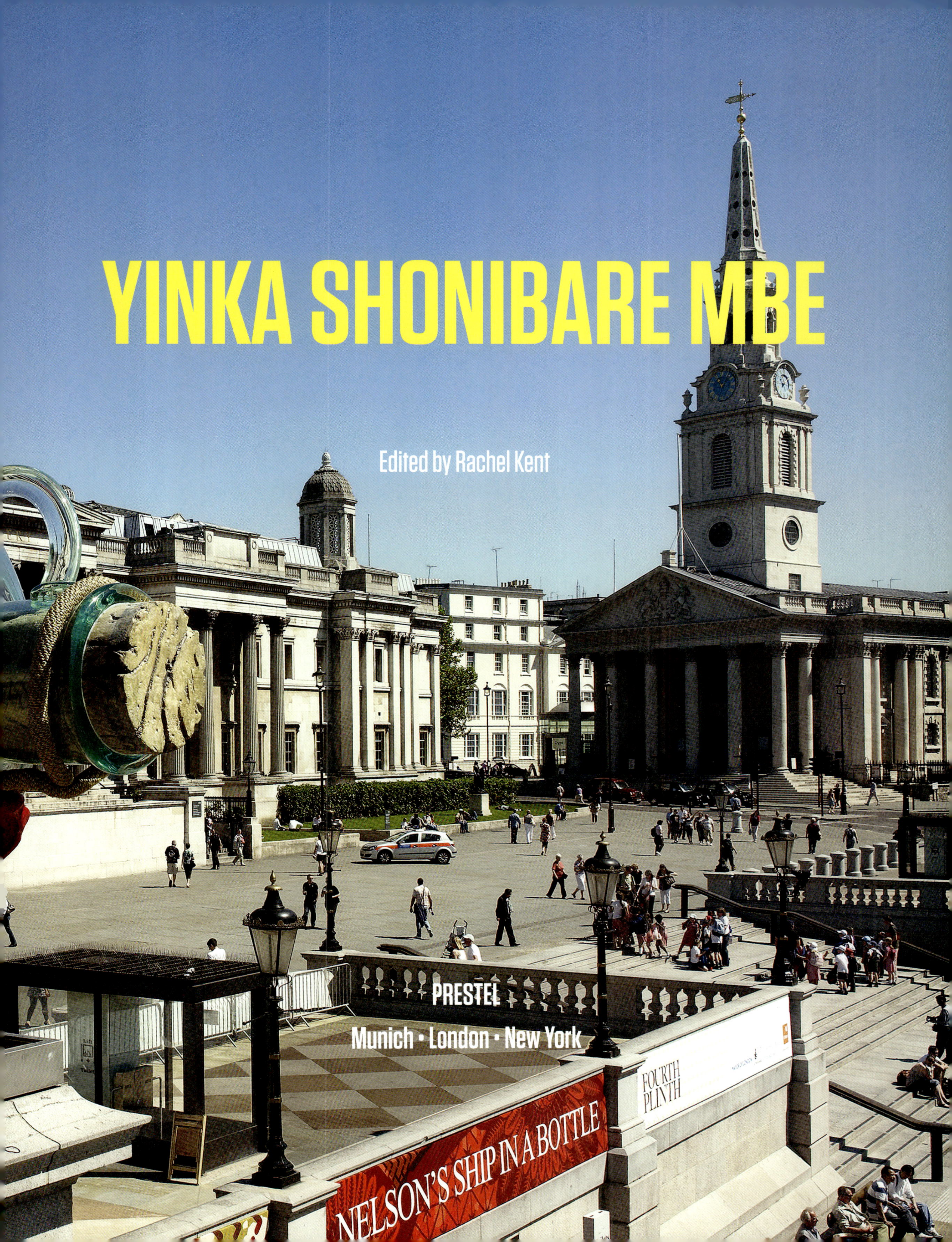

PRESTEL
Munich · London · New York

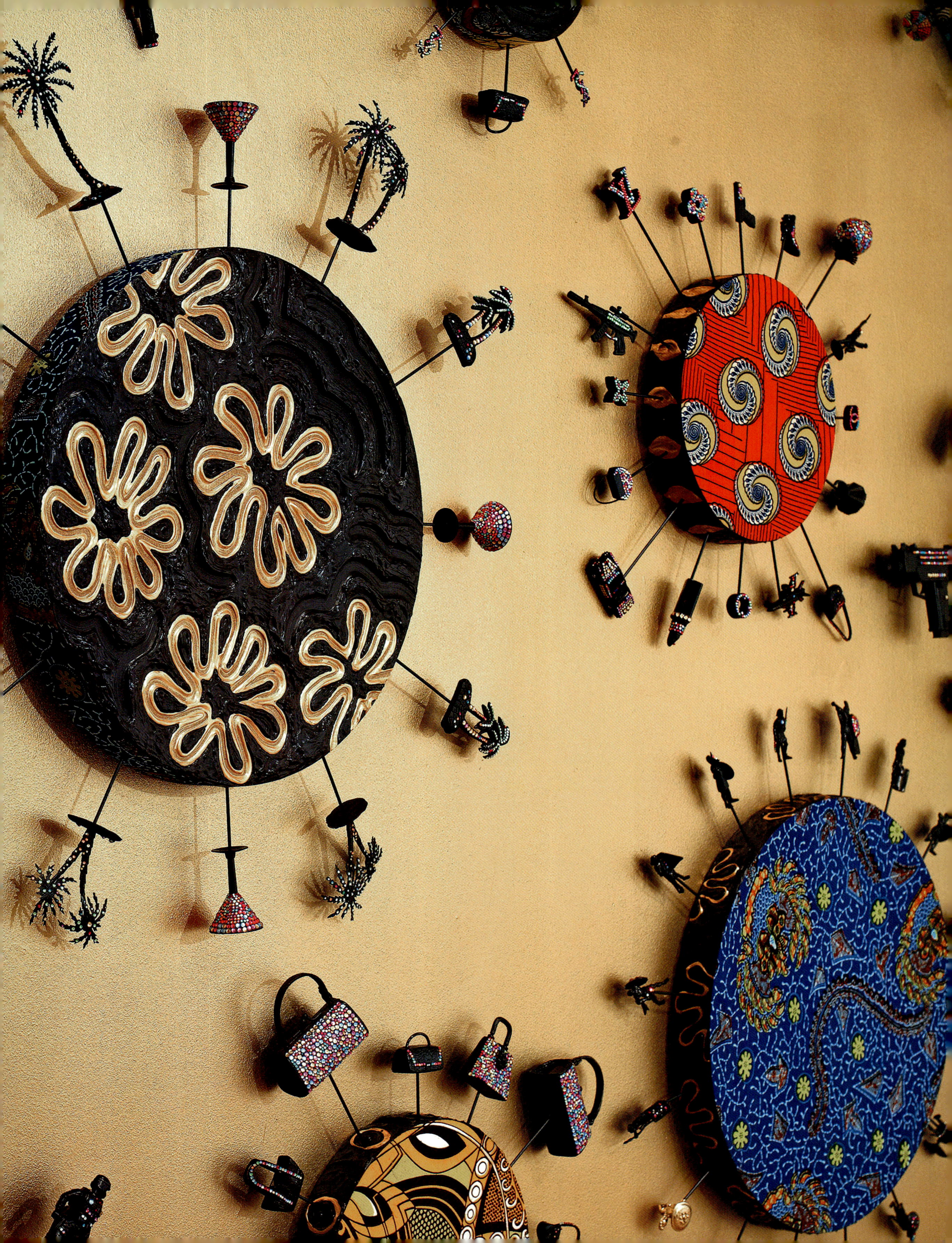

CONTENTS

PLATES

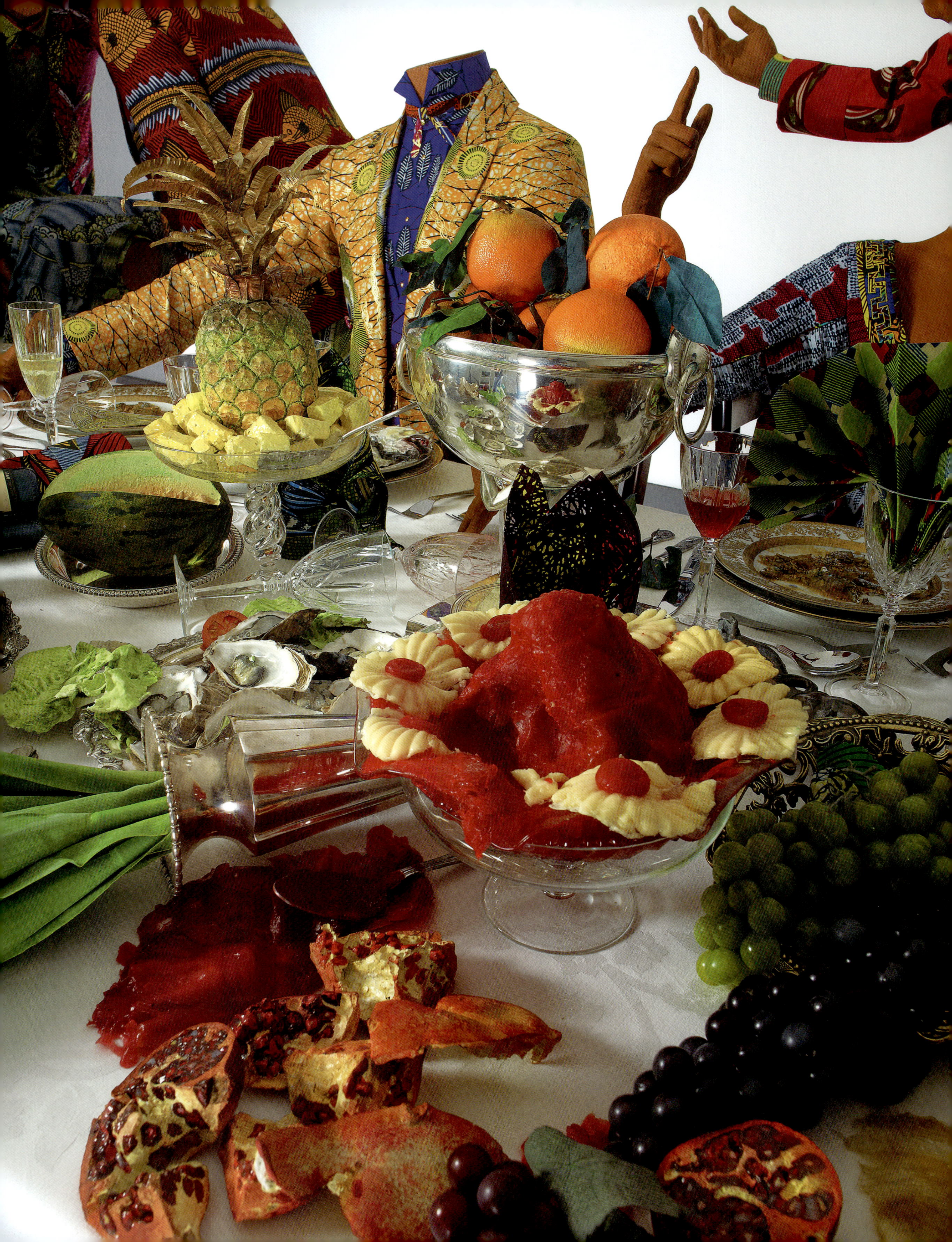

Time and Transformation in the Art of Yinka Shonibare MBE

Rachel Kent

Every human problem must be considered from the standpoint of time. Ideally, the present will always contribute to the building of the future.

—Frantz Fanon[1]

Yinka Shonibare MBE is a British-born Nigerian artist who works across the media of painting, sculpture, photography, and filmmaking. He is a master of technical and visual versatility, well known for his embrace of richly patterned Dutch wax textiles, which are applied to the surface of canvases and three-dimensional landscapes, fashioned into elaborate period costumes upon headless mannequins, and used to clothe performers in sweeping cinematic tableaux. Underpinning the artist's work is an engagement with themes of time: of history and its legacy for future generations, of how we live in the present, and of cycles or patterns that repeat across time despite their often destructive consequences. In this way he pricks the consciences of those who encounter his art, using beauty and seduction instead of words as his chosen weapons.

Much has been written about Shonibare's strategic use of Dutch wax fabric, its history, and its symbolism. Though it is commonly described as "African-print" fabric, its complex origins and production encompass the continents of Asia, Europe, and Africa. Inspired by Indonesian batiks, manufactured in the Netherlands and Manchester, and marketed in the nineteenth century to West African buyers, Dutch wax fabrics have become a signifier of authentic African identity, particularly in the wake of 1960s decolonization and the rise of Pan-African nationalism. This might seem ironic in light of their European colonial origins, yet it is precisely this sense of ambiguity and hybridity that has drawn Shonibare to their colorful, stylized images of Western consumer goods, African political leaders, and abstract geometric patterning. Speaking of their tangled transcontinental history, he says, "What that means to me is a metaphor . . . of interdependence."[2] Origins and authenticity, high art and popular culture are recurring themes in Shonibare's art, brought into focus through the symbolism of Dutch wax fabric and its deployment across two- and three-dimensional forms. Shonibare, who purchases his fabrics at London's Brixton Market, adds, "When you realise they are designed and produced by people in Dutch and English factories, then that completely destroys the methodology of this seductive African thing. Therefore it is important I don't go to Africa to buy them, so that all African exotic implications remain fake. And I actually like that fakeness."[3]

The story of Shonibare's first experimentation with Dutch wax fabric in the mid-1990s is an oft-recounted one and serves to set the ground for much discussion of his subsequent practice. Born in the United Kingdom to Nigerian parents, who returned to Lagos with Shonibare and his siblings when he was three, Shonibare relocated to London at the age of seventeen and later undertook tertiary studies in art. While at art school he was questioned by a lecturer about his choice of subject matter and why it was not "African" in theme. Surprised and then intrigued by the perception that, as a person of African origin, he should therefore be expected to make "African" art, he began to think about stereotypes as well as wider issues

Last Supper (after Leonardo) (detail), 2013. Thirteen life-size mannequins, Dutch wax printed cotton, reproduction wood table and chairs, silver cutlery and vases, antique and reproduction glassware and tableware, fiberglass and resin food; 158 x 742 x 260 cm. VandenBroek Foundation, Sassenheim of authenticity and its flip side—selecting his fabrics to illustrate the muddiness that underlies such preconceptions. What would it mean to make an African-style art, and is there really such a thing in this day and age? For a middle-class Nigerian Londoner with deep roots in both countries, these questions opened up a host of possibilities as well as complexities. He says, "As an artist of African origin . . . there is an expectation that I am still connected to traditional African art, even though I am a twenty-first-century person and it would be rather odd to imagine that a French or English artist is remotely interested in medieval art."[4] *Contamination* is a word that Shonibare has used in describing his methodological approach, noting that "this purity notion is nonsense."[5] Working across cultures and seamlessly integrating the language of contemporary art with that of popular culture, fashion, literature, and cinema, he suggests a range of gray areas rather than simple "categories" for the framing of ideas.

Shonibare's early paintings illustrate these concerns well. Comprising neat rows of small, square canvases wrapped in Dutch wax fabric instead of linen, they are overlaid with pigment and then arranged en masse upon a monochromatic background square (see pp. 201–3). They draw upon Minimalism's use of seriality, repetition, and the grid while breaking down the grandiosity of scale and gesture associated with its (predominantly white male) practitioners. Subsequent paintings by Shonibare have consisted of small roundels upon circular or oval painted backgrounds (p. 200), and two paintings of 2006 (see pp. 196–97) have broken down the notion of the border or edge altogether with their glistening black splatter-forms across the gallery wall. Referencing "black gold," or Africa's rich oil resources, they also recall the extravagant splashes and drips of the American Abstract Expressionist Jackson Pollock, to which they form a riposte. Discussing "fragmentation" as an element of impurity, Shonibare observes, "There is no need for me to make one big heroic painting. I can actually take the language of this big abstract painting and produce it in very small pieces, in fragments. I can actually break it down and reconstruct it."[6] For an artist with a physical disability, the reduction of scale is equally a practical solution. Additional parallels have been drawn between the artist's use of the grid and the geometric patterning and warp and weft of traditional West African textiles,[7] whereas Robert Hobbs has eloquently addressed the profound significance of Nigerian Yoruba culture for Shonibare in his essay in this publication.

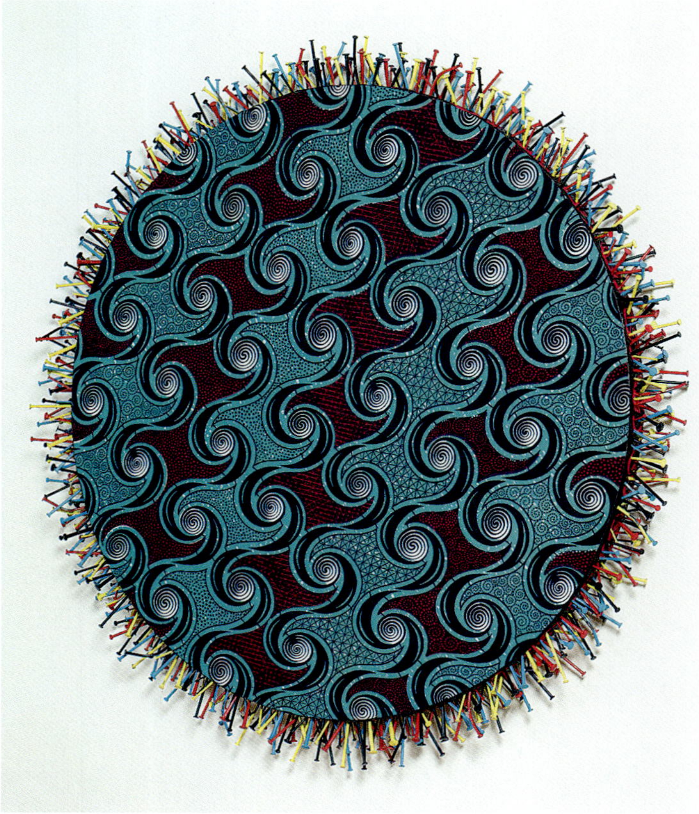

Fig. 1. Yinka Shonibare MBE, *Circular Fetish Painting with Nails 2*, 2012. Acrylic and acrylic aerosol spray paint on Dutch wax printed cotton, steel and aluminum nails, Medite MDF; 118 x 118 x 10 cm

Indeed, some of Shonibare's most recent paintings have moved off the gallery wall and onto the floor, taking the form of leaning panels or "totems," their edges surrounded by spiky, protruding nails. Recalling his first considerations of authenticity and stereotyping while at art school, and people's expectations in relation to "Africanness," the *Totem Paintings* (2011, p. 189) play with notions of the tribal in their menacing ornamentation. His series *Circular Fetish Paintings with Nails* (2012, fig. 1, p. 188) continues this exploration.

Shonibare has spoken at length about the influences upon his art. He cites feminist theory and deconstructionist literature as significant, particularly Jacques Derrida's writings and "the debate about the grand narrative."[8] Fracturing this narrative into small pieces quite literally through his paintings—and then exploding it across the wall with an irreverent splash—he has also sought to dismantle grand narratives in history through his sculptures and installations, photographs, and films. Two of Shonibare's sculptures of 1998–99 take the form of alien, rather than human, subjects. Carefully stitched and

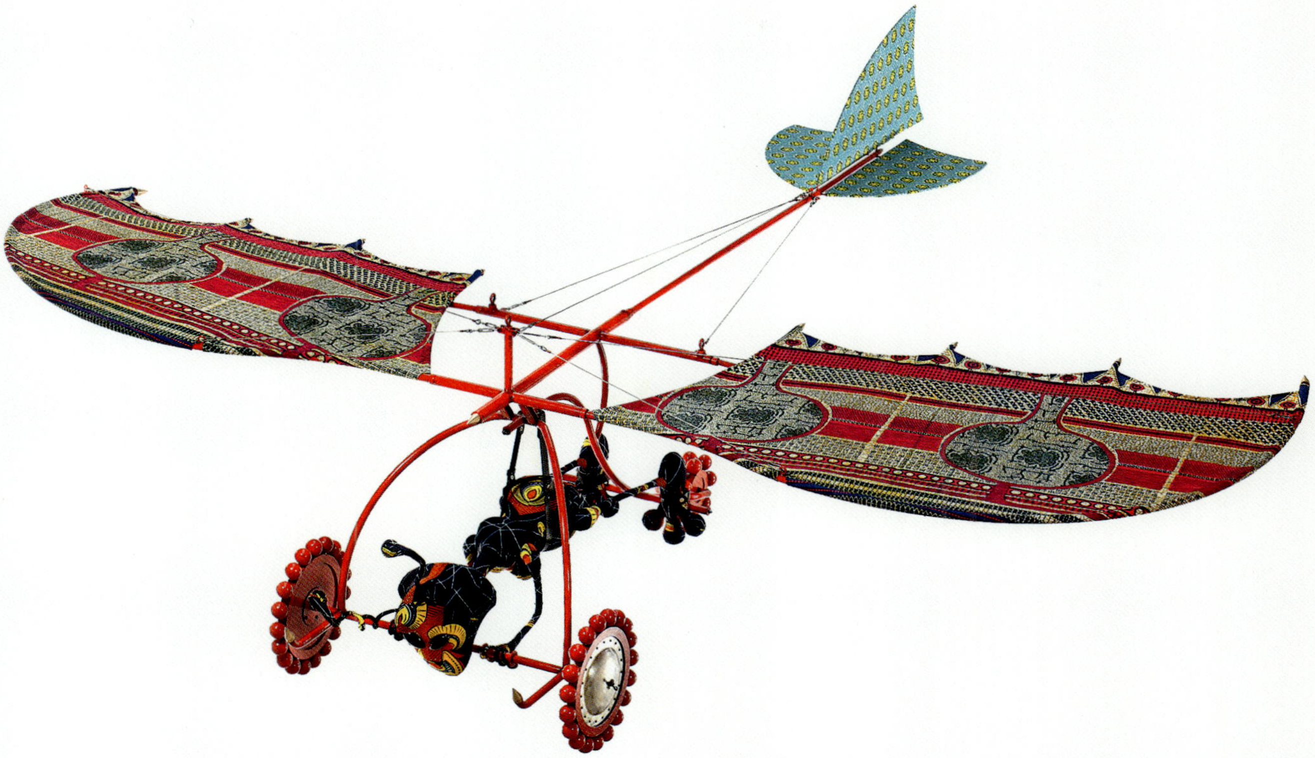

Fig. 2. Yinka Shonibare MBE, *Alien Woman on Flying Machine*, 2011. Steel, aluminum, brass, Dutch wax printed cotton, rubber; 150 x 450 x 400 cm

attired in a colorful skin of Dutch wax, his *Alien Obsessives* (p. 176) and *Dysfunctional Family* (p. 177) illustrate the idea of the outsider: of masquerading within the dominant culture while remaining peripheral or external to it. An experience common to so much of Britain's own ethnically and culturally diverse population, the idea of "difference"—with its inevitable questions of tradition, assimilation, contamination, and exchange—is tackled in Shonibare's work with a combination of allusion and wit. Two sculptures of 2011 return to this theme, featuring an alien man and woman in anachronistic flying machines (fig. 2, pp. 84–85). The works make cheeky reference to the notion of "alien invasion" and the arrival of people from diverse cultures on British shores as well as those of its former colonial outpost, Australia, which has a less-than-glowing record on the treatment of asylum seekers. This theme is further extended through his 2011 mural-scale *Alien Toy Painting* (pp. 192–93), with its characteristic monochromatic background and fabric-covered roundels, which are decorated with plastic children's sci-fi figurines that fan around the perimeter of the paintings like halos.

Despite its intentionally benign exterior, the notion of the "alien" resonates for Shonibare with the language of immigration and exile. It echoes the literature of the prominent black writer James Baldwin, who famously wrote, on the subject of living in Europe, "I was a kind of bastard of the West . . . an interloper," and it also recalls Ralph Ellison's semifictional "invisible man," adrift and alone in subterranean New York.[9] Describing the alien as "the colonial figure par excellence" and alien-invasion films as revealing the underlying fears of a nation, Shonibare concludes, "In the United States for a long time, the fear of communism prevailed. There is a lot of talk about 'bogus' asylum seekers in Britain now."[10] Some of his sculptures invert this logic, instead projecting their human subjects out into deep space, handsomely attired in Dutch wax astronaut suits and bubble helmets. *Vacation* (2000, p. 164) presents the recognizable image of a nuclear family, but

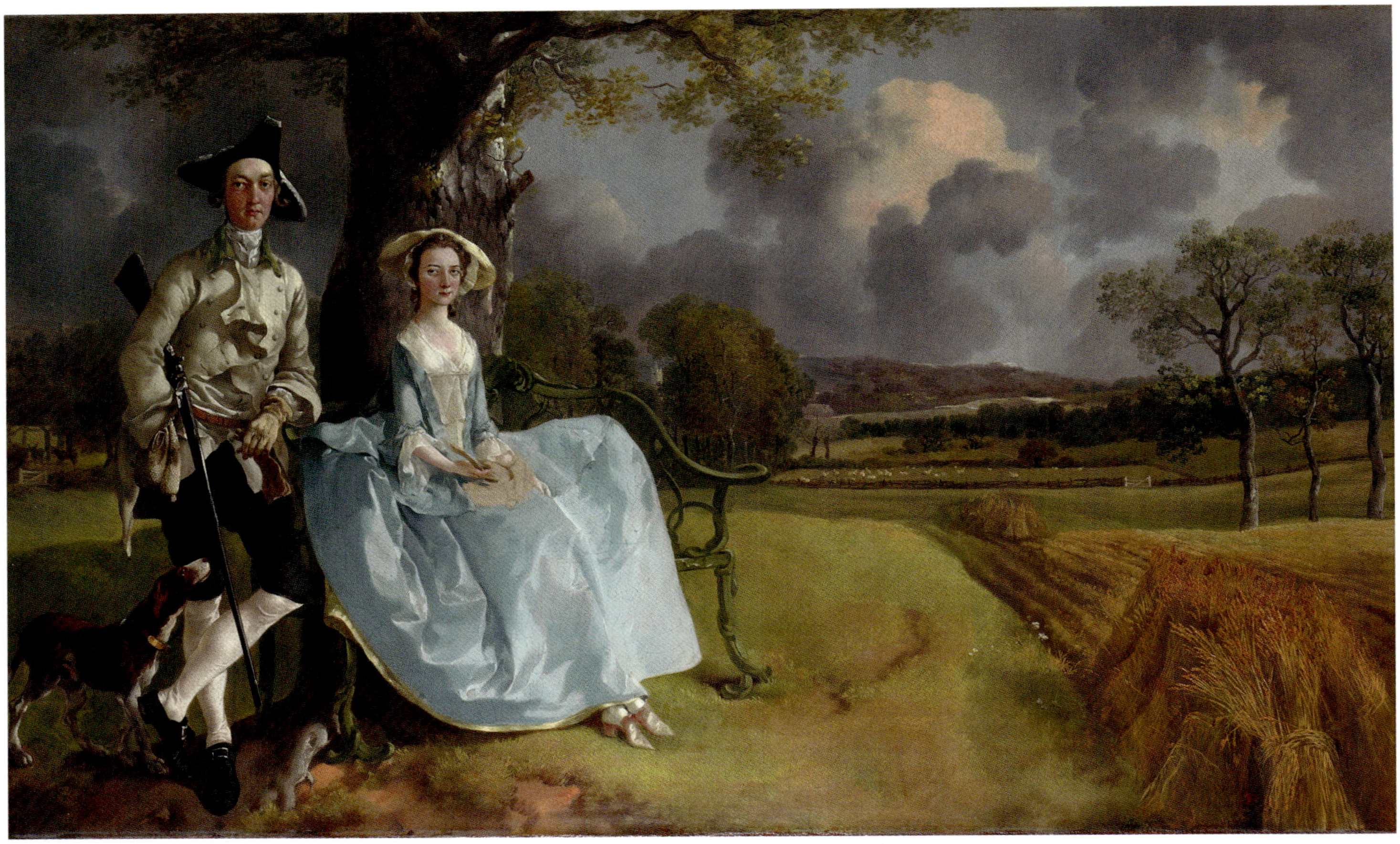

Fig. 3. Thomas Gainsborough, *Mr. and Mrs. Andrews*, ca. 1750. Oil on canvas, 69.8 x 119.4 cm. National Gallery, London, bought with contributions from The Pilgrim Trust, The Art Fund, Associated Television Ltd, and Mr. and Mrs. W. W. Spooner, 1960

their holiday destination is far, far away. Playing on notions of the foreign and the exotic, this work also evokes the cultural tourism of the "well-to-do" to distant places they see only through the window of an air-conditioned car or hotel.

Art history has provided another rich source of subject matter for Shonibare, who has transformed well-known European paintings into three-dimensional *tableaux vivants* with a twist since the late 1990s. One example is Thomas Gainsborough's *Mr. and Mrs. Andrews* (ca. 1750, fig. 3). This painting represents a wedding portrait as much as it does a statement about Britain's landed gentry, embodied by the figures of a young couple seated before their vast estate. In Shonibare's sculptural response of 1998 (p. 178), the couple is presented minus their heads—a playful reference to the beheading of the French aristocracy and the revolutionary redistribution of power and land scarcely forty years after Gainsborough's painting. Shonibare comments, "It amused me to explore the possibility of bringing back the guillotine in the late 1990s . . . for use on the historical icons of power and deference."[11] He has further noted that the absence of heads in his sculptures removes direct connotations of race. Fascinated by the culture of eighteenth-century Europe and its aristocrats, with their love of frivolity and excess, Shonibare also cites the Rococo artist Jean-Honoré Fragonard as particularly influential. Fragonard's paintings and sculptures are characterized by lavish depictions of the upper class at play, pursuing love, and enjoying the material comforts of their wealth. It cannot be lost on Shonibare that their vogue was ultimately short-lived and that Fragonard died in relative obscurity in 1806, while a number of his wealthy patrons met their fate at the guillotine the decade before.

Shonibare's sculptural installation *The Swing (after Fragonard)* (2001, pp. 168–69) responds to Fragonard's 1767 painting of the same name (fig. 4), depicting the sensual abandon of a privileged young woman at her leisure. The woman's airborne slipper, kicked high as she swings back and forth before her lover, underlines the decadence of the original scene. A garter is exposed to view beneath her billowing dress and,

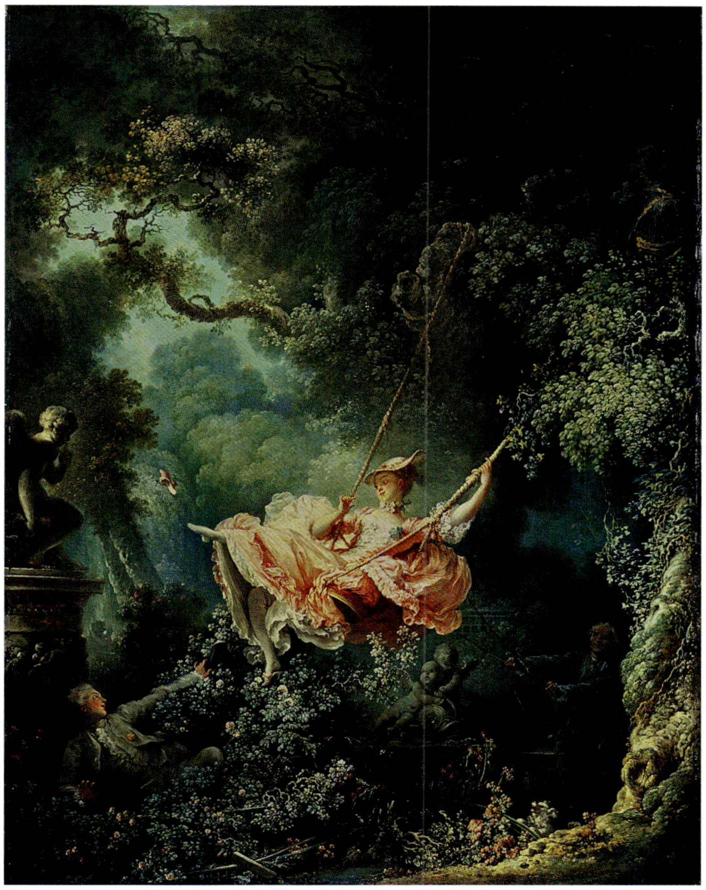

Fig. 4. Jean-Honoré Fragonard, *The Swing*, 1767. Oil on canvas, 81 x 64.2 cm. The Wallace Collection, London

scandalously, she is assisted in her tryst by a priest who obligingly pushes the swing. The concept of leisure is particularly significant for Shonibare. He observes: "To be in a position to engage in leisure pursuits, you need a few bob. . . . You need spare time and money buys you spare time. While the leisure pursuit might look frivolous . . . my depiction of it is a way of engaging with that power. It is actually an expression of something much more profoundly serious insofar as the accumulation of wealth and power that is personified in leisure was no doubt a product of exploiting other people."[12] Shonibare's ice-skating cleric of 2005 (fig. 5, pp. 64–65, 150–51), meanwhile, draws upon Sir Henry Raeburn's painting *Reverend Robert Walker Skating on Duddingston Loch* (ca. 1795, fig. 6). Depicting an unexpected pastime for a reverend, who would normally be painted in a more pious or solemn moment, Raeburn's painting and Shonibare's sculptural response combine playfulness and seriousness while turning conventional expectations upside down. Interestingly, Raeburn and his painting are often spoken of within the context of the Scottish Enlightenment, a fact that will not be unknown to Shonibare. Linked to the accumulation of knowledge and, with it, power, wealth, and territorial expansion, the Enlightenment period has become a strong focus in Shonibare's recent sculpture and photography.

Other related works by Shonibare include a "leisure lady" promenading with her canine companions (p. 173) and another, more ostentatiously, with three leashed ocelots (p. 170). Eighteenth-century fashionability, a love of exoticism, and the taming (or subordination) of wild nature are themes embodied in these sculptures. Speaking more widely about stereotypes and notions of the exotic, Shonibare drily observes: "These members of the aristocracy . . . are objects of curiosity, in a kind of reverse way. So the fetish for me, as an African, is the eighteenth-century European culture, whilst their fetish is the African mask!"[13] Sculptures of an English foxhunt (p. 172) and of exquisitely dressed adults and children fishing, walking with stilts (pp. 148, 149), and riding unicycles (pp. 128, 129) continue the artist's interest in leisure pursuits and their attendant associations of class.

With their high visual aesthetic and meticulous finish, it is very easy to be seduced by Shonibare's paintings and sculptures. Underscored by themes of power and privilege, however, they reveal on closer inspection a less savory commentary on history and its repetitions. Shonibare has frequently cited his use of beauty as a device to draw in viewers and gain their attention before confronting them—ever so gently—with less palatable truths about the world in which we live. Describing himself foremost as "an aesthete, an artist" and claiming that "beauty . . . is just as important as the content," he revels in the "paradox or contradiction" contained within his art.[14] Shonibare's labyrinthine exhibition *Jardin d'Amour* (*Garden of Love*, 2007) at the Musée du quai Branly, Paris, re-created a suite of allegorical paintings by Fragonard (pp. 138–39, 140, 141). The works draw a sharp parallel between prerevolutionary France and the contemporary culture of greed and excess that divides rich from poor and permeates the first world at the expense of the third. Selecting for his costumes Dutch wax fabrics patterned with luxury-goods logos, car designs, dollar bills, and coins, Shonibare says of the installation, "I am deliberately taking this period as a metaphor for the contemporary situation . . . showing very wealthy Europeans in very wealthy clothes, but because I changed their clothes into African textiles, I give an indication

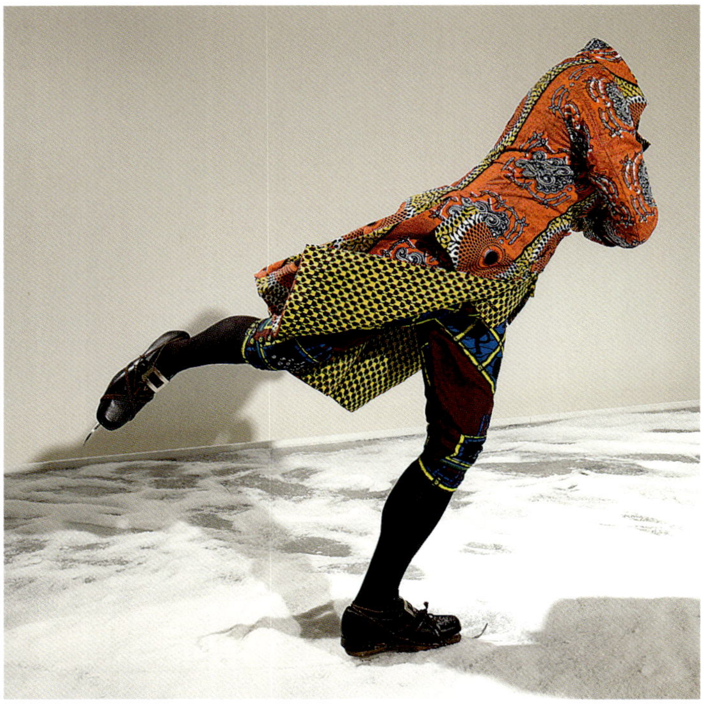

Fig. 5. Yinka Shonibare MBE, *Reverend on Ice*, 2005. Life-size mannequin, semi-opaque synthetic polymer resin, Dutch wax printed cotton, wool, leather, wood, steel; 160 x 402.3 x 601.5 cm. National Gallery of Victoria, Melbourne, purchased with the assistance of NGV Contemporary, 2006

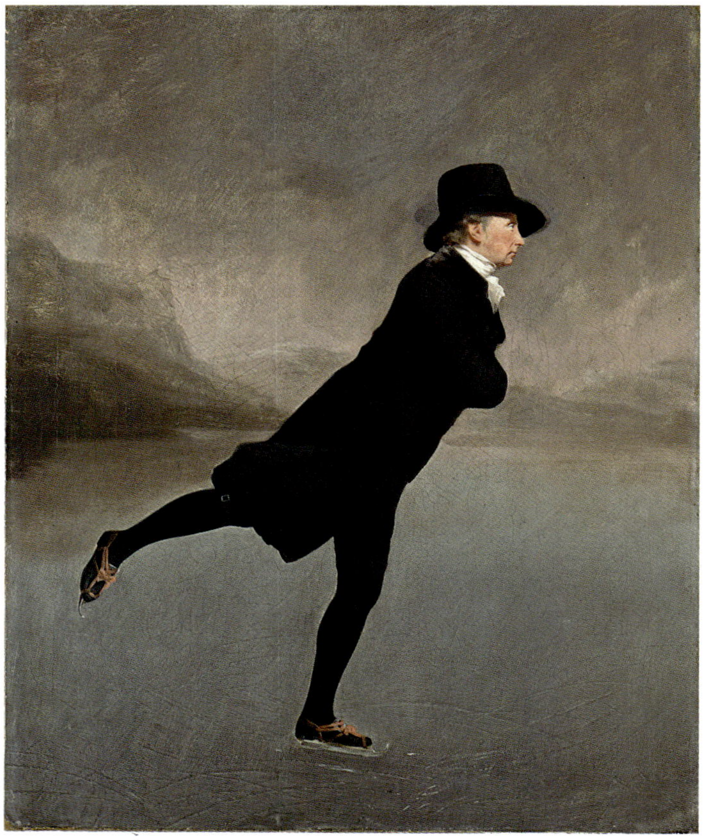

Fig. 6. Sir Henry Raeburn, *Reverend Robert Walker Skating on Duddingston Loch*, ca. 1795. Oil on canvas, 76.2 x 63.5 cm. Scottish National Gallery, purchased 1949

that the luxury they enjoy, the labour of making the clothes is supplied by others who are less fortunate."[15]

Shonibare's installation is inspired by Fragonard's 1771–73 painting cycle *The Progress of Love*, which was commissioned and then rejected by King Louis XV's mistress, Madame du Barry, for her opulent château at Louveciennes. A commoner and a courtesan, Du Barry was famed for her extravagant taste and fashion while she was consort to the king. Like her regal rival Marie Antoinette, she eventually went to the guillotine in 1793 during the Reign of Terror—famously screaming and pleading on the scaffold, to the chagrin of her executioner. Shonibare's interpretation of Fragonard's vignette *The Progress of Love: The Lover Crowned* is particularly ironic as his own sculptural figures are of course already headless. A floral wreath held aloft (fig. 7) equally shifts in its meaning. Shonibare has described contemporary Europe as a "fruit basket" or "rich garden" to which other cultures look but are increasingly denied access.[16] The ever-widening gulf between rich and poor and themes of discrimination and exclusion are symptomatic of the post-9/11 world we occupy. Refusing to take an overtly confrontational stance, unlike many of his contemporaries, Shonibare instead invites us to consider these polarities through the lessons of history and taste.

Shonibare's *Jardin d'Amour* captures the last carefree moments of a regime on the brink of destruction, a theme that resonates powerfully in the present era of financial irresponsibility and collapse led by the banking institutions of America and Europe. The economic catastrophe that engulfs large parts of the Western world and its governments in 2013—Spain, Greece, Portugal, and Italy, for example—is a salient reminder of history's repetitions and our inability to learn from the past. Greed and decadence are indeed recurring motifs in Shonibare's art, and they find particular expression in scenes of feasting, excess, and merriment. *Party Time: Re-imagine America* (2008–9, pp. 114, 115) was commissioned for the centenary celebration of New Jersey's Newark Museum and presented in the dining room of the museum's 1885 Ballantine House, its festive table the site around which much adult misbehavior takes place. Another sculptural installation, *Last Supper (after Leonardo)* (2013, pp. 6, 70–71, 72–73), re-creates one of art history's great themes, substituting Jesus and the apostles with thirteen men and women in ribald couplings around an overladen table.

Speaking of his dinner-party works, Shonibare has described *Party Time* as ironic—a celebration of excess in a society that is failing. In his *Last Supper*, Christ is replaced by Bacchus, the Greek god of wine, and his "disciples" are represented in varying states of intoxication. Building on these installations are the *Champagne Kid* sculptures (2013, pp. 68, 69), also presented in states of inebriation. Perched upon their shoulders are globes that show graphs of financial markets around the world and chart the collapse of the banking system. A related sculpture (pp. 66, 67) depicts a finely dressed gentleman festively popping a champagne bottle; its contents spurt outward in a semenlike arc, a satirical reference to the contemporary "banker wanker." In stark contrast are the artist's *Food Faerie* sculptures of 2010 (pp. 92, 93), which carry food in their tiny baskets to distribute to the hungry of the world, and his *Homeless Man* (p. 75) and *Homeless Boy* (p. 74) of 2012. Both figures are bowed under the weight of the stacked suitcases upon their shoulders, and celestial globes in place of their heads bear inscriptions by the great Victorian-era novelist Charles Dickens. The artist's 2008–11 sculptures of young children balancing upon globes of the Earth (pp. 118–19) depict infrared heat maps of regions affected by climate change, a bitter outcome of our excess consumption and exploitation of the planet's fragile, finite resources—a critique continued in his 2009 series of collaged *Climate Shit Drawings* (pp. 194, 195).

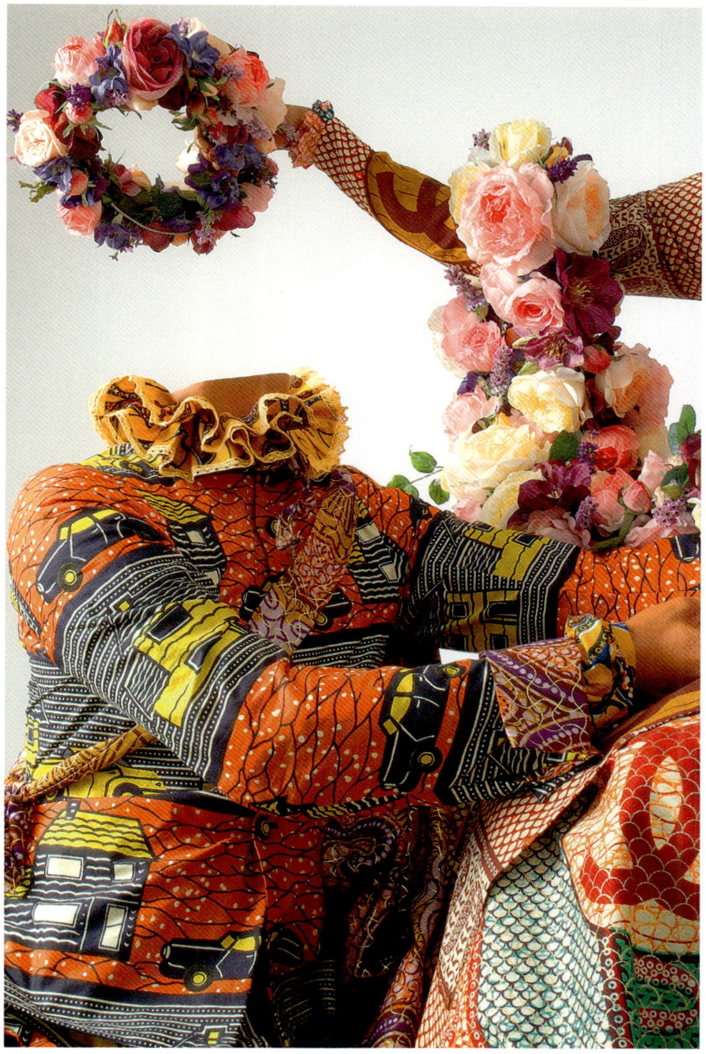

Fig. 7. Yinka Shonibare MBE, *The Crowning* (detail), 2007. Two life-size mannequins, Dutch wax printed cotton, shoes, coir matting, artificial silk flowers, mixed media; 160 x 280 x 210 cm. Commissioned by the Musée du quai Branly, Paris, for the exhibition *Jardin d'Amour*

While the eighteenth-century culture of excess has remained a persistent theme in Shonibare's art, the expansionist era heralded by the nineteenth century holds an equally strong appeal. Introducing his major book on the subject, the historian A. N. Wilson observed, "The Victorians are still with us."[17] As a person living in England, surrounded by the vast architectural and technological legacy of the Victorian age, Shonibare has focused in considerable depth upon this defining period in the country's history. The cultural inheritance of the era—of "Victorian" morality, manners, social structures, and notions of class—has been particularly significant and forms a recurring theme within Shonibare's art. He says, "Living in England with my colonial relationship to this country one cannot escape all these Victorian things, because they are everywhere: in architecture, culture, attitude. . . . In the eighties, Margaret Thatcher started talking about bringing back Victorian values, the time when everything was so proper-proper. And I started to think: what do these Victorian ideas mean, why do we need to bring them back, what was so good about it all?"[18] To view Shonibare's comments as a simple critique would be erroneous. Instead they reveal a profound ambivalence toward the Victorian era that he has described as "a sort of love-hate thing,"[19] acknowledging himself to be its product and inheritor.

Scramble for Africa (2003, pp. 27, 154–55, 156, 157) is a pivotal work for Shonibare in its exploration of late Victorian England and its territorial expansion into Africa during the 1880s. Wilson writes, "It has been observed by one of its liveliest historians that 'the scramble for Africa bewildered everyone, from the humblest African peasant to the master statesmen of the age, Lord Salisbury and Prince Bismarck." In a speech in May

1886, Salisbury stated that when he left the Foreign Office in 1880 "nobody thought about Africa," but when he returned to it five years later "the nations of Europe were almost quarrelling with each other as to the various portions of Africa which they could obtain. I do not exactly know the cause of this sudden revolution."[20] The scramble for Africa by leading European and world powers resulted in the carving up of a continent, an act that was formalized at the Berlin Conference of 1884–85.[21] Shonibare's work depicts this historic gathering, capturing the various statesmen huddled around a table with a large map of Africa, eagerly staking their claims. In Shonibare's interpretation, the heads of state are characteristically headless—and equally mindless in their hunger for what King Leopold II of Belgium called "a slice of this magnificent cake."[22]

The artist's subsequent paintings *Black Gold I* (pp. 196–97) and *Black Gold II* (both 2006) continue themes of colonial domination and exploitation, bringing them into the twentieth and twenty-first centuries as multinational companies greedily extract and export Africa's natural resources while its people suffer and starve. The image of Cecil Rhodes, colonial politician and founder of De Beers Diamonds, also comes to mind. Immortalized in 1892 by the satirical magazine *Punch* as the rapacious "Rhodes Colossus," he is shown straddling the African continent like his planned transcontinental telegraph service from Cape Town to Cairo (fig. 8). Rhodes once famously remarked, "I would annex the whole world. . . . I would if I could. . . . The planets . . . yes, the planets, if I could. I often think of that."[23] This wishful thinking was not so far removed from the colonial reality—or that of the next century, with its space travel and moon landings. Needless to say, one of the first acts documented by NASA's Apollo astronauts on their unwieldy Hasselblad cameras was the planting of the American flag on lunar soil (fig. 9).

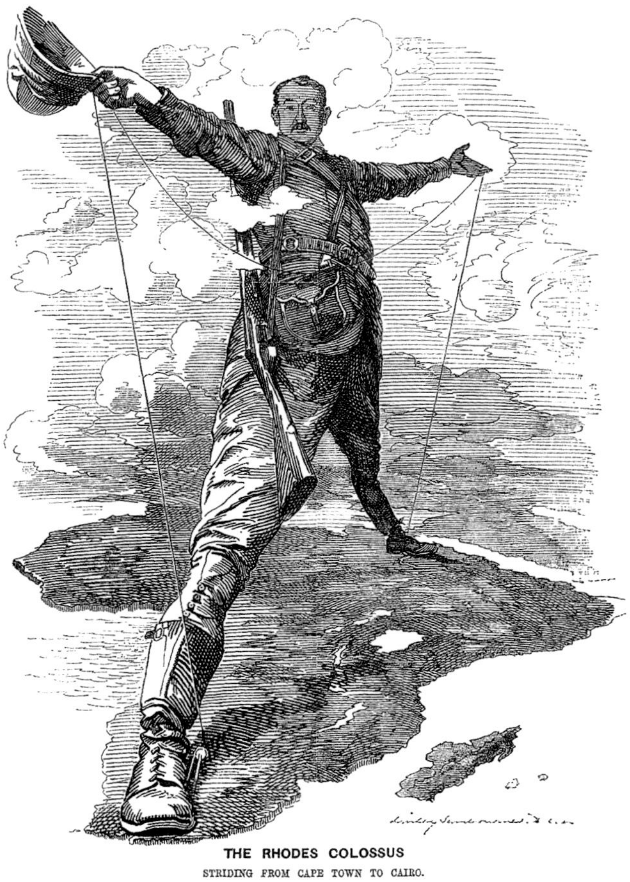

Fig. 8. "The Rhodes Colossus: Striding from Cape Town to Cairo," from *Punch* magazine, December 10, 1892

Shonibare's large installation *The Victorian Philanthropist's Parlour* (1996–97, pp. 181, 182–83) extends the theme of wealth and its creation in the nineteenth century. Designed like a stage set that viewers can walk around, its provisional wall panels and floor supports reveal an opulent interior setting and furniture upholstered with Dutch wax fabrics. In the context of the work, the absent philanthropist is a double-edged entity who has likely generated his wealth through the labor of others. His philanthropic redistribution presumably does not equal the vast sum of his worth, and the motives for his largesse are unclear. The repeated motif of the black athlete appears upon the parlor's Dutch wax wallpaper, inviting associations of "patronage" and the relationship between the colonial "haves" and the colonized "have-nots."[24] The Victorian era was a time of enormous economic growth and prosperity for some. For others it was a time of grinding poverty, reaching a peak late in the century as England's territorial ambitions stretched across the globe. *The Victorian Philanthropist's Parlour* continues the artist's interest in class and privilege. Its deliberately setlike presentation alludes, moreover, to our own fascination with the lives of the rich through history, as encountered through period re-creations and television dramas. A subsequent site-specific installation, commissioned for the period rooms of the Brooklyn Museum, features sculptures of well-to-do children hidden playfully amid the furniture of their parents' homes (pp. 100–113). Titled *Mother and Father Worked Hard So I Can Play* (2009), the presentation referenced the material aspirations of settler arrivals in the "new world"

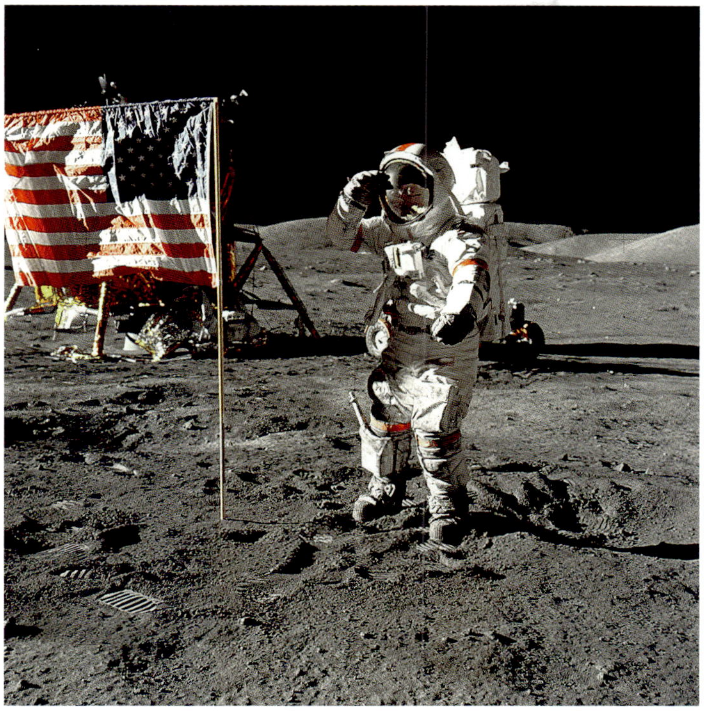

Fig. 9. *Cernan Jump Salutes Flag*, 1972. Eugene A. Cernan, Commander, Apollo 17, salutes the flag on the lunar surface during extravehicular activity (EVA) on NASA's final lunar landing mission. Digital photograph, NASA

of America and the luxurious indulgence of their beneficiaries, who may never need to work again.

Victorian morality represents a subject of much literary discussion. Equal if not greater interest has been aroused by its indiscretions and sexual mores, from the rumored relationship between Queen Victoria and her Scottish manservant John Brown to the flamboyant sexuality of cultural figures such as Oscar Wilde. Running distinctly contrary to the "proper-proper" Victorian veneer of manners and social acceptability—twin polarities described by A. N. Wilson as "appearance and reality"[25]—the many inherent contradictions of Victorian culture have provided rich subject matter for Shonibare, culminating in his vast 2002 installation *Gallantry and Criminal Conversation* (pp. 158–59, 160, 161, 162–63). Inspired by the phenomenon of the Grand Tour, a seventeenth- and early eighteenth-century travel itinerary for the European upper classes, this work pulls back the curtain on Victorian propriety to reveal hidden intimacies and exchanges, including adultery (or "criminal conversation," as it was then called).

"Grand Tourists" traditionally sought to improve and enlighten themselves through the study of European art, culture, and history, visiting popular destinations such as Paris, Rome, and Venice. In Shonibare's work, the Grand Tour is simultaneously revealed as a kind of covert sexual tourism, calling to mind, in turn, ugly contemporary connotations of foreign and exotic places and the (typically) white men who frequent them. Interestingly, historical references to "criminal conversation" commonly position women as active agents while their male companions are presumably excused from culpability (the lonely downfall of nineteenth-century adulteresses Emma Bovary and Anna Karenina comes to mind). This is an ironic inversion of Victorian attitudes to homosexuality, which Queen Victoria famously criminalized in 1885 for men but not for women, in the purported belief that same-sex female relations could not exist. As Shonibare's fabulously attired 1999 sculptures *Victorian Couple* (p. 175), *Gay Victorians* (fig. 10), and *Affectionate Men* (p. 174) demonstrate, with their references to prominent Victorians of all sexual persuasions, nothing could be further from the truth.

Notions of contamination and contradiction are central to Shonibare's artistic practice, and are expressed both in the use of Dutch wax fabric and in the conceptual basis of individual works. Writing on Shonibare's art for the 2002 solo exhibition *Double Dutch*, Manthia Diawara described the Nigerian concept of the *been-tos*, "those Africans who adopted the English manners, the Queen's English and Victorian style of dress." Identifying the been-to as "a fake, a false Englishman; one who is a caricature of Englishness and therefore cannot be authentic," he concluded that in today's world, definitions have become so confused and communities so enmeshed that "it has become impossible to tell who is English and who is not, based on appearance, accent, and way of life alone. For Shonibare, the stereotype is all we have left to invoke Englishness, its different histories and futures."[26] Shonibare's photographs engage extensively with ideas about stereotype, as well as duality and masquerade, through the personae of the Victorian "dandy" (or social aspirant) and Oscar Wilde's antihero Dorian Gray. Both "fakes" and rakes, the dandy and Gray are portrayed by Shonibare himself in the photographs, assuming costumes and theatrical makeup, with a cast of supporting actors.

Shonibare's ambitious photographic suite *Diary of a Victorian Dandy* (1998, pp. 218–19) has frequently been considered in relation to the satirical art of William Hogarth. A well-known painter and caricaturist of the eighteenth century, Hogarth

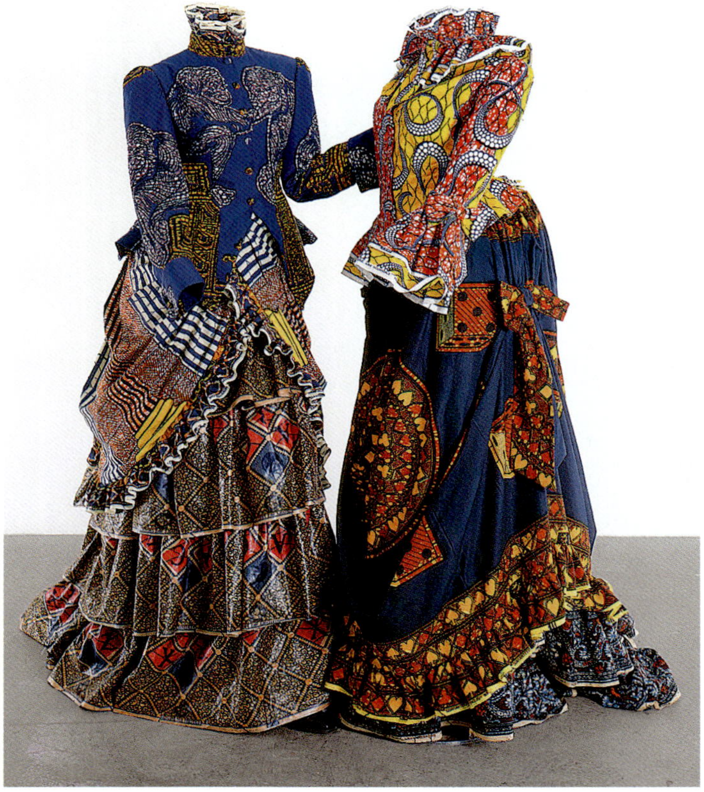

Fig. 10. Yinka Shonibare MBE, *Gay Victorians*, 1999. Two life-size mannequins, Dutch wax printed cotton, mixed media; 165.1 x 63.5 x 106.7 cm, 165.1 x 73.7 x 109.2 cm. Collection of Vicki and Kent Logan, fractional and promised gift to the San Francisco Museum of Modern Art

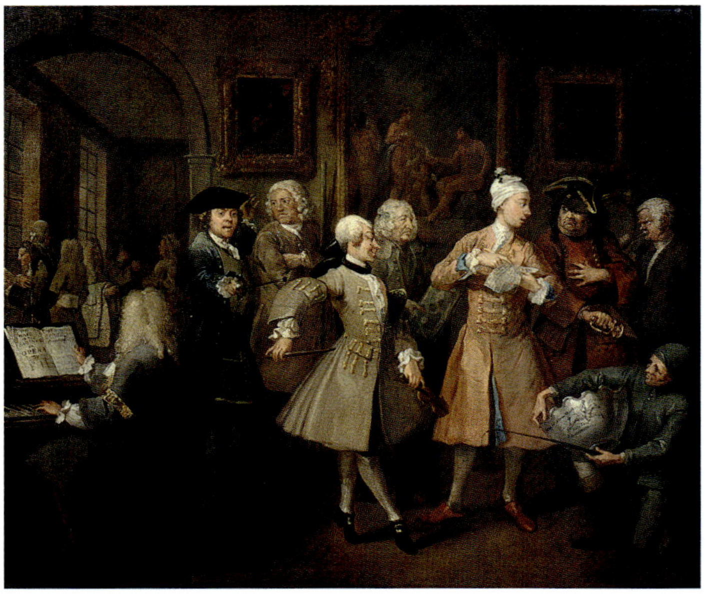

Fig. 11. William Hogarth, *The Rake's Progress: 2. The Rake's Levée*, 1734. Oil on canvas, 63 x 75.5 cm. Sir John Soane's Museum, London

lampooned the rich and moralized to the poor through his art. He produced various didactic bodies of work first as paintings and then as prints, including *The Harlot's Progress* (1731); its sequel, *The Rake's Progress* (1734, fig. 11); *Marriage à-la-mode* (1743–45), with its ridiculing of upper-class vanities; and *Beer Street and Gin Lane* (1751). Shonibare's photographs resonate with *The Rake's Progress*, transposing the central character into the nineteenth century and following just one day in his life, unlike Hogarth's chronicle of Thomas Rakewell from his humble origins to success, dissipation, and eventual madness. Shonibare's work also avoids the moralizing tenor of Hogarth, celebrating excessiveness and decadence while inverting the stereotype of otherness through the figure of the black dandy, with his fawning white servants and acolytes. He says, "Rakewell spends his father's money extravagantly, gets into debt and ends up in a madhouse. My *Diary of a Victorian Dandy* is the opposite of that. My dandy has a wild time, has wild orgies, but he gets away with it. He challenges the notion of bourgeois morality."[27] Shonibare's work invokes contemporary associations of black social mobility. Parallels may also be drawn between the plush attire of Shonibare's dandy and the high style and "bling" of a new black social elite. The symbolic meanings of clothing and its transformative powers are many, and Shonibare's deep interest in fashion predates his career as an artist.[28] The acclaimed fashion designer Vivienne Westwood is particularly pertinent in this regard with her acute eye for "Britishness" and its deconstruction through style, wit, and unrepentant sexuality.

Diary of a Victorian Dandy is one of several works by Shonibare that do not feature Dutch wax fabric costumes. Instead the artist and his supporting cast wear conventional Victorian clothing, although any sense of authenticity is swiftly undermined by the exaggerated theatricality of each image. Originally shown as a commissioned project in the London Underground train network, *Diary of a Victorian Dandy* differs structurally from Shonibare's paintings and sculptures. It constructs a clear durational narrative through five large prints, each numbered according to the hour at which it is set. Thus we learn that the dandy rises from bed at 11 a.m., conducts his business at 2 p.m., plays billiards at 5 p.m., attends a musical recital at 7 p.m., and indulges in sexual pleasures at 3 a.m. Themes of leisure and frivolity, self-invention, and social mobility are played out through the dandy, a contentious figure in English life whose circulation in upper-class circles was often linked to his style and wit. Shonibare has described his attraction to the dandy as an "outsider" figure who "upsets the social order of things,"[29] a notion echoed by Charles Baudelaire: "They all partake of the same characteristic quality of opposition and revolt."[30] *Diary of a Victorian Dandy* extends the artist's interest in ambivalent states of being, touching on early works with their consideration of exclusion and otherness as well as later works with their focus on inclusion through class and privilege.

One recent interpretation has proposed the figure of Olaudah Equiano as a "poignant shadow" behind Shonibare's dandy.[31] Equiano was an educated, literate African slave who bought his freedom and settled in England. He married a white woman, campaigned tirelessly for the abolition of slavery, and chronicled his own experiences in an acclaimed autobiographical work of 1789. A "precursor" of sorts because of his outsider status and inversion of the social order, Equiano was one of few black figures in eighteenth- and nineteenth-century English society who occupied positions of visibility and influence. Within a Pacific context there is the equally poignant shadow of Omai, a high-ranking political exile from Raiatea in the Society Islands. Omai accompanied Captain Cook on the ship *Adventure* from Tahiti to Portsmouth, England, in 1774. He was the first Pacific Islander to visit London, where he caused a stir among its upper-class circles. A "social lion" noted for his gracious manners and extensive tailor's bills,[32] he was presented to King George III, painted by Joshua Reynolds, and even became the subject of a hugely popular pantomime, *OMAI: Or, the Trip Round the World*, at the Theatre Royal in Covent Garden in 1786. Omai's good fortune was, however, very short-lived, and he returned to the Society Islands in 1776 to political turmoil and unrest, abandoned by his former British patrons on Huahine, an island that was not his own. There his experiences in London were met with local indifference. He was unable to reclaim his father's Raiatean estate and reportedly died of disease in 1779.

Shonibare's second photographic suite considers the late Victorian literary creation Dorian Gray. Oscar Wilde, considered a consummate dandy of the Victorian age, completed his only novel, *The Picture of Dorian Gray*, in 1890 while at the height of his social and literary career. Wilde's novel tells the story of a handsome young man who sells his soul to the devil in order to remain forever young, a hidden portrait painting capturing the effects of his age and increasing moral corruption over the next eighteen years. Themes of decadence and late Victorian aestheticism permeate the book, while the duality of its protagonist finds literary parallels in other Victorian-era novellas, including Robert Louis Stevenson's *The Strange Case of Dr. Jekyll and Mr. Hyde*, published four years earlier and admired by Wilde.

Like Stevenson's book before it, Wilde's *Dorian Gray* was the subject of stage adaptations and in 1945 became a Metro-Goldwyn-Mayer film under the direction of Albert Lewin. It is this predominantly black-and-white film adaptation that fuels Shonibare's own photographs as much as the original novel. In choosing to make all but one of his photographs black and white (unlike the colorful *Victorian Dandy* photographs), Shonibare emulates the look of the film still and relates the idea of duality back to the black-and-white film medium. Another duality or inversion is evident in Shonibare's substitution of the original Dorian Gray, a nineteenth-century white Englishman, with his own countenance. It is interesting to note that in his preface to the novel, Wilde invokes Shakespeare's *Tempest* with its black trickster and "wild man," Caliban, a character that Shonibare has since addressed obliquely in his recent works.

In a pivotal moment in Lewin's film, an ever-youthful Dorian Gray stands before his wizened, corrupted portrait and understands that a symbolic transference has taken place between himself and his image. In that brief moment we see the portrait in vivid Technicolor: eyes bulging, hair on end, and hands bloodied. Shonibare's solitary color photograph depicts the artist as Dorian Gray standing before a gilded mirror and encountering his own reflection. The face that stares back is hideously scarred and disfigured like the portrait, in contrast to Shonibare's black-and-white image of the same encounter. Tellingly, Wilde says in his preface, "The nineteenth-century dislike of Realism is the rage of Caliban seeing his own face in a glass. The nineteenth-century dislike of Romanticism is the rage of Caliban not seeing his own face in a glass."[33] James Baldwin's poignant observation in *Notes of a Native Son* (1955) forms a fitting response: "When, beneath the black mask, a human being begins to make himself felt one cannot escape a certain awful wonder as to what sort of human being it is. . . . It is one of the ironies of black-white relations that, by means of what the white man imagines the black man to be, the black man is enabled to know who the white man is."[34]

Notions of the "fake" and the "trickster" are variously explored in the literature surrounding Shonibare, with some accounts citing the Yoruba trickster-god Eshu and his two-sided black-and-red hat as a reference point.[35] Inextricably linked to the artist's ideas about authenticity and contamination, Shonibare's dandy and villain are essentially ambivalent creations, the latter manifesting his duality as a confrontation between art (imitation) and origin (the "real") through the symbolic motif of the portrait painting. They are also fakes twice removed, first from the original they sought to emulate (an aristocrat, a beautiful young man) and second by Shonibare's own revision. If Shonibare sees an element of himself within the characters that he occupies, then it is one defined by masks and mutation, suggesting that individual identity is in a constant state of play.

Two subsequent photographic series by the artist extend these themes: one through the character of Willy Loman, the troubled protagonist of Arthur Miller's 1949 play *Death of a Salesman*, and the other through Admiral Horatio Nelson, the celebrated naval commander who led the British to victory against the French at the Battle of Trafalgar in 1805. *Willy Loman: The Rise and Fall* (2009, pp. 208, 209) is Shonibare's only photographic series so far that is situated firmly within the present. It unfolds in an unadorned warehouse with a concrete floor and whitewashed walls, and most of its characters are naked except for Loman, who wears a Dutch wax jacket and trousers. Reflective of a new austerity precipitated by the European financial crisis, it situates Loman in the seven circles of hell, with each photograph modeled upon an etching by Gustave Doré. *Willy Loman* offers a flip side to Shonibare's Victorian dandy, its protagonist being instead a man of profound self-doubt and delusion who does not "get away with it" and eventually commits suicide by crashing his car at the play's conclusion. He is, however, a rake and a fake, like his Victorian-era counterpart, something that only his son Biff recognizes when he cries angrily, "You fake! You phony little fake! You fake!"[36] Shonibare's photographs are augmented by a life-size sculpture of the fated car, tilted to one side with its headless driver slumped behind the wheel. The notion of fakery is playfully extended in Shonibare's latest photographic series, *Fake Death Pictures* (2011, fig. 12, pp. 204–5, 206, 207): five highly theatrical images that insert the figure of Admiral Nelson into historical paintings of death scenes, among them Henry Wallis's *The Death of Chatterton* (1856) and Édouard Manet's *The Suicide* (1877–81). In three of the *Fake Death Pictures,* Nelson perishes by his own hand, like Willy Loman at the wheel of his car, although the resulting images revel in pomp and overt artifice. In their representation of the great naval leader's death, Shonibare's staged photographs echo the demise of the social order itself. Speaking about the works, he has also suggested that they reflect the zeitgeist of the times, the death of colonial power, and the rise of new regional superpowers such as India and China. As old powers such as England fade, the developing countries become like "new colonials," building stature and wealth—and so the wheels of history turn once more.

A related sculpture, *Cannonball Heaven* (2011, pp. 80–81), literally softens, or neutralizes, Nelson's (and thus empire's) power. Based upon the cannons on HMS *Victory,* the work features two headless gentleman soldiers firing colorful fabric balls into the corner of the gallery. Shonibare comments that wars rarely happen in order to protect human rights. Rather, they occur in order to secure power, territory, and big economic agendas—such as Britain's control over the seas and thus trade. *Cannonball Heaven* presents a futile scenario and also a paradox: one in which war is suggested but effectively unable to be realized. One might also conclude that, here, the men of power (and their balls) are rendered impotent.

Writers on Shonibare's art have so far paid little attention to its cinematic aspects. They bear further examination, however, particularly in light of recent film works that tease out the relationship between still and moving art forms. Extending the range of his practice, Shonibare made his first film, *Un Ballo in Maschera* (*A Masked Ball*) (pp. 226–27) in 2004, inspired by the 1792 assassination of King Gustav III of Sweden at a masked ball in Stockholm. An elaborate costume drama featuring performers in Dutch wax ball gowns, frock coats, and ornate Venetian-style masks, Shonibare's film represents one of his most technically complex projects to date. Aristocracy and play, frivolity and excess are themes within the film, which takes its title from Giuseppe Verdi's 1859 opera on the same subject. *Un Ballo in Maschera* is followed by a second film, *Odile and Odette* (2005, pp. 224, 225), a considerably more pared-back production featuring two ballerinas who face each other on either side of a gilded frame. Their graceful movements mirror each other as though they are a single body in reflection, a notion that is disrupted only by the contrasting colors of the women's skin.

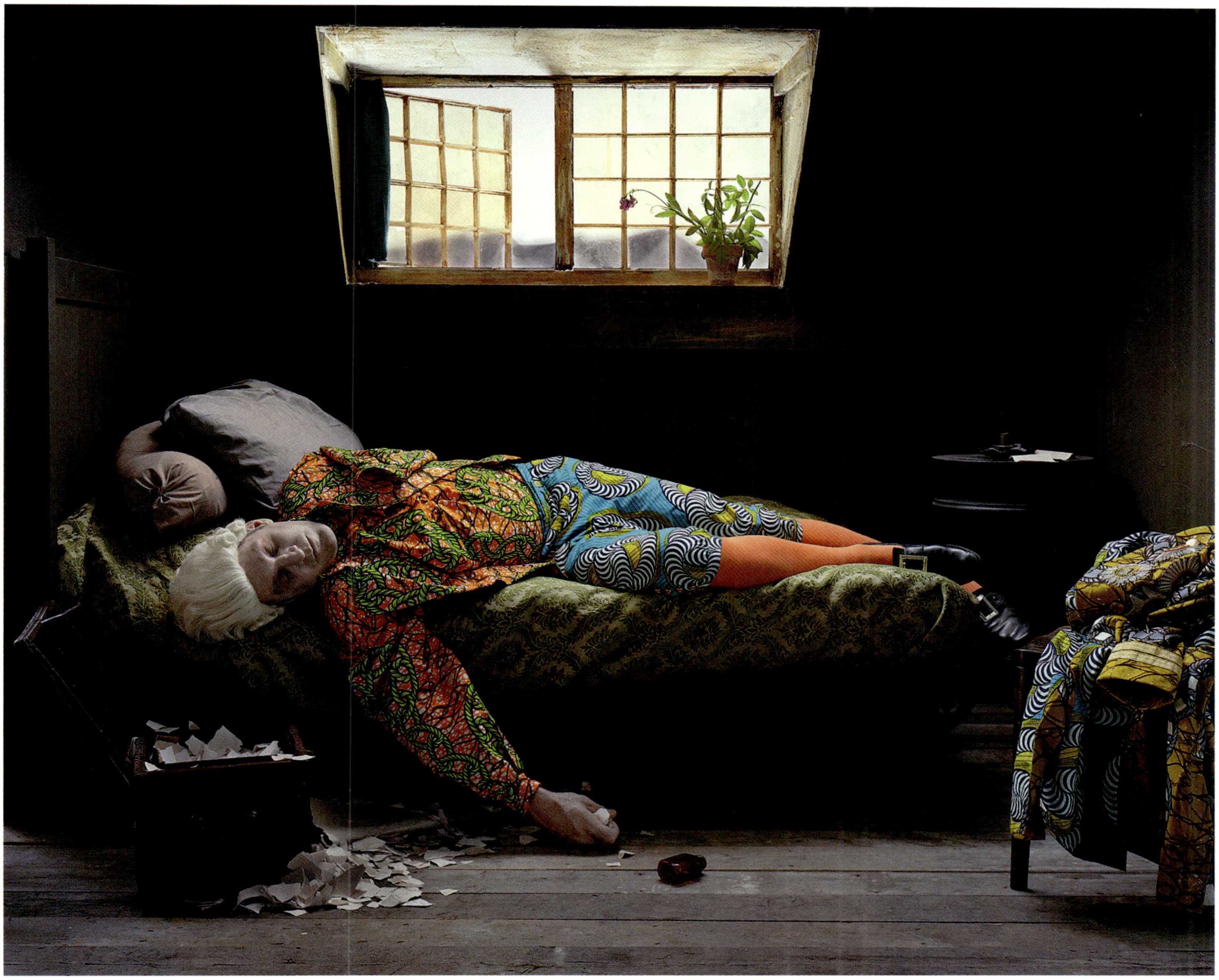

Fig. 12. Yinka Shonibare MBE, *Fake Death Picture (The Death of Chatterton—Henry Wallis)*, 2011. Digital chromogenic print, ed. of 5; 194 x 148.9 cm (framed)

Odile and Odette is inspired by Tchaikovsky's ballet *Swan Lake*, which premiered in Moscow in 1877. In the ballet the princess Odette has been cursed by the evil sorcerer Von Rothbart to live as a swan by day and a woman by night. Von Rothbart disguises his daughter, Odile, to resemble Odette, except that she wears black instead of white, and Prince Siegfried mistakenly swears to marry her, leading to tragedy for Odette and Siegfried. In Tchaikovsky's ballet, the roles of Odile and Odette are traditionally performed by one ballerina with two costumes. Shonibare's interpretation extends the theme of blackness and whiteness in his juxtaposition of the two dancers, and calls into question the Western binary opposition in which negative or "dark" forces are polarized against positive, "light" ones. A third, more recent film titled *Addio del Passato* (2011, pp. 220–21, 222–23) furthers Shonibare's exploration of the moving-image format. In this work, a black female opera singer has been "blind cast" by Shonibare to play the role of Admiral Nelson's estranged wife, singing Violetta's famed death lament from *La Traviata* by Verdi (1853). Her lament is repeated three times with subtle variations in staging, recalling the narrative loop of *Un Ballo in Maschera*, and is periodically intercut by watery images of Nelson with his consort, Lady Hamilton. It is further disrupted by meticulous restagings of Shonibare's *Fake Death Pictures* of Nelson's demise. It will not be lost on the artist that Nelson's greatest naval triumph at Trafalgar also resulted in his death, shot through the spine onboard the HMS *Victory*. History painters have represented the idea of the noble death and apotheosis, or transformation from the human to the divine realm, in depictions of Captain Cook (who was famously murdered by the "natives" at Kealakekua Bay, Hawaii) and Admiral Nelson after Trafalgar. Shonibare's film and alternative *Fake Death* scenarios puncture the nationalistic rhetoric and reification of the great naval hero, using mimicry and repetition instead to signal the decline of an empire.

Shonibare's embrace of film over the last decade marks a significant turning point for the artist. Moving between static and time-based art forms, he explores the idea of film as a "moving tableau" or animated painting with its luminous surfaces, sumptuous attention to detail, and strong compositional effects. The link between Shonibare's photography and film is equally strong, shifting between color and black and white and between the notion of the film still versus the moving tableau. Narrative is a central concern for Shonibare, introduced by the diaristic format and titling of his *Victorian Dandy* photographs and the sequential, cinematic presentation of his *Dorian Gray* images. Inversion and doubling also figure strongly, as illustrated by the cyclical, looped format of Shonibare's films: King Gustav III, for example, gets up to dance once more after being assassinated, while Nelson's wife repeats her lament over and over. Shonibare expressed his interest in film and narrative structures in the detailed interview that is included within this publication, noting, "I did not want to make a film with a beginning, middle, and end; instead, I wanted to explore the reflexivity of the film and how it reflects back on itself."[37] Speaking of *Un Ballo in Maschera*, he could equally have been referring to *Odile and Odette*, with its literal mirroring of form and content, or *Addio del Passato*. Shonibare also cites the French New Wave directors, including Alain Resnais and Jean-Luc Godard, as significant. Akira Kurosawa's cinematic masterpiece *Rashomon* (1950), with its self-referential structure and four alternating perspectives on one story, might offer another interesting counterpoint. In the latter film a brutal rape and murder in ancient Japan are replayed through the eyes of a bandit, a samurai and his wife, and a woodcutter. One character is the crime's perpetrator, one is its witness, and two are its apparent victims, yet each account varies greatly and the truth remains indistinct. Ambiguity and contradiction—key themes for Shonibare—are central to the film, as is its nonlinear, story-within-a-story format. Shonibare, like Kurosawa, cross-examines truth and fiction in his art, ultimately revealing "history" itself as a malleable human construction.

Like truth and fiction, reason and its opposite are recurring motifs for Shonibare. Embodied in the principles of the Age of Enlightenment, they are explored in depth in the artist's sculptural and photographic works of 2008 and beyond. As the eminent scholar Peter Gay observed, "The Enlightenment may have been a consequence and expression of a revolution in men's minds; it was also one of its principal causes."[38] Enlightenment thinking affected powerfully the political, economic, scientific, and social fabric of eighteenth-century Europe. Fluid as a "movement" and comprising many contradictory voices, the Enlightenment was nonetheless pivotal in shaping intellectual attitudes about the nature of man, rationality, and individual will versus authority. Shonibare's 2008 *Age of Enlightenment* sculptures (pp. 120–25) take five *philosophes* as their subjects: Immanuel Kant, Antoine Lavoisier, Jean le Rond d'Alembert, Adam Smith, and Gabrielle Émilie Le Tonnelier de Breteuil, Marquise du Châtelet. Each sculpture is given a physical disability, a rare autobiographical reference to Shonibare's own disability and equally a suggestion that even reason has its vulnerabilities.[39] Thus we encounter Kant as a double amputee, Smith with a hunchback, Lavoisier in a wheelchair, and d'Alembert and Le Tonnelier with wood prosthetic limbs. With his extensive makeup effects, Shonibare's *Dorian Gray* is perhaps an unlikely precursor (or "shadow") for the disfigurements presented in these works. Yet the earlier work, with its emphasis on duality and the nature of man, is interesting on both a personal and empirical level.

Shonibare's 2008 photographs *The Sleep of Reason Produces Monsters* (fig. 13, pp. 210–11, 212, 213) rework Francisco de Goya's 1799 etching *The Sleep of Reason Produces Monsters* (fig. 14). In the original etching we see Goya asleep at his desk, a billowing mass of creatures rising about him as irrational nocturnal fears take their hold. Goya's etching served as the frontispiece for his print suite *Los Caprichos*, a satirical critique of Spanish moral values, political corruption, and the debauchery of the clergy. Shonibare's interpretation restages the original image in five variations, each representing a world continent (Europe, Africa, America, Asia, and Australia). The sleeping figure differs in each photograph and is at odds with the continent he represents: a white man for Africa, an African man for Asia, and so forth. These images bring together the

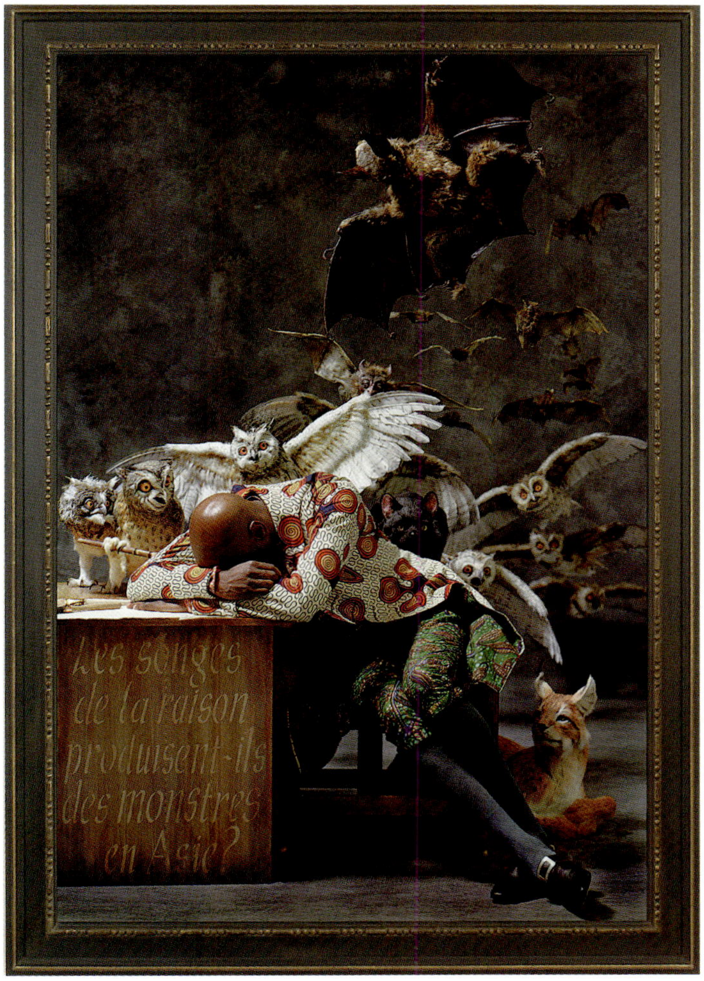

Fig. 13. Yinka Shonibare MBE, *The Sleep of Reason Produces Monsters (Asia)*, 2008. Chromogenic print mounted on aluminum, ed. of 5; 207 x 147.3 cm (framed)

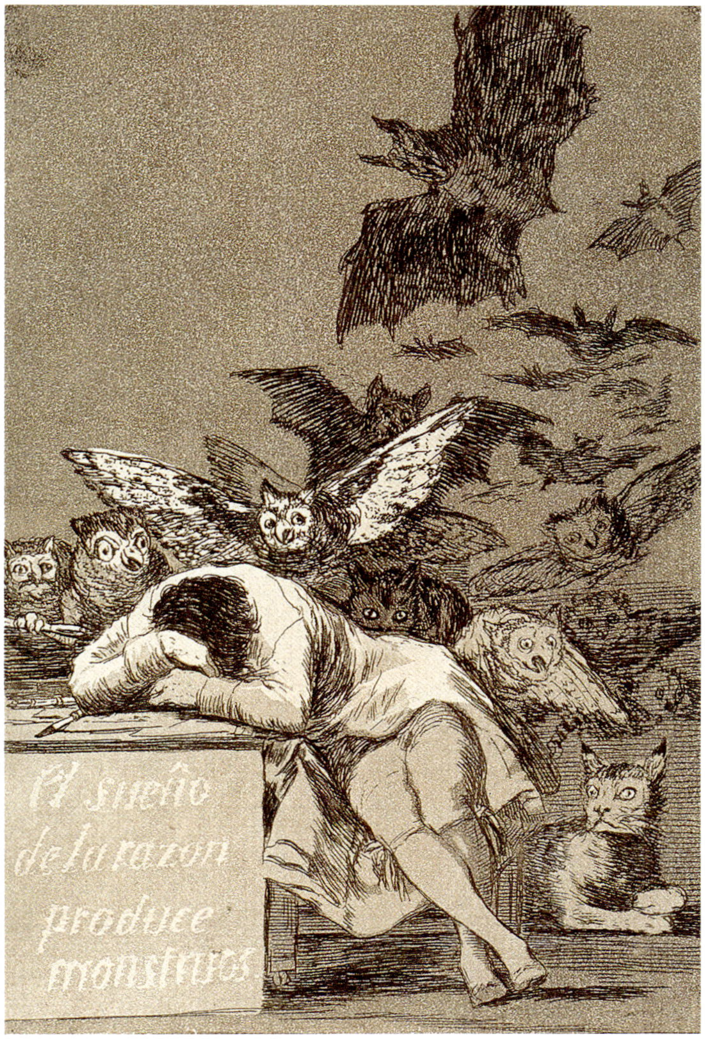

Fig. 14. Francisco de Goya, *The Sleep of Reason Produces Monsters* (*El sueño de la razón produce monstruos*), plate 43 from *Los Caprichos* (*The Caprices*), first edition, 1799. Etching and aquatint printed in sepia ink, 18.3 x 12.2 cm. National Gallery of Victoria, Melbourne, Felton Bequest, 1976

concerns that have shaped Shonibare's art since the mid-1990s, with their breaking down of grand narratives and contamination of ideas. In all five of them the specter of unreason hovers nearby, its presence a constant reminder that we humans are not perfect, rational, or enlightened all the time.

In his 1784 essay "An Answer to the Question: What Is Enlightenment?" the philosopher Kant cried, "Sapere aude! 'Have courage to use your own reason!'—that is the motto of enlightenment." Explaining that the individual must learn to think independently, "unfettered" by authority, he proposed that enlightenment "is the freedom to make public use of one's reason at every point."[40] Shonibare draws a literary parallel between the Enlightenment ideal of reason (or "illumination") and its "dark" opposite through the presence of Caliban, Prospero's deformed slave in *The Tempest*. Introduced as "a freckled whelp . . . not honoured with a human shape,"[41] Caliban is the orphaned "bastard" offspring of a witch called Sycorax. A large 2008 sculpture by Shonibare of a keeling ship (p. 127) alludes to the play's central narrative, in which a group of royal Italian seafarers is shipwrecked upon Caliban's magical island.[42]

Written as a comedy, Shakespeare's play contains serious themes about the intersection of reason and irrationality, darkness and light. Initially Prospero seeks to "civilize" Caliban, teaching him his European religion and language. When Caliban errs, however, Prospero enslaves him. Caliban's resistance may be read as the confrontation between colonizer and colonized, and his words are revealing: "You taught me language, and my profit on't / Is, I know how to curse. The red plague rid you / For learning me your language!"[43] The cultural theorist Homi K. Bhaba's observations resonate at all levels:

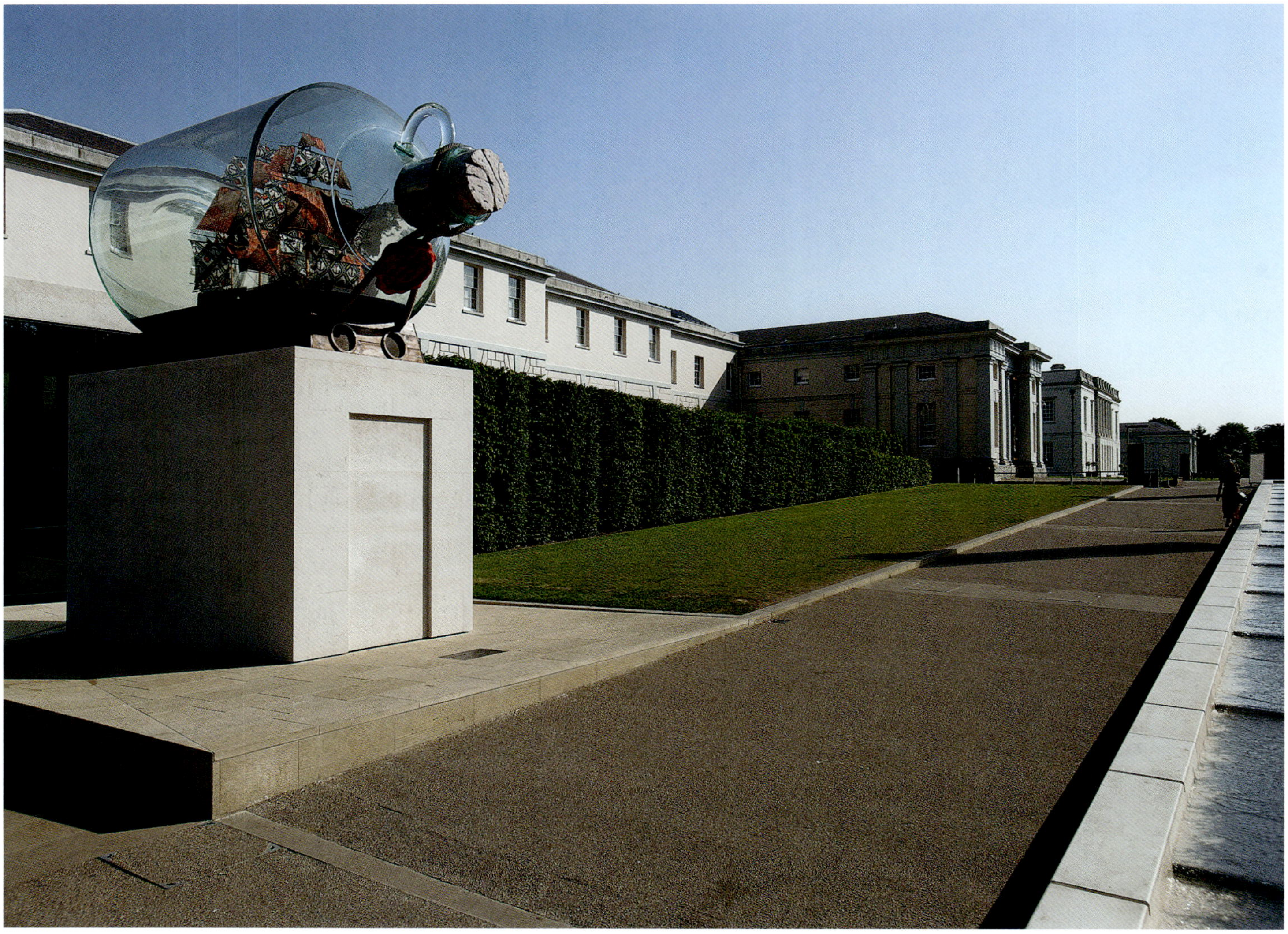

Fig. 15. Yinka Shonibare MBE, *Nelson's Ship in a Bottle*, 2010. Fiberglass, steel, brass, resin, UV ink on Dutch wax printed cotton, linen rigging, acrylic, wood; 290 x 525 x 235 cm. National Maritime Museum, Greenwich, London. Installation view, National Maritime Museum, Greenwich, 2013

"The discriminatory effects of the discourse of cultural colonialism . . . do not simply refer to a 'person,' or to a dialectical power struggle between self and Other, or to a discrimination between mother culture and alien cultures. Produced through a strategy of disavowal, the *reference* of discrimination is always to a process of splitting as the condition of subjugation: a discrimination between the mother culture and its bastards, the self and its doubles, where the trace of what is disavowed is not represented but repeated as something *different*—a mutation, a hybrid."[44] Caliban's physical disfigurement, echoed by Shonibare's *philosophes*, becomes both a metaphor and a mirror. Like his ambivalent "freckled" skin, it reflects meaning and similitude back onto those who impose it under the guise of rationality and civilizing force.

In 2008 Shonibare was selected for the prestigious Fourth Plinth commission in London's Trafalgar Square, a project that was unveiled in 2010 to critical acclaim. A replica of the HMS *Victory* with Dutch wax sails (pp. 2–3, 60–61), Shonibare's monumental ship in a bottle used its proximity to Nelson's Column to generate public awareness and debate, and has since come to rest permanently at the National Maritime Museum in Greenwich (see fig. 15), which houses an extensive collection of Nelson memorabilia. Since the success of his Fourth Plinth project, Shonibare has undertaken several major public commissions that expand his practice beyond the museum and into the public domain. This new dimension to the artist's career is significant, for it has widened his audience and provided complex conceptual and technical challenges. *Globe Head Ballerina* (2012, pp. 52–53, 59), commissioned by the Royal Opera House, is one of his first kinetic works and is permanently installed upon the facade of the company's Covent Garden headquarters like an oversize snow dome;

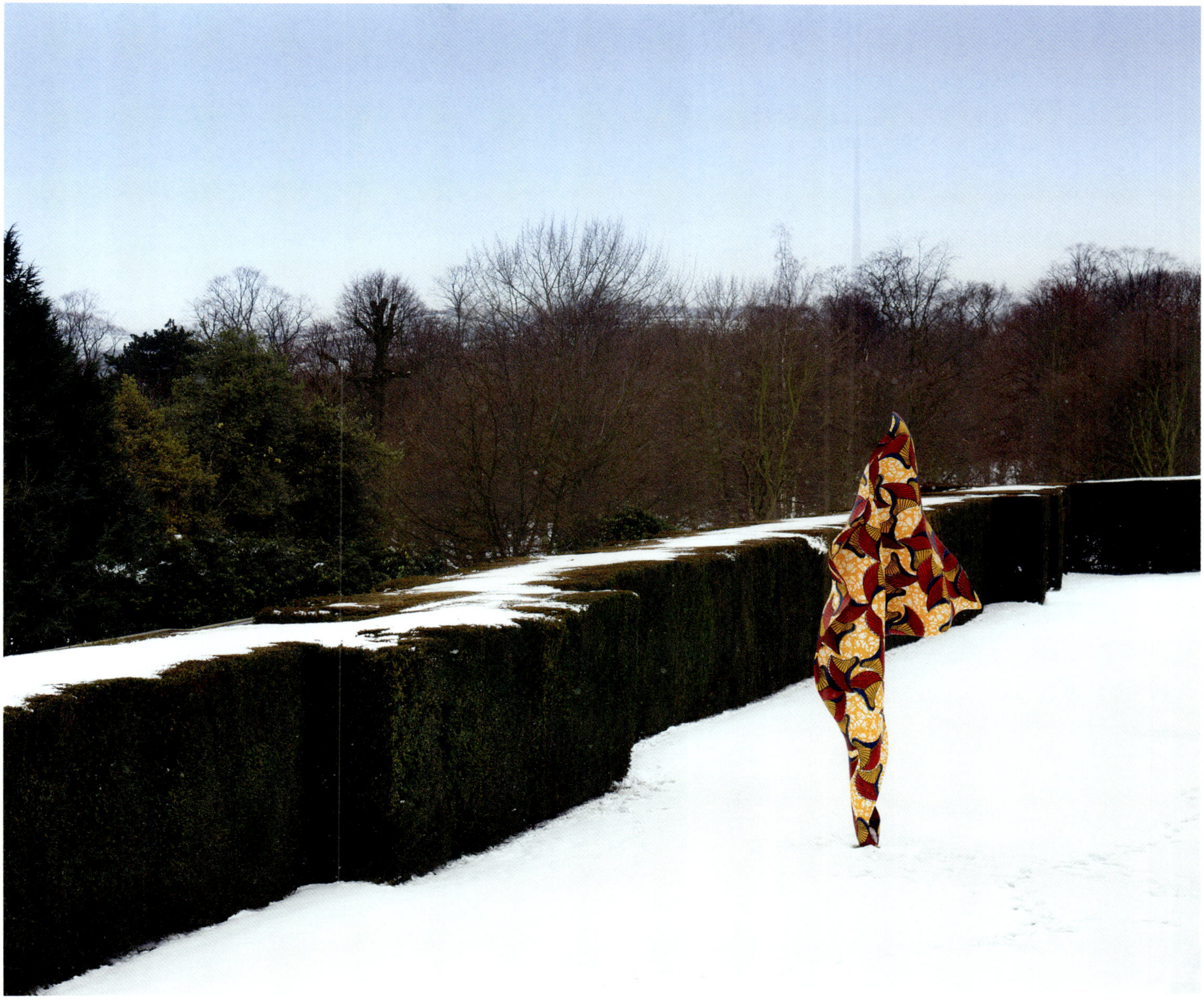

Fig. 16. Yinka Shonibare MBE, *Wind Sculpture 1*, 2013. Steel armature with hand-painted fiberglass resin cast, 610 x 340 x 80 cm. Commissioned by Yorkshire Sculpture Park, Wakefield, UK, for the exhibition *Yinka Shonibare MBE: FABRIC-ation*. Installation view, Yorkshire Sculpture Park, 2013

his two six-meter-high *Wind Sculptures* (fig. 16, pp. 54–55, 56–57), realized for the Yorkshire Sculpture Park in 2013, are constructed from fiberglass painted with Dutch wax patterns. There is something particularly whimsical about these works in their attempt to capture the impermanent, invisible nature of air itself. Reflecting Shonibare's ongoing fascination with flight, as illustrated by his flying aliens, Victorian inventors/adventurers, and modern-day astronauts, they are perhaps obliquely self-referential as well. Humankind's dream, he says, has been to achieve the impossible: to fly, like Icarus. In his desire to sculpt wind, Shonibare creates something tangible from the intangible and gives expression to the human spirit, transcending physical constraints and imperfections.

Yinka Shonibare was awarded a Member of the Order of the British Empire in 2005. He accepted the award with relish, deciding to use it as his "platform" despite—and because of—its obvious irony. Working against expectations, this gesture is particularly fitting within the context of his artistic practice and provides added means to communicate his message. Shonibare's art engages with history in order to draw attention to important issues in the present. Embracing a broad spectrum of material and conceptual forms, it works across cultural perspectives and introduces ambiguity and complexity in the place of rigid definitions. Shonibare has previously described the idea of the dandy as compelling because of its "Trojan Horse relationship to the aristocracy."[45] The artist similarly, indeed strategically, locates himself both within and outside the structures he critiques. In doing so, he stimulates the senses, engages the mind, and encourages careful thought for the future.

Rachel Kent is chief curator at the Museum of Contemporary Art Australia in Sydney. She has presented exhibitions in Australia, New Zealand, Japan, the United States, and Canada. She speaks and publishes widely on contemporary art and curated the survey exhibition *Yinka Shonibare MBE*, which opened at the MCA Australia before touring to the Auckland Art Gallery, New Zealand; the Brooklyn Museum, New York; and the National Museum of African Art, Smithsonian Institution, Washington, DC, in 2008–10.

Notes

1. Frantz Fanon, *Black Skins, White Masks*, trans. Charles Lam Markmann (1952; New York: Grove Press, 1967), 13.

2. Bernard Miller, "Interview with Yinka Shonibare MBE," in *Yinka Shonibare, MBE: Jardin d'Amour / Garden of Love*, ed. Germain Viatte (Paris: Musée du quai Branly / Flammarion, 2007), 14.

3. Jaap Guldemond and Gabriele Mackert, "To Entertain and Provoke: Western Influences in the Work of Yinka Shonibare," in *Yinka Shonibare: Double Dutch*, ed. Jaap Guldemond and Gabriele Mackert with Barbara van Kooij (Rotterdam: Museum Boijmans Van Beuningen; Vienna: Kunsthalle Wien; Rotterdam: NAi Publishers, 2004), 41.

4. Miller, "Interview with Yinka Shonibare MBE," 19–20.

5. Guldemond and Mackert, "To Entertain and Provoke," 37.

6. Ibid., 37.

7. See Suzanne Landau, "Yinka Shonibare's Garden of Pleasure," in *Yinka Shonibare: Double Dress*, ed. Suzanne Landau (Jerusalem: The Israel Museum, 2002), 11–12.

8. Guldemond and Mackert, "To Entertain and Provoke," 38.

9. James Baldwin, "Autobiographical Notes," in *Notes of a Native Son* (1955; Boston: Beacon Press, 1984), 6–7; Ralph Ellison, *Invisible Man* (1952; London: Penguin Books, 2001).

10. Clive Kellner, "Interview with Yinka Shonibare," in *Yinka Shonibare* (Johannesburg: Camouflage / Coartnews Publishing, 2001), 9.

11. Anthony Downey, "Setting the Stage: Yinka Shonibare MBE in Conversation with Anthony Downey," in this volume, 45.

12. Ibid.

13. Miller, "Interview with Yinka Shonibare MBE," 21.

14. Ibid., 12.

15. Ibid.

16. Ibid.

17. A. N. Wilson, *The Victorians* (London: Hutchinson, 2002), 1.

18. Guldemond and Mackert, "To Entertain and Provoke," 38.

19. Ibid.

20. Wilson, *The Victorians*, 487.

21. The "Act of the Berlin Conference on West Africa" was signed in February 1885 by key European powers as well as the United States and Turkey. See M. E. Chamberlain, *The Scramble for Africa*, Seminar Studies in History (London: Longman, 1974), including 124–25.

22. Wilson, *The Victorians*, 489.

23. Sarah Gertrude Millin, *Rhodes* (London: Chatto and Windus, 1933), 138.

24. See Downey, "Setting the Stage," in this volume, 43.

25. See chapter 40 in Wilson, *The Victorians*, 548–71.

26. Manthia Diawara, "Independence Cha Cha: The Art of Yinka Shonibare," in *Yinka Shonibare: Double Dutch*, 21.

27. Kellner, "Interview with Yinka Shonibare," 9.

28. See the documentary *Yinka Shonibare* (London: Illuminations, 2005), DVD.

29. Downey, "Setting the Stage," in this volume, 47.

30. Baudelaire expanded, "Dandyism appears above all in periods of transition, when democracy is not yet all-powerful, and aristocracy is only just beginning to totter and fall." Charles Baudelaire, "The Painter of Modern Life" (1863), in *The Painter of Modern Life and Other Essays* (London: Phaidon Press Ltd., 1964), 28.

31. Jean Fisher, "The Outsider Within: Shonibare's Dandy and the Parasitic Economy of Exchange," in Landau, *Yinka Shonibare: Double Dress*, 31–32.

32. Michelle Hetherington, "The Cult of the South Seas," in *Cook and Omai: The Cult of the South Seas* (Canberra: National Library of Australia, 2001), 6.

33. Oscar Wilde, preface to *The Picture of Dorian Gray* (London: Wordsworth Classics, 2001), 4.

34. James Baldwin, "Stranger in the Village," in *Notes of a Native Son*, 167.

35. See Fisher, "The Outsider Within," 33–35.

36. Arthur Miller, *Death of a Salesman* (London: Penguin Books, 1949), 95.

37. Downey, "Setting the Stage," in this volume, 48.

38. Peter Gay, *The Enlightenment: An Interpretation*, vol. 2, *The Science of Freedom* (London: Weidenfeld and Nicolson, 1969), 3–4.

39. Faye Hirsch, "Yinka Shonibare at James Cohan," *Art in America*, no. 6 (June–July 2008): 189.

40. Immanuel Kant, "An Answer to the Question: What Is Enlightenment?" (1784), in *What Is Enlightenment? Eighteenth Century Answers and Twentieth Century Questions*, trans. and ed. James Schmidt (Berkeley: University of California Press, 1996), 58–64.

41. William Shakespeare, *The Tempest*, ed. Martin Butler (London: Penguin Books, 2007), 18.

42. The ship is in fact *La Méduse*, which was famously shipwrecked in 1816 and depicted by Géricault in his painting *Raft of the Medusa* (1819).

43. Shakespeare, *The Tempest*, 21.

44. Homi K. Bhaba, "Signs Taken for Wonders," in *The Post-Colonial Studies Reader*, ed. Bill Ashcroft, Gareth Griffiths, and Helen Tiffin, 2nd ed. (Oxford: Routledge, 2006), 42.

45. *Yinka Shonibare* DVD.

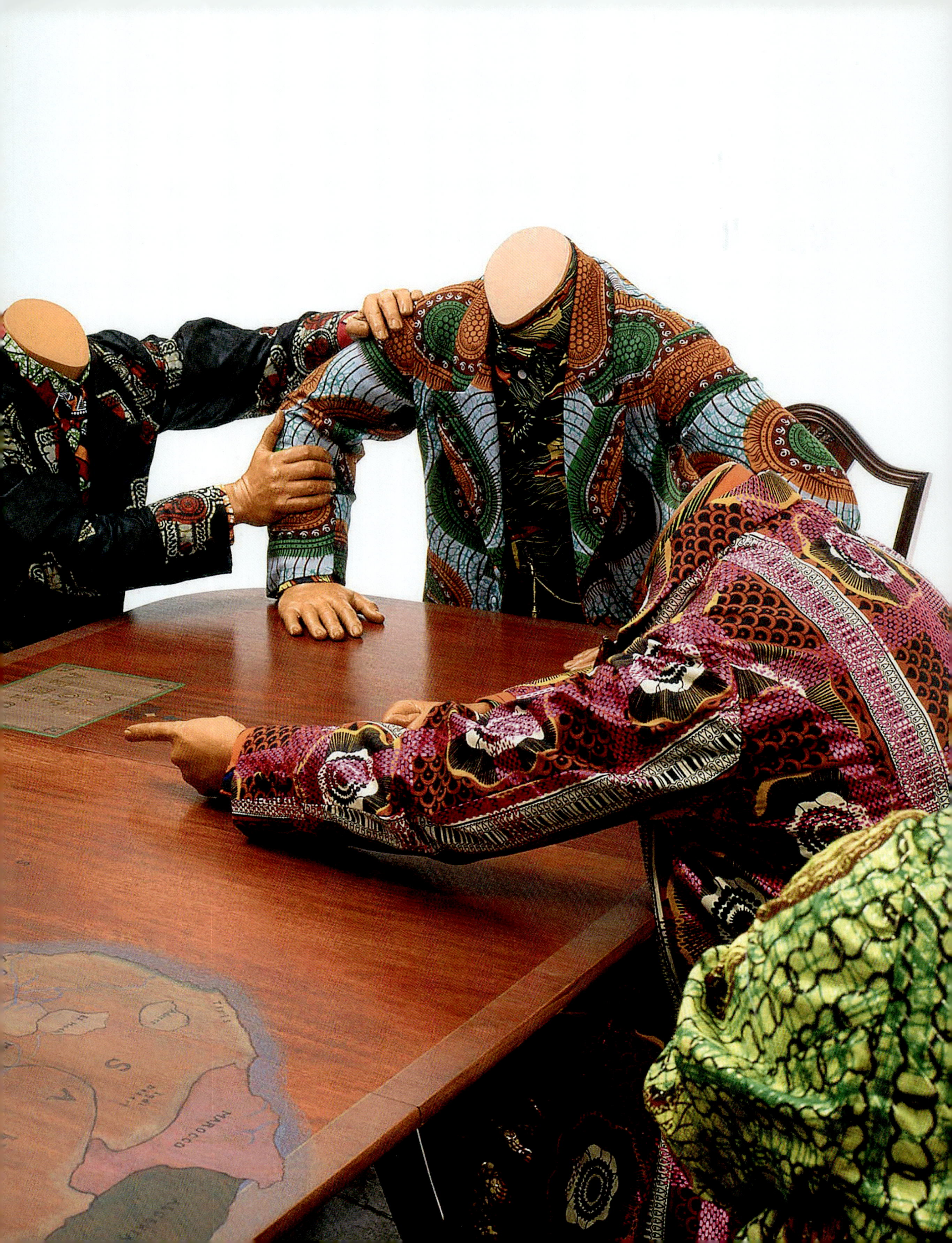
MAROCCO

Yinka Shonibare MBE: The Politics of Representation

Robert Hobbs

Although I speak Yoruba very well, I think in English sometimes and it's rather strange, you know. You move from one way of thinking. Then you think in Yoruba: sometimes you think in English and you dream in English sometimes. It's that kind of existence that in a way my work tries to talk about . . . my work is actually not about the representation of politics but the politics of representation.

—Yinka Shonibare MBE, in John Picton, "Laughing at Ourselves," 2004

The art of the London-based Nigerian expatriate Yinka Shonibare MBE has been ratified as belonging to the contemporary canon. In the past twenty-four years it has been included in hundreds of group shows and has been the focus of more than fifty solo museum and gallery exhibitions; and in the last decade it has been featured on the covers of *ARTnews* (2002), *Artforum* (2003), *Sculpture* (2006), and *Art in America* (2008), as well as an elaborate *New York Times Style Magazine* spread (2005). With all this coverage, plus being made in 2005 a Member of the Order of the British Empire (MBE), a government-initiated honorific for his services to art, and receiving prominent commissions for public sculpture installations at London's Trafalgar Square (2010), Royal Opera House (2012), and the Yorkshire Sculpture Park (2013), one would think the most relevant questions about Shonibare's work have been posed and answered. This is not the case. In the many perceptive responses to his work, the overall emphasis, with few exceptions, has been focused rather than panoramic. It has looked at distinct bodies of work rather than considering how this artist's work builds on such larger aesthetic issues as excess and beauty and such broad-based political concerns as imperialism, postcolonialism, and globalism. In order to appreciate Shonibare's remarkable contributions to recent art in particular and art's increasing awareness of its own contributions to knowledge in general, it is essential to consider the contrapuntal nature of this work that keeps dialectics open rather than allowing its meanings to be closed off. This work is notable not only for those high art and popular cultural elements that it privileges but also for those Western aspects of the artist's Yoruba background that it reconsiders from an international point of view.

Scramble for Africa (detail), 2003. Fourteen life-size mannequins, fourteen chairs, table, Dutch wax printed cotton; 132 x 488 x 280 cm. The Pinnell Collection, Dallas; commissioned by the Museum for African Art, New York

Instead of looking at Shonibare's work as comprising discrete and autonomous objects, I will use a wide-angle lens to consider the perspectives that it permits and enhances as well as those it precludes. This approach assumes an understanding of aspects of the French theorist Michel Foucault's definition of the author's function as the point of entry to a socially ratified discourse, which in turn depends on the French linguist Émile Benveniste's theory of enunciation, pertaining to the position that subjects must assume within language if their information is to be construed as knowledge. In addition, I will emphasize the ways that Shonibare relies on Jacques Derrida's theory of deconstruction. In doing so he employs "excessive beauty in his work" as well as evades the limits of established thinking—concepts derived from the French theorist Georges Bataille—as a means for undermining and redirecting such polarities as past and present, high and popular art, and first and third world cultural conventions.

Even though Shonibare's family and early development have had an impact on the overall direction of his work, there has been little appreciation of the important role that his traditional Yoruba background plays in his art, an approach that will be discussed at the end of this essay. This lacuna no doubt results in part from a commendable deference to the artist's insistence that his British citizenship has been the major influence on his work:

> Geographically and contextually I'm British now. I pay British taxes, I'm subject to the same weather, I watch the same telly.
>
> I'm absolutely certain that the way my work looks has very particularly to do with its London context. It wouldn't have developed in the same way anywhere else. It reflects a multiculturalism that's unique to London—you won't even find it in New York, because it's far more ghettoized than London.[1]

This critical nod to Shonibare's British affiliations has been buttressed in recent years by his insistence on adding the initials *MBE* to his name when it is used professionally, signifying his membership in the Order of the British Empire. Speaking of this distinction, Shonibare has reminisced, "Some of my friends were shocked that . . . I accepted it, though not half as shocked as they were when they found out that I was going to make it part of my artistic identity. . . . But I like that contradiction."[2]

Despite Shonibare's wholesale ironic embrace of his London address and MBE status, he remains proud of his Yoruba heritage and his international upbringing in Lagos. He has recalled his descent from the renowned nineteenth-century Yoruba king Kosoko of the Lagos tribe, even though he has admitted that this chief, like many others at the time, was regrettably a slave owner. This is not surprising when one considers that Lagos was a major center for the slave trade from the early eighteenth century to the middle of the nineteenth century. More pertinent to Shonibare's artistic practice: his grandfather was a tailor. In the late 1950s and 1960s his parents were part of a new Nigerian elite, which benefited from the country's independence in 1960 and continued membership in the British Commonwealth. About the same time that this country's sovereignty was becoming a reality, the Shonibares moved to London to prepare for leadership positions in Nigeria. Shonibare's father became a successful corporate lawyer and worked with companies going into receivership, while his mother was employed briefly as an executive secretary before becoming a full-time parent. Yinka, the couple's third child, was born in 1962 in London; when he was three years old, the family moved to Lagos, then Nigeria's capital. Because his parents, like many other expatriate students, had the forethought and funds to purchase a London town house while living there, the family regularly summered in this house while Yinka was growing up. His father could afford to send the three children to excellent Western schools in Lagos where only English was spoken. And while his father wore business suits and spoke English during the day, at home he changed into African robes—sure signs of national pride—and spoke Yoruba. Like their father, Yinka and his siblings were divided between European and Nigerian cultures, albeit in different ways. They spoke Yoruba at home; however, instead of embracing traditional African dress, they preferred wearing only Western clothes, and in their free time they relished mixing first and third world popular culture. According to Shonibare:

> We mixed listening to local Yoruba music, watching Yoruba drama on television, and watching *Hawaii 5-0* and programs coming from the U.S. I drank Coca-Cola like everybody else. In my home, my father reads *National Geographic*, *The Economist*, and *Time*. It was totally natural for a modern African. That's how I evolved as a child. There was nothing about my upbringing that was traditionally African, if you can put it that way.[3]

In addition to immersing himself in mainstream and Nigerian pop culture, Shonibare began to be interested in art while still in elementary school. He took classes at the Lagos Museum, which focused on Western-style painting even though the museum featured collections of tribal objects.[4] During this time he was intrigued by comic-book graphics such as those appearing in *Spider-Man*, *Captain America*, and *Asterix*. He also would buy art instruction manuals, so that he learned the conventional ways of drawing flowers, for example, or painting seascapes. As he grew older, he copied paintings by Paul Cézanne and read Vincent van Gogh's letters.

In 1978 Shonibare's parents decided to send him to an elite English boarding school for his last two years of preparatory school. He was sixteen at the time and was astonished by the influx of impoverished Yoruba expatriates, who were moving to the UK for jobs. "I was actually surprised when I came to England," Shonibare later recalled, "and found out that there was this notion that if you were black you were somehow disadvantaged—I thought that was hilarious. But then you either dwell on those issues or turn them to your advantage."[5] In his study of Yoruba living in the UK, the African studies specialist B. Akíntúndé Oyètádé notes that from 1960 to the early 1990s, "the population of Nigerian residents in the UK has grown from less than 1,000 to almost 300,000, of whom 80 percent are Yoruba,"[6] and points out, "it is impossible to avoid hearing conversation in Yorùbá in places like . . . Brixton market,"[7] where they are only partially assimilated. Shonibare later did turn the new face of the Yoruba in London to his advantage when he began purchasing African-print fabric for his art from a Portuguese merchant's shop in Brixton.

In 1981, three years after moving to London and during his first year at art school, Shonibare contracted a viral infection leading to the rare neurological disorder known as transverse myelitis, which results in inflammation and permanent damage to the spinal cord. Because of this condition, he was completely paralyzed for a month and remained hospitalized for an entire year. After being confined to a wheelchair for three years, he was once again able to walk, even though his overall mobility and use of his left side have remained impaired. Recalling his slow convalescence, Shonibare explained, "I had to learn to do everything again—to dress myself, feed myself . . . everything . . ." and added, "but as things got better . . . I figured the only way I could really carry on was to get back into art school and pick up where I left off."[8] Two decades later Shonibare summarized the overall impact of his illness on him and his work:

> It's certainly affected my method. . . . I've become very good at delegating and have a number of people who facilitate my priorities. Also . . . I wouldn't want to be presumptuous—but I think the experience may have made me more acutely aware of my mortality than most. That's why I view pleasure as so important, and use it in my work as an intellectual basis for questioning a lot of things I believe very deeply.[9]

As one might expect, the journey from suffering a severe physical setback to assuming a philosophic stance toward it and then later recognizing the value of enjoyment was long and demanding. Shonibare's attitude shortly after his illness when he was studying at the Byam Shaw School of Painting and Drawing in London is revealed by his response to an instructor who questioned his use of perestroika in his art. In the mid-1980s, the general secretary of the Soviet Communist Party, Mikhail Gorbachev, initiated a sweeping reform of the USSR's policy of centralized economic planning by encouraging both groups and individuals to embrace aspects of Western capitalism. Tentatively approached during the years 1985–87 and then mandated into law in 1987, perestroika not only provided opportunities to open up the Soviet Union and its satellites to foreign capital but also led to the Soviet Union's dissolution. Shonibare may have been struck by the idea that in many respects this transformation of the Soviet Union encapsulates, in a remarkably short time, the type of transitions that had taken place earlier in the century and over a period of several decades when European empires were being broken up. In a tutorial the Byam Shaw instructor asked Shonibare, "Why are you making art about Russia? Why don't you produce authentic African art?"[10] At first Shonibare viewed these queries as exclusionary and prejudicial because of the implicit assumption that Africans should need to declare their ethnicity in their work. Fortunately, he was not prepared to make this concession. As he thought about his professor's queries, he recognized how much they hinged on residual imperialist views of authenticity.

Shonibare's realization was in sync with a then full-scale debate about the status of so-called primitive art. *Artforum* editor Tom McEvilley initiated this conversation when he severely criticized the treatment of third world art included in the blockbuster exhibition *"Primitivism" in 20th Century Art*, which curators William Rubin and Kirk Varnedoe opened in 1984 at New York's Museum of Modern Art (MoMA). McEvilley's response to this exhibition became the focus of exchanges between the two parties published in the February and May 1985 issues of *Artforum*. McEvilley's approach was largely endorsed by curators, art historians, anthropologists, and artists around the world intent on separating lingering modern assumptions about art from postmodern goals.

For McEvilley and others, the exhibition wrongfully perpetuated an out-of-date imperialist approach since it regarded tribal objects only as sources of inspiration for vanguard artists. Rubin in particular, in the modernist section of the exhibition, attempted to achieve parity between tribal and Western objects even as he relegated the latter to a universal category unconcerned with differences between cultures, individual artists, and dates. Despite Rubin's attempt to characterize the relationships between tribal and Western objects as affinities, the exhibition presented them in the supportive role of decontextualized foundations for modern artists' inspiration. Rubin ignored postmodernism's foundational premise that art's meaning must be subject to ongoing and open-ended debates between different parties and dissimilar points of view.[11] In one of his rejoinders to Rubin and Varnedoe, McEvilley summarized this postmodern approach in language that anticipates aspects of Shonibare's mature work:

> What we must learn is to see a doubleness, the two aspects at once, simultaneously feeling these objects as art, which is our way of appreciation, and maintaining a sharp and constant awareness of the fact that the people of their own culture did not so feel them. This keen awareness of cultural relativity and of the arbitrariness of one's own horizon is simply the necessary step in maturation for our culture.[12]

Years after MoMA's exhibition attempted to demonstrate the relevancy of tribal objects in museums devoted to contemporary art, this show continued to elicit strong reactions from curators and scholars.

Differing from MoMA's show, the catalogue for *Yoruba: Nine Centuries of African Art and Thought*, a 1989 exhibition at the Center for African Art, New York, included an Egungun mask that made fun of a European male, thus presenting an African point of view. One of this exhibition's goals was "to dispel the notion of a fictional, timeless, 'ethnographic present' by illustrating continuities and/or changes over several centuries in 'shapes of time' and thought."[13]

In 1992 the British art historian Sidney Littlefield Kasfir, writing in *African Arts*, characterized the controversies generated by *"Primitivism"* and the Centre Georges Pompidou's 1989 *Magiciens de la Terre* as a "debate about African art . . . concern[ing] its role as a mirror of Western colonial history." The exhibition attempts "to demonstrate the 'affinities' between 'the tribal and the modern,' Third World and First World," while "postmodern critics have used these exhibitions . . . to comment upon the intellectual appropriation of African and other Third World art by Western museums."[14] Kasfir ties the issue of the authenticity of African art—a topical subject in the late 1980s and early 1990s—to the commodity culture of dealers and art collectors who decide which objects will be considered as legitimate. She dryly concludes, "The Western connoisseur is the essential missing factor that transforms artifact into art."[15] The criteria for this person's judgment, she notes, depend on viewing African artists as anonymous and eternally unchanging screens on which their tribe's essential ethos is projected.[16] This quest for authenticity has necessitated removing from contemporary photographs and films of African peoples evidence of non-African cultural connections that Shonibare and his peers in Lagos and other parts of Nigeria had enjoyed while growing up.

This reactionary view of traditional African art, which was packaged as "tribal art" and regarded as the only truly authentic African art, was increasingly lambasted in the 1980s. Shonibare's approach was anticipated by the critical attitude toward modern art that was the subject of work being made in the 1980s by the New York East Village commodity artists—Ashley Bickerton, Peter Halley, Jeff Koons, Haim Steinbach, and Meyer Vaisman—whose work was known collectively as Neo-Geo. Their effort to evaluate commodification's effects without being co-opted by its spurious values was a delicate balance that sometimes worked and just as often made these artists, particularly Koons, with his seemingly generous acceptance of kitsch, appear to be colluders rather than critics. In addition to artists questioning the excesses of commodity culture, market researchers, who were similarly influenced during the 1980s by the French theorist Jean Baudrillard's reworking of Marxist production in terms of late capitalist consumption, were looking at the ways consumers were acquiring signs and symbolic power when purchasing goods and thereby ratifying distinct social meanings while doing so. Their emphasis on consumption as a mode of ratifying particular sign systems and on interactions between shopping rituals and fine art protocols as a way of setting up meaningful situations was to have an enormous impact on Shonibare's work, which focuses on the different ways of approaching a commercial product: African-print fabrics. But before we look at the polyvalent role commodification plays in his art, it helps to consider briefly the overall cultural phenomenon of Afrocentrism because Shonibare's art plays with the expectations and attitudes of this broad-based informal movement, which first achieved an international following in the 1980s.

Afrocentrism, also known as "nativism," revives aspects of 1930s-era Pan-Africanism and Negritude, which had largely been confined to artists and intellectuals, and dilutes the program of Black Power nationalism, which had appealed in the 1960s to a relatively small number of political radicals. Like these movements, Afrocentrism is predicated on a discourse of authenticity. In the 1980s it became a largely middle-class movement in both the UK and the US. For blacks wishing to support a cultural heritage based on race and self-esteem, Afrocentrism played an important role. In her capacity as the curator of the Studio Museum in Harlem, Thelma Golden characterized Afrocentrism's hold on the black middle class. Although she described a situation in the US, her remarks also apply to the UK version that the worldwide hip-hop phenomenon helped to catalyze and perpetuate. Golden writes:

> Afrocentrism had entered the mainstream of black American life, and its influence could be felt everywhere: in the lyrics of conscious hip-hop, in the dubious, growing popularity of Kwanzaa (an "African" holiday invented by the black nationalist Maulena Karenga), in the fact that we now called ourselves African American rather than black. (The "African" in African American represented a desire as much as a fact, a reaffirmation of a bond that history had severed.) This Afrocentrism had a distinctly commercial bent. African Americans proudly bought and collected African artifacts, tangible symbols of their cultural ancestry. There was a hope in this hunger for symbols, hope that the erasure of our heritage—symbolized most vividly by the "X" in Malcolm's name—could be reversed by patient, determined effort, by a kind of cultural renaissance. African Americans wrapped themselves in all things African, and, in the process, often imagined a place that bore little resemblance to the real Africa . . . constructing a spiritual homeland that was pure, authentic, and almost as imaginary as the Dark continent in the writings of Eurocentrism, but also, strangely enough, its mirror image.[17]

African Americans as well as Afro-English youth signaled their Afrocentrism by wearing shirts, robes, headscarves, and caftans made of the intensely patterned African-style cotton fabrics that had been embraced two to three decades earlier by African nationalists. Even though these textiles connoted African solidarity, they were, until recently, designed and mostly manufactured in Europe.

Shonibare's education at Goldsmiths College, University of London, where he enrolled in 1989, put him in a position to demonstrate how this African-style fabric might serve as a sliding signifier of authenticity and simulation. He entered the college the same year Damien Hirst graduated, and he subsequently exhibited with the group of artists around Hirst known as YBAs (Young British Artists) in a number of shows, most notably Charles Saatchi's controversial *Sensation* exhibition at the Royal Academy. But he has never been considered one of its members, probably because his advocacy of excessive beauty and ironic, polite restraint differs from their shock tactics. As he later explained, "Yes, okay, I am here to protest, but I am going to do it like a gentleman. It is going to look very nice. You are not even going to realise that I am protesting, you are going to invite me to your museum because the work is nice."[18]

Because Goldsmiths' students focused on conceptual art strategies and held feminist theory in high regard, Shonibare soon became acquainted with the work of the American artists Jenny Holzer, Barbara Kruger, Cindy Sherman, and Nancy Spero. Their work empowered him to view racist stereotypes as subjects that his art could probe and critique. "I realised," Shonibare reflected, "that I didn't have to accept my designation as some sort of doomed other, I could challenge my relationship to authority with humour and parody in mimicking and mirroring."[19] His familiarization with their work also enabled him to look at the ways identity can be constructed and, at the same time, undermined through using African-print fabrics.

Since most of Shonibare's art after 1992, with the notable exception of his photographic cycles *Diary of a Victorian Dandy* (1998, pp. 218–19) and *Dorian Gray* (2001, pp. 216, 217), has incorporated African-print fabric in paintings, sculptures, installations, and photographs, it is crucial to understand the complex and at times little-understood background of the material that affects the way it is read. African-print fabric has been as important to Shonibare's art as automotive parts have been to John Chamberlain, since both types of materials furnish ongoing and offstage sets of signs that impact the work these two artists have made. The meaning of African-print fabric in Shonibare's work is in part predicated on its history, the process by which it is manufactured and merchandised, and the way it has been traditionally used in Africa as well as more recently in the UK and US, where it has become a sign of Afrocentricism. Before looking at this product's history, a brief view of the product names used for this material helps, in part, to explain why its references to authenticity and place of manufacture have proven such a rich resource for Shonibare. Standard names generally used for this fabric are the same ones employed by the Dutch manufacturer Vlisco Company, the producer of the finest versions of African-print textile since 1846, and the fabrics that Shonibare utilizes for his work. These names are "Super Wax," which Vlisco inaugurated in 1973, and "Real Dutch Wax," or "Véritable Wax Hollandais Vlisco" (for French-speaking Africans), which the company introduced in 1980 when it was printed on the fabric's selvage to signify its origin.[20] As one might expect, there are a number of permutations of these brand names, testifying to their importance, in addition to generic references such as "industrial batik" and "African-print fabric."

The history of the distribution of European and Southeast Asian printed cottons in sub-Saharan West and Central Africa is sketchy at best. According to Kevin Matthews of the UCLA African Studies Center, "European and Indian-produced textiles . . . served as exchange currency in the gold, ivory and slave trades."[21] The distribution of these fabrics began in the late sixteenth century when the Portuguese sold Indian cotton textiles; late in the nineteenth century French merchants exported "guinea cloth" to this region. In order to compete with Indian fabrics, particularly calicoes from Calcutta, which were often traded for African slaves, European manufacturers in the mid-nineteenth century began improving on the designs commonly used for Yoruba resist-dyed textiles and other regional fabrics. When the Dutch recruited West African mercenaries over the extraordinarily long period of 1837–72 to help take back Indonesia, these soldiers returned home with Eastern batiks, which were already known in West Africa through trade, and this nineteenth-century influx further enhanced the popularity of the batiks already familiar to sub-Saharan Africans.

An often-told story is that Dutch manufacturers began producing batiks in the nineteenth century to compete with the Indonesian market's indigenous producers. When the Dutch product failed to meet the high standards of the Indonesian markets, it was pawned off on less discerning West and Central African buyers. This new market was supposedly delighted with the veining and spotting that developed as a result of the dyeing used instead of the traditional wax batik method. But this narrative is inconsistent with Vlisco's historical account,[22] even though it is apparently true of other companies such as the Belgian Previnaire & Co.[23] According to Vlisco, which was known as PF van Vlissingen & Co. before 1964, completely hand-printed textiles were produced until about 1910–11, when the company introduced its first wax printing machine. Vlisco had begun exporting its completely hand-printed wax batiks to the Dutch East Indies in 1852 and only started introducing its designs in Africa in 1876. Problems with the Dutch East Indian market began in 1900 when Indonesians developed stamps, which lowered production costs, and when the Indonesian Dutch government protected local productions by imposing stiff tariffs, thus forcing Vlisco and other Dutch companies to develop markets elsewhere, including Africa, which became Vlisco's major focus.

In 1932 the director of Vlisco visited West Africa and discovered ways his products could appeal even more to local preferences, with the result that the company was ultimately able to dominate the West African market. In the 1950s, as independent countries emerged in Africa, enterprising businesspeople in West Africa began building printing mills, thus undermining all European factories except for the ones owned by Vlisco and ABC, based in Hyde, Cheshire, just outside Manchester. In 1966 Vlisco began taking steps to cut down on the labor-intensive process of hand-printing, which involved as many as twenty-seven steps, and stopped producing hand-printed designs at its main site in 1993, although it apparently still continues to employ hand-blockers at its subsidiary Ghana

Textile Printing.[24] The company estimated in 2006 that 75 percent of all wax fabric sold in Africa used Vlisco designs, but noted that their patterns were being illegally produced by a number of Asian and African companies.

Though Vlisco's innovative designs number in the thousands and are thus ubiquitous in sub-Saharan West and Central Africa, and the quality of its production has outdistanced that of its competitors, its continued imperial approach to its African market may be another reason why Shonibare employs this material for his work. The company does not hire African designers, though it did regularly solicit the opinions of African wholesalers until the 1970s.[25] Producing on average about 150 new designs each year, the company sends its designers, who, according to the company's head of design, Frans van Rood, "must have a keen interest in the exotic," into the field in Africa every two to three years to talk to Vlisco distributors, wholesalers, and people frequenting the marketplaces. In 2000 Van Rood characterized the firm's product in anachronistically imperialistic terms. Noting that "most Africans appreciate innovations that come from abroad, not those that come from within," he pointed out that Vlisco's textiles are African only in inspiration: "We interpret what we see in the African streets, and we see what our own imagination comes up with. We mix the two, and that provides for a constant process of creation and innovation that wouldn't happen otherwise."

These popular simulacra are considered effective in providing contemporary Africans with a more compelling image of themselves than their own designers could. The situation resembles the tantalizingly obtuse circularity outlined by Kobena Mercer, a cultural studies specialist focusing on modes of representation in the African Diaspora. He pointedly asks, "What happens when ethnics appropriate others' appropriations of ethnicity?"[26] Van Rood elaborates on this same situation by subscribing to the long overworked authenticity ideology that continues to encumber Africans and others with conventional thinking:

> In our view, African designers are too dependent on traditions. From olden days, African artists have been, first and foremost, the people to [give] voice to the traditions. In many societies, they are the keepers of history. . . . [T]hey are craftsmen rather than artists.

Consistent with their view that they can provide their African market with an exoticism its artists do not have the aesthetic distance to discern, Vlisco designers have found ways to improve on the art of the "perfect imperfection":

> If we use lines or a raster of lines, instead of putting them at exact geometrical angles, we give the lines a slightly odd angle, sometimes hardly visible with the bare eye. The effect is that the screen, instead of being stable, is unstable and much more lively. It dances in front of your eyes.

Relying on the highly artificial simulacra of African tastes, Shonibare's use of Vlisco fabrics enables him to avoid modern art's quest for essentials as he puns the different levels of fabrication involved in the creation, marketing, and use of these textiles. Not only do the textiles result from an involved fabrication based on a combination of local needs and international business interests, but they are also concerned with constructing shorthand signs for local narratives that take the form of letters, depicted and written proverbs, and pictures of rulers and visiting dignitaries, as well as emblems of government authority, political parties, wealth, status, and timely issues. Thus people wearing the cloth are able to demonstrate physically, through their dress, an allegiance to different facets of the social and political fabric constituting their cultural universe. In addition to serving as a visual/verbal pun, Shonibare's African-print cloth, with its assumptions of a constructed Africanness, is a readymade with the built-in joke of authenticity that even Marcel Duchamp would have appreciated, even though others might argue from a Wittgensteinian perspective that applied use, rather than a product's origin, is a function of meaning.[27] Apropos this line of reasoning, the African art specialist John Picton has recalled seeing groups of people in West Africa attending political and family celebrations all dressed in the same African-print fabric.[28] And in his exploration of the Yoruba in London, Oyètádé has noted the prevalence of these African prints during the summer and at special events such as housewarmings, weddings, and naming ceremonies where they appeared to epitomize the subject of Yorubaland, since he and others were under the mistaken impression that the shops in Brixton had imported all these fabrics from Nigeria.[29]

Because there is a great difference in the quality and consequent price of African-print textiles, which range from the least expensive screen prints to moderately priced resin-resist-dyed fabrics with hand-blocked colors to the relatively costly wax-dyed fabrics, responses to the significance of this fabric in Shonibare's art have ranged from discussions of its working-class affiliations to estimations of the considerable price that purchasing six-meter lengths of Vlisco textiles (the quantity required for a traditional woman's dress and head-scarf) would entail. West Africans have been known to invest in the best products as hedges against inflation, since Real Dutch Wax and Super Wax, along with gold and diamonds, have held their value during times of financial insecurity. As an example of the relative values separating high- and low-end markets, in 2000 journalist Matt Steinglass compared Real Dutch Wax, which then sold for about US$90 for a six-meter length in Togo, to an Asian knockoff that was deceptively referred to as "Real Wax—Printed as [*sic*] Holland," which sold for one-tenth of this amount.[30] Since the average Togan yearly income was then around $350, one can readily appreciate the type of luxury product Vlisco's textiles represent. The differences between low and high grades not only stem from the printing techniques employed but are also apparent in the stability of the fabric's dyes after repeated washings. As one might expect, the cheapest materials fade after one washing whereas the best retain their quality after repeated use.

From this discussion, one can conclude that when Shonibare uses Real Dutch Wax or Super Wax for his sculptures, he is not so much mixing low and high elements, similar to Neo-Geo artists like Koons, as he is employing an identifiable high-end polyvalent sign of colonialism, nationalism, and globalism. He does so in order to reference the luxury and expense of both European imperial powers and colonized elites, whose combined wealth during imperialism was derived from the political trajectories that they had set on their course and perpetuated. Considered in this way, Shonibare's work connects the aristocracy of Europe with the colonized wealthy class, which benefited from Western educations and international connections. Regarding the aristocracy and their role in his work, Shonibare has pointed out, "I'm not moralistic about the aristocracy. . . . I crave the trappings of wealth like anyone else, but politically I do question the means by which that is achieved."[31] In addition, when Shonibare has his figures constructed, he elides strict differences in skin tones so as to avoid racial tagging and also to indicate complicity between both groups. In this way, his assessment is double-edged, demonstrating the necessary collusion—one of his main yet still unappreciated subjects—that supports the wealth and power of both groups.

Shonibare's first exhibited work to incorporate African-print fabric is *Installation*, which was a finalist in the 1992 Barclays Young Artist Award annual exhibition, featuring work by recent London art school graduates. Since this exhibition was held from February 7 to March 8, 1992, at the Serpentine Gallery, a highly visible and respected London venue for cutting-edge work, and since Shonibare's piece was the subject of a three-page *African Arts* review that concludes with the artist speculating about "what might happen when he takes his kind of art to Nigeria,"[32] the dialectics between mainstream and formerly colonized venues that MoMA's curators had totally ignored eight years earlier are now duly noted. *Installation* comprises twenty-three randomly placed and differently sized rectangles of stretched fabric: some are painted with hardware-store paint to resemble monochromes, while others remain densely patterned. Situated on two perpendicular white walls, the unpainted pieces of cloth present a range of subjects, including soccer players, flowers, alphabet letters, images of playing cards, cosmic diagrams, and tribal symbols. Both the fabric and its subject matter sustain Shonibare's earlier goal to connect Africa with the modern world in his art. Following the example of the 1980s New York commodity artist Haim Steinbach, Shonibare's works of the late 1980s and early 1990s juxtaposed images of tribal artifacts found in the British Museum with modern home appliances selected from an Argos catalogue. These include such pairings as an Ife head with a coffeemaker as well as a Lega stool with a telephone, which he titled *Caryatid Figures Rafia Colour Motif with Viscount from British Telecom*. These unusual combinations also perpetuated Victor Shklovsky's early twentieth-century Russian Formalist ideal of distancing images from familiar contexts so that they might be seen afresh.[33]

After creating *Installation*, Shonibare continued attaching stretched African prints to small square stretchers, which he could physically handle with ease, and then over-painted some of them with emulsion and house paint (see pp. 201, 202, 203). At this stage in his development, his conceptual grounding in feminism enabled him to regard painting as a means of signifying the subjects of African-print fabrics as popular-culture phenomena rather than as a set of personally generated

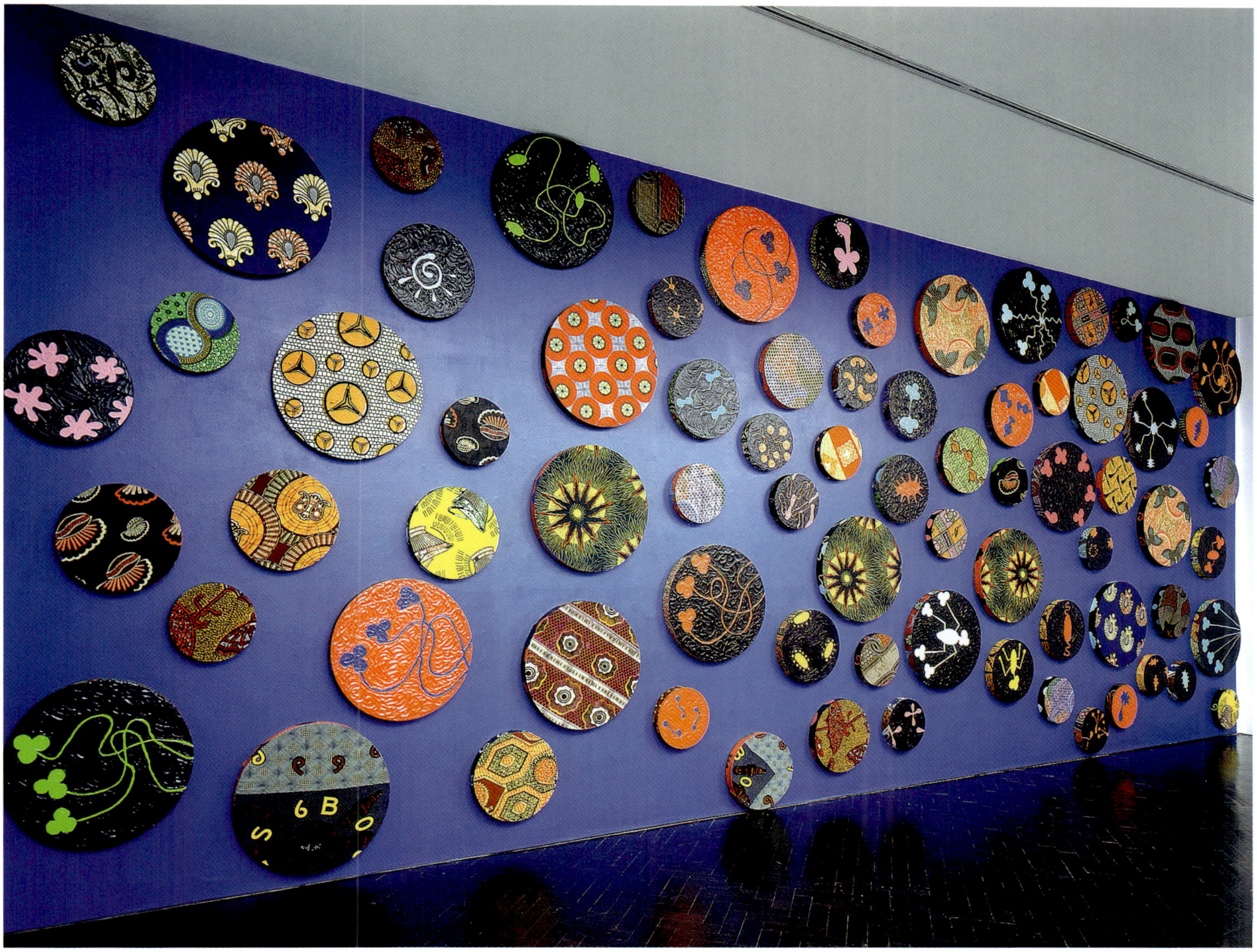

Fig. 17. Yinka Shonibare MBE, *Maxa*, 2003. Emulsion and acrylic on seventy-five Dutch wax printed cotton canvases, acrylic on wall; 330 x 805 x 5 cm. Collection of Melva Bucksbaum and Raymond Learsy

symbols. This in turn enabled him to subvert the idea of universality that is part of the modern tradition. "What I started to do when I began to use African fabric in my work," he later reminisced slyly, "was to contaminate the modernist idea of painting."[34] During this period he was intrigued with the work of the 1980s New York postmodern abstract painter Jonathan Lasker, who cast different abstract styles within the same painting as distinct protagonists in the nonobjective theater he was creating.[35] Shonibare's approach to African-print fabric in *Installation* led to the gridlike assembly of small rectangles against an intense pink wall in *Double Dutch* (1997, p. 203), the randomly sized circles against an indigo background in *Maxa* (2003, fig. 17), and the giant black splatter representing oil, which is superimposed with overlapping roundels of African-print fabric and hung on a white wall, in *Black Gold I* (pp. 196–97) and *Black Gold II* (both 2006).

In 1995 Shonibare began using African-print fabric for Victorian clothing in *Five Under Garments and Much More* (fig. 18). In this piece he plays on the fact that Great Britain's then prime minister Margaret Thatcher had extolled the Victorian era as a time when bedrock British values were developed and thus advocated returning to them.[36] He has noted that this era was also the peak period of British imperialism and a time when Africa was being divvied up by various European powers, an act he later solemnized in *Scramble for Africa* (2003, pp. 26, 154–55, 156, 157). In regard to Victorian values, Shonibare had this to say:

> Of course I realised, as an African, that Victorian values for me, were very draconian. . . . The

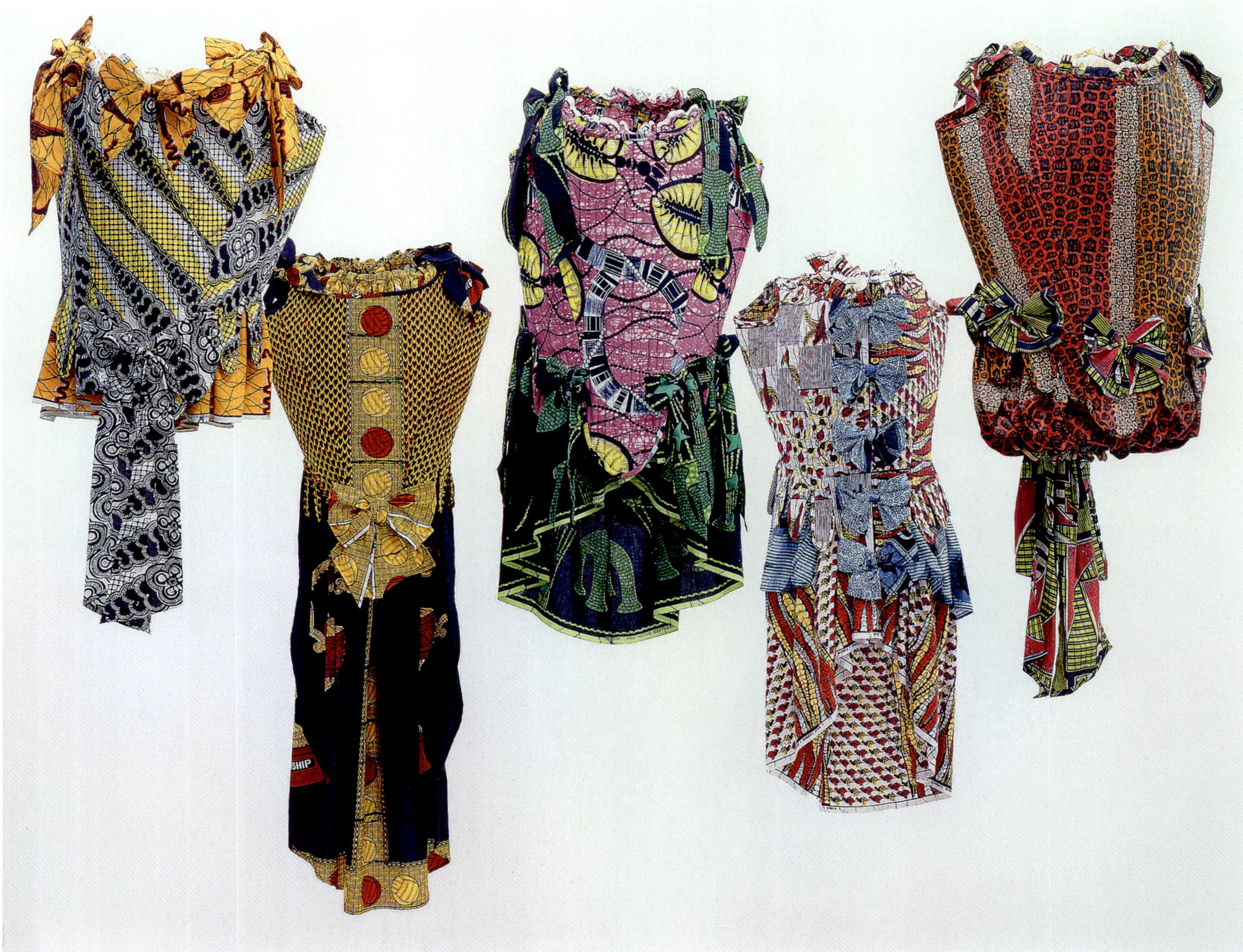

Fig. 18. Yinka Shonibare MBE, *Five Under Garments and Much More*, 1995. Dutch wax printed cotton, Rigilene, fishing line, interlining; five garments, each 130 x 95 x 95 cm. Tailored by Sian Lewis

> Victorians colonised Africa. Basically the Victorians made Africans work to produce a great empire. So Victorian values[,] to me, were values of repression, values of making me feel inferior.[37]

In addition to constructing individual Victorian garments in African prints so that they would serve as a synecdoche for the artist's act of undressing and revealing imperialism's chameleon-like nature and could be read by turns as European, African, and Diasporic (as his *Cha Cha Cha* [1997], with its Latin theme, clearly indicates), Shonibare began to present his African-print fabric Victorian costumes on dressmakers' dummies in *How Does a Girl Like You Get to Be a Girl Like You?* (1995). This work repeats as its title the famous line Cary Grant's character, Roger O. Thornhill, says to the spy Eve Kendall, played by Eva Marie Saint, in Alfred Hitchcock's *North by Northwest* (1959). In my opinion, Shonibare's dressmakers' dummies should be considered elaborate puns on the mindless acts of historic players (dummies) who are not so much active forces as unthinking participants whose lives provide ready and willing screens on which historical events are projected. Two years later Shonibare continued subscribing to this common dressmaker's model in *Dressing Down* (p. 179), but only began creating his painted and sculpted headless mannequins the following year (1998), when he conceived *Mr. and Mrs. Andrews without Their Heads* (p. 178), a three-dimensional play on a famous early Thomas Gainsborough painting of ca. 1750 in London's National Gallery, which commemorated the marriage of

Robert Andrews and Frances Carter by situating them before their combined property (see fig. 3).

Published writings on Shonibare's work have readily adopted his explanation for using headless figures in his work. His most complete explanation reads as follows:

> During the French Revolution, the heads of the aristocrats were chopped off using the guillotine. Basically, it started as a joke. . . . It's witty in a knowing sort of way. It adds more ambivalence.[38]

When one compares his statement with the phrase "without their heads," which was part of Shonibare's title for his three-dimensional riff on Gainsborough's painting cited above, the joke is an obvious reference to the symbolic killing of aristocrats, even those living more than forty years before the Reign of Terror, like Robert Andrews and his fiancée, and in England, where such extreme measures never took place. Because Shonibare's headless figures are dressed so ostentatiously in variegated overlays of usually three different African-print patterns, one is encouraged to move almost immediately from his guillotine joke to his statement about the political roles that excess and seduction play in his work:

> This is my own way of dealing with ideology. The use of excess, seduction, and pleasure in my work always remains political but without preaching politics, which is a different thing. I'm never moralistic. Instead it's a question of working through political issues as well as being seduced by the actual form, a question of provoking and seducing.[39]

Although this statement connects politics with excess and seduction, it suggests a far more complex relationship between these different elements than is usually attributed to them and makes one wonder about a common source for them.

And there certainly is a place where excess, seduction, and headlessness meet, and that is in the thought of the French writer, archivist, librarian, and sometime philosopher and Surrealist Georges Bataille, whose work has assumed increasing importance in art and literary studies over the past decades and was at its height in the late 1990s. In 1936 Bataille started the magazine *Acéphale*, published in five issues from 1936 to 1939,

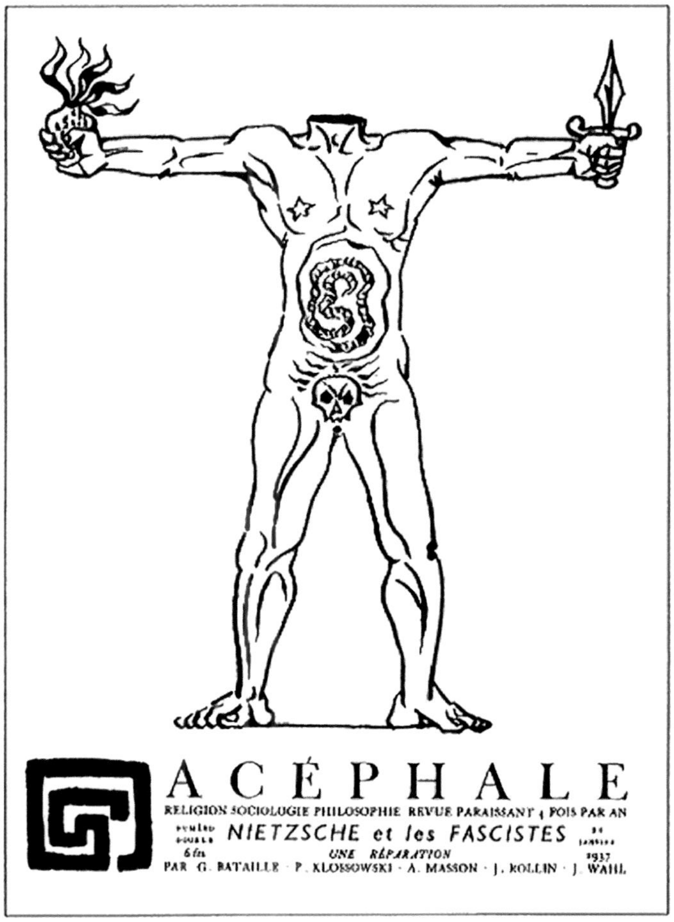

Fig. 19. André Masson, cover of *Acéphale: Religion, Sociologie, Philosophie*, 1937. Magazine published June 1936–June 1939

and a secret society of the same name, both of which honored the beheading of the French king Louis XVI as a fitting symbol of a new nonhierarchical form of life that celebrated the dispersion of power throughout society. Those individuals associated with either the *Acéphale* publication or the secret society indirectly opposed both the leadership of the high pope of Surrealism, André Breton, and contemporaneous fascist developments in Germany. On each of *Acéphale*'s covers there appeared the same headless image (fig. 19) drawn by André Masson, who had worked out its iconography while he was in close contact with Bataille.

Rather than supporting either Leonardo da Vinci or Robert Fludd's Renaissance-era views of a heroic man ruled by his spirit or mind, *Acéphale* (from the Greek *a-cephalus*, meaning, literally, "headless") advocated a new form of anarchy that became the basis for an irreverent theory of sovereignty and nonknowledge, which culminated in the publication of Bataille's 1949 two-volume *The Accursed Share*. In this study

Bataille reverses the direction of classical economics as he moves from traditionally conceived "restrictive" economies, based on scarcity, to "general" ones characterized by excess. Recognizing that successful economies all create excess goods and money that then need to be expended in various forms of waste, such as wars, the pastimes of autonomous rulers, and works of art, Bataille theorizes that both sovereign economies and human beings depend on recklessly spending surplus moneys and using up goods in ecstatic and unpremeditated ways.[40] When they do so, they move away from the limitations of and distance from life associated with setting goals and cogitating, toward living fully in the moment. Embracing life in this fashion, they attain sovereignty. Bataille's thinking about this type of wanton expenditure depends in part on his earlier theory of base materialism as an unsettling form of matter that disrupts high and low polarities by subverting their foundations. An energetic dynamic incapable of being subsumed under opposing individual political views, base materialism is an unwieldy third term that assumes a trickster-like wiliness and bears a surprising resemblance to Derrida's deconstruction.

Bataille's chimerical base materialism functions in Shonibare's work in terms of the African-print fabric that assumes a chameleon-like role since it can be viewed, depending on one's perspective, as African, European, colonial, imperialist, and even global. In Shonibare's works this material in particular and his art in general can be cast in the role of either "purloined seduction or pretend identity."[41] This material's changeability, in combination with the ostentatious luxury offered by Vlisco's Real Dutch and Super Wax textile designs, is used to clothe headless figures that outrageously reenact famous historical paintings by Gainsborough, Fragonard, and Raeburn that attempt to take possession of family property, carry on courtships while swinging, and enjoy the personal autonomy afforded by skating. In Shonibare's art, the polarities of signs referring to colonizing powers, as well as colonized and postcolonized peoples, are undermined by the excess of their costumes and gestures that unites them into a totality that partially eradicates the firmly held political positions of any one group.

In Bataille's system, then, the sovereign human subject is sacrificed to the dissipation of excess energy that necessarily mindless consumption, he theorizes, entails. Similarly, in Shonibare's work the sovereign subject transcends capitalism's limits even as it consumes and consummates itself in doing so. This ultimately transcendent act is a catharsis in which imperialism is deconstructed through the base materialism of Shonibare's elaborate and excessive costumes in African-print fabric that join in the figures' joyous ecstasy (*jouissance*) and sacrifice (their headlessness). Apropos the overall transgressive jouissance found in his work, Shonibare has opined, "Excess is the only legitimate means of subversion. . . . Hybridisation is a form of disobedience, a parasitic disobedience on the host of the species, an excessive form of libido, it is joyful sex."[42] The complex process of sovereignty and sacrifice that he constructs is evident in the eleven uncanny life-size headless figures making up *Gallantry and Criminal Conversation* (2002, pp. 158–59, 160, 161, 162–63), which, according to the artist, refers to sexual encounters occurring to youths making the Grand Tour.[43] Apropos this type of work, Shonibare has concluded, "I consider myself a hedonist. . . . I think that pleasure is king—as well as a very strong basis for being subversive."[44]

The state of headlessness in Shonibare's work can also be considered a postcolonial refutation of Thomas Hobbes's *Leviathan*, which served as a frontispiece for his mid-seventeenth-century study of political theory bearing the same title (fig. 20). In this engraving, on which Hobbes collaborated with the Parisian printmaker Abraham Bosse, the Leviathan takes the form of a giant's upper torso whose body is composed, like an Arcimboldo, of the citizens sanctioning his power. Although this image is intended to demonstrate the conflicting role of the body politic, which is dependent on the giant that it has helped to create, the mixture of public and private interests representing this composite image of state head and bourgeois citizenry has been extended over the centuries to represent imperial powers and their colonies. Once the body politic is seen without its powerful head, one moves from imperialism to postcolonialism as Shonibare's acephalous figures poignantly suggest.

Viewed in concert with the postmodern tradition that empowered critics of MoMA's *"Primitivism" in 20th Century Art* exhibition to reflect on the substantially different perspectives of mainstream modernists, tribal initiates, and well-informed anthropologists, Shonibare's art is predicated on the capacity of his African prints to be viewed from radically different perspectives, depending on whether they are

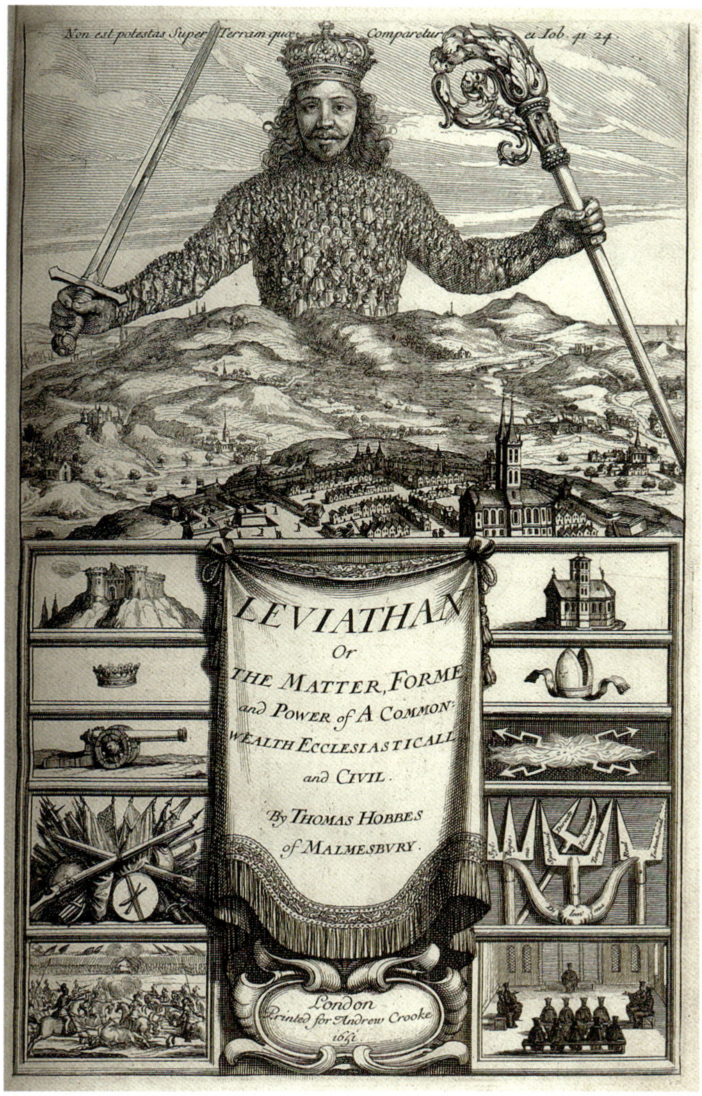

Fig. 20. Frontispiece to Thomas Hobbes, *Leviathan, or the Matter, Forme and Power of a Commonwealth, Ecclesiasticall and Civil*, 1651. Line engraving, 24.1 x 15.6 cm. The Library of Virginia

contemplated by mainstream Westerners or Yoruba versed in traditional culture. Considered also in terms of Benveniste's theory of enunciation, referred to earlier, Shonibare's dialectical work can be comprehended in terms of both Western and traditional Yoruba artistic protocols, which legitimate in different ways their subjects' entries into their own socially authorized perspectives. In the critical writing on Shonibare's headless figures, it is both surprising and unfortunate that the traditional Yoruba outlook has been passed over, particularly since this tribe considers the head to be the seat of the soul and consequently the most important part of the body. According to the Nigerian art historian Babatunde Lawal, the head in traditional Yoruba culture is "the lord of the body" and is "given pride of place," even in Yoruba art, where "it is almost always the biggest and most elaborately finished part of a typical figure sculpture, often adorned with a crownlike coiffure or headgear."[45] Because Shonibare's work so obviously veers away from this tradition, one wonders if his refutation of it was a conscious decision or was otherwise motivated. At any rate, the Yoruba's view of the head as enclosing inner and outer parts would predispose tribal members schooled in Yoruba traditions to view Shonibare's headless figures as much more transgressive and alarming than would mainstream audiences. Adding to Shonibare's negation of this tradition is a narrative cycle of photographs on the subject of Dorian Gray (pp. 216, 217) that could be considered a devilish reframing of the Yoruba tradition of inner (spiritual) and outer (secular) heads and the invocation "May my inner head not spoil my outer one," which seems to parallel so appropriately Oscar Wilde's tale of an ageless Edwardian dandy with his hidden portrait (his inner head, so to speak) mirroring the effects of his dissolute life. In addition to the importance placed on the head in Yoruba culture, this tribe's view of the past as both readily available and wholly indispensable to the present suggests important resonances with Shonibare's desire to rethink in his art aspects of imperialism and its impact on postcolonialism and contemporary globalism.

In addition, the Yoruba could well view Shonibare's use of African-print cloth as a secular updating of the Yoruba Egungun masquerades, particularly when one considers his memory of seeing them in Lagos while he was growing up.[46] Just as Egungun dancers are completely hidden underneath costumes comprising multiple layers of cloth that connect the Yoruba to the spiritual power of their ancestors, who are capable of affecting their future, so Shonibare's sculptures are defined by their clothing, which looks back to imperialism and forward to global networks. The assessment of the African scholar John Pemberton III that "it is the [Egungun] costume, not the performance, that carries the expressive weight"[47] of the masquerade makes one consider how the Yoruba might regard Shonibare's dramatic use of African-print fabrics to reposit, in terms of excessive consumption, imperialism's continued legacy. One might also reflect on how Yoruba tribe members, who build shrines in marketplaces to the trickster Eshu, might regard Shonibare's use of commercial fabric to symbolize the conflicted motivations and needs characterizing imperial and global networks. Similar to Eshu, who symbolizes the impulsive and destabilizing forces of commercial transactions, passageways, and transitions and, as a preeminent trickster, combines lighthearted dancing with fury and unsettling sexuality with inspired moments of intimacy, Shonibare's sculptures bring together conflicting points of view.

In considering the possibility of regarding Shonibare's art from a Yoruba perspective, we might conclude that his work is definitely polyvalent in the dialectical views it permits and global in terms of the different network protocols it elicits. Poised on differences, it can be regarded in multiple ways that accord with postmodernism's eminent hybridity and differ markedly from modernism's univocal generalities. "Speaking as a self-confessed beauty hugger," Shonibare once explained, "I would like to add that I have found beauty one of the most radically subversive strategies to counter a Eurocentric hegemony on the use of beauty. The debates on aesthetics cannot be narrowly defined as a modernist concern; the politics of aesthetics is directly related to issues of globalisation."[48]

Robert Hobbs, PhD, holds the Rhoda Thalhimer Endowed Chair in Art History at Virginia Commonwealth University and is a regular visiting professor at Yale University. He has published widely on contemporary art in general and African American art in particular. He is the author of monographs on such artists as Alice Aycock, Beverly Pepper, Sterling Ruby, Robert Smithson, Frank Stella, Kara Walker, and Kehinde Wylie, among others.

Notes

The author gratefully acknowledges the thoughtful help provided by Timothy Andrus, former Thalhimer Research Assistant, Virginia Commonwealth University.

1. Hephzibah Anderson, "Art of Africa," *Evening Standard*, October 14, 2004, http://www.standard.co.uk/showbiz/art-of-africa-7235111.html?origin=internalSearch (accessed May 28, 2013).

2. Rachel Campbell-Johnston, "Dandy in the Undergrowth," *The Times* (London), November 28, 2006, http://www.thetimes.co.uk/tto/arts/article2392147.ece (accessed May 28, 2013).

3. Jan Garden Castro, "In Art, Anything Is Possible: A Conversation with Yinka Shonibare," *Sculpture* 25, no. 6 (July–August 2006): 25. On other occasions Shonibare has acknowledged watching the Australian program *Skippy the Kangaroo*, the US-originated *Batman*, and *Soul Train*. Pernilla Holmes, "The Empire's New Clothes," *ARTnews*, October 2002, 119–20. In addition to these programs he also watched at different times during his childhood in Lagos *The Muppets* and the BBC Masterpiece Theatre serialized production *Upstairs, Downstairs*. See also Anderson. In 2005 he told the critic Ingrid Sischy, "I grew up with this constant flow between two cultures. . . . I would listen to the music of Fela Kuti, but I would also play James Brown." See Sischy, "The Artist Formally Known for Prints," *New York Times Style Magazine*, February 20, 2005, http://www.nytimes.com/2005/02/20/style/tmagazine/TW1372137.html (accessed May 28, 2013).

4. Yinka Shonibare, interview with author, New York City, April 12, 2008. This and the following discussion about Shonibare's early schooling in art come from this interview.

5. Holmes, "The Empire's New Clothes," 120.

6. B. Akíntúndé Oyètádé, "The Yorùbá Community in London," *African Languages and Cultures* 6, no. 1 (1993): 76–77.

7. Ibid., 73.

8. Holmes, "The Empire's New Clothes," 120.

9. Ibid., 119.

10. Sischy, "The Artist Formally Known for Prints," 188.

11. In 1991 the British art historian Norman Bryson emphasized the MoMA exhibition's "elision of cultural differences," which "conveniently disremembers the brutal era of European colonialism" and chalks up the exhibition's major blind spot to "the ideology of colonialism, past and present." Cf. Norman Bryson, "The Politics of Arbitrariness," in *Visual Theory: Painting and Interpretation*, ed. Norman Bryson, Michael Holly, and Keith Moxey (New York: Icon Editions / HarperCollins Publishers, 1991), 99.

12. Thomas McEvilley, "Thomas McEvilley Replies," in "Letters: On 'Doctor Lawyer Indian Chief': *'Primitivism' in 20th Century Art* at The Museum of Modern Art in 1984," *Artforum* 23 (February 1985): 51. McEvilley is guilty of oversimplifying tribal art when he says that its creators and users did not look at their work as art.

13. Henry John Drewal, "Contested Realities: Inventions of Art and Authenticity," in Philip L. Ravenhill, V. Y. Mudimbe, Henry John Drewal, and Sidney Littlefield Kasfir, "More on African Art and Authenticity," *African Arts* 25, no. 4 (October 1992): 26.

14. Sidney Littlefield Kasfir, "African Art and Authenticity: A Text with a Shadow," *African Arts* 25, no. 2 (April 1992): 41.

15. Ibid., 44.

16. Ibid., 41, 44, 72.

17. Thelma Golden, introduction to *Yinka Shonibare*, ed. Thelma Golden (New York: The Studio Museum in Harlem, 2002), 7–8.

18. Jaap Guldemond and Gabriele Mackert, "To Entertain and Provoke: Western Influences in the Work of Yinka Shonibare," in *Yinka Shonibare: Double Dutch*, ed. Jaap Guldemond and Gabriele Mackert with Barbara van Kooij (Rotterdam: Museum Boijmans Van Beuningen; Vienna: Kunsthalle Wien; Rotterdam: NAi Publishers, 2004), 41.

19. Holmes, "The Empire's New Clothes," 120.

20. See http://www.vlisco.com/Timeline (accessed June 3, 2008).

21. Kevin Matthews, "Q&A: Nina Sylvanus," UCLA African Studies Center (April 2007), at http://www.international.ucla.edu/africa/article.asp?parentid=67940 (accessed May 28, 2013).

22. http://www.vlisco.com/Timeline (accessed May 5, 2008).

23. John Picton, "Laughing at Ourselves," in Guldemond and Mackert, *Yinka Shonibare: Double Dutch*, 50.

24. Cathryn Poff, "Dutch Wax," in "West African Days: Venturing to Ghana and Beyond," April 2, 2005, http://reportersabroad.org/ghana/archives/2005/04/dutchwax.php (accessed April 5, 2008).

25. See Wyger Wentholt, "The Real Dutch Wax . . . the Company That Clothes Africa," *New African*, March 2000, 28–31. The following discussion regarding Vlisco's approach to design relies on information in this essay.

26. Kobena Mercer, "Art That Is Ethnic in Inverted Commas," *Frieze*, no. 25 (November–December 1995), http://www.frieze.com/issue/article/art_that_is_ethnic_in_inverted_commas/ (accessed May 28, 2013).

27. Sylvanus actually does make this point. "I would actually argue," she has stated, "that it's not the origin of the fabric that designates its capacity to become 'African,' but the way an object is used and integrated into a local context." Matthews, "Q&A: Nina Sylvanus."

28. Picton, "Laughing at Ourselves," 57.

29. Oyètádé, "The Yorùbá Community in London," 74.

30. Matt Steinglass, "Out of Amsterdam," *Metropolis*, December 2000, http://www.metropolismag.com/html/content_1200/ent.htm (accessed May 5, 2008).

31. Holmes, "The Empire's New Clothes," 119.

32. Elsbeth Court, "Yinka Shonibare: Finalist, Barclays Young Artist Award," *African Arts* 26, no. 1 (January 1993): 79–81.

33. Victor Shklovsky, "Art as Technique," in *Russian Formalist Criticism: Four Essays*, trans. Lee T. Lemon and Marion J. Reis (Lincoln: University of Nebraska Press, 1965), 12. Shklovsky writes, "The technique of art is to make objects 'unfamiliar,' to make forms difficult, to increase the difficulty and length of perception because the process of perception is an aesthetic end in itself and must be prolonged."

34. Suzanne Landau, "Yinka Shonibare's Garden of Pleasure," in *Yinka Shonibare: Double Dress*, ed. Suzanne Landau (Jerusalem: The Israel Museum, 2002), 9.

35. Cf. Robert Hobbs, "Jonathan Lasker's *Dramatis Personae*," in *Jonathan Lasker: Paintings, Drawings, Studies* (Madrid: Museo Nacional Centro de Arte Reina Sofía; Düsseldorf: K20 Kunstsammlung Nordrhein-Westfalen, 2003). This essay may be accessed on http://roberthobbs.net.

36. Holmes, "The Empire's New Clothes," 121.

37. "Nigerian Artist's Victorian Values," *BBC News*, December 2, 2004, http://news.bbc.co.uk/2/hi/africa/4061281.stm (accessed May 28, 2013).

38. Castro, "In Art, Anything Is Possible," 26.

39. Lars Bang Larsen, "1000 Words: Yinka Shonibare Talks about *Un Ballo in Maschera*, 2004," *Artforum* 43, no. 5 (January 2005): 173.

40. In terms of Shonibare's focus on imperialism and the relation of his work to Bataille's general economy of excess, it is worth noting that the philosopher Hannah Arendt assesses imperialism in terms consistent with Bataille's theory. She writes: "Innocently enough, expansion appeared first as the outlet for excess capital production and offered a remedy, capital export. The tremendously increased wealth produced by capitalist production under a social system based on maldistribution had resulted in 'over saving'—that is, the accumulation of capital which was condemned to idleness within the existing national capacity for production and consumption. This money was actually superfluous, needed by nobody though owned by a growing class of somebodies. The ensuing crises and depressions during the decades preceding the era of imperialism had impressed upon the capitalists the thought that their whole economic system of production depended upon a supply and demand that from now on must come from outside of capitalist society. . . . [C]apitalists had to decide either to see the whole system collapse or to find new markets, that is, to penetrate new countries which were not yet subject to capitalism and therefore could provide a new noncapitalistic supply and demand." See Arendt, *The Origins of Totalitarianism* (1951; New York: Harcourt, Brace and World, 1966), 147–48.

41. Mercer, "Art That Is Ethnic in Inverted Commas."

42. Jean Fisher, "The Outsider Within: Shonibare's Dandy and Parasitic Economy of Exchange," in Landau, *Yinka Shonibare: Double Dress*, 27.

43. Holmes writes, "The work is based on the artist's study of the Grand Tour, an 18th- and 19th-century English aristocratic rite of passage . . . according to Shonibare, the trip turned into an exercise in sexual liberation." Holmes, "The Empire's New Clothes," 121.

44. Ibid., 119.

45. Babatunde Lawal, "Àwòrán: Representing the Self and Its Metaphysical Other in Yoruba Art," *The Art Bulletin* 83, no. 3 (September 2001): 501.

46. Shonibare, interview with author, April 12, 2008.

47. John Pemberton III, "Egungun Masquerades in the Igbomina Yoruba," *African Arts* 11, no. 3 (April 1978): 46.

48. Tim Griffin, James Meyer, Francesco Bonami, Catherine David, Okwui Enwezor, Hans-Ulrich Obrist, Martha Rosler, and Yinka Shonibare, "Global Tendencies: Globalism and the Large-Scale Exhibition," *Artforum* 42, no. 3 (November 2003): 163.

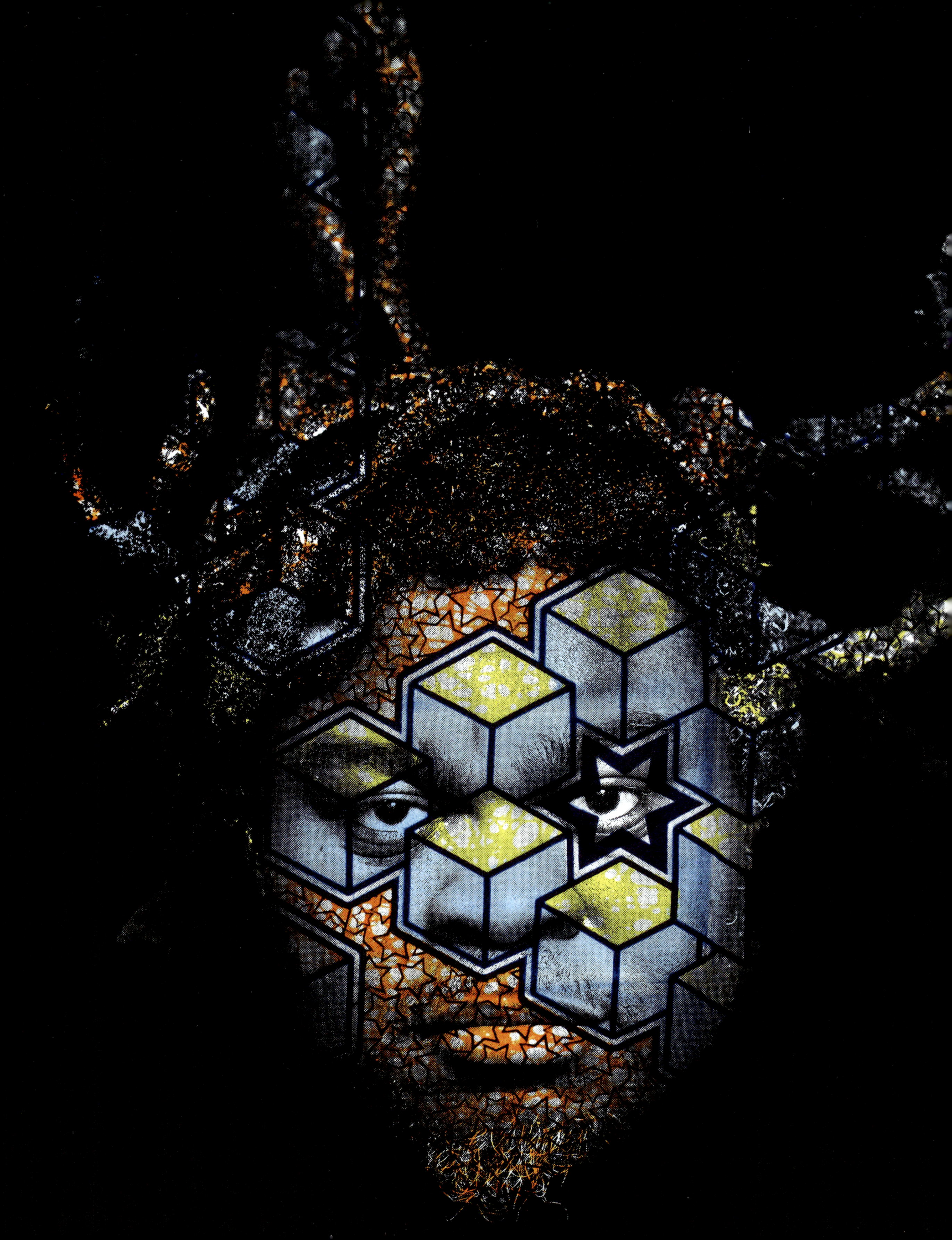

SETTING THE STAGE

Yinka Shonibare MBE in Conversation with Anthony Downey

ANTHONY DOWNEY: I have always been particularly interested in *The Victorian Philanthropist's Parlour* (1996–97, pp. 181, 182–83), the most notable aspect of which is that everything is covered with Dutch wax fabric. Can you elaborate upon why you chose that specific material?

YINKA SHONIBARE: The fabrics are signifiers, if you like, of "Africanness" insofar as when people first view the fabric, they think of Africa. When I was at college in London, my work was very political. I was making work about the emergence of perestroika in the then Soviet Union, and I was also quite intrigued by the idea of the Cold War coming to an end. However, my tutor, upon seeing this work, said to me: "You are African, aren't you; why don't you make authentic African art?" I was quite taken aback by this, but it was through the process of thinking about authenticity that I started to wonder about what the signifiers of such "authentic" Africanness would look like. The fabrics, in this context, happen to be the one obvious thing that people think of when they think about Africa, so I went to Brixton Market where the fabrics are sold. I started to speak to people who sold them and they told me that they were influenced by Indonesian batiks that the Dutch had later mass-produced. The intention was to sell these mass-produced batiks back to the Indonesians but, for largely political and cultural reasons, the Indonesians wanted to promote their own locally produced and better-quality batiks. So the industrially produced versions were largely sold in West Africa in the nineteenth century where they subsequently became very popular, and today they are seen as a signifier of Africa. It was with this in mind that I started to explore precisely what was meant by authentic in the context of Africa.

Yinka Shonibare MBE, *Self-Portrait (after Warhol) 1* (detail), 2013. Unique screen print, digital print, hand-painted linen; 134.5 x 134 cm. Collection of George and Margot Grieg

AD: The other notable aspect of *The Victorian Philanthropist's Parlour* is that it references the Victorian period (ca. 1830–90), as does a significant amount of your work. Why is the Victorian period such an important point of reference for your work?

YS: Let me begin to answer that question by noting that I am an African speaking English to you. The reason for that is because of the colonial period, empire building, and the British encounter with Africa. The Victorian era in Africa coincided with the height of the British Empire, so there are historical reasons for my interest in the period and its legacy in Africa. There are also more immediate reasons: in the 1980s the then prime minister, Margaret Thatcher, started to talk about Victorian values. My first instinct upon hearing these comments was to flee or run from this idea of Victoriana because it seemed so repressed and so far away from me. But then, on the other hand, I thought it would be ironic to play with precisely that notion of Victorian "values." There was a way of subverting that idea of the historical authority of the Victorian period by appropriating it or being complicit with it. As for the idea behind *The Victorian Philanthropist's Parlour*, it is relatively simple: the philanthropist wants to help the less fortunate; however, in this opulent environment of the parlor, where he has decorated his walls with images of black footballers, there will always be a relationship of patronage—or, if you like, a relationship between the "haves," the colonial philanthropist, and the so-called have-nots, the poor colonials. Philanthropy is more about dominance in the colonial context that it is about altruism; it is more of a condescending idea where the power relationship is never equal.

AD: This is interesting insofar as your work would appear not only to deconstruct notions of so-called authentic African signifiers but also the notion of Victorian values and the legacy of the Victorian period in contemporary politics and culture.

YS: Yes, I agree. I am very interested in that legacy, and being a Londoner moving around the city of London, you quickly begin to realize that the buildings you see—from the Tate to the National Gallery to Lloyd's insurance offices, not to mention the entire banking system of this country—were based firstly on the trade in slaves and thereafter on forms of inequitable trading practices. And, of course, there has always been a relationship between Europe and Africa; and the maintenance of a so-called developed and civilized Europe through these various institutions is underpinned by an uneven relationship with the less fortunate—not unlike the practice of Victorian philanthropy.

AD: In the context of trade or exchange, there is also a cultural dimension that you draw upon: the trade in ideas, for example. And as much as your work looks at colonial history, the legacy of slavery, and the aftermath of imperialism, it also looks at Western art history for its sources. I am thinking here of works such as *The Swing (after Fragonard)* (2001, pp. 168, 69) which is now actually part of the Tate's collection in London. What attracted you to Fragonard?

YS: I was drawn to Fragonard because—like the Victorian period—it is one of the references you would least expect. Although I cannot recall my first actual encounter with Fragonard, it seems to have been there forever; it was an iconic art historical image. More specifically, I like the frivolity of the image and the wild abandon of the lady on the swing. I wanted to reference frivolity over profundity, but in choosing frivolity I wanted to make a comment on profundity itself. This reply might need a more immediate historical reference inasmuch as the generation working before me, the so-called Black Art Movement that included Eddie Chambers and Keith Piper, was dealing with a lot of really important political issues but in a largely serious way that some people have described as being didactic. I wanted to come to things from a different angle and look at the notion of frivolity and playfulness; however, my playfulness has an inverted form of politics underlining it. Being a black artist looking at frivolity and playfulness is the least expected thing I could do—and that has a political resonance in light of the history of black artists working in Britain. I think this is why I accepted an MBE [Member of the Order of the British Empire] when it was offered: it was the last thing you would have expected of me and it also sets up a series of expectations of behalf of others about who I am and what I do—expectations that, I hope, are being constantly put into question by my work.

AD: This point references further issues. Firstly, Fragonard is widely viewed as part of the Rococo movement, which critics then viewed in derogative terms as both frivolous and merely fashionable. And there has always been a dichotomy in art history between frivolity, fashionability, decoration, and the apparent profundity of high art. It seems to me that you play with this in a way that disarms the viewer.

YS: Looking back to art history for images is central to my work insofar as it often yields unexpected images and resonances. If we look at another of my works, *Reverend on Ice* (2005, fig. 5, pp. 64–65, 150–51), which is after Henry Raeburn's *Reverend Robert Walker Skating on Duddingston Loch* (ca. 1795, fig. 6), you get some sense of both this frivolity and seriousness. In the original painting, the reverend is both a "man of the cloth," a reverend, and a "man of the book." He is a serious chap and to be respected. And yet this painting has caught him in a moment of frivolity and playfulness—a moment when he thinks no one else is looking at him and he can be a bit naughty. It is the last thing we would expect from him, this joyousness and our catching him in the act of being joyful. I also like the play on words in the title, *Reverend on Ice*, which gives a sense of the reverend being frozen in time and space, or being "kept on ice" for this one surprising outing.

AD: It is almost as if we, too, have come across him unexpectedly, and this is the last thing we are expecting from him, this most frivolous of gestures.

YS: Yes, he is indeed a very irreverent reverend!

AD: Let's further explore this notion of irreverence here as it seems important in your work.

YS: It was certainly the twin poles of irreverence and reverence that drew me to the original painting, and with a lot of the references that I use there is a degree of both reverence and irreverence on my part. If I work with a Thomas Gainsborough painting such as *Mr. and Mrs. Andrews* (ca. 1750, fig. 3), then that painting historically stands for something, and in using it in my work *Mr. and Mrs. Andrews without Their Heads* (1998, p. 178), I am appropriating a degree of its power while at the same time offering up a critique of it. In the contemporary world, Gainsborough's painting is an anachronism of sorts insofar as a man stands next to his belongings, in this case his wife, dog, and gun—in no particular order—and displays the extent of his land ownership in the background. The view of his estate in the background indicates a society where reverence, if not deference, is absolute. This painting is first and foremost a celebration of deference, and I want to deflate that somehow. I think I achieve that by beheading them, which is an allusion to the French Revolution and the beheading of the French landed gentry and aristocracy. It amused me to explore the possibility of bringing back the guillotine in the late 1990s, not for use on people, of course—my figures are mannequins—but for use on the historical icons of power and deference.

AD: In adopting that iconic image of Gainsborough's *Mr. and Mrs. Andrews,* there would appear to be a form of complicity with the power of the image but also a very irreverent take on that image, too, which brings us back to your practice as an artist of adopting the iconography of power to deconstruct power itself. In a show in 2007 you were invited to display your work in the hallowed halls of the National Gallery in London—becoming in turn one of the few living artists to have been extended such an honor. Could you talk a little bit more about how you felt about being invited into such a venerable establishment, which houses, among other works, Gainsborough's *Mr. and Mrs. Andrews*?

YS: That was an interesting experience for sure. I later heard that when my show opened, some of the board members refused to come to the opening because they felt very strongly that the National Gallery is not a place for contemporary art. As for my work being placed in that context, the curators looked for works within their collection that had a relationship to the slave trade—bearing in mind that 2007 was the bicentenary anniversary of the abolition of the slave trade—and asked me to engage with them. They found two portraits, one of Colonel Tarleton and the other of Mrs. Oswald, both of whom had had connections to the slave trade. These works were removed and I put my work *Colonel Tarleton and Mrs. Oswald Shooting* (2007, pp. 130–31, 132–33) in their place. Both are life-size mannequins, dressed in Georgian outfits made of Dutch wax fabric, and both have just blown apart an unfortunate pheasant—an activity that relates to their social status and the leisured classes. The part of the gallery where the work was placed is a very busy part. It acts as a center point, so I decided to do an installation that would happen above people's heads, where it could be seen by all. The fact that they are shooting a pheasant that has exploded "blood" on people's heads also gives it a comic element, which would have no doubt further displeased some of the National Gallery board who had objected to it in the first place.

AD: It would seem that quite a number of your chosen subjects are actively engaged, so to speak, in leisure pursuits. I am also thinking here of *Leisure Lady (with Ocelots)* (2001, p. 170) and *Hound* (2000, p. 172).

YS: Yes, that is obviously intentional. To be in a position to engage in leisure pursuits, you need a few bob. You cannot be a peasant and be off shooting for a day because you would have had work to do. You need spare time and money buys you spare time. While the leisure pursuit might look frivolous—we are back to that word again—my depiction of it is a way of engaging with that power. It is actually an expression of something much more profoundly serious insofar as the accumulation of wealth and power that is personified in leisure was no doubt a product of exploiting other people.

AD: It also appears that leisure may lead to a degree of ennui if not the breakdown of social order on behalf of the so-called leisured classes; a degree of dysfunctionality that results in the scenario represented in *How to Blow Up Two Heads at Once (Ladies)* (2006, p. 143), in which two individuals literally blow each other's head off.

YS: *How to Blow Up Two Heads at Once* is the perfect duel with a 100 percent result because these two Victorians simultaneously shoot each other's head off and guarantee a form of Mutually Assured Destruction [MAD]. The work was in part a reaction to the world we live in today. We are living in a post-9/11 environment that has recently seen war in Afghanistan and subsequently Iraq, and what it has came down to in popular cultural and political terms is the pitching on one side of the Americans and on the other side militant Muslims. This seems reductive to me and this work may initially appear humorous and perhaps frivolous, but it is examining the pointlessness of conflict in general. It is not just about the Iraq War but an opportunity to think about what happens when conflict turns to violence: you literally blow each other's heads off because no one actually comes out of a war a winner, not even the victor.

AD: One of the things that strikes me about all of these works is their sheer unabashed theatricality and their frieze-like appearance. Each has a centralized narrative that appears to be suspended in time. I am thinking here of *Scramble for Africa* (2003, pp. 26, 154–55, 156, 157), which draws upon the mise-en-scène of colonial history and visualizes it as if on a stage of sorts.

YS: Theatricality is certainly a device in my work. It is a way of setting the stage; it is also a fiction—a hyperreal, theatrical device that enables you to reimagine events from history. There is no obligation to truth in such a setting, so you have the leeway to create fiction or to dream. *Scramble for Africa* examines how history repeats itself, and when I was making it I was really thinking about American imperialism and the need in the West for resources such as oil, and how this preempts the annexation of different parts of the world. This is what happened in the 1880s with Africa, which was carved up arbitrarily by European powers. I thought about a historical equivalent for what is happening today, and that historical equivalent was the so-called Scramble for Africa, whereby a conference in Berlin (1884–85), attended by the then European superpowers, decided which Europeans could trade in Africa and who would get which territory. *Scramble for Africa* is about people having a conference about a continent that was not theirs and deciding how they are going to divide it up without any form of consultation with those who would be most affected—the Africans.

AD: The strangeness of the image also appeals to me—fourteen headless men sitting around a table with a contested map of Africa on it. I first saw this piece in a room at Stephen Friedman Gallery in London and it was not easily forgotten. I found this strangeness in another of your works, *Gallantry and Criminal Conversation* (2002, pp. 158–59, 160, 161, 162–63), when I first saw it in Documenta 11. I was initially intrigued by the impossibility of it all, which you have mentioned in previous conversations: the impossibility of headless people having sex, for example, or the impossibility of eighteenth-century costumes made of African fabric.

YS: I enjoy presenting "impossibility," but the reality of *Gallantry and Criminal Conversation* is more concerned with power relationships and how the exploitation of Africa had a counterpart of sorts in the Grand Tour—the latter being an original form of tourism that was popular from the mid-seventeenth century onwards and which mostly involved the upper classes traveling to Venice and Rome for reasons of "improvement." The Grand Tour was also a form of sex tourism that belied the cultural tone of its apparent purpose. This is also about power; you could relate it to the present-day relationship between the so-called first world and third world. I am thinking here about people making trips to Thailand and elsewhere for the purpose of having sex; that is a power relationship that finds expression in sexuality. Although I read books such as *Ladies of the Grand Tour* (2001), I made up the title myself: criminal conversation is what people used to be accused of if they committed adultery in the eighteenth century.

AD: I was also thinking here of the sheer excessiveness of the work—there is a lot of it and it is very theatrical in its excess. There is, for one, a full-sized carriage floating over the scene.

YS: Excess generates its own reactions and forms of critique that are not immediately apparent. When you think about Africa and about being an African artist, people most likely think about poverty and political struggle; they also think about independence and civil rights. None of those things actually sit well with the ideas of frivolity or excess, and so this returns us to notions of the unexpected. It is saying, "Look, I'm not going to be where you expect me to be, I'm not going to play victim, and I'm not going to play nature to your culture"—the last phrase is a reference to Barbara Kruger's work *We Won't Play Nature to Your Culture* (1983) and the possibility of adopting a stance that questions not only the status quo but your own assumptions about that status quo.

AD: And this brings us back to the sense of unexpectedness in your work, in terms of its sources, the way it is presented, and the positions you take in relation to historical and contemporary events. One of the other unexpected angles to your work is the fact that you started out as a painter and periodically return to that form.

YS: Yes, I did start off as a painter and it is something I still do. There is the tactile aspect to it and the use of materials.

There are also the two opposing forces of decoration and abstraction, which reflect the history of modernism and Greenbergian notions of what painting was supposed to be. I try to marry those two things in the kind of paintings I have chosen to do, which are neither just decorative nor just abstract—they are both. They also play with the idea of the Minimalist grid, so that the rigid structure is played within a manner that is very much Postminimalist.

AD: You have also referenced people like Rothko and that motif of the heroic white male—to what extent is a painting such as *Deep Blue* (1997, p. 201) engaging with that legacy?

YS: In a purely physical way, and bearing in mind I have a disability, it is much easier for me to paint things that are broken down into smaller pieces. And so rather than actually trying to make some heroic large painting, what I do is fragment that heroism by reducing it to smaller manageable chunks.

AD: Which is, in certain ways, a complicity with art history, an adoption of certain codes and the authority associated with those codes in order to disrupt them—not unlike your use of Gainsborough's *Mr. and Mrs. Andrews*.

YS: Yes, you could put it that way.

AD: I am also interested here in the way you have adopted and adapted the code of the dandy in your work, a figure that returns us to the Victorian period but also—in its soi-disant demeanor and display of wit—a somewhat excessive and unexpected figure. I am thinking here of *Diary of a Victorian Dandy* (1998, pp. 218–19) and *Dorian Gray* (2001, pp. 216, 217).

YS: Historically, the dandy is usually an outsider whose only way in is through his wit and his style. Coming from a middle-class background, the dandy aspired to aristocratic standing so as to distinguish himself from both the lower and middle classes. In this sense, his frivolous lifestyle is a political gesture of sorts, containing within it a form of social mobility. Needless to say, Oscar Wilde is a good example of the dandy, and he played that role well; he used his wit and his style to progress within English society and was brutally penalized in the end for his apparent frivolity. His apparent lack of seriousness, of course, belied an absolute seriousness, and that attracts me to the dandy as a figure of mobility who upsets the social order of things. As a black man living in the UK, I find myself in a position where I am not so-called upper class; however, in Nigeria I would be considered upper class. And this got me thinking about social and class mobility in the context of the dandy. The dandy can remake himself again and again; he can do that through the image, he can remake his own image and thereafter re-create and remake himself.

AD: I was reminded of two quotes here, one from Oscar Wilde, whom you just mentioned, and his notion that "One should either be a work of art, or wear a work of art," and one from Charles Baudelaire, who wrote that "the dandy is one who elevates aesthetics into a living religion." Again, just as the figure of the dandy alluded to a politics of sorts, aesthetics always has a political context; the adoption of clothing, for example, being the means to go beyond one's allotted class in a time where such mobility was rigorously policed. To identify with such a figure would suggest an inclination toward role-playing for political purposes and an intention to disrupt certain accepted ways of seeing things—would you agree with that?

YS: All identity construction is a form of reenactment. You are playing a role and to do so you have to construct that role. The dandy is a figure who not only lives out this fact but he is also both an insider and an outsider who disrupts such distinctions. When *Diary of a Victorian Dandy* was first shown, it was in the London Underground and the audience for that was in excess of three million people. Again, the sheer unexpectedness of this image had a huge impact. The organization that commissioned the piece, InIVA [Institute of International Visual Arts], did a survey where they asked people who they thought the character in the photographs was. And some people either imagined that he was a real Victorian character who existed, and some people thought that they were posters for a film. I enjoyed that open-endedness and the disruptiveness in the display of the image insofar as it already depicted a figure, the dandy, who is a sign of disruption.

AD: These images could be seen in terms of visual disruption, an unexpected image, but could they also be seen as a moment of historical revisionism—a moment of going back in time and pointing out that Victorian society was not as monocultural as we think it was?

YS: I would not necessarily go with that reading because I do not really go for that kind of revisionism; for me, that would come across as merely illustrative and it is more about disruption and unexpectedness. It is not about expressing something that once existed but that people did not know about. The images in *Diary of a Victorian Dandy* are fakes—it is pure theater and it is Yinka Shonibare in that picture, not some obscure historical character. It is a contemporary person doing this and it is playing with this idea of making people look twice and re-engage in what they are looking at.

AD: Let's take this notion of fakery further. I was reminded just now of a quote from an interview of yours from some years back in which you said, "To be an artist, you have to be a good liar."

YS: I think that sometimes people have a problem distinguishing artifice from so-called reality. Artifice is not reality; they are two different things and I think that once that is understood you can perhaps read into the work of the artist a bit better. For me it is about providing people with alternative possibilities and that sometimes requires the device of the lie.

AD: Which brings us to another aspect of your work, your use of film—often seen in terms of artifice and alternative realities—in works such as *Un Ballo in Maschera* (*A Masked Ball*) (2004, pp. 226–27) and *Odile and Odette* (2005, pp. 224, 225). What has film enabled you to do that you cannot do in, say, painting and sculpture?

YS: In the most basic sense, it has allowed me to explore movement. There is an aesthetic quality with movement and the resonance of the image that you cannot get when it is presented as a still image. There is also the sense of repetition and, in *Un Ballo in Maschera*, for example, I did not want to make a film with a beginning, middle, and end; instead, I wanted to explore the reflexivity of the film and how it reflects back on itself.

AD: Which recalls the films of the French New Wave period.

YS: Yes, very much so, and I am thinking here of Jean-Luc Godard's works and in particular Alain Resnais's *Last Year at Marienbad* (1961), which is a film that had a great influence on me because of the way it consistently draws the viewer back to the filmic moment and refers to the fact that it is a film and not a reality in itself. It also does this with its repetitive, almost incomprehensible, structure and plot and the blurring of the distinction between truth and fiction, artifice and fact. It is a very modernist approach, I guess, and in *Un Ballo in Maschera* I use devices such as repetition to draw attention to the filmic nature of what we are seeing.

AD: Could you describe that a little bit more, because the film examines a relatively obscure event—that is, the assassination at a masked ball of the Swedish King Gustav III in 1792.

YS: In the 1780s and '90s, Gustav III was attempting to expand Sweden's borders into Russia. These attempts were not only costly and divisive but drew attention away from poverty at home and his own extravagances. One of Gustav III's major preoccupations was going to the ball, another frivolity, I guess, and I thought of this as a metaphor for the kind of imperialist figure who, like in Rome before, is "fiddling" while the seat of empire is burning. However, things are of course more complicated than that inasmuch as he was also a great patron of the arts. In the film, and this returns us to the formal devices mentioned above in relation to the French New Wave, I use repetition and open-ended narratives to suggest alternative readings. In one, he dies as a result of the assassination; in the other, he lives. And the narrative repeats itself so it is not closed by any means; rather, it is open-ended and the outcome depends on where the audience wants to stop viewing it or indeed how they want to view it. If you stop viewing after his assassination you do not see him rise up again and the whole thing start over again.

AD: This notion of repetition, in part, brings us to your second film, *Odile and Odette*, which is taken from Tchaikovsky's *Swan Lake* (1875–76). Could you describe what attracted you to *Swan Lake* and, in particular, what attracted you to the relationship between Odile and Odette?

YS: This film is more about doubling than repetition. In the original story, Odile is Von Rothbart the magician's daughter and Odette is the beautiful swan that Prince Siegfried has promised to marry. Siegfried and Odette have an agreement between them that they would stay faithful, but Von Rothbart dresses his daughter Odile—who bears an uncanny resemblance to Odette—to trick Siegfried into kissing her at a ball at the palace. Odette sees this and their union is broken forever. There are a number of endings, one involving Siegfried throwing himself from the castle ramparts when he realizes his mistake, whereas another has Odette do the same thing after she has seen Siegfried kiss Odile. What interested me most here is that when the ballet is performed, it is usual that the two roles of Odette and Odile are danced by one performer. Odile is usually in black, signifying a certain malign intent, while Odette is traditionally in white. In my version of the ballet I have used two dancers, one black and one white, and composed them so they appear to be mirror reflections of one another. They synchronize each other's movements in a framed "mirror" to give the impression that it is a mirror we are looking at. The idea is that one woman is the reflection of the other woman, so that although you are seeing two different ballerinas, essentially you are seeing one person.

AD: It seems that *Odile and Odette* personifies precisely what you said earlier in relation to the medium of film giving you the ability to look at movement and the ambiguities of narrative and time with the context of film itself.

YS: Yes, very much so; it is difficult to fully portray that in painting and sculpture.

AD: Your most recent work went back further than the Victorian age to a time broadly commensurate with the Enlightenment period and the high-water mark of European reason and rationality. In *The Sleep of Reason Produces Monsters* (2008, fig. 13, pp. 210–11, 212, 213), you have produced a series of photographs after Goya's series of etchings *Los Caprichos*, which he produced in the 1790s (see fig. 14), but there is also a broader reference to the figure of Caliban, who figures prominently in Shakespeare's *The Tempest* (ca. 1610–11).

YS: The Enlightenment period is a time of being liberated from the Dark Ages, from the shackles of tradition into the empirical methods of science and rationality. Our traditional notions of democracy were refined in this period and emerged in the Age of Enlightenment alongside the ideals of liberalism. However, it is precisely the arrogance of liberal democracy that has been used as a justification for a number of wars and, most recently, the war in Iraq. The appeal to a transcendentalist notion of democracy has effectively presaged an unjust war. The arguments are familiar from a colonial period: they, the other, are an "uncivilized" people and we, enlightened Europeans that we apparently are, will endeavor to enlighten them. However, like Caliban in *The Tempest*, they refuse to be enlightened so we will force democracy upon them by the gun. This act is irrational in itself: the arrogance of liberal democracy has led to the most irrational acts of genocide. In *The Sleep of Reason Produces Monsters*, I have taken the text from Goya's original aquatint prints and their formal composition. I have turned the original statement, reproduced on the desk where a figure sleeps, and put a question mark after it so that it reads in French, "The sleep of reason produces monsters in America?" The original statement becomes rhetorical, and I used French in particular here as it was the French who gave America its Statue of Liberty. There are five images in all, representing five continents. In Africa, it is an image of an old white man, rather than an African, asleep at the desk. In Asia, the figure is a black man. In the most basic terms I am suggesting that irrational aggression, born out of a form of Enlightenment rational reasoning, toward a race that you do not understand produces a sleep of "reason" out of which comes monsters—and the term *monsters* could be substituted here with any amount of atrocity. Your enlightened intentions, in sum, do not necessarily produce enlightened results.

AD: When this work was first shown in 2008 in New York, it was under the collective title *Prospero's Monsters*—what is the reference to Caliban, the figure in the play that you just mentioned?

YS: There were no images in that show depicting Caliban, or Prospero for that matter, but I felt it was a good title to frame the exhibition with because in a broader context I am talking about the relationship between the other and the master. I was attracted to the play because in it Caliban refuses to be civilized; he fights back and is not as passive as is often portrayed. He not only fights back but refuses to learn Prospero's language and the codifications that go with it. When he does learn the language he learns only the swear words, which is very irreverent of him. And that, I thought, was a form of empowerment.

AD: In that show you also had a series of figures more closely associated with the Enlightenment, including Adam Smith, often seen as the father of modern economics, and the eighteenth-century physicist and philosopher Jean le Rond d'Alembert. In each case, these figures, of which there are five in all (see pp. 120–25), have been given disabilities—why was this?

YS: I'm doing two things there; one is an autobiographical device. I have my own physical disability but also the Enlightenment scientists and philosophers had their own human frailties, too; however, it is the human, the sense of frailty that is too irrational and disorganized, that is often factored out of discussions about reason and rationalism. Because it is unpredictable, disability does not lie well with the essence of Enlightenment certainty—bearing in mind the overarching empiricism associated with the time. In giving Adam Smith and Jean le Rond d'Alembert disabilities, alongside the figures of Antoine Lavoisier, Gabrielle Émilie Le Tonnelier de Breteuil, and Immanuel Kant, I wanted to use it as a device for showing how these figures, who were partly responsible for defining otherness in the context of the Enlightenment, could also be "othered" in the context of disability.

AD: It seems that these works question the empiricist underpinnings of the Enlightenment period and invert its processes of thinking about otherness and how we look at other cultures.

YS: That is very much part of what I am doing there.

AD: Finally, can I ask you what you are working on presently?

YS: At present I am rereading Jonathan Swift's *Gulliver's Travels* (1726), which interests me on a number of levels. I am particularly interested in the question of Gulliver's empathy with the different cultures he encounters. He sees that they are different and they see that he is different, and they are trying to learn from his culture and he is trying to learn from their culture. He rarely seems to come down in favor of one group over the other before he has had a chance to listen to both sides of the story. I am at a relatively preliminary stage in my thinking about this and rereading a book I first read as a child, but it holds a number of points of interest for me at this moment in time—and will no doubt provoke some thoughts on my behalf. Gulliver's voyages also see him becoming involved in internal power struggles in the lands he visits, but he himself is also, at various stages, both powerful and powerless depending on the context. Which brings us back to the question of power and its contexts and how we assume and in some cases are beholden to power itself.

Anthony Downey is director of the Master's Program in Contemporary Art at Sotheby's Institute of Art, London. He is editor of *Ibraaz* (www.ibraaz.org), a research forum for visual culture in North Africa and the Middle East, and sits on the editorial board of *Third Text*. This conversation was conducted in 2008 in advance of the touring retrospective *Yinka Shonibare MBE*.

Yinka Shonibare MBE, *Self-Portrait (after Warhol) 2* (detail), 2013. Unique screen print, digital print, hand-painted linen; 134.5 x 134 cm. Collection of John and Amy Phelan

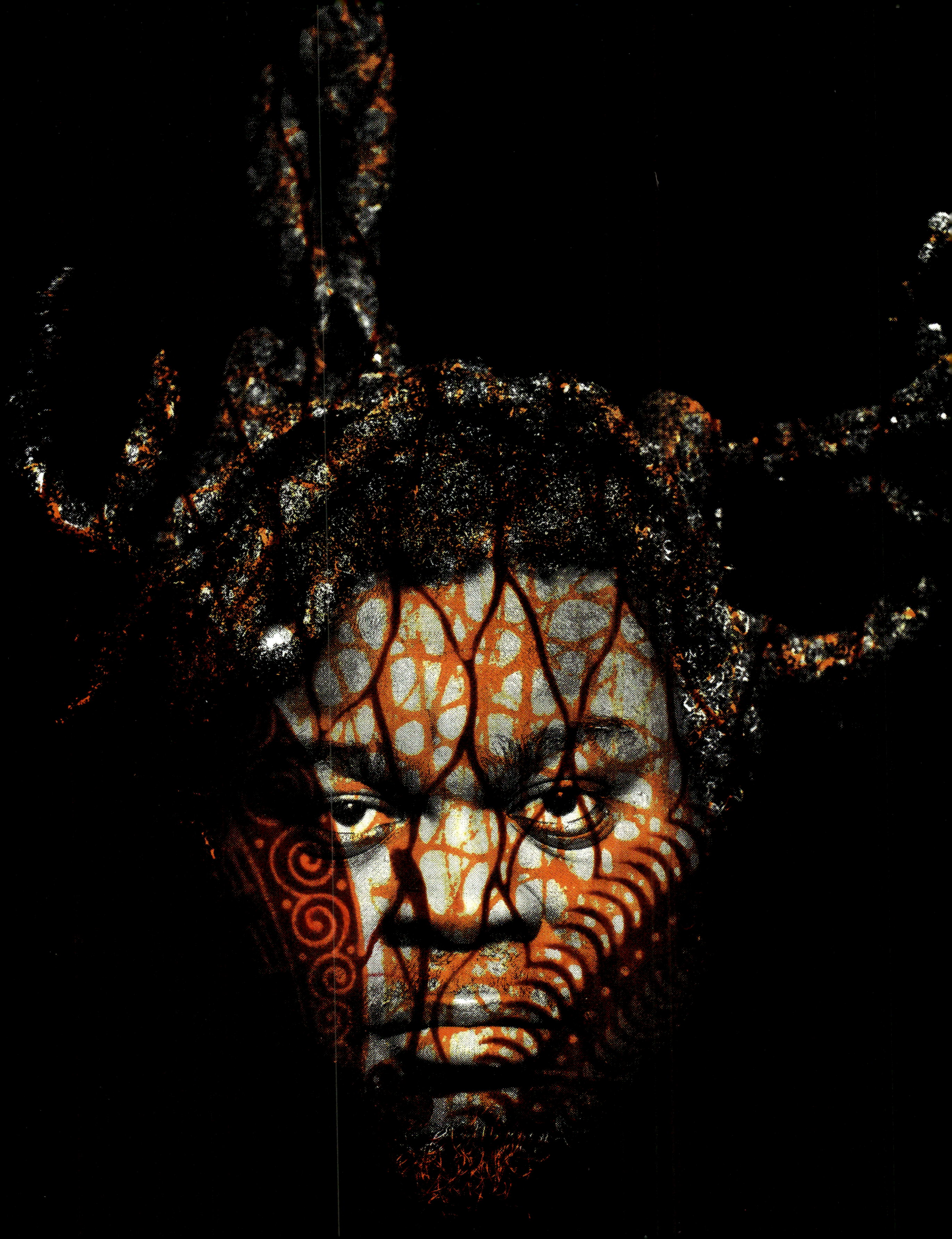

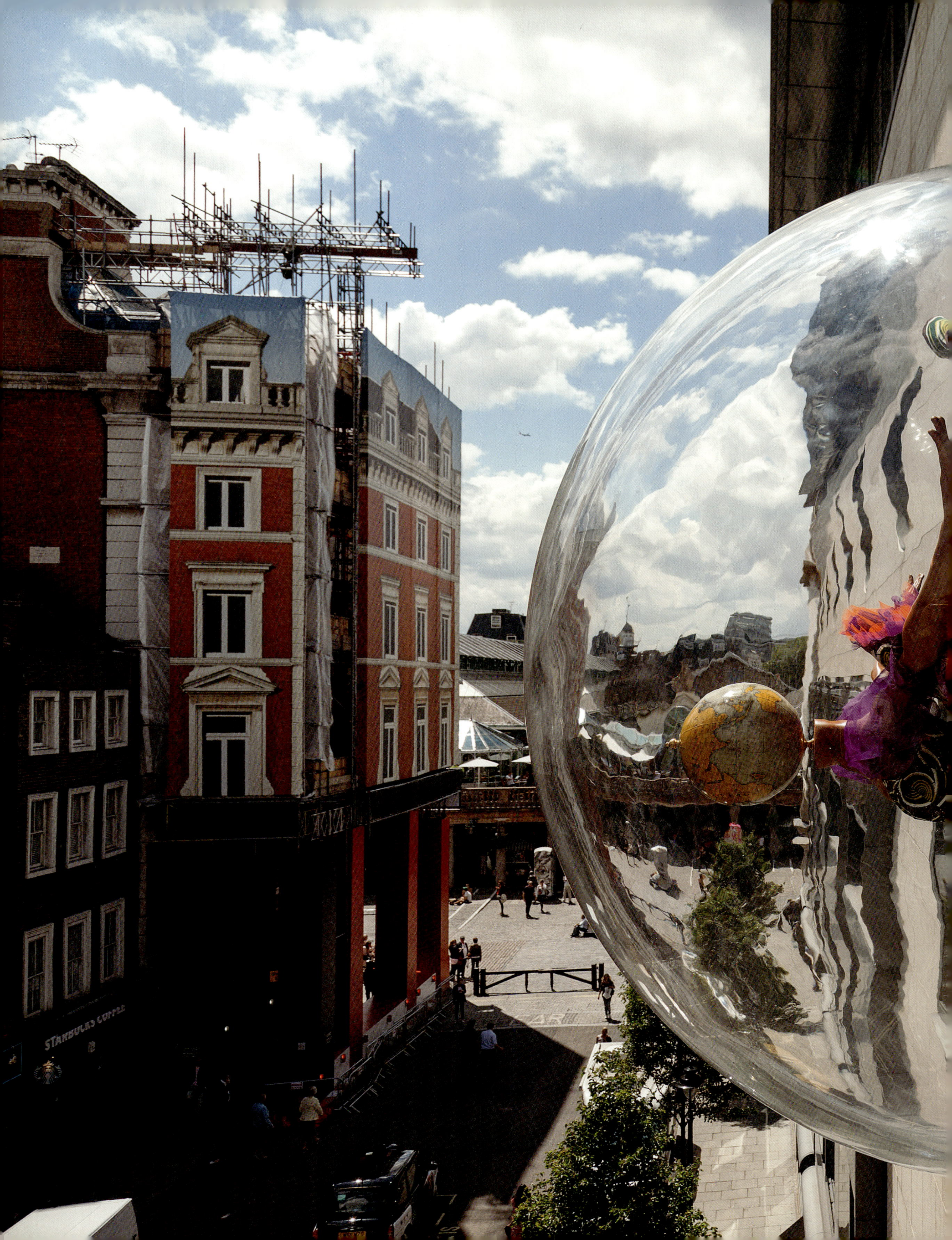
STARBUCKS COFFEE

PUBLIC ART

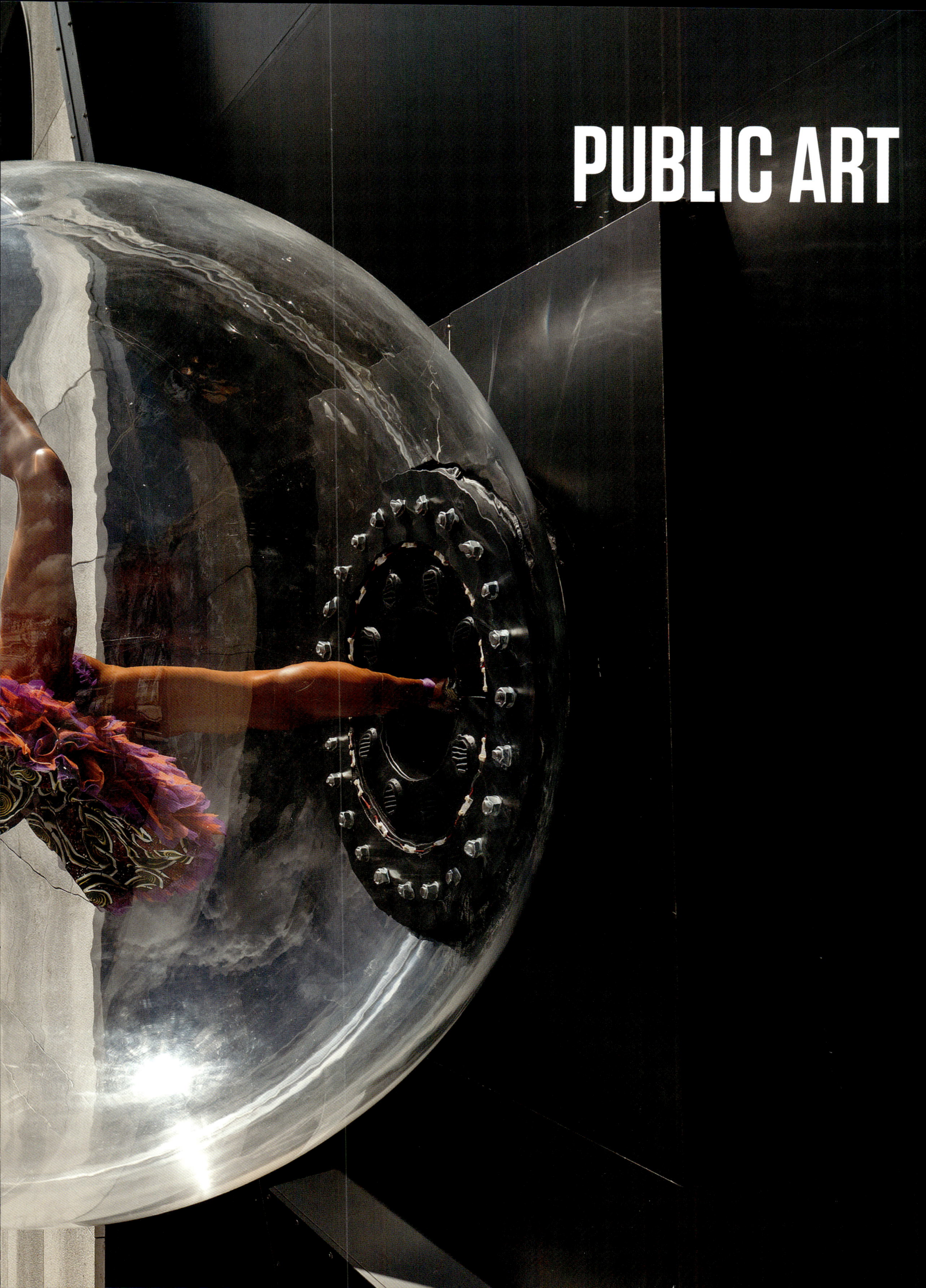

Preceding spread:

Globe Head Ballerina, 2012

Acrylic, mannequin, Dutch wax printed cotton, globe, rotor
200 x 200 x 200 cm
Commissioned by the Royal Opera House, London
Installation view, Royal Opera House, London, 2012

Wind Sculpture 1, 2013

Steel armature with hand-painted fiberglass resin cast
610 x 340 x 80 cm
Commissioned by Yorkshire Sculpture Park, Wakefield, UK, for the exhibition *Yinka Shonibare MBE: FABRIC-ation*
Installation view, Yorkshire Sculpture Park, 2013

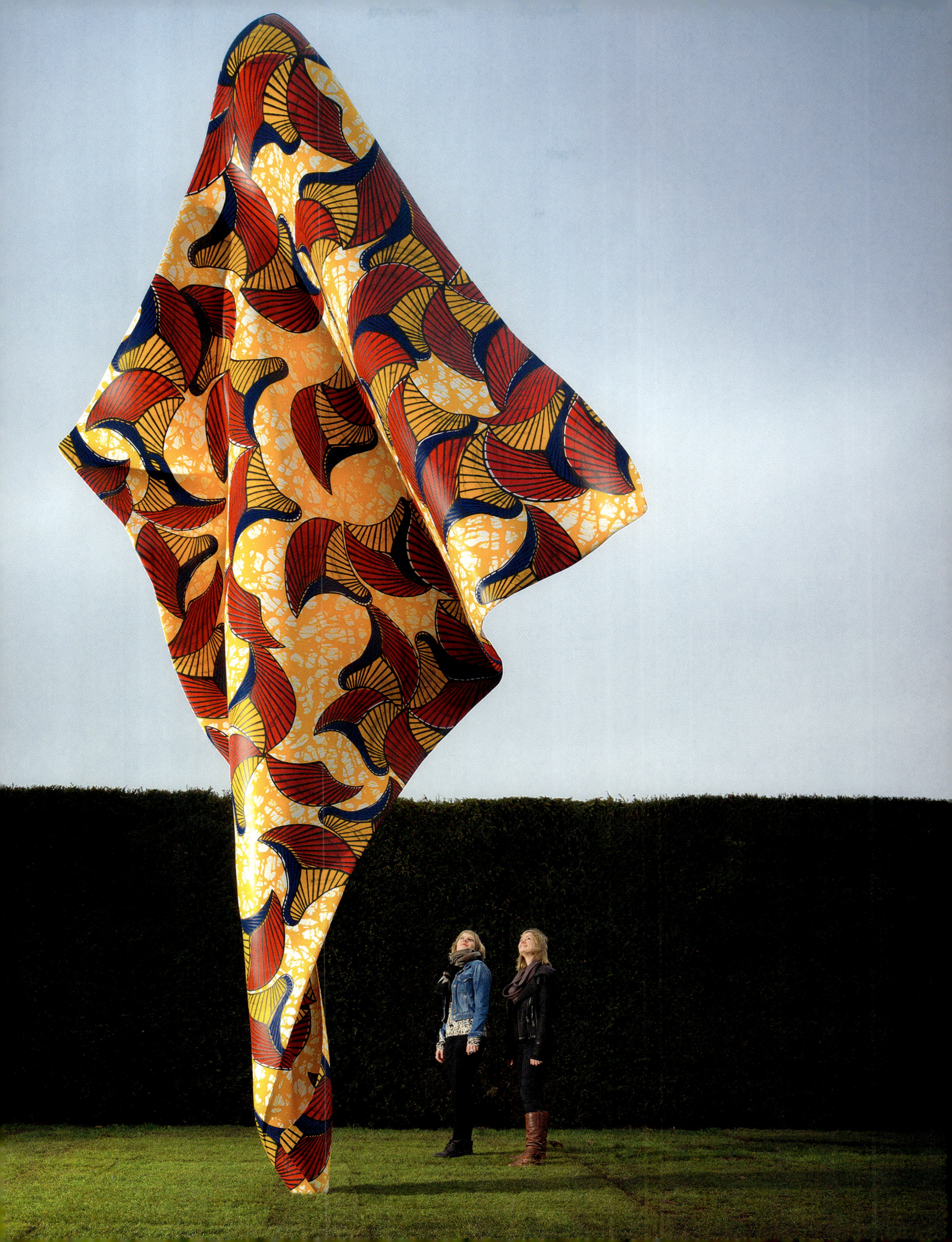

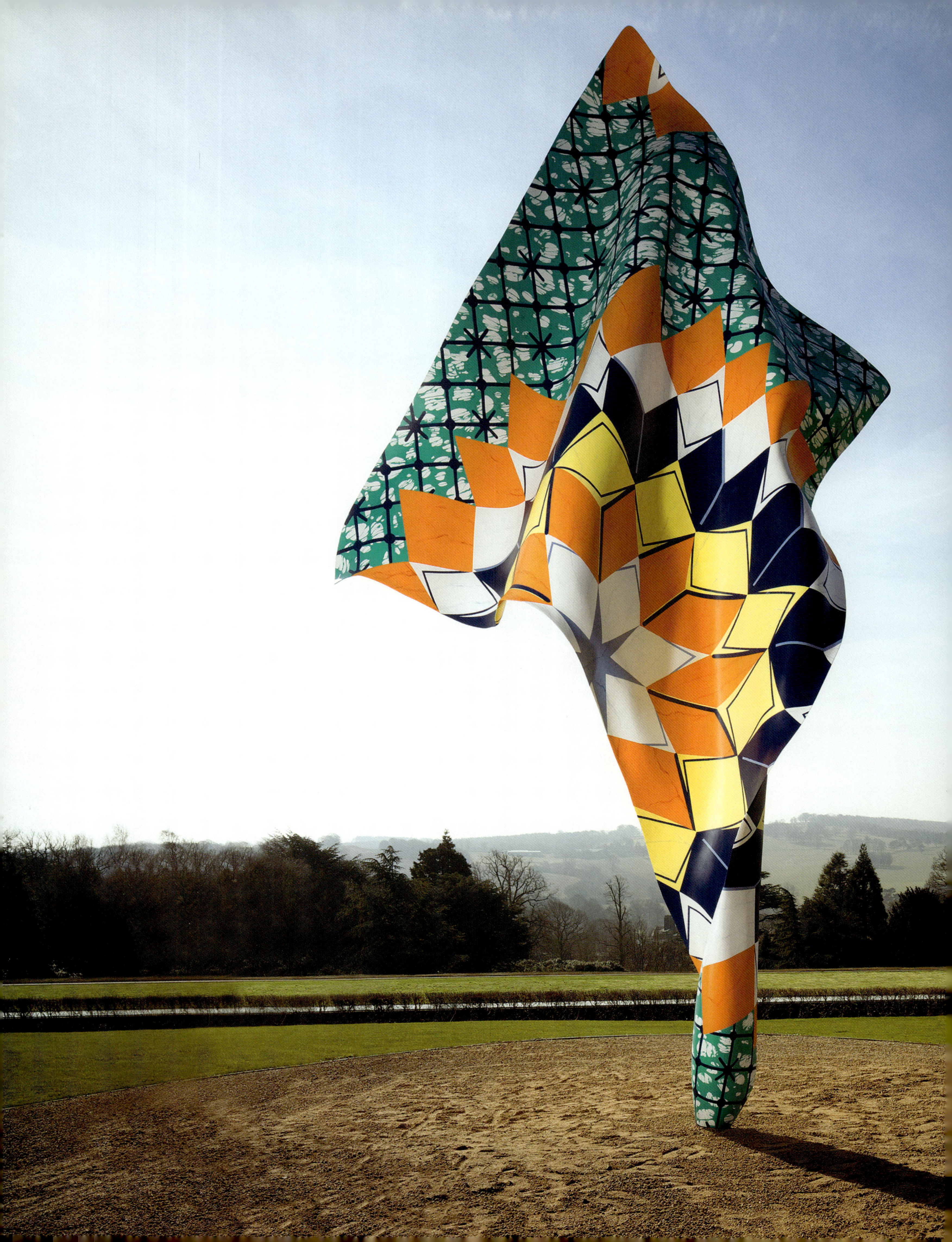

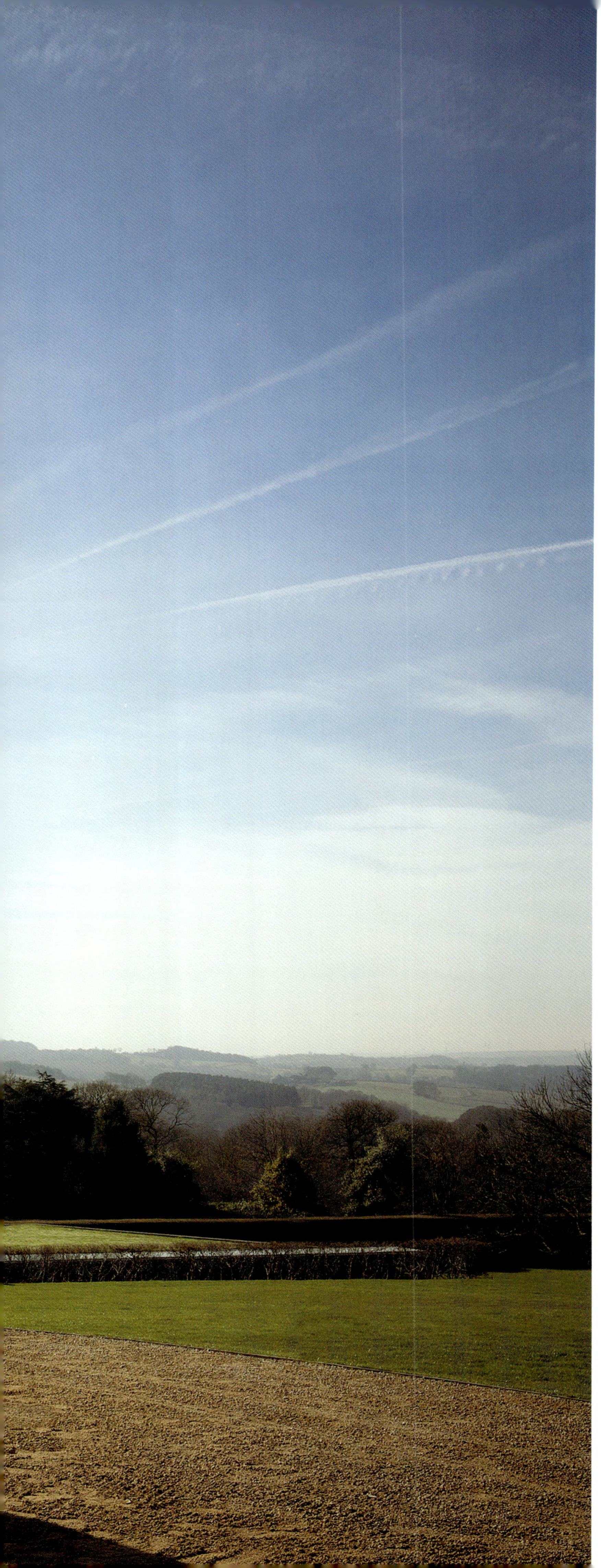

Wind Sculpture 2, 2013

Steel armature with hand-painted fiberglass resin cast
610 x 340 x 80 cm
Commissioned by Yorkshire Sculpture Park, Wakefield, UK, for the exhibition *Yinka Shonibare MBE: FABRIC-ation*
Installation view, Yorkshire Sculpture Park, 2013

Globe Head Ballerina, 2012

Acrylic, mannequin, Dutch wax printed cotton, globe, rotor
200 x 200 x 200 cm
Commissioned by the Royal Opera House, London
Installation view, Royal Opera House, London, 2012

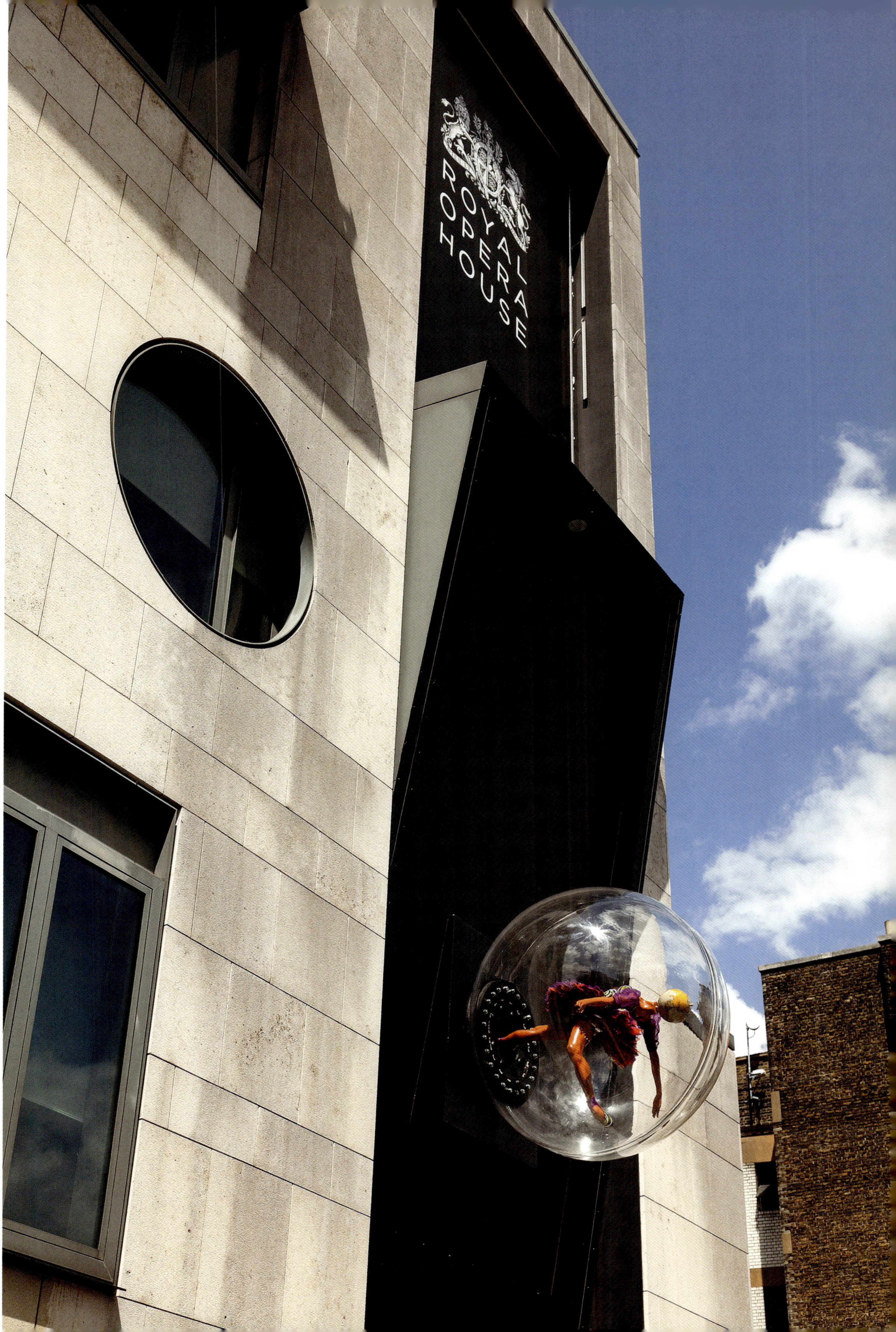
ROYAL
OPERA
HOUSE

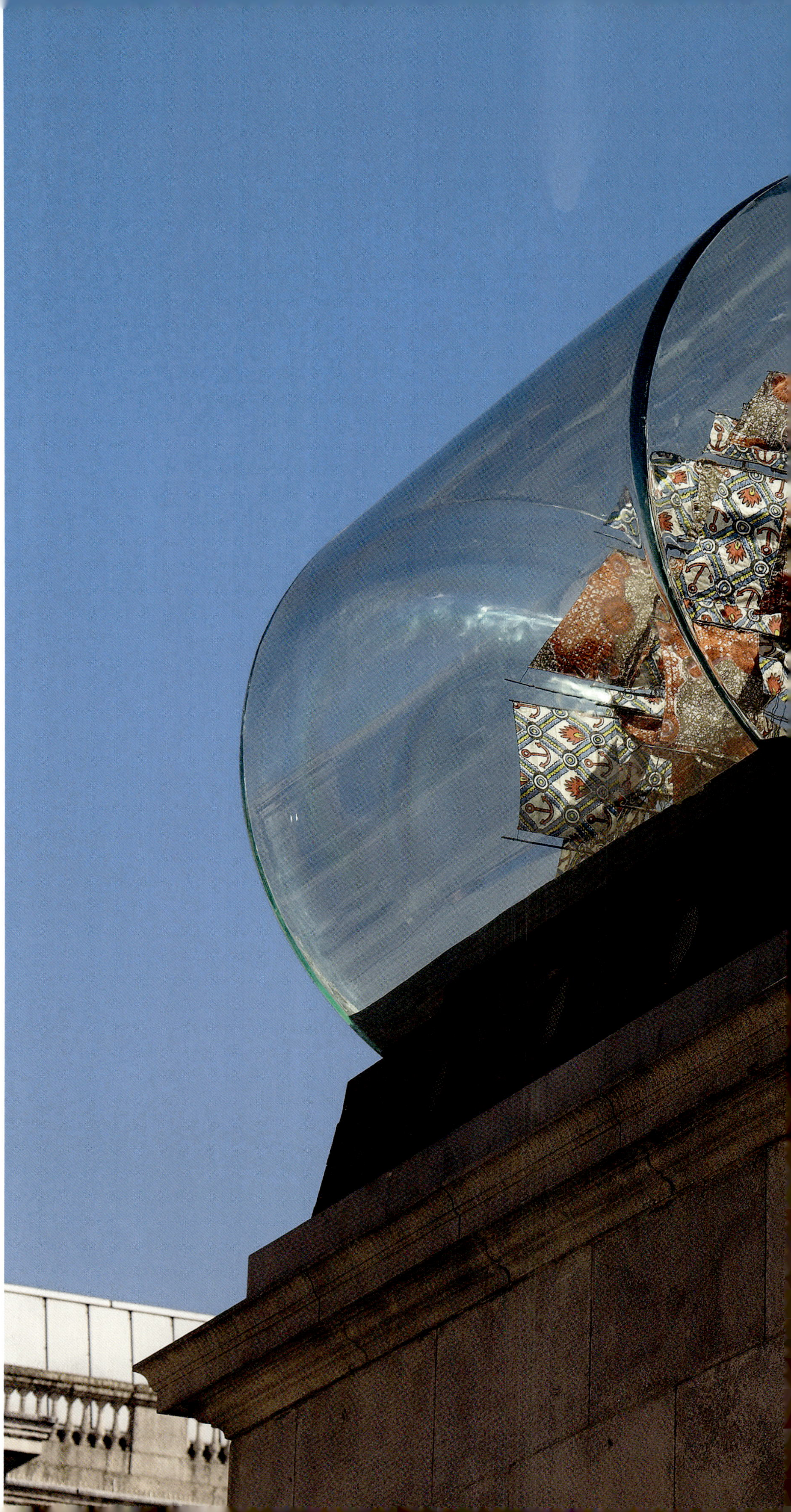

Nelson's Ship in a Bottle, 2010

Fiberglass, steel, brass, resin, UV ink on Dutch wax printed cotton, linen rigging, acrylic, wood
290 x 525 x 235 cm
National Maritime Museum, Greenwich, London
Installation view, Fourth Plinth, Trafalgar Square, London, 2010

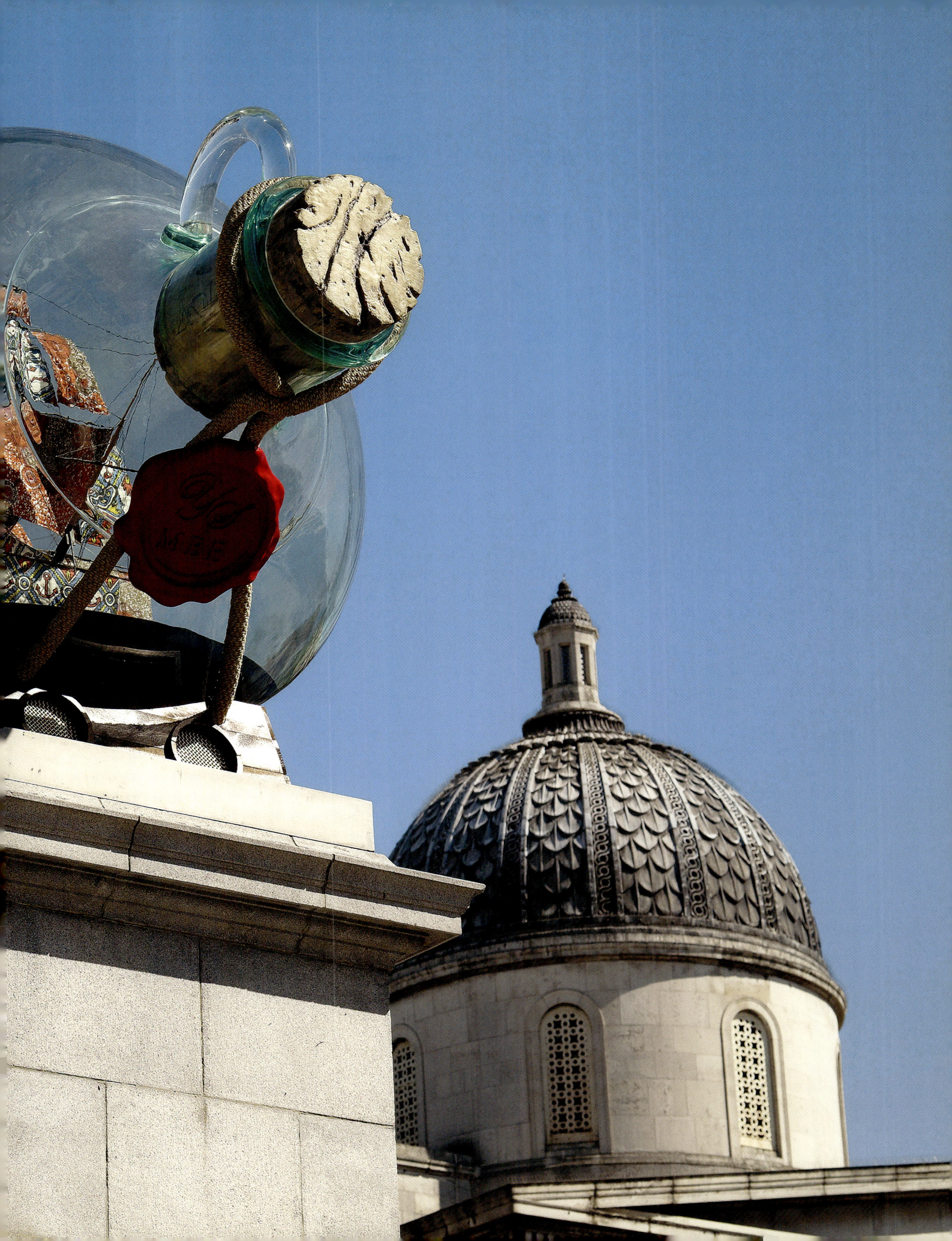

Wall, 2010

Dutch wax design or building facade
Dimensions variable
Commissioned by South London Gallery for the exhibition
Nothing Is Forever
Installation view, South London, 2010

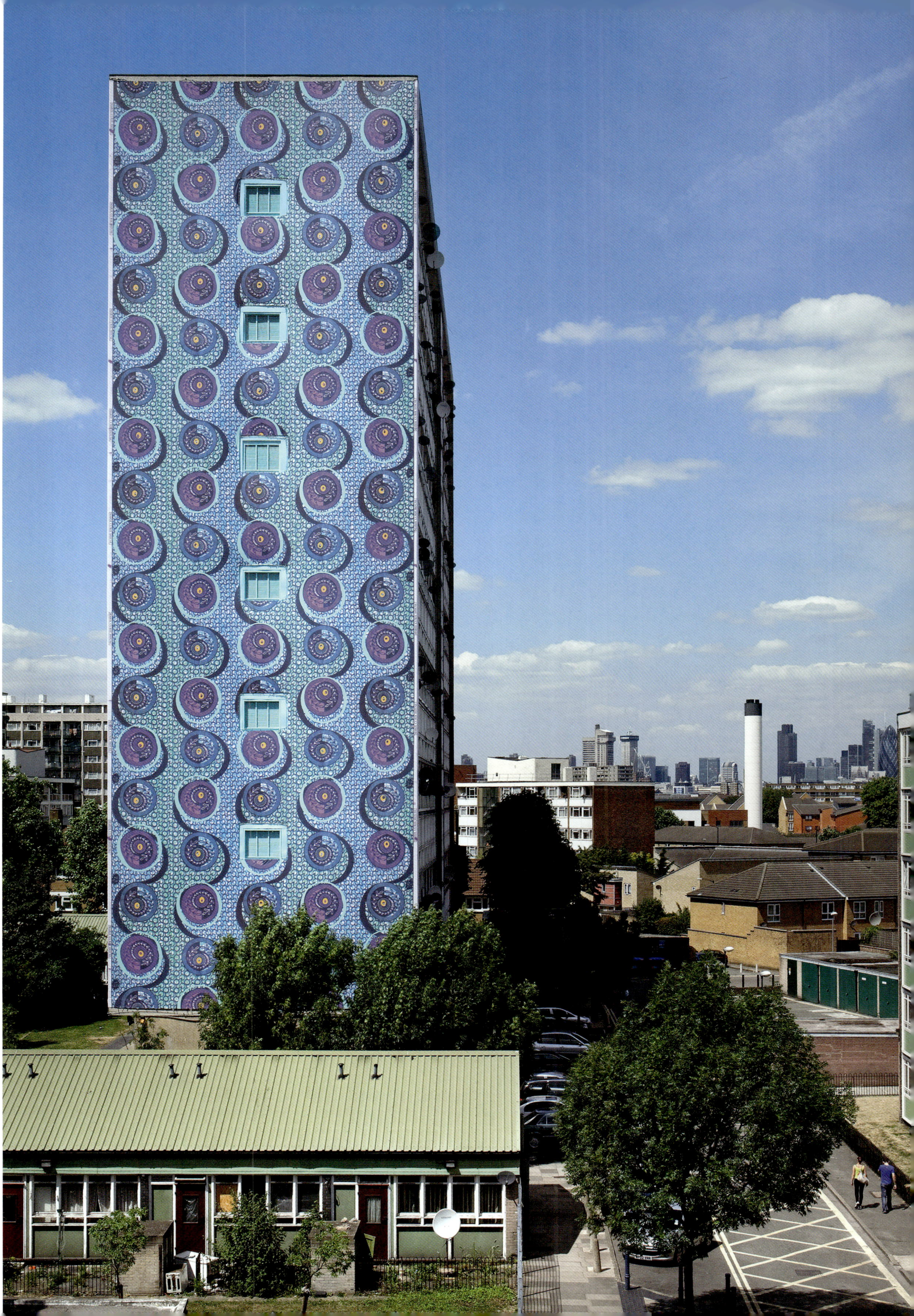

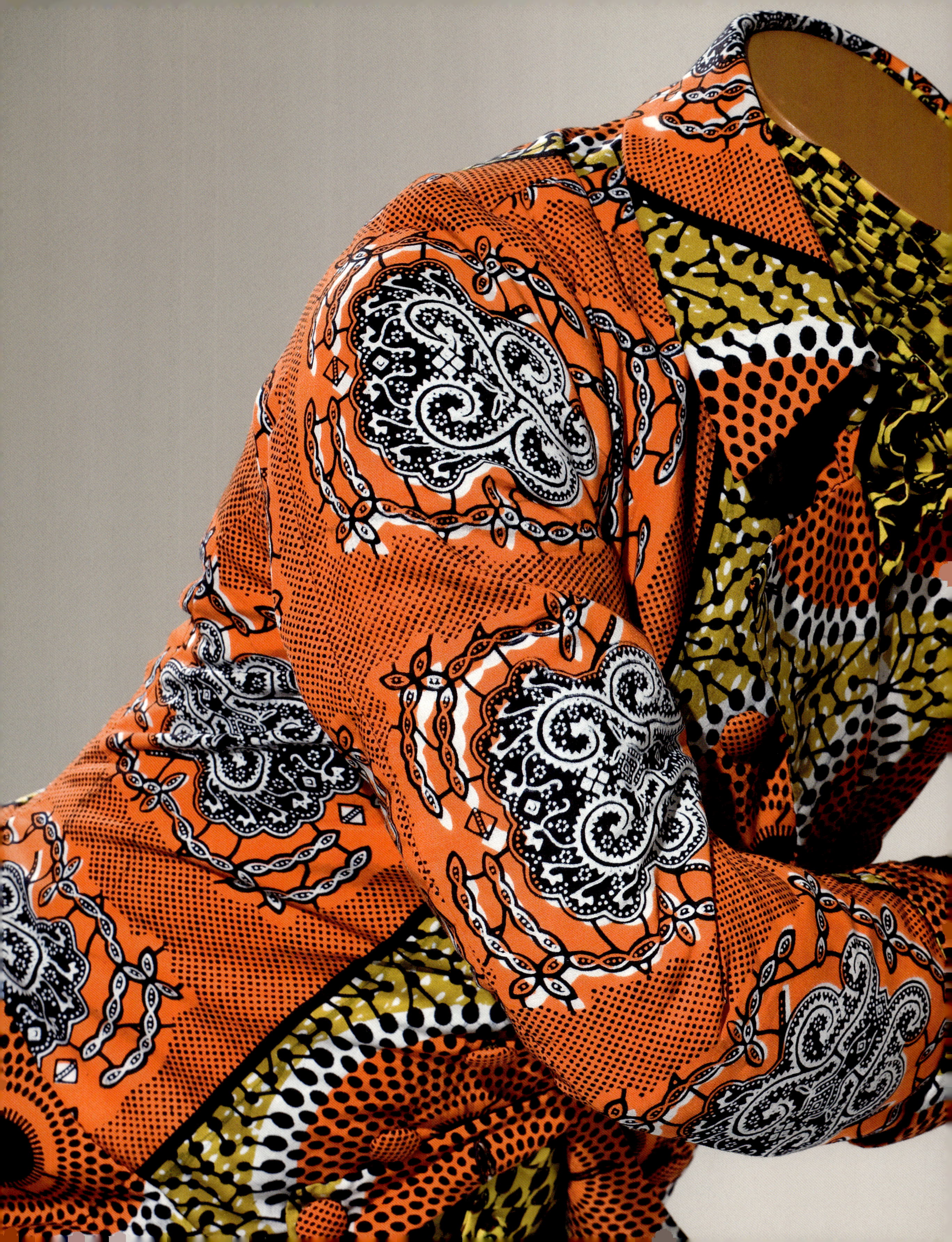

SCULPTURE

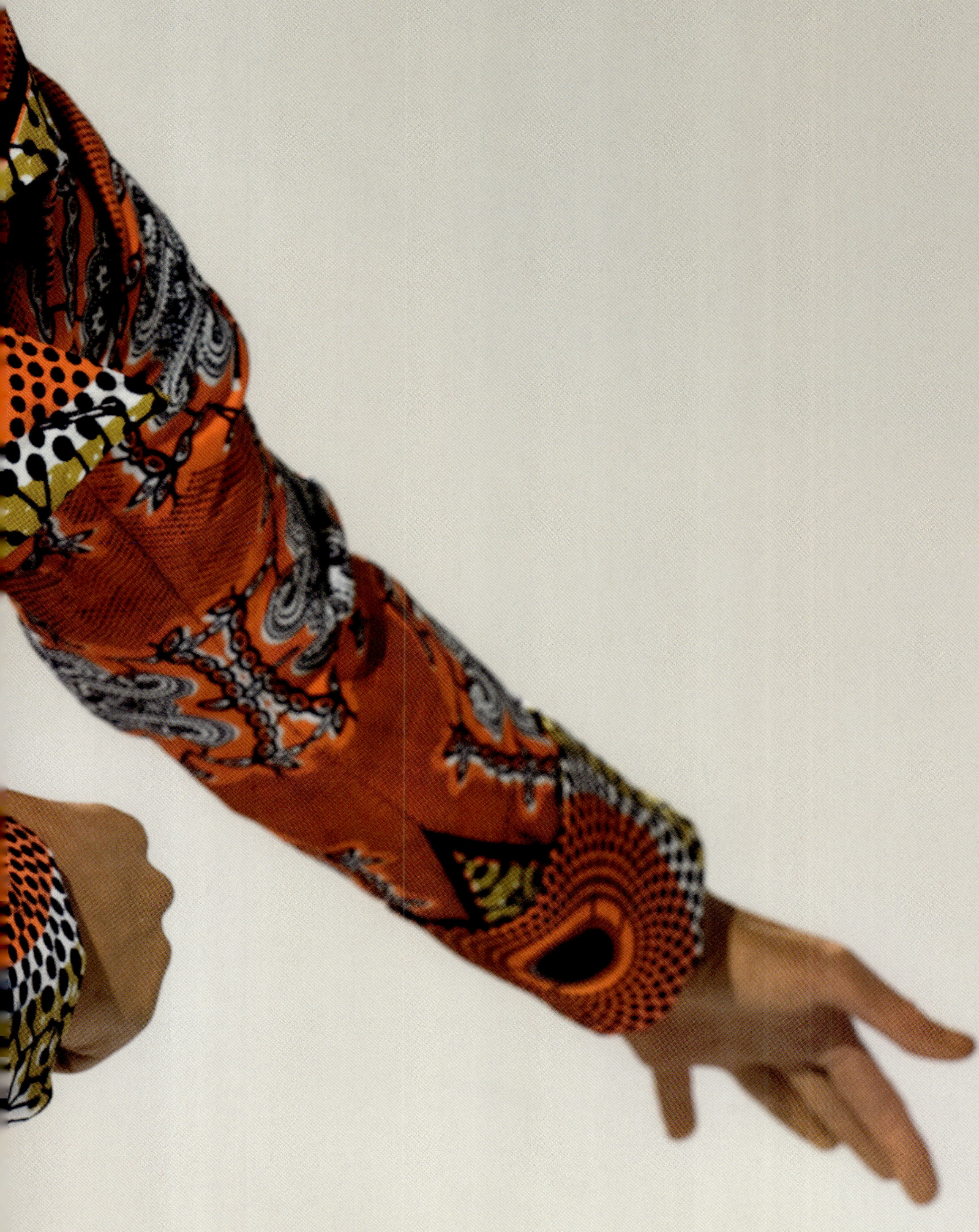

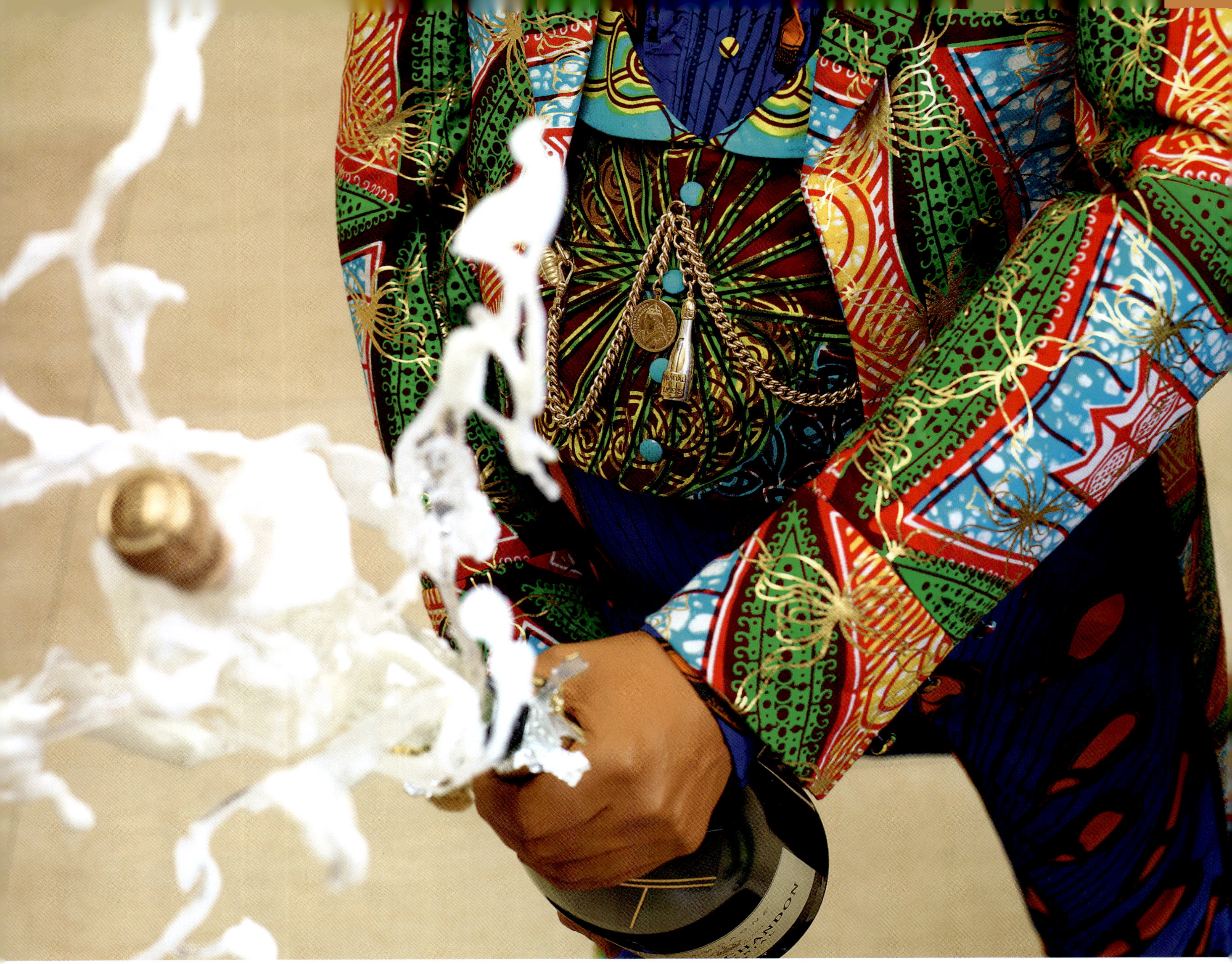

Preceding spread:

Reverend on Ice, 2005

Life-size mannequin, semi-opaque synthetic polymer resin, Dutch wax printed cotton, wool, leather, wood, steel
160 x 402.3 x 601.5 cm
National Gallery of Victoria, Melbourne, purchased with the assistance of NGV Contemporary, 2006

Above and opposite:

B(w)anker, 2013

Life-size mannequin, Dutch wax printed cotton, champagne bottle, resin, fiberglass
157 x 96 x 110 cm
Collection of John and Amy Phelan

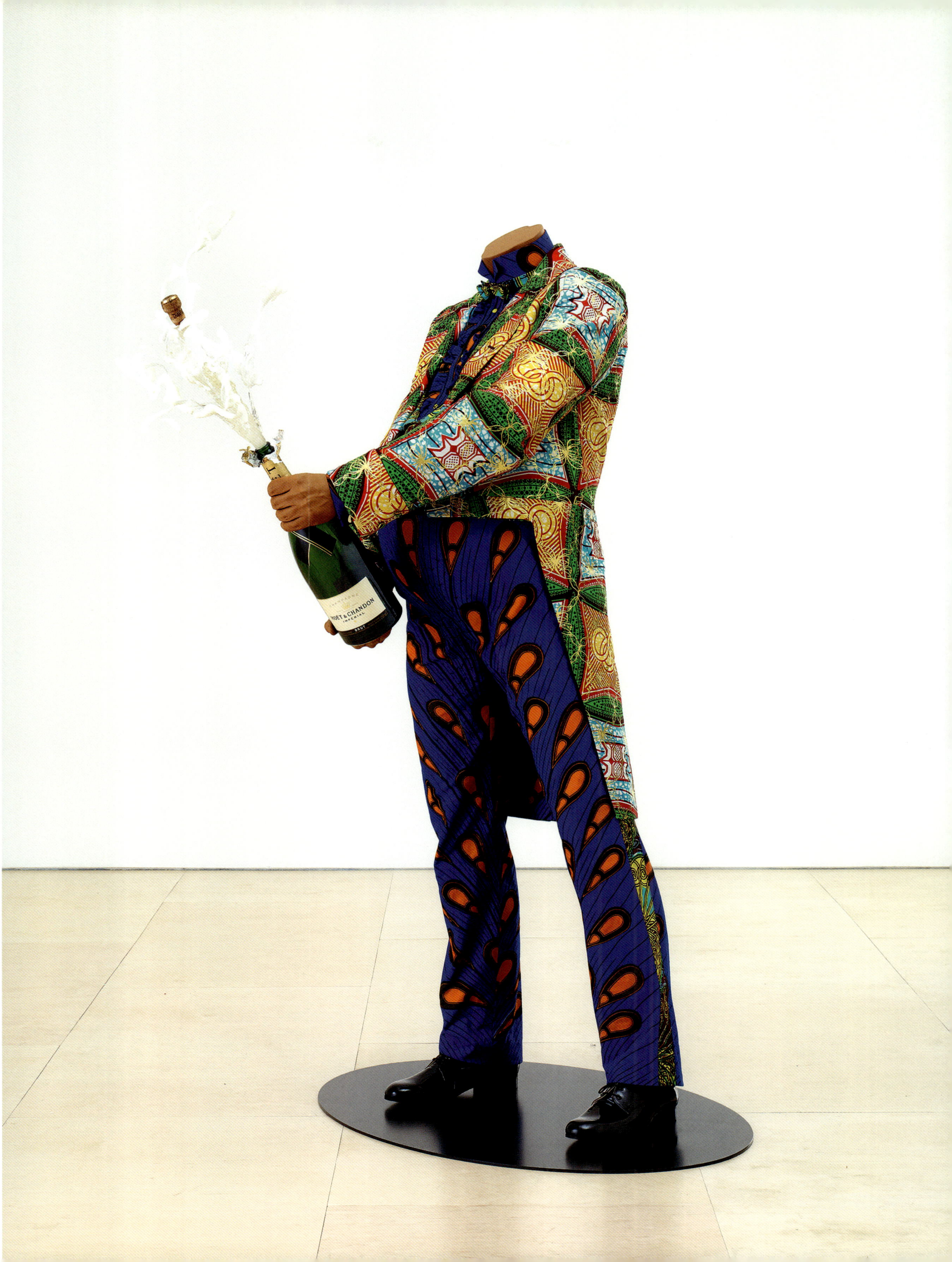
CHAMPAGNE
MOËT & CHANDON
IMPERIAL
BRUT

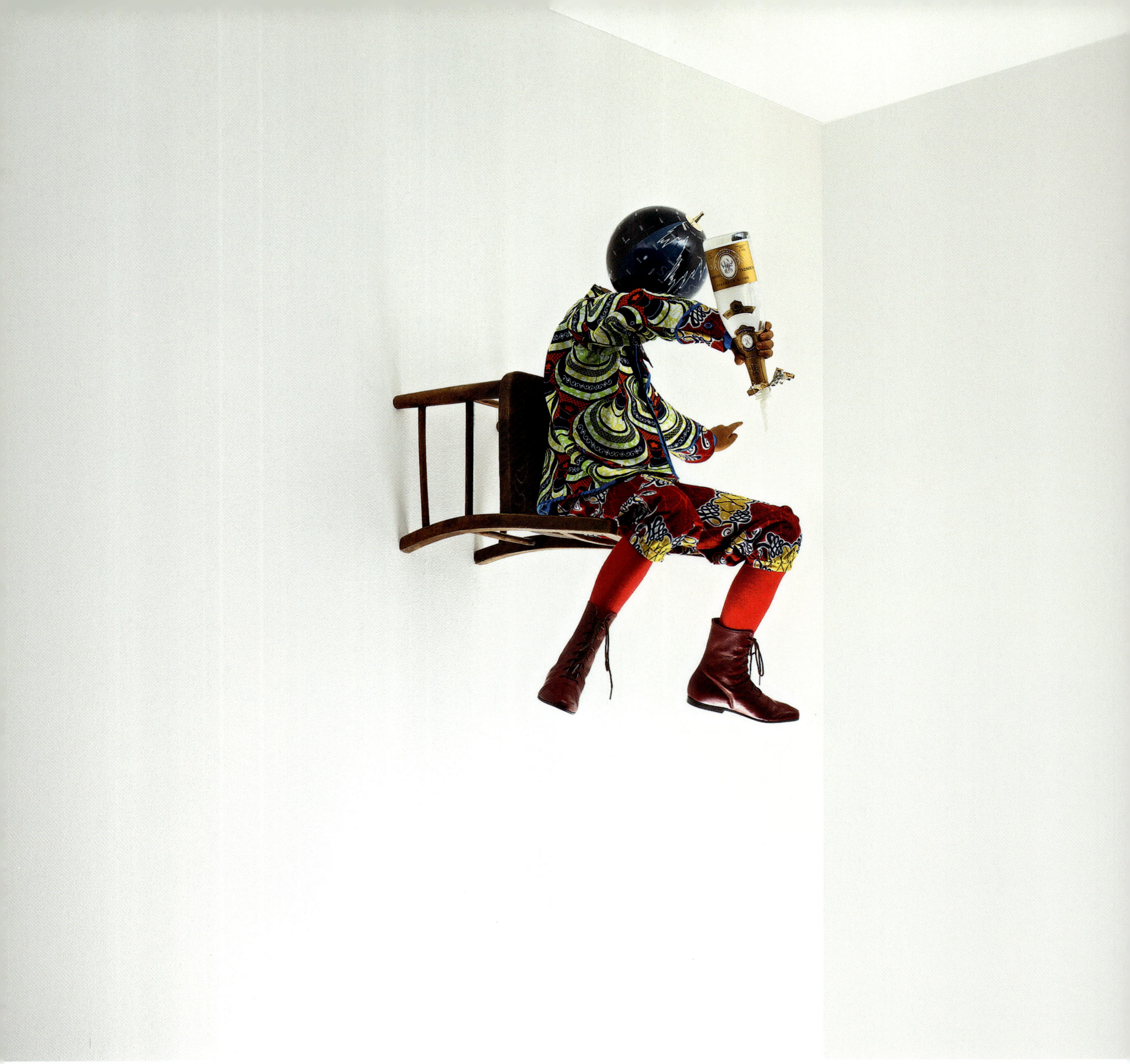

Above:

Champagne Kid (Perching), 2013
Life-size mannequin, Dutch wax printed cotton, chair, champagne bottle
98 x 95 x 89 cm
Private collection, Germany

Opposite:

Champagne Kid (Leaning), 2013
Life-size mannequin, Dutch wax printed cotton, chair, champagne bottle
118.5 x 84 x 134 cm
Guttman Collection, Belgium

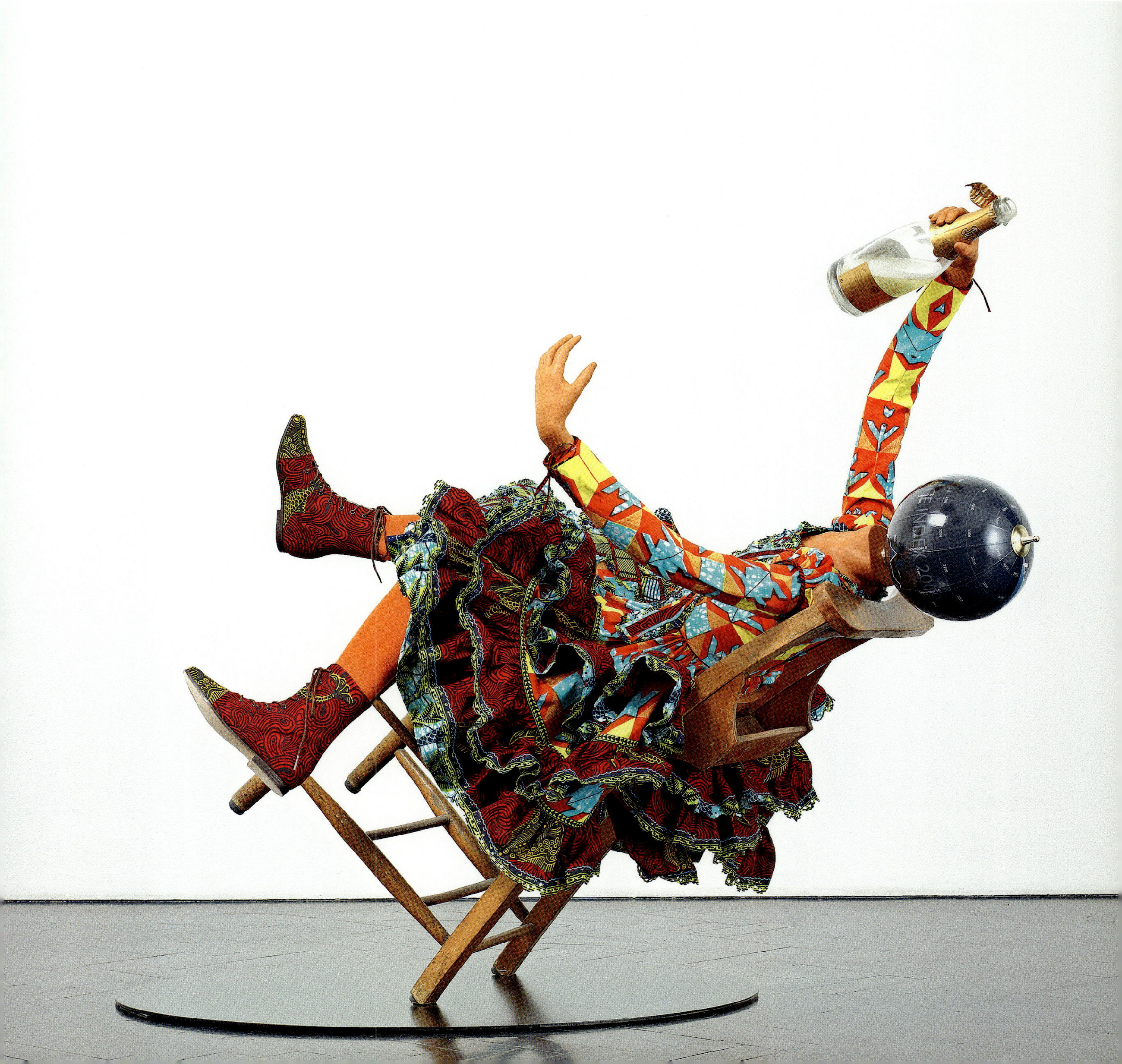

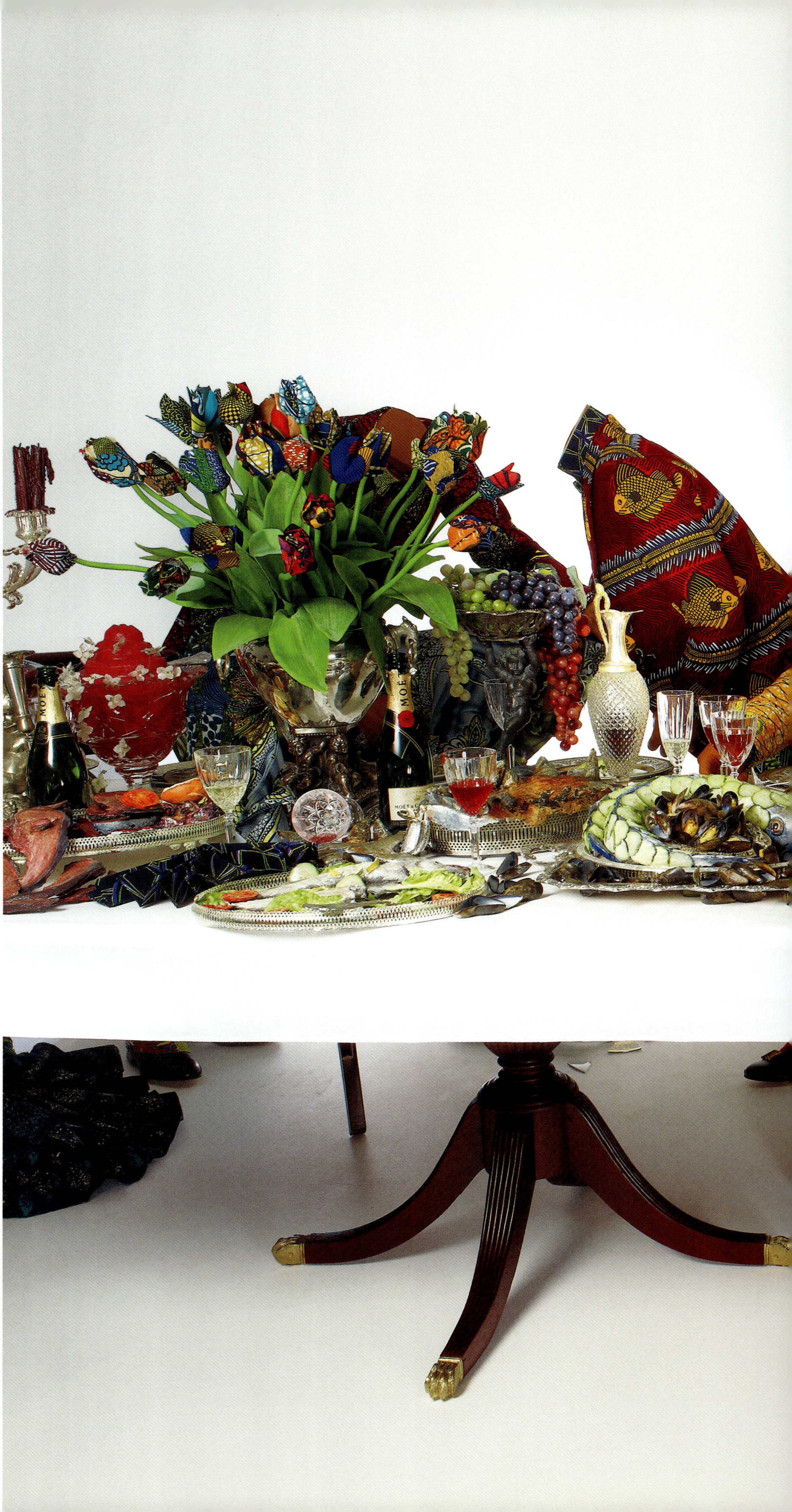

Opposite and overleaf:

Last Supper (after Leonardo), 2013

Thirteen life-size mannequins, Dutch wax printed cotton, reproduction wood table and chairs, silver cutlery and vases, antique and reproduction glassware and tableware, fiberglass and resin food
158 x 742 x 260 cm
VandenBroek Foundation, Sassenheim

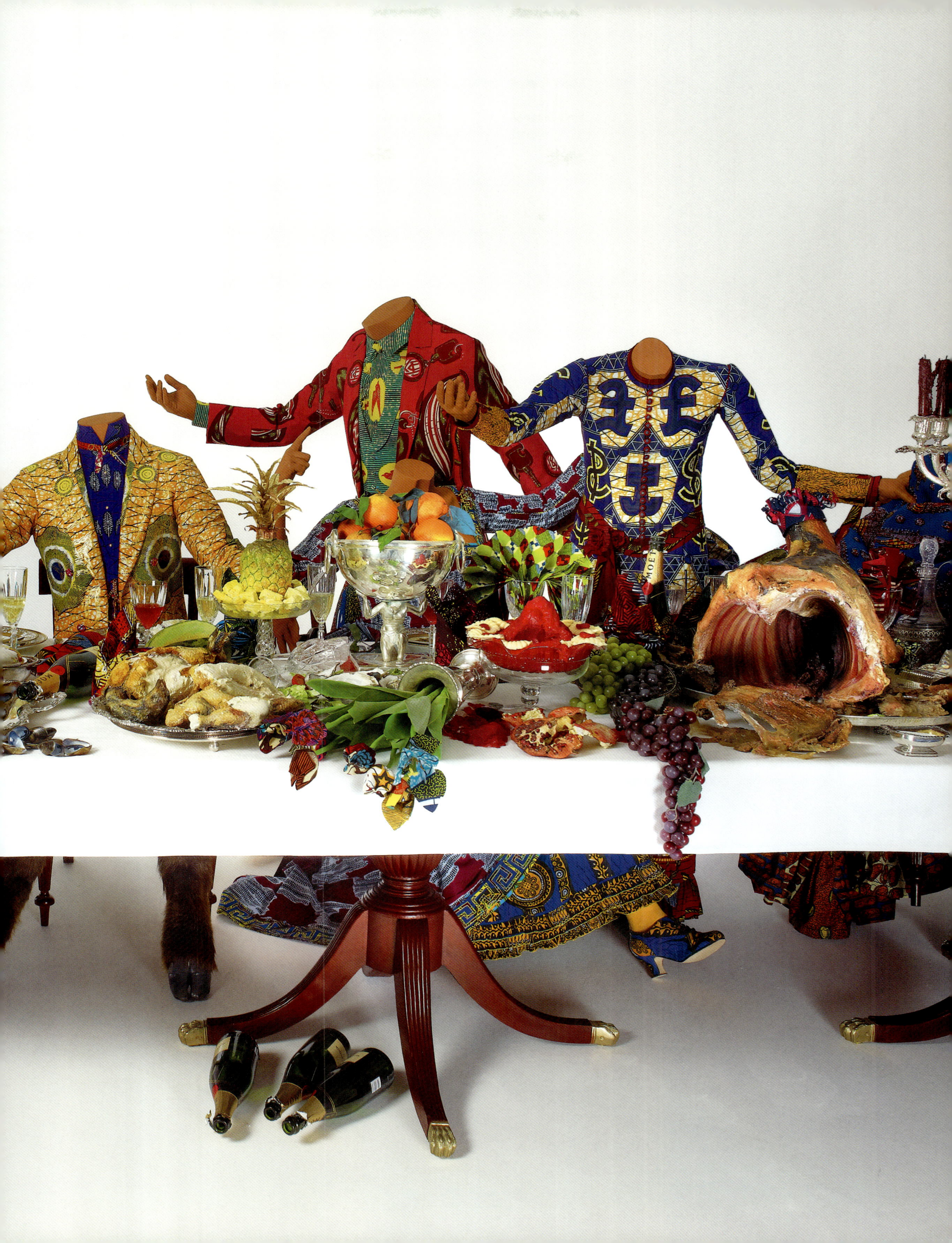

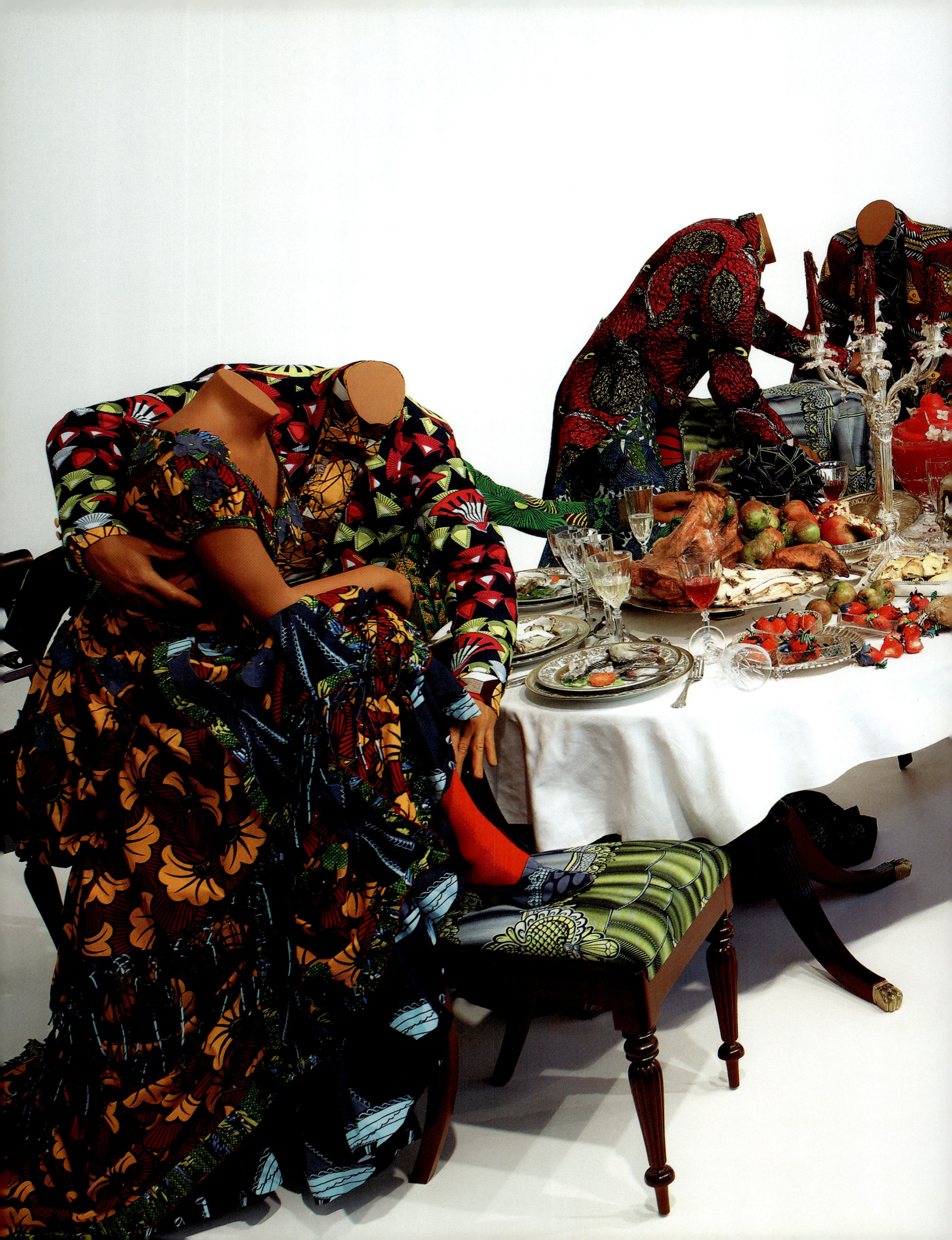

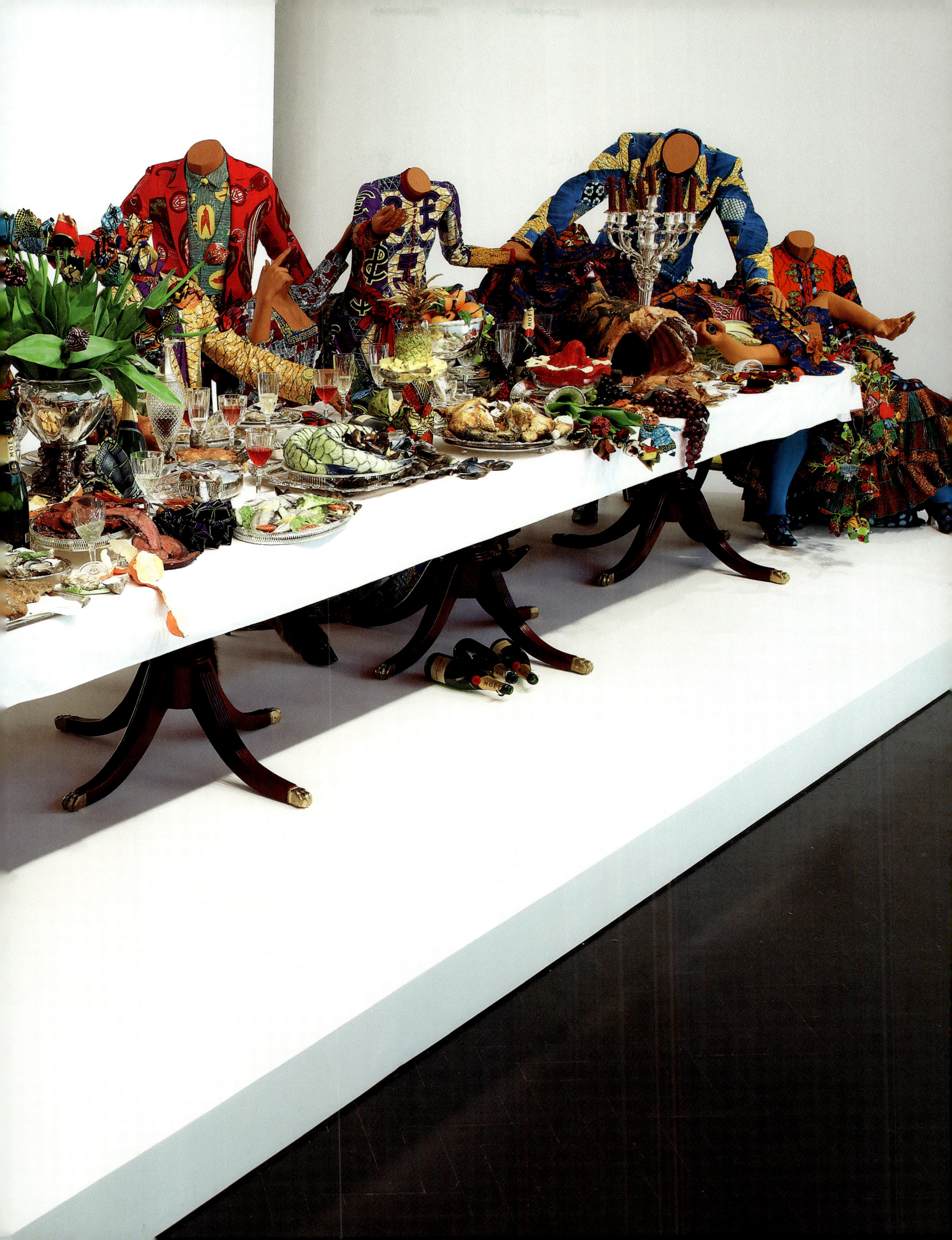

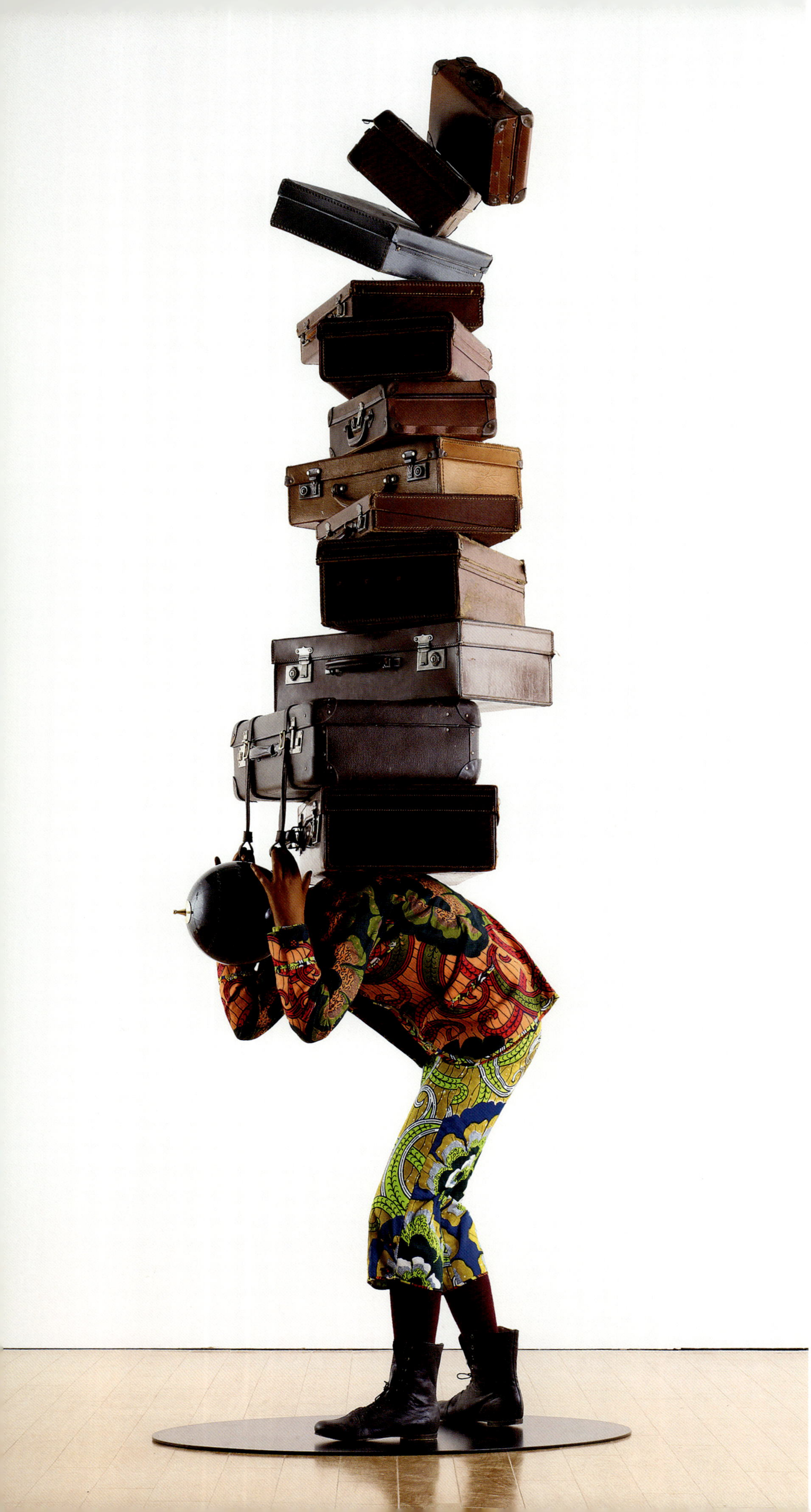

Homeless Boy, 2012

Life-size mannequin, Dutch wax printed cotton, leather suitcases, globe, metal base
270 x 65 x 100 cm

Opposite:

Homeless Man, 2012

Life-size mannequin, Dutch wax printed cotton, leather suitcases, globe, metal base
320 x 80 x 115 cm

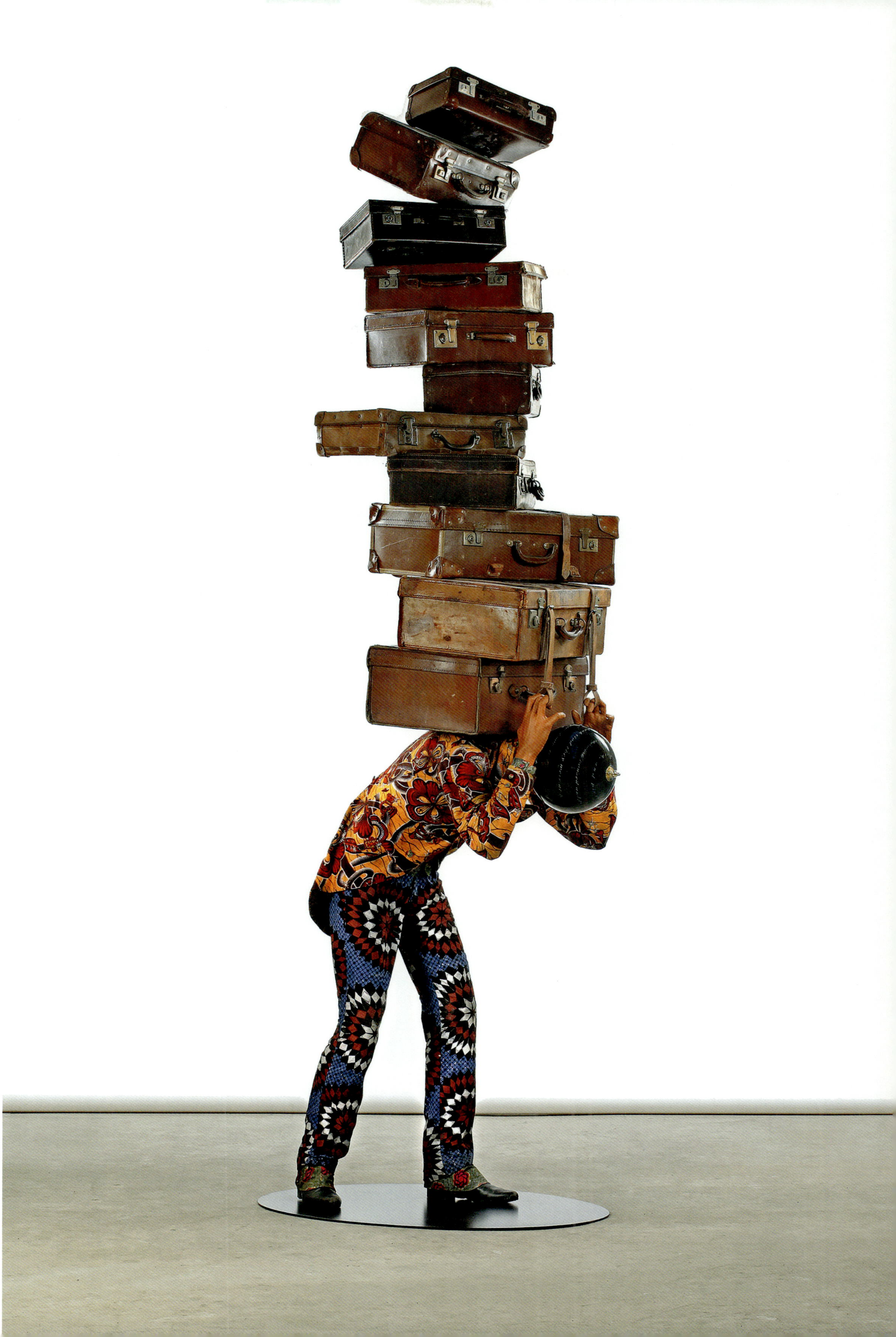

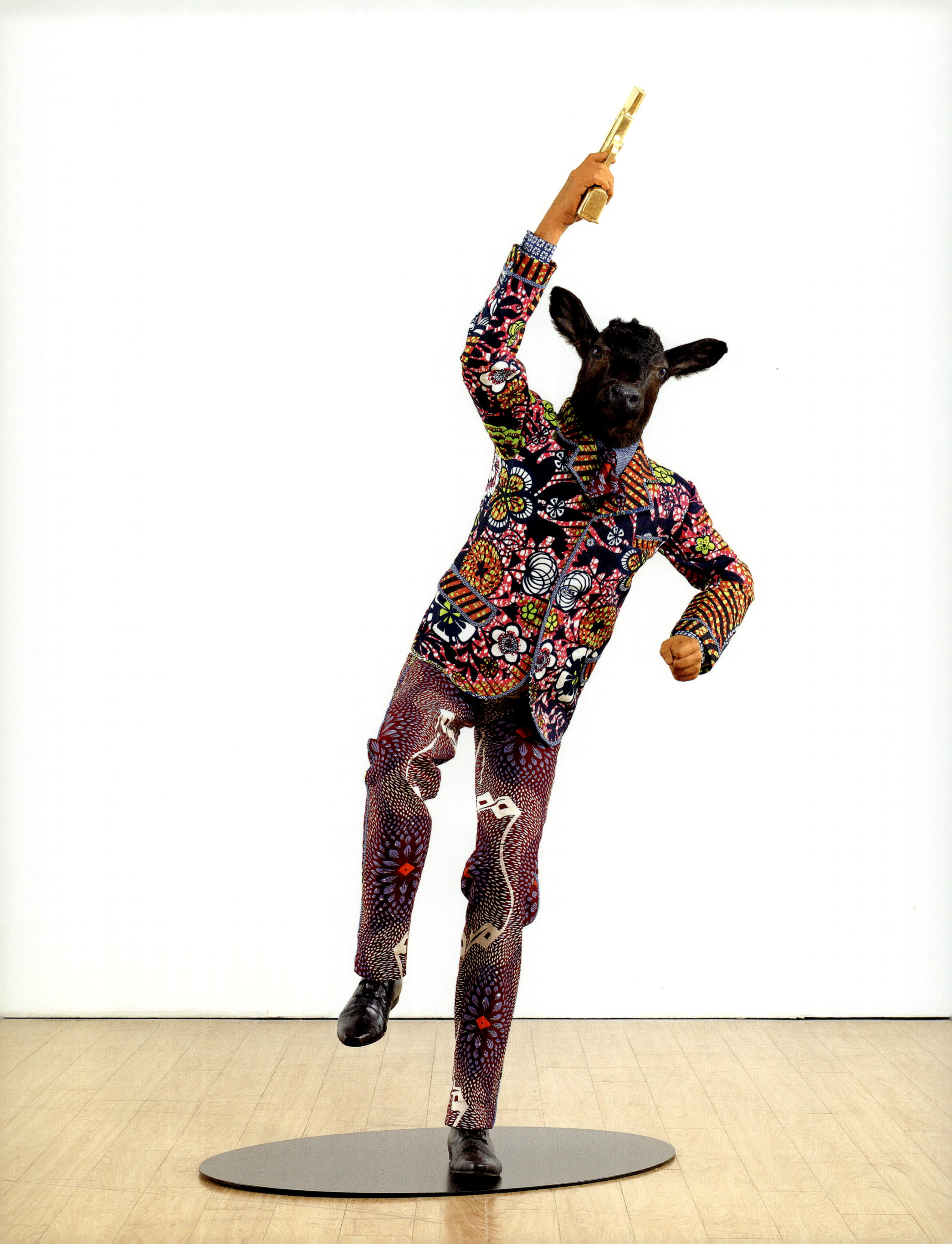

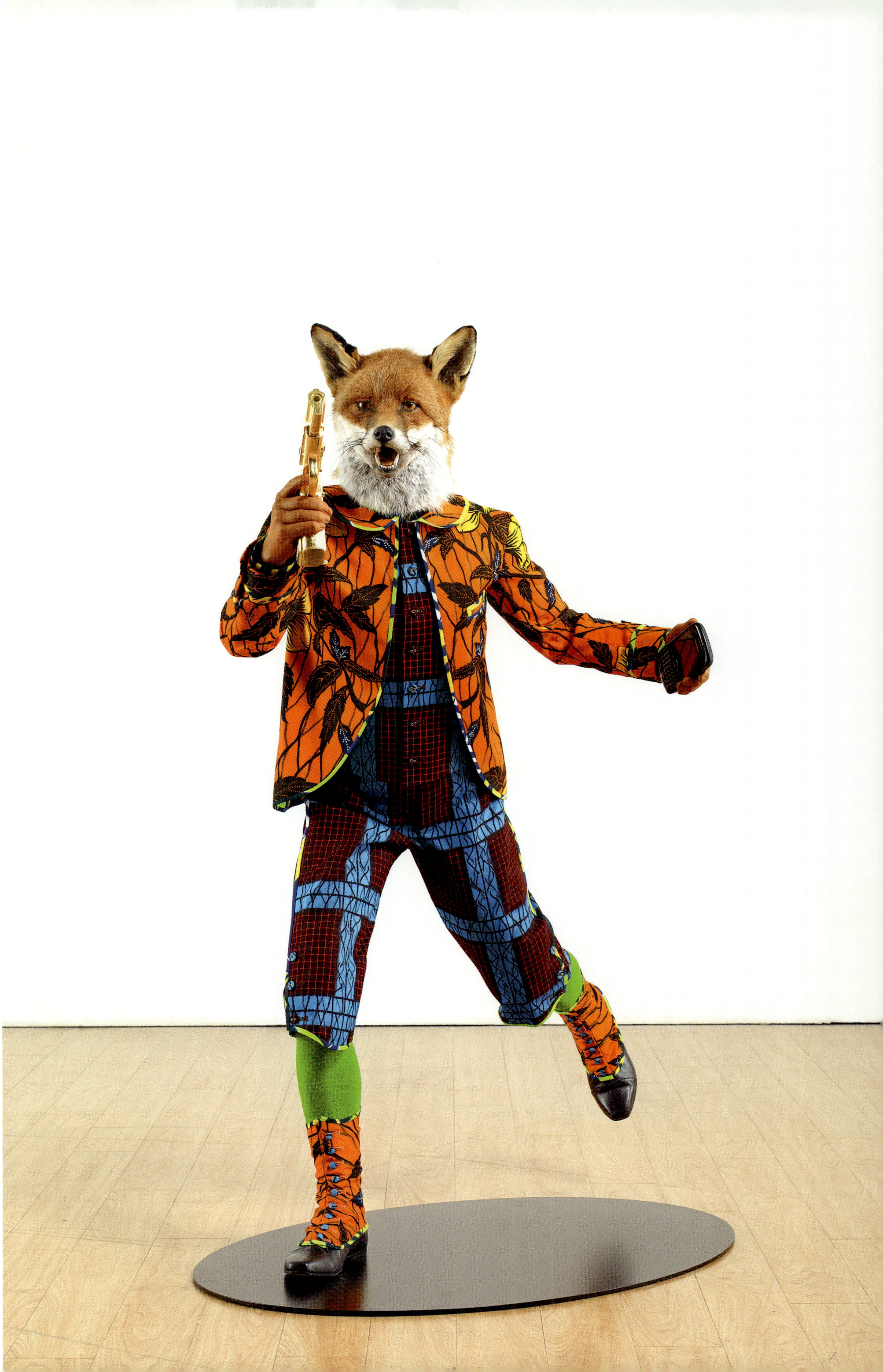

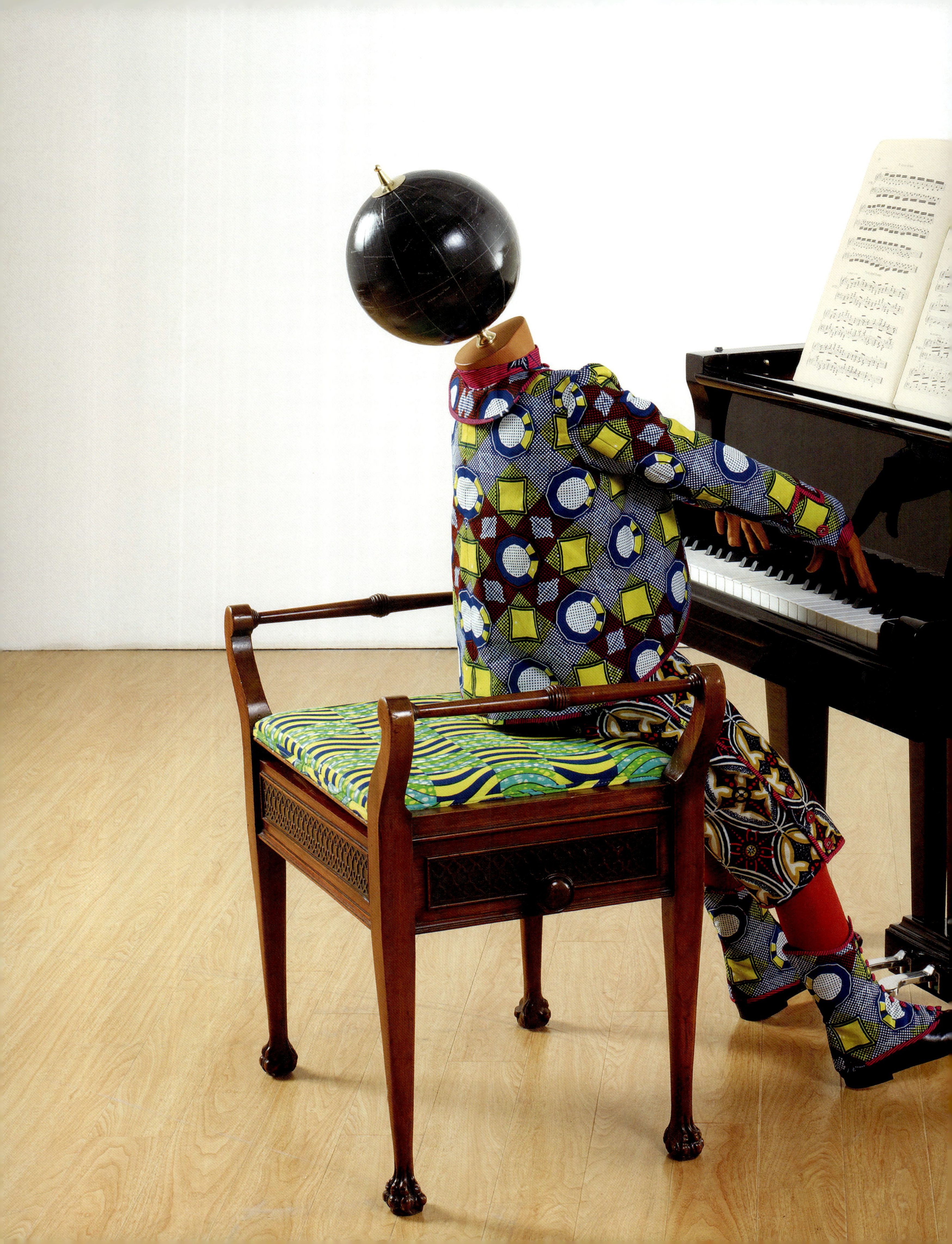

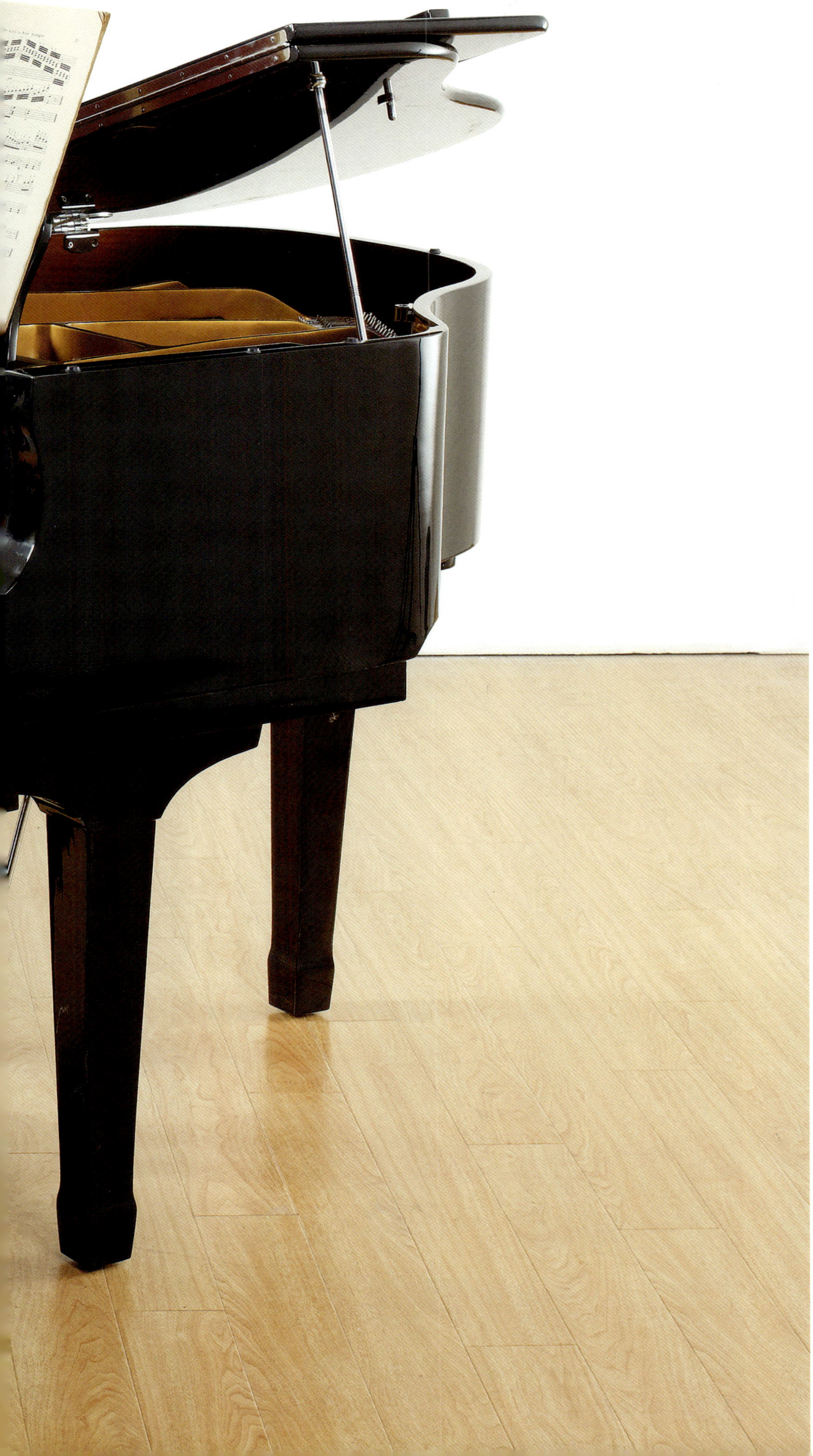

Preceding spread, left:

Revolution Kid (Calf), 2012

Life-size mannequin, Dutch wax printed cotton, fiberglass, leather, taxidermy calf head, 24-carat gilded gun
165 x 64 x 53 cm

Preceding spread, right:

Revolution Kid (Fox), 2012

Life-size mannequin, Dutch wax printed cotton, fiberglass, leather, taxidermy fox head, BlackBerry, 24-carat gilded gun
119 x 66 x 120 cm
Museum Beelden aan Zee, The Hague

Planets in My Head, Music, 2012

Life-size mannequin, fiberglass, Dutch wax printed cotton, child's grand piano, Victorian stool, Victorian sheet music, leather
115 x 90 x 176 cm

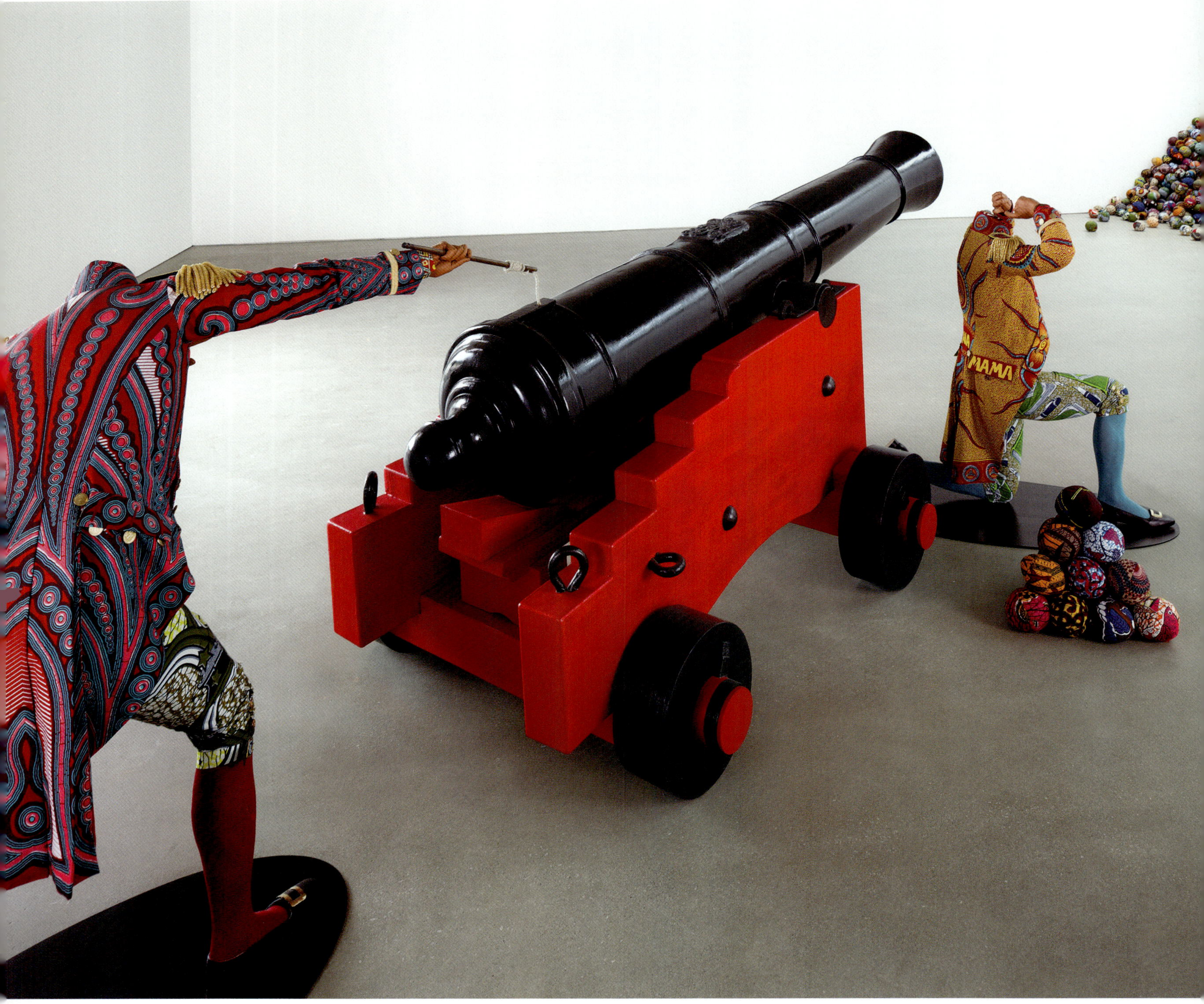

Cannonball Heaven, 2011

Two life-size mannequins, Dutch wax printed cotton, leather boots, 600 foam balls, fiberglass reproduction cannon
Dimensions variable
Commissioned by La Comunidad de Madrid for the exhibition *Yinka Shonibare MBE* at Sala Alcalá 31, Madrid

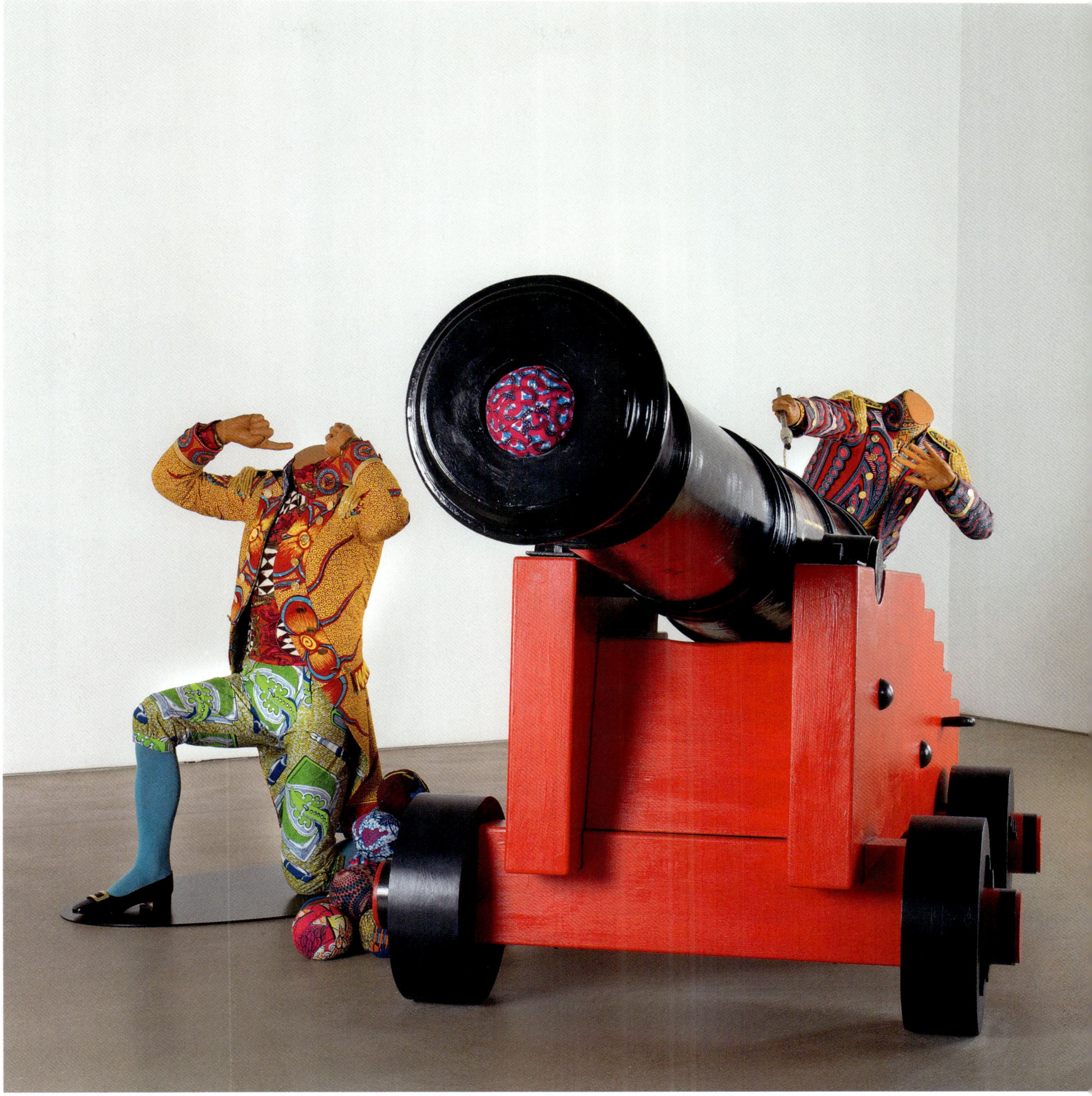

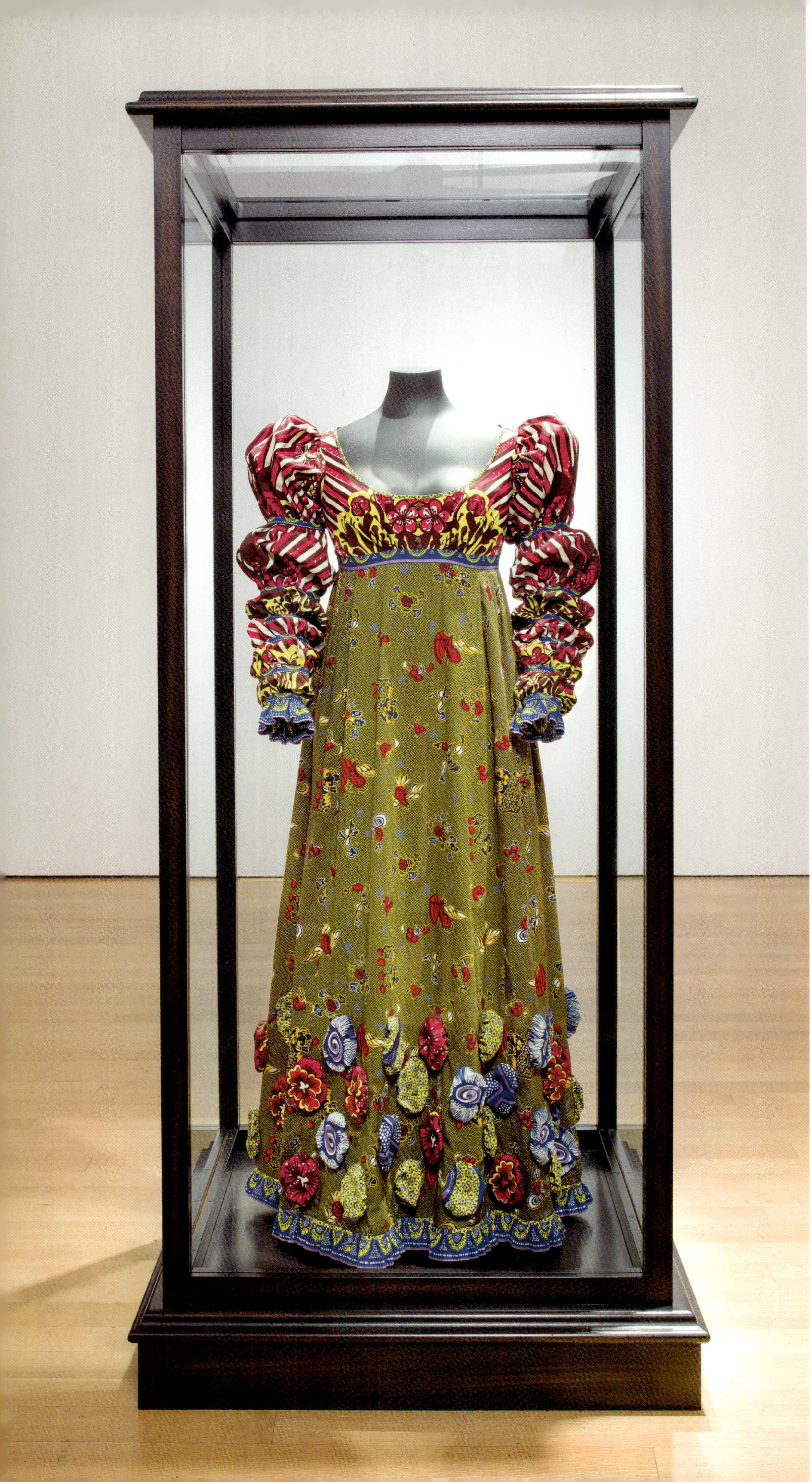

Fanny's Dress, 2011

Dutch wax printed cotton, fiberglass mannequin, wood and glass vitrine
207.7 x 91.4 x 91.4 cm

Opposite:

Nelson's Jacket, 2011

Dutch wax printed cotton, fiberglass mannequin, wood and glass vitrine
207.7 x 91.4 x 91.4 cm

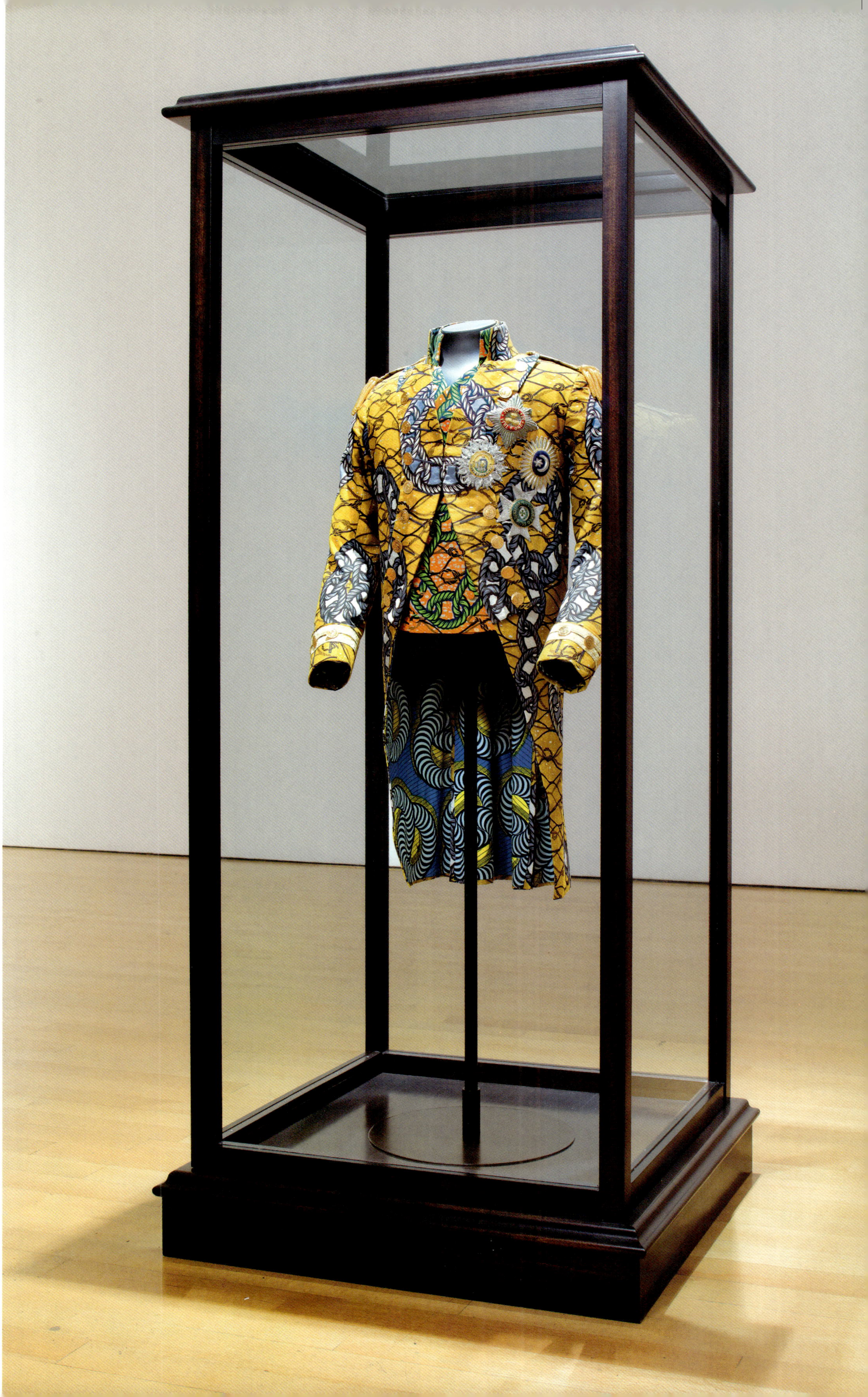

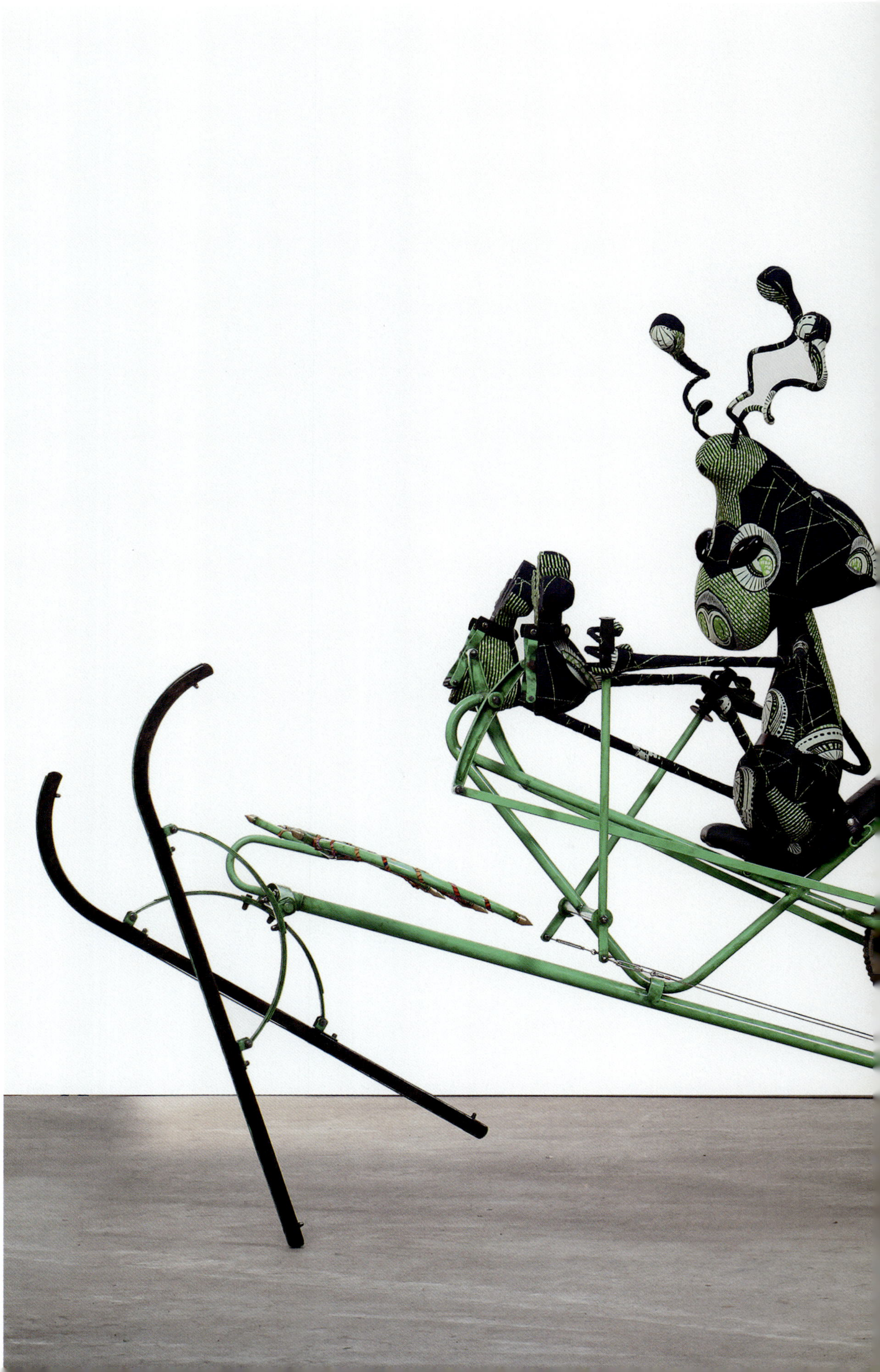

Alien Man on Flying Machine, 2011

Steel, aluminum, brass, Dutch wax printed cotton, rubber
250 x 450 x 450 cm

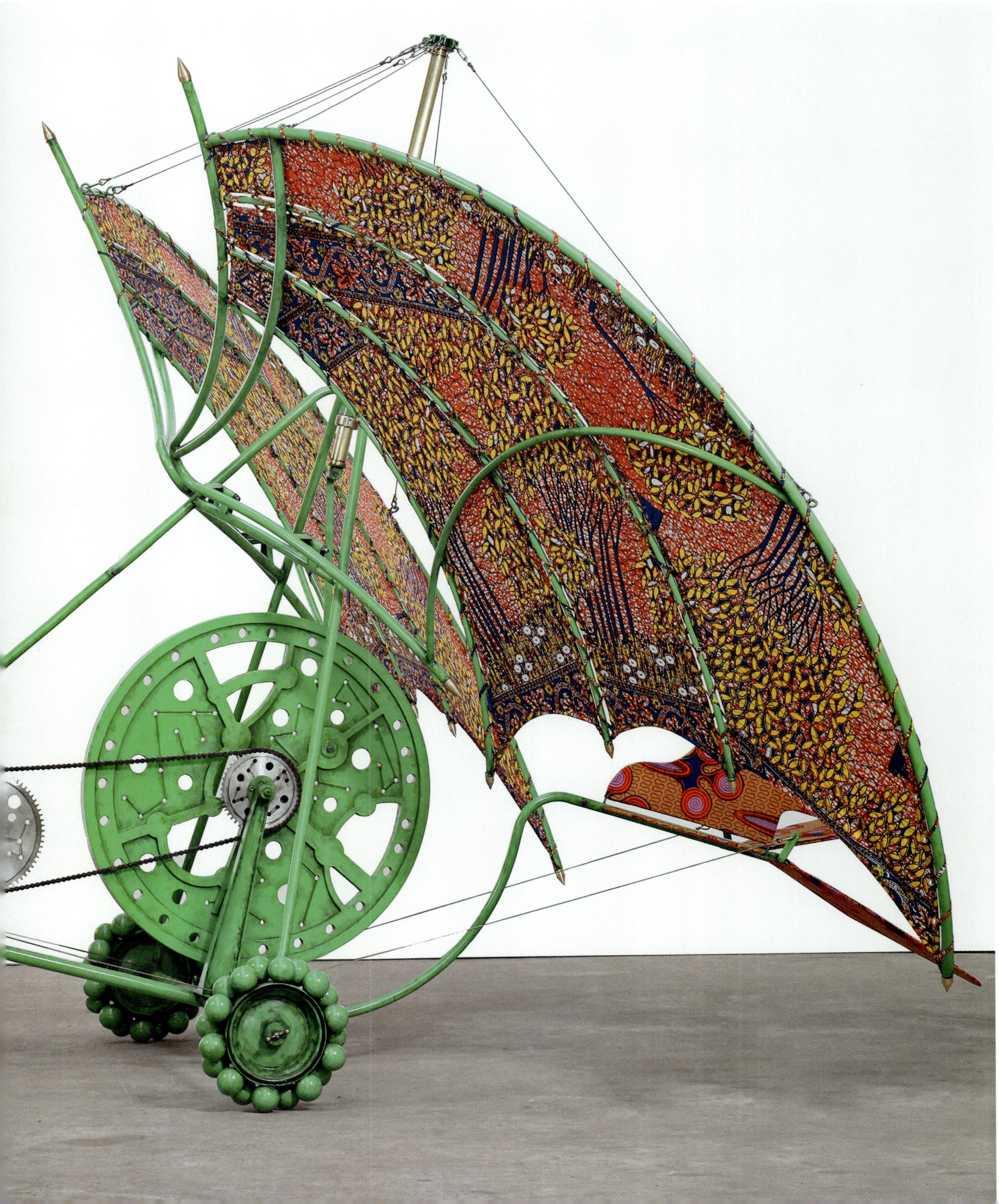

Fire, 2010

Life-size mannequin, Dutch wax printed cotton, leather, wood, brass lamp stanc, glass lamp shade, circuit board, LED, metal base
184 x 110 x 70 cm
Commissioned by the Israel Museum, Jerusalem, for the exhibition *Yinka Shonibare: Earth, Wind, Fire, and Water*

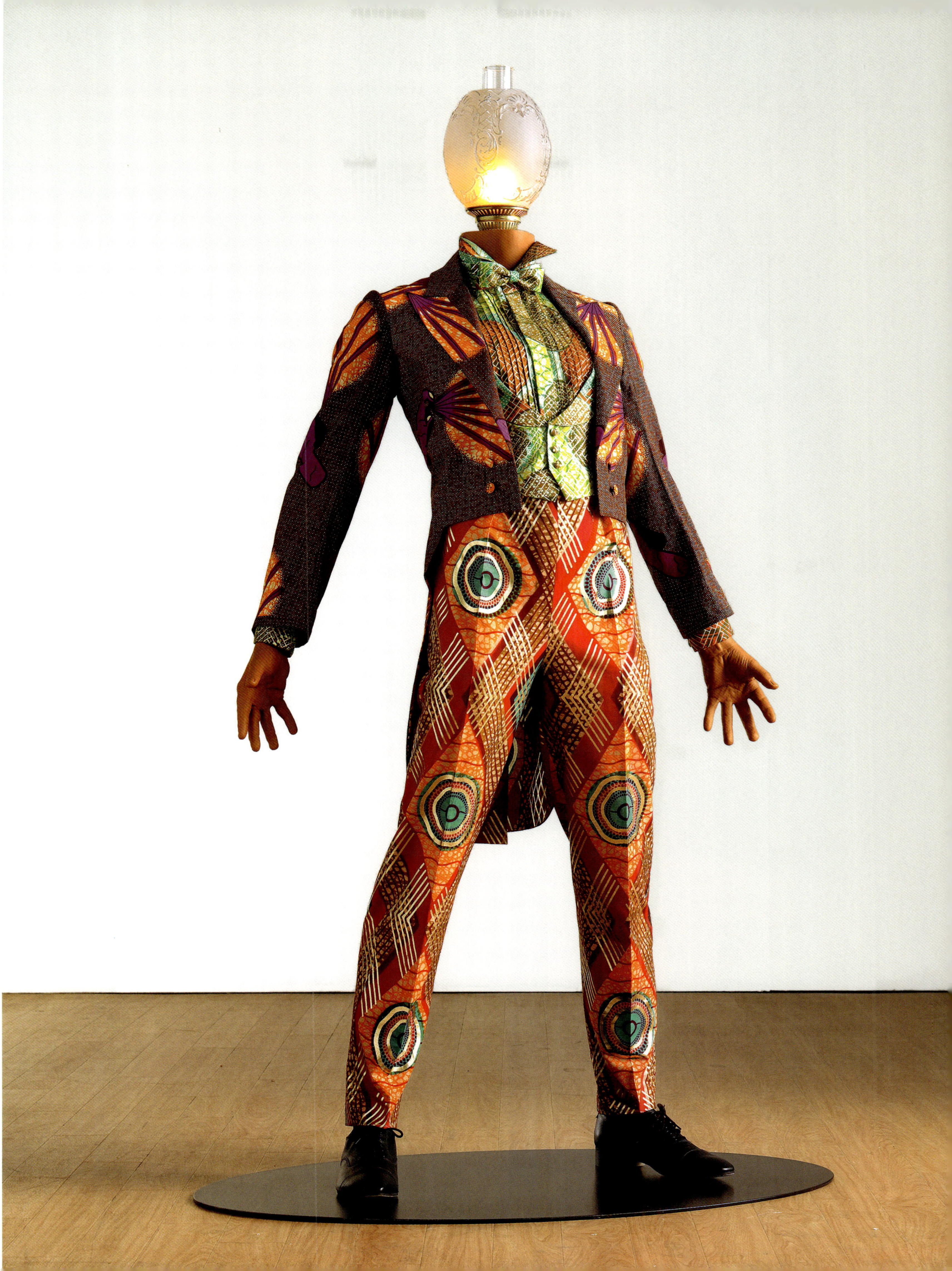

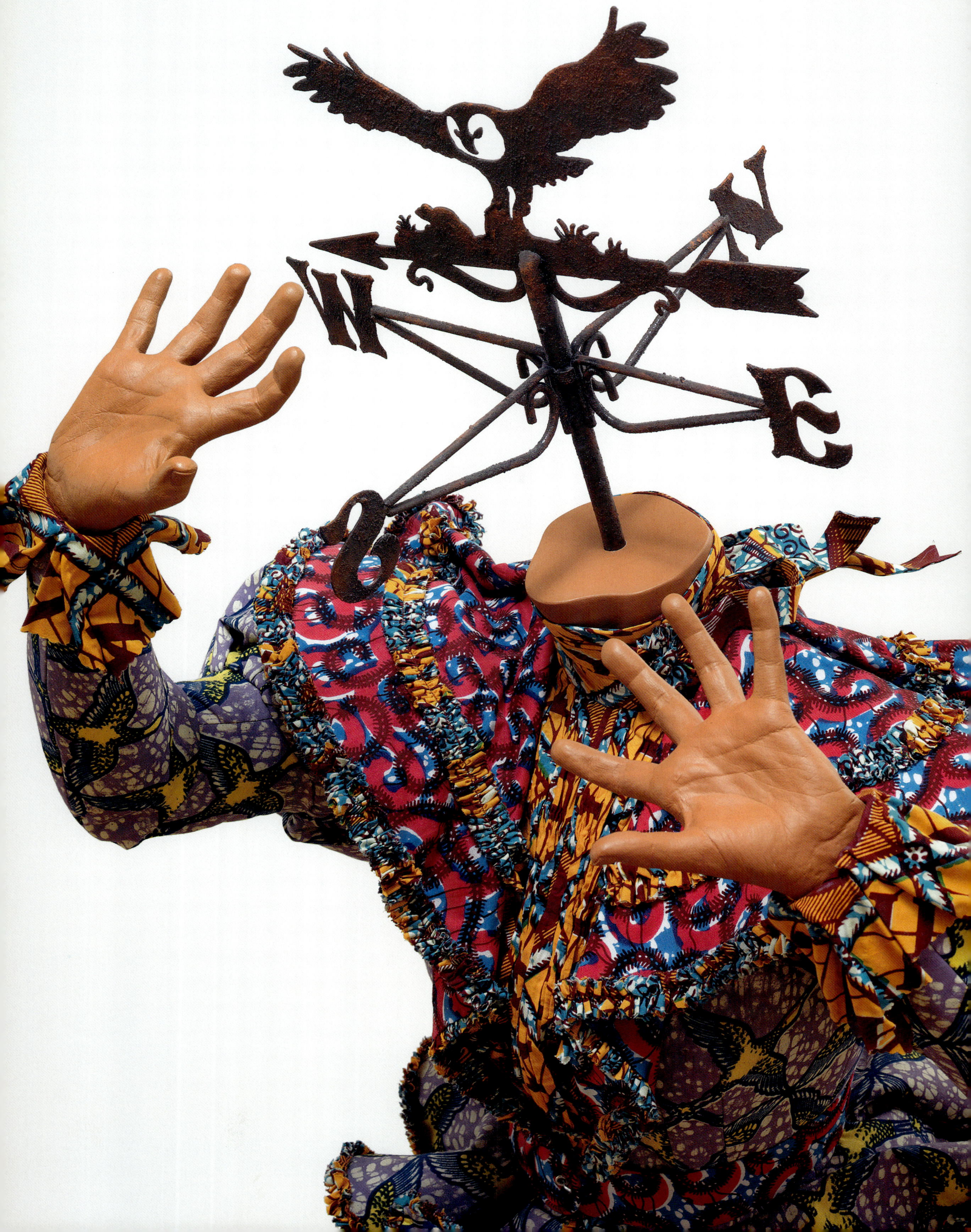
N
E

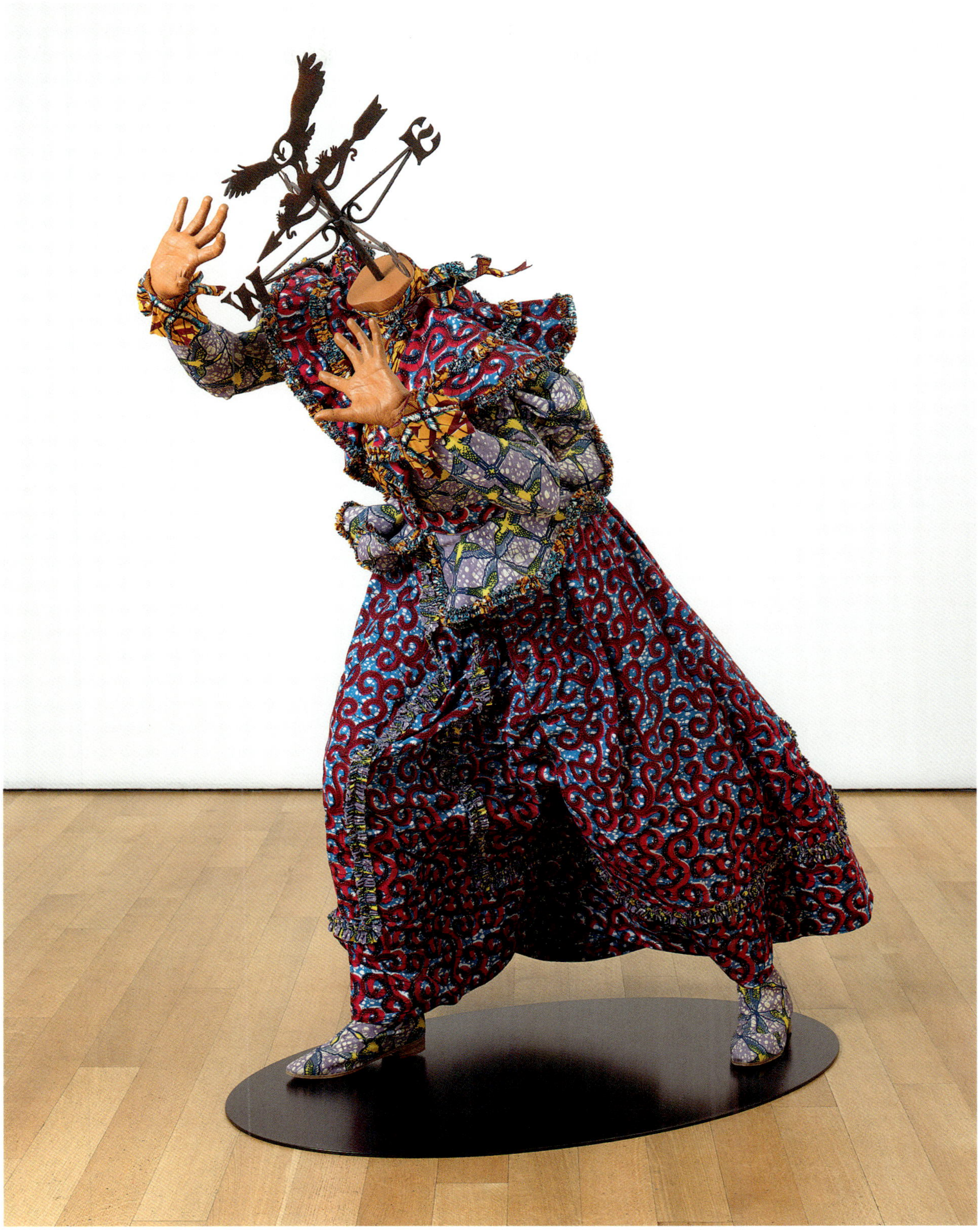

Opposite and above:

Air, 2010

Life-size mannequin, Dutch wax printed cotton, leather, wood, metal weather vane, metal base
180 x 70 x 130 cm
Private collection

Overleaf, left:

Earth, 2010

Life-size mannequin, Dutch wax printed cotton, leather, wood, globe, metal base
183 x 140 x 165 cm
Commissioned by the Israel Museum, Jerusalem, for the exhibition *Yinka Shonibare: Earth, Wind, Fire, and Water*

Overleaf, right:

Water, 2010

Life-size mannequin, Dutch wax printed cotton, leather, wood
143 x 75 x 88 cm
Private collection

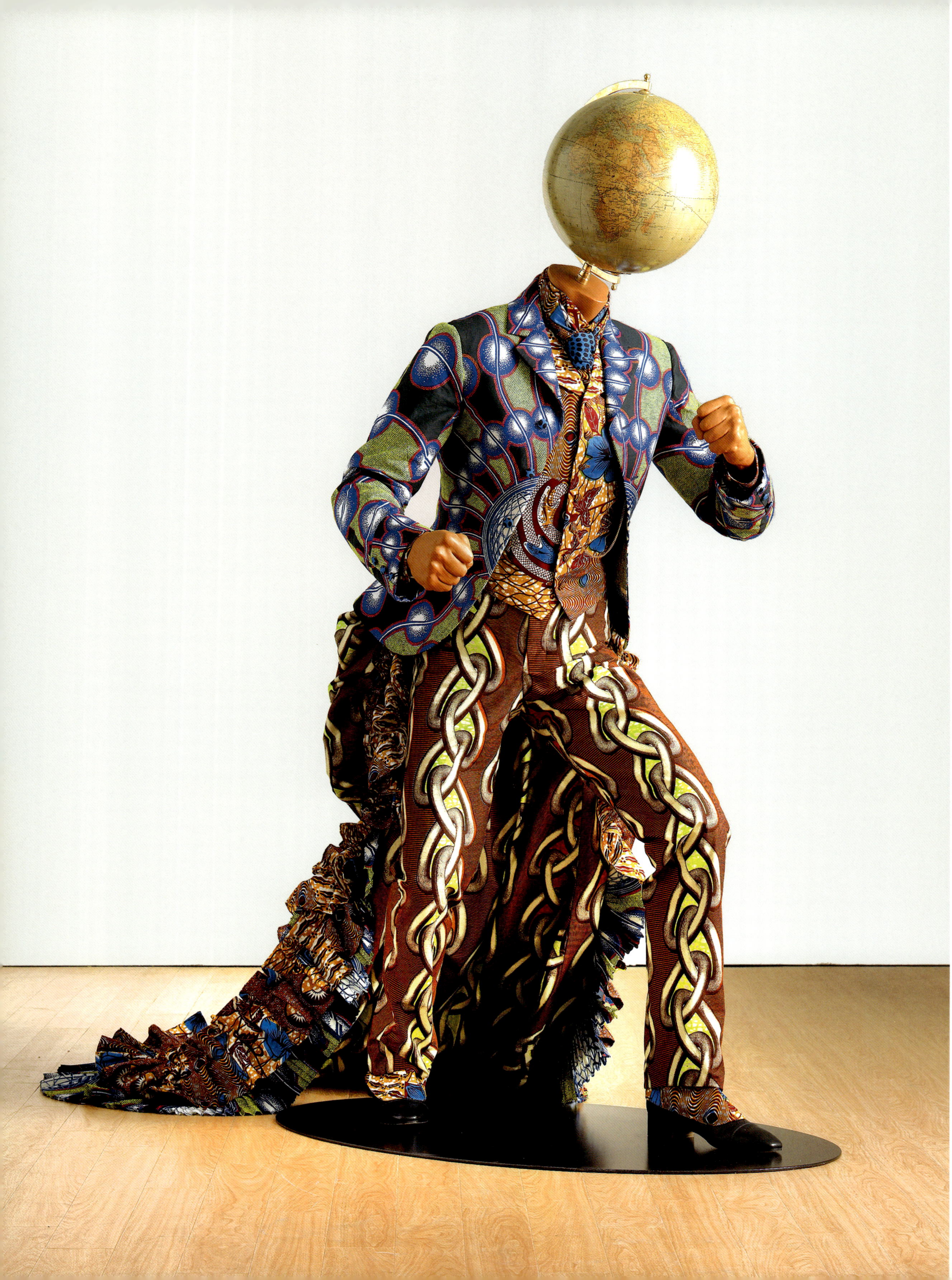

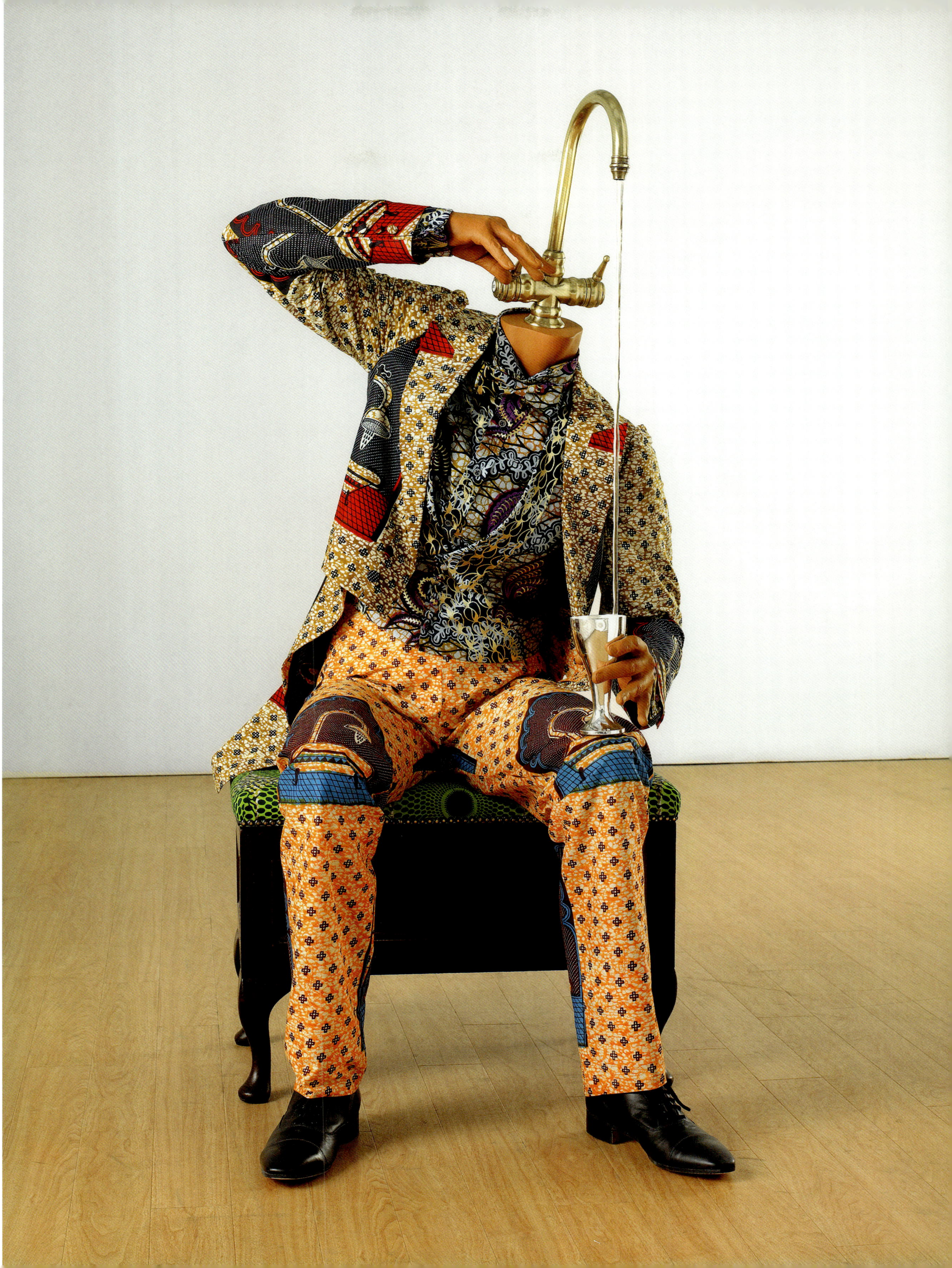

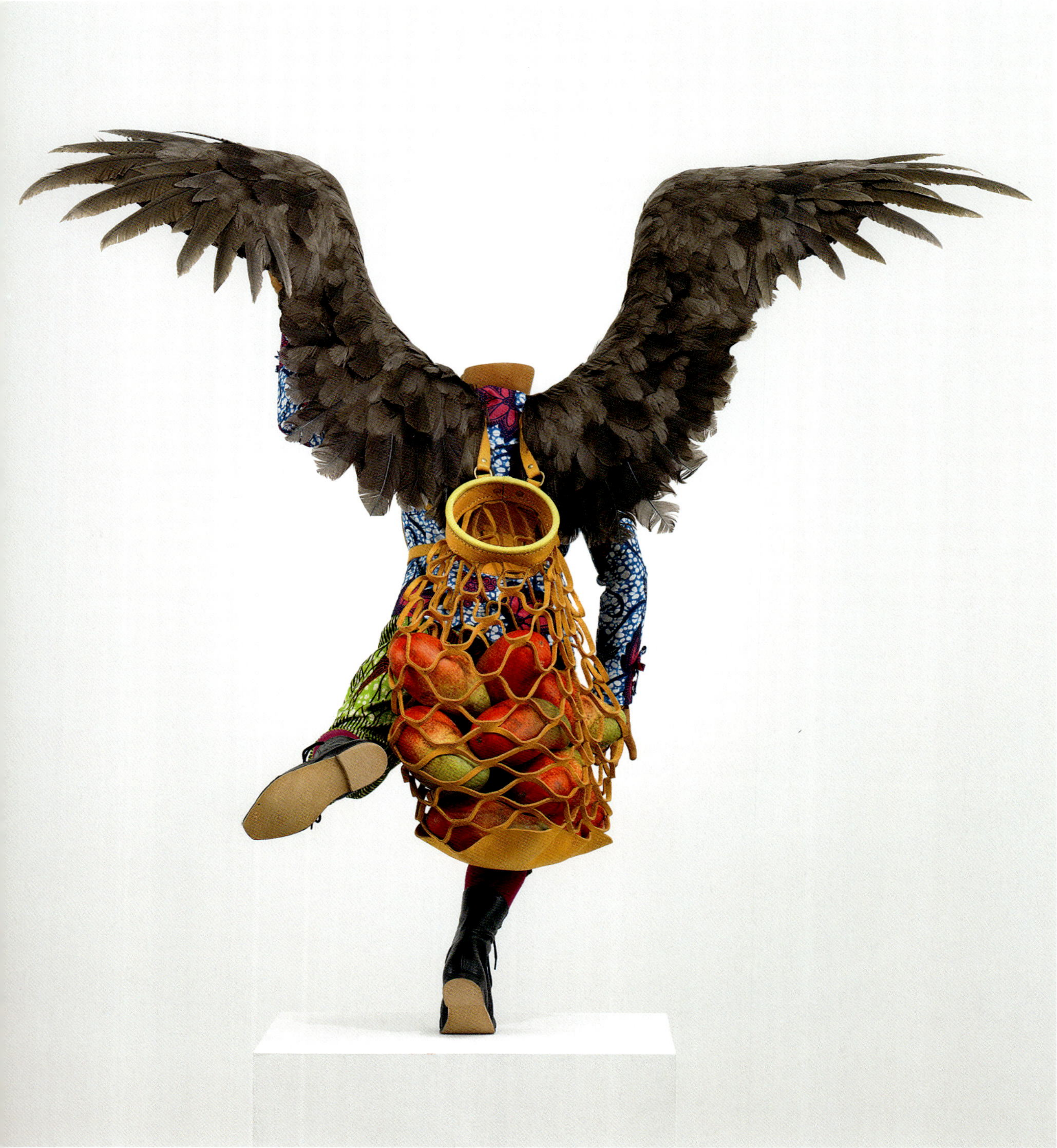

Food Faerie, 2010

Life-size mannequin, Dutch wax printed cotton, leather, artificial fruit, fiberglass, goose feathers
84 x 50 x 119 cm
Private collection

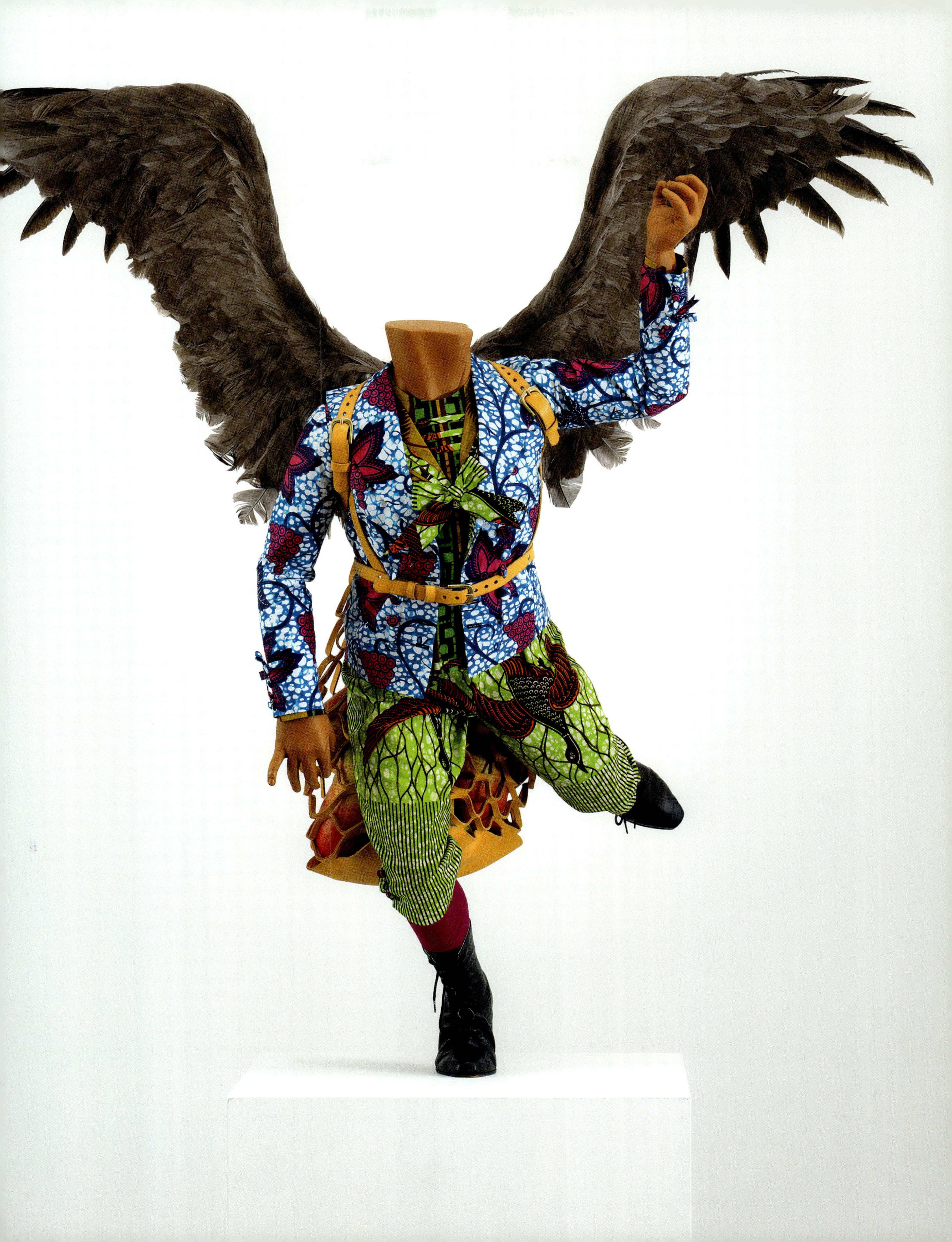

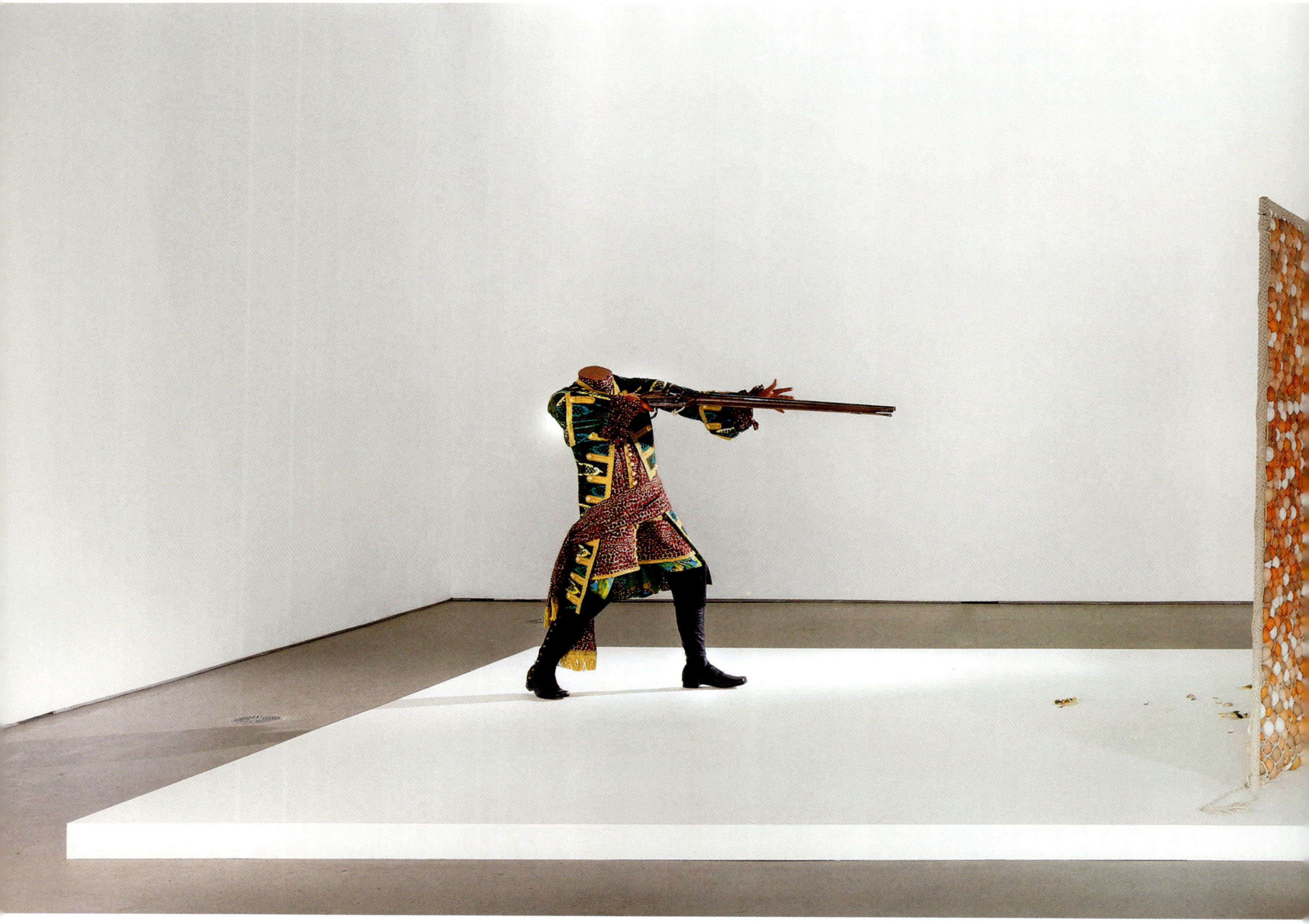

Egg Fight, 2009

Two life-size mannequins, Dutch wax printed cotton, leather boots, guns, rope, polystyrene eggs, silicon
Dimensions variable
Commissioned by Dublin City Gallery The Hugh Lane

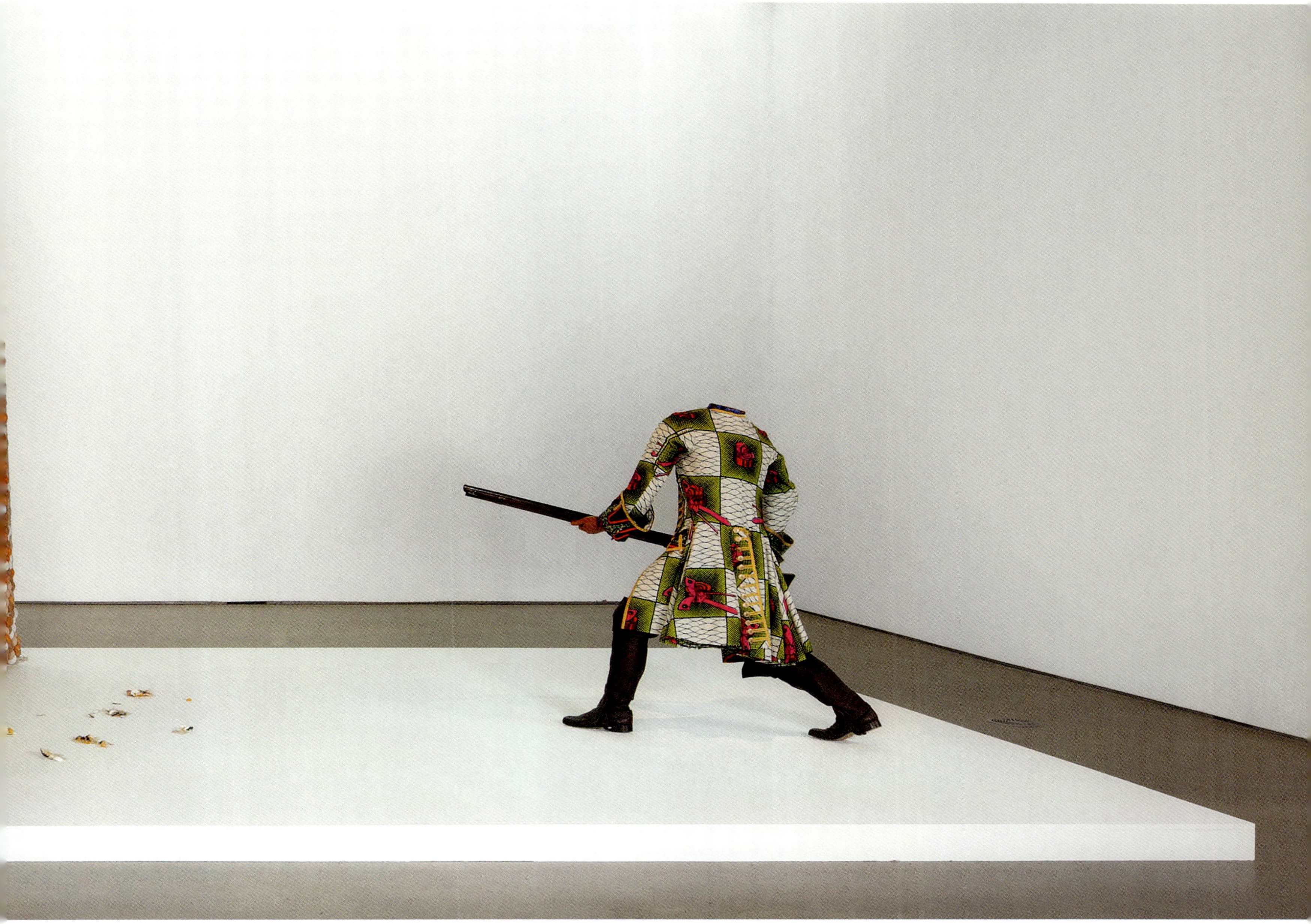

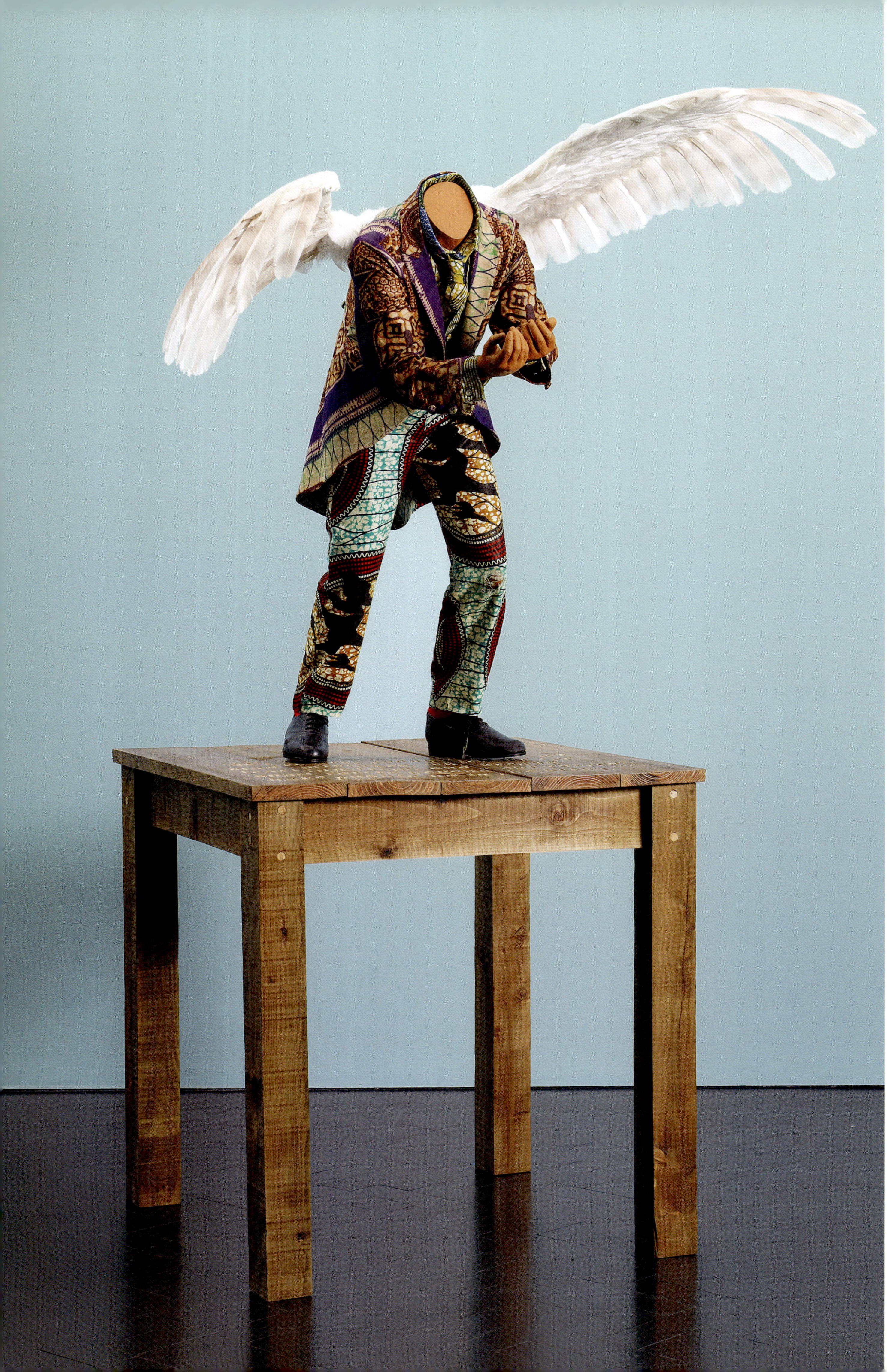

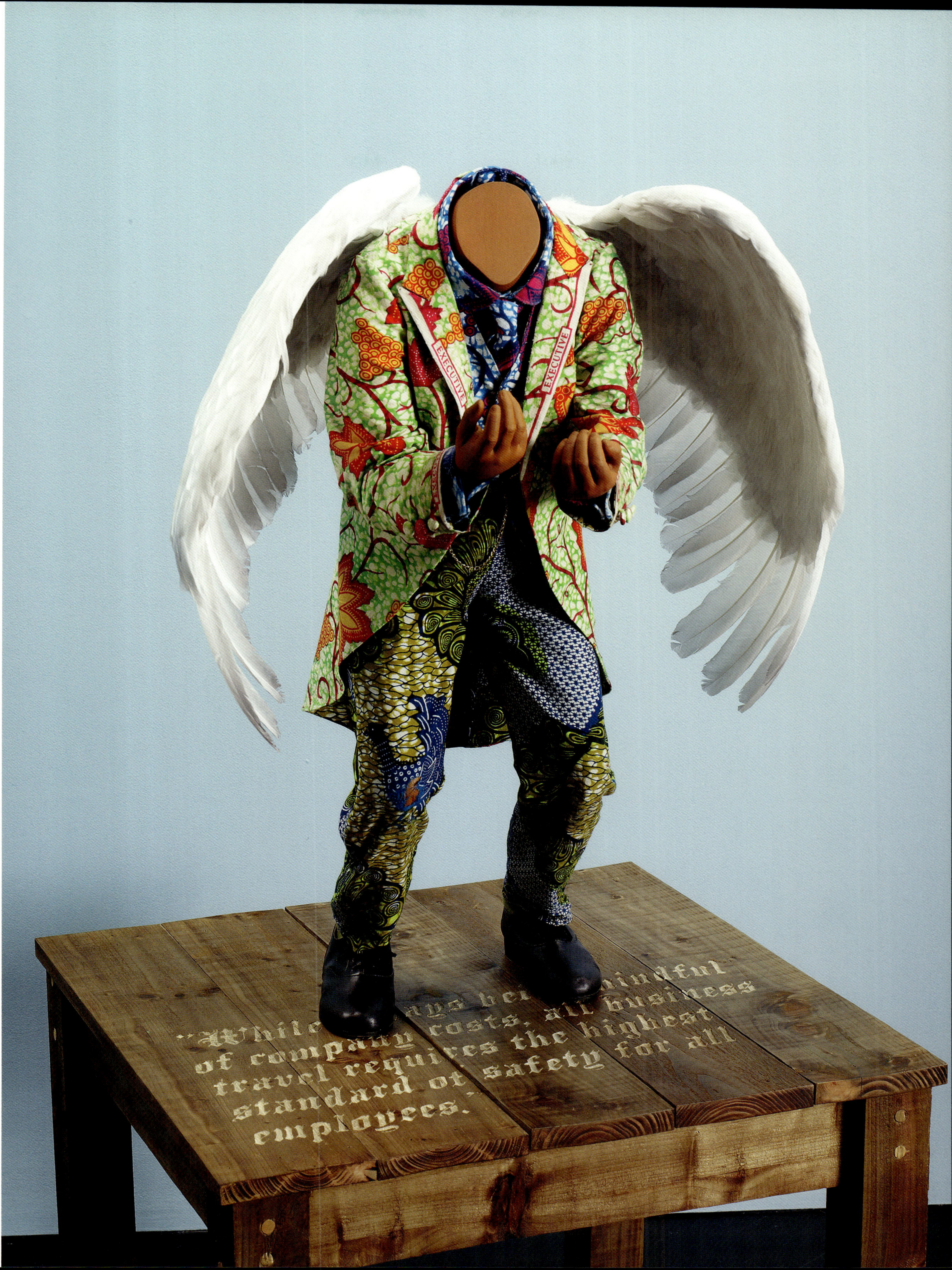
EXECUTIVE
EXECUTIVE
of company costs, all business
travel requires the highest
standard of safety for all
employees.

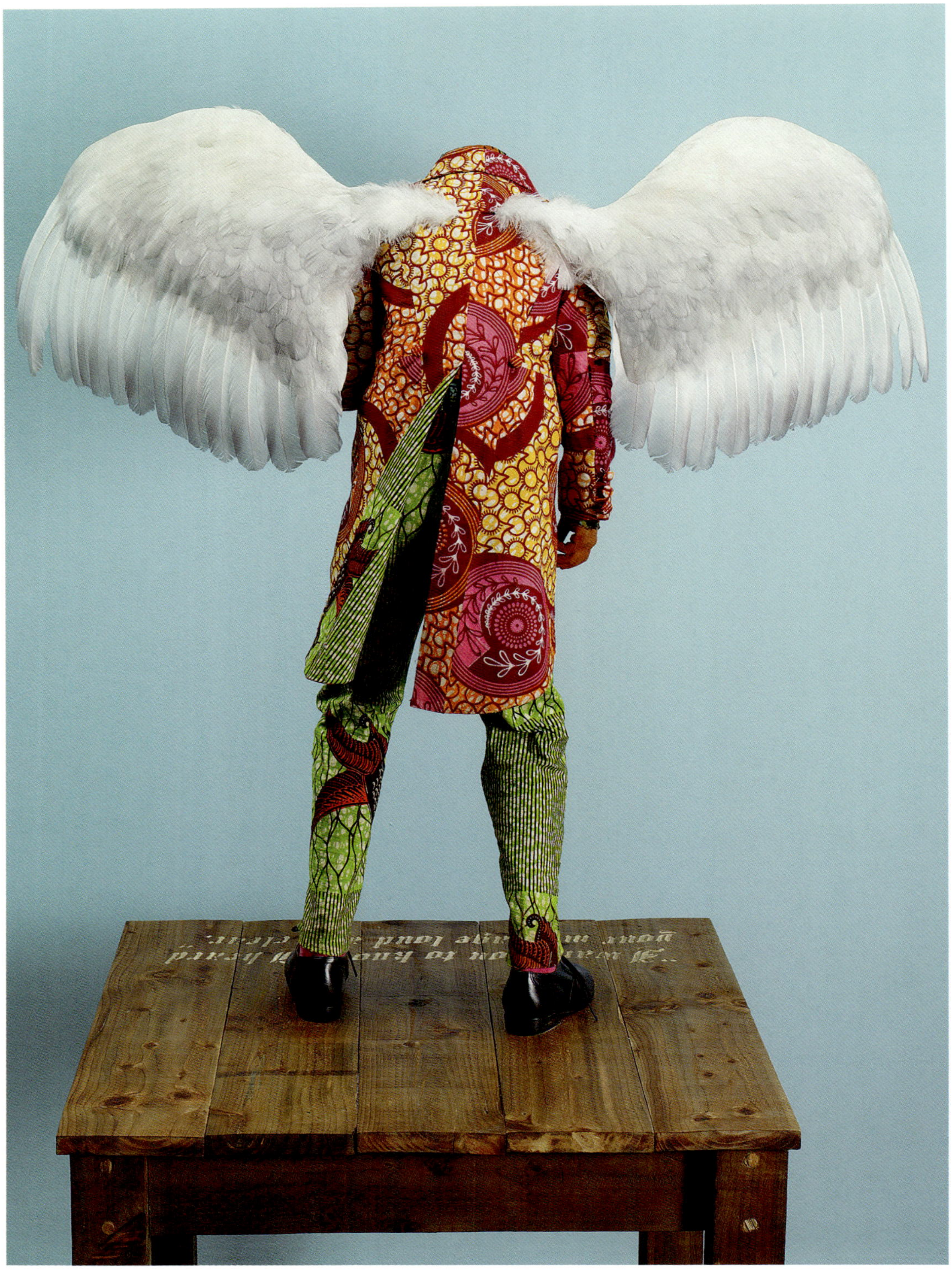

Preceding spread, left:

The Big Three (General Motors), 2009

Life-size mannequin, Dutch wax printed cotton, leather, wood
177 x 112 x 114 cm
Collection of John and Amy Phelan

Preceding spread, right:

The Big Three (Chrysler), 2009

Life-size mannequin, Dutch wax printed cotton, leather, wood
177 x 112 x 114 cm
Collection of John and Amy Phelan

Above and opposite:

The Big Three (Ford), 2009

Life-size mannequin, Dutch wax printed cotton, leather, wood
175 x 120 x 89 cm
Collection of John and Amy Phelan

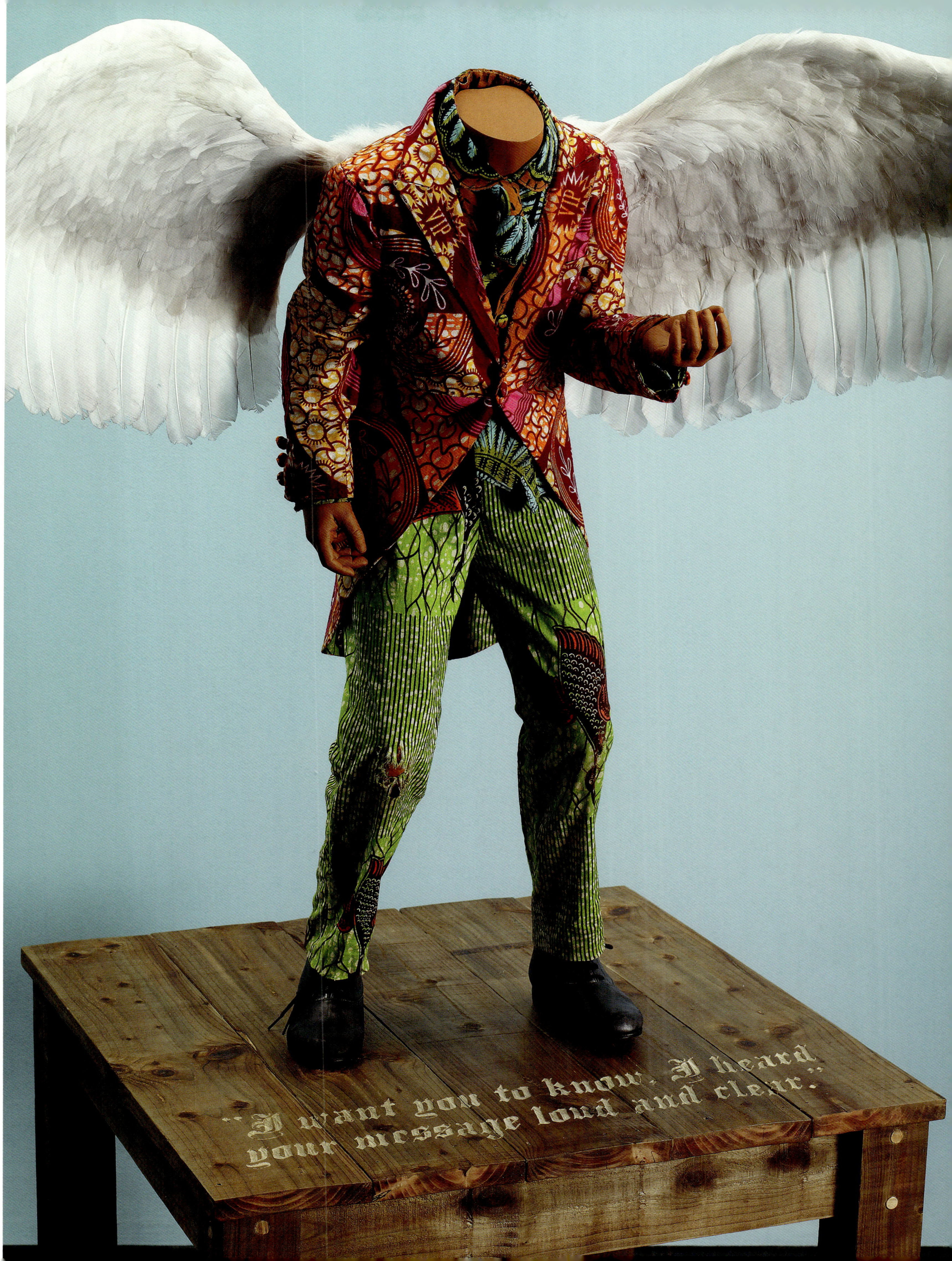
"I want you to know, I heard
your message loud and clear."

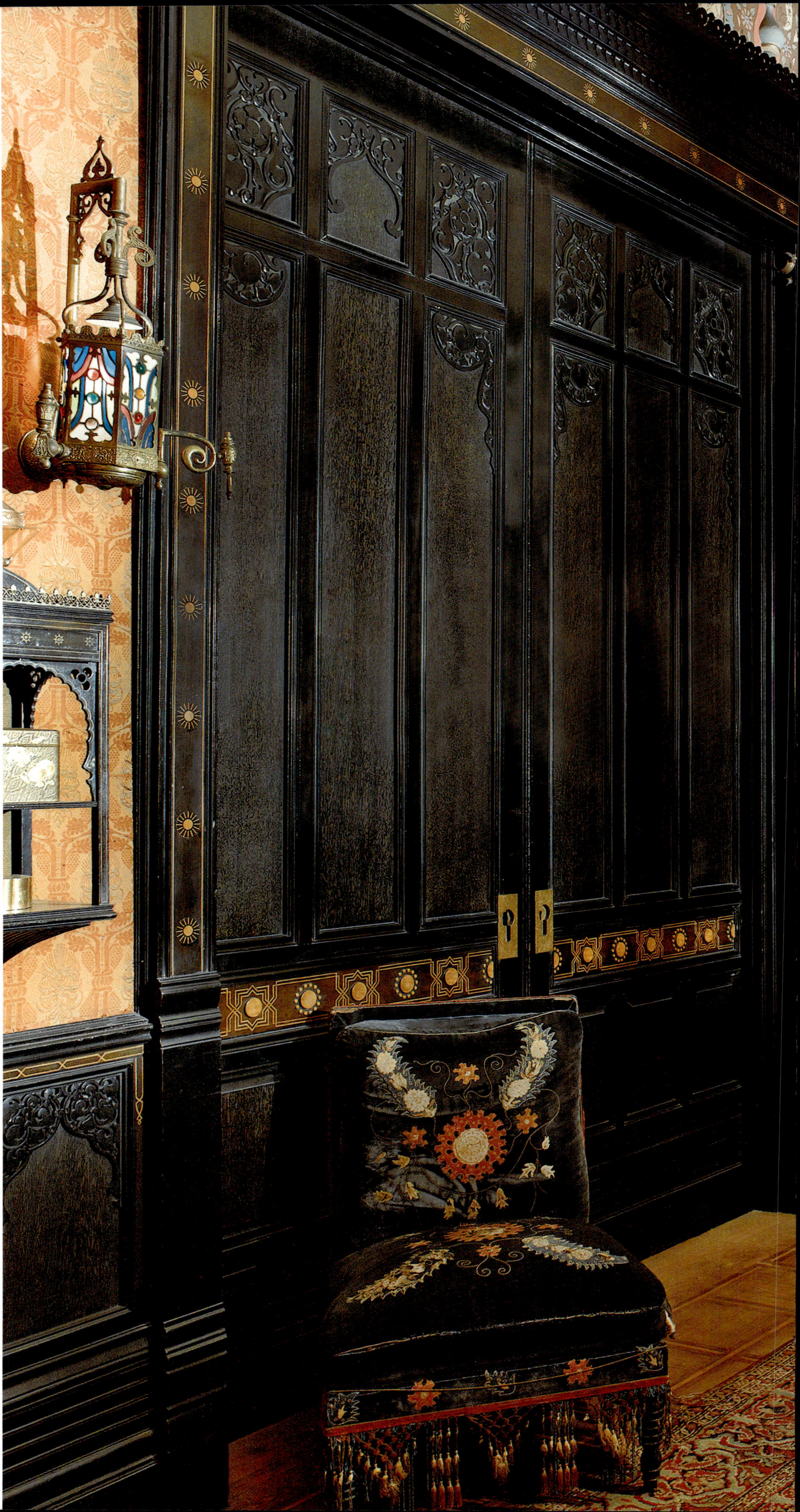

Skipping Girl, 2009

Life-size mannequin, Dutch wax printed cotton, mixed media
127.6 x 73.7 x 109.2 cm
Brooklyn Museum of Art
Installation view, Brooklyn Museum, New York, 2009

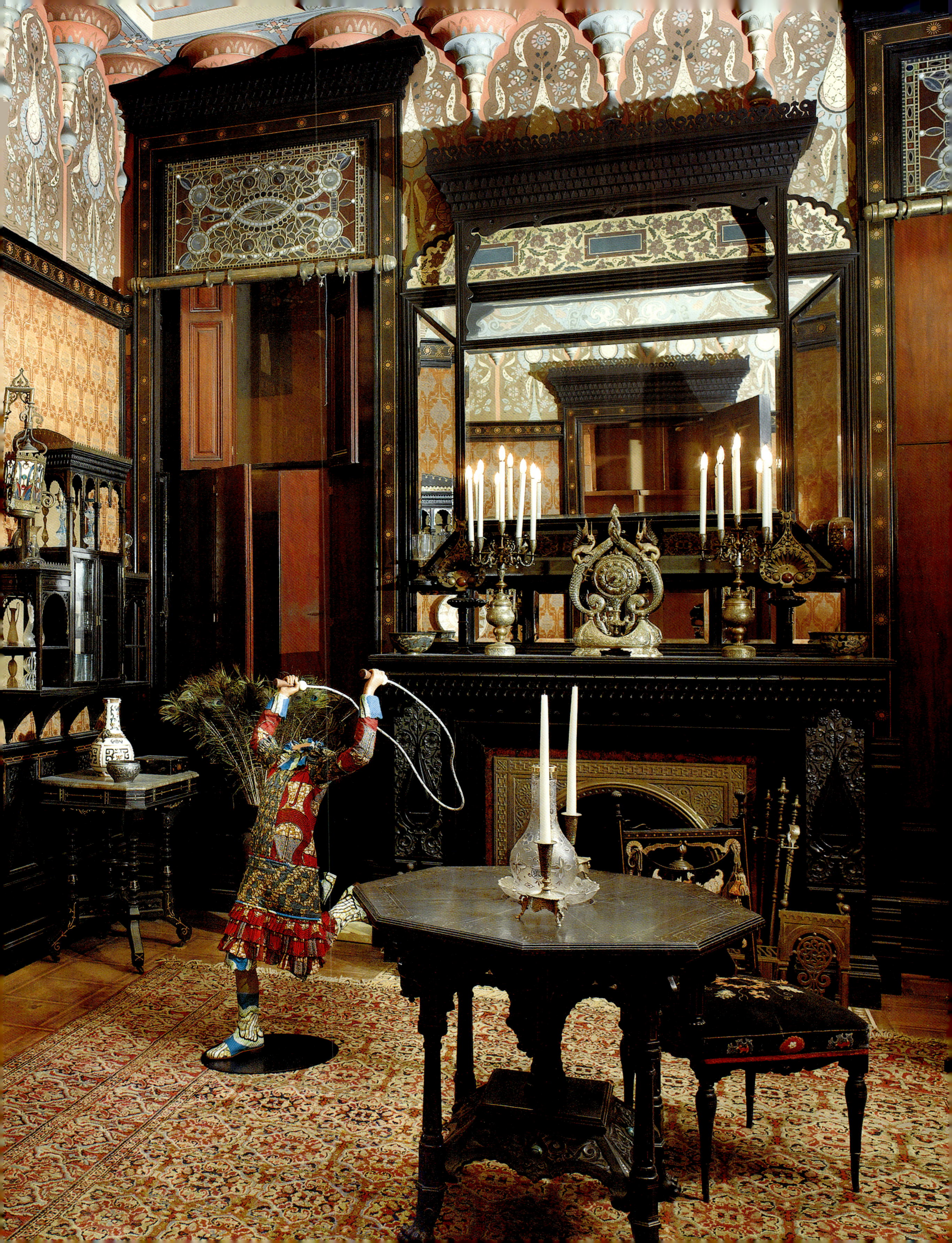

Boy with Marionette, 2009

Life-size mannequin, Dutch wax printed cotton, mixed media
113 x 48.3 x 106.7 cm
Collection of Theodor and Isabella Dalenson, Stockholm
Installation view, Brooklyn Museum, New York, 2009

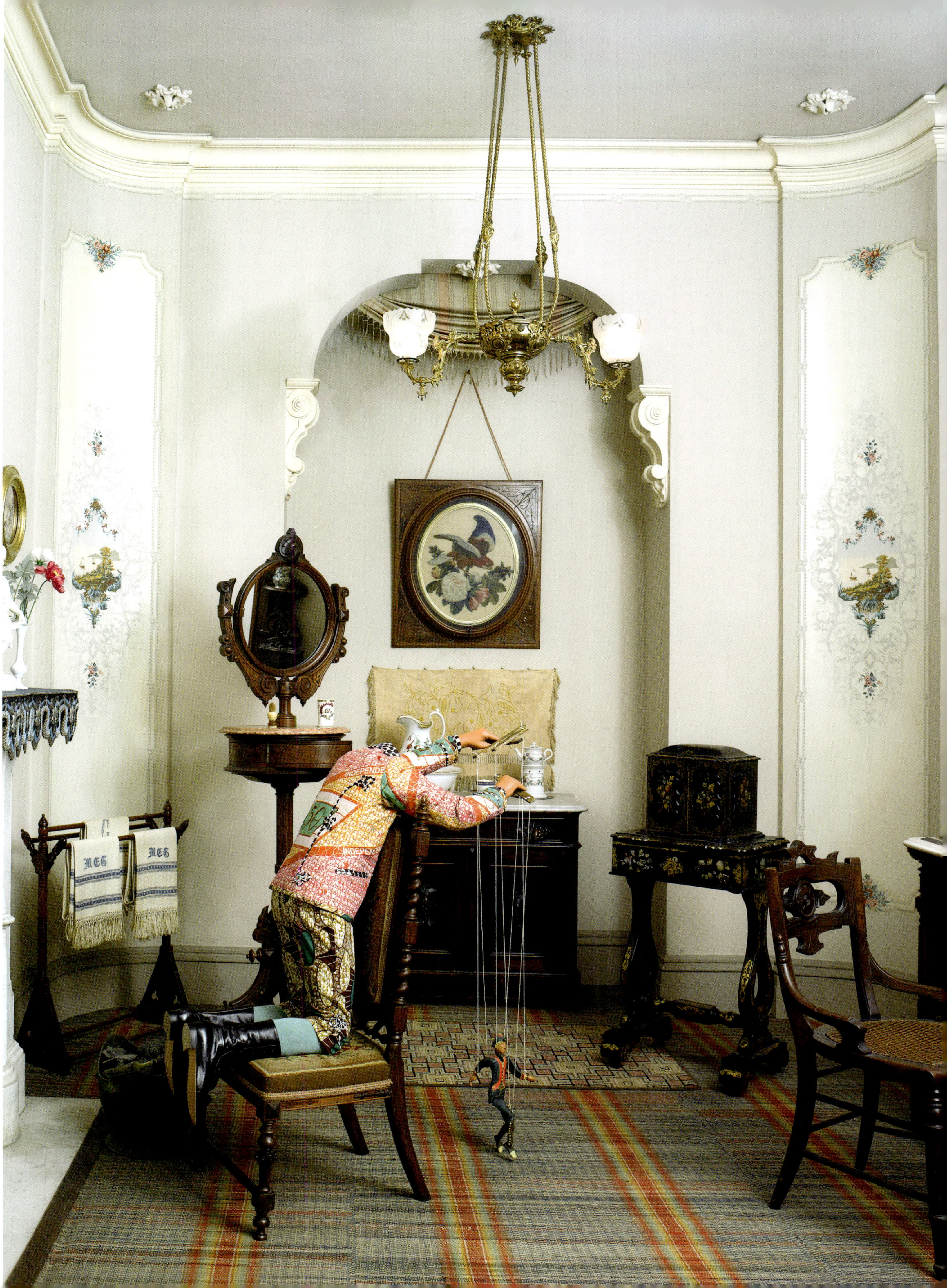
MEG
MEG

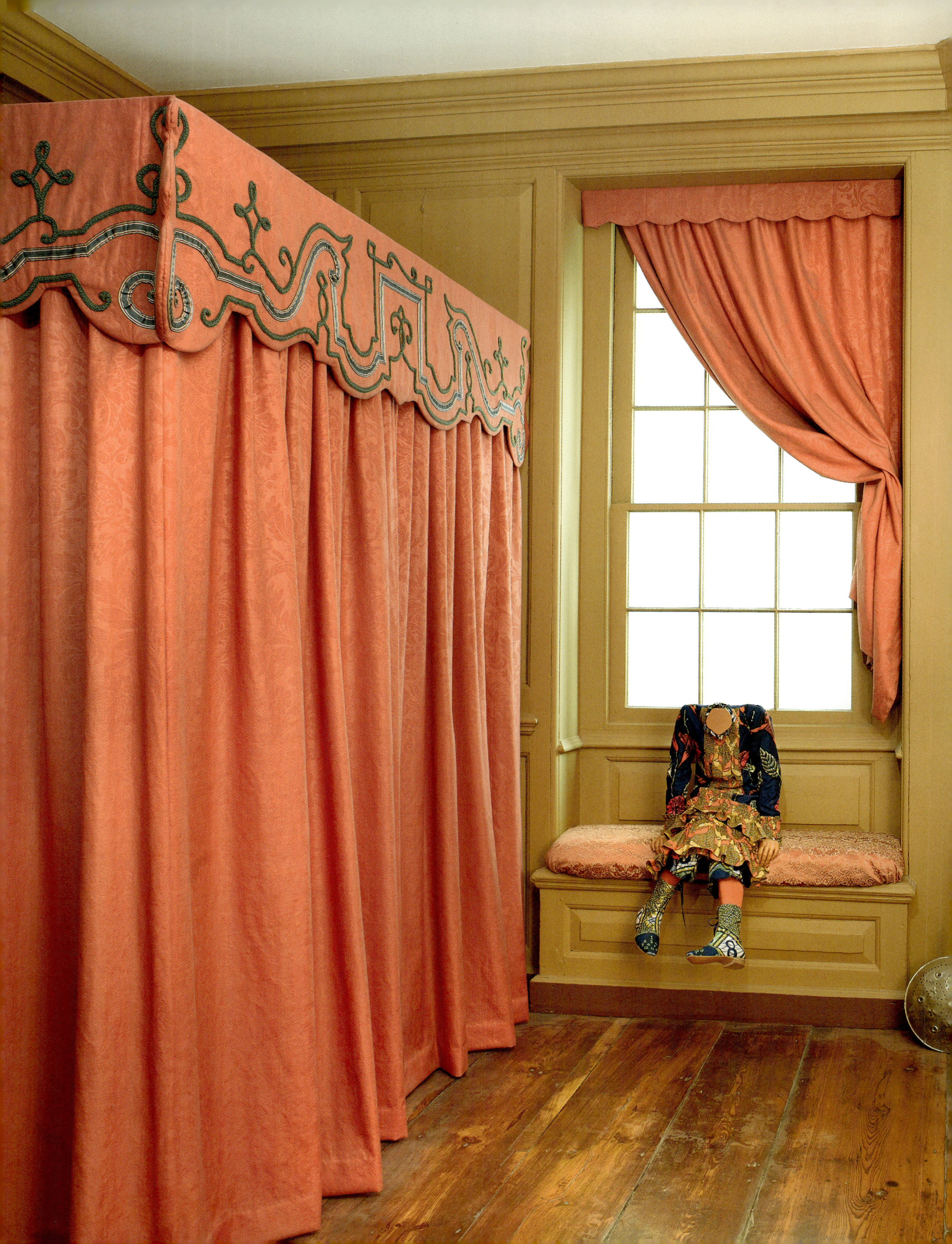

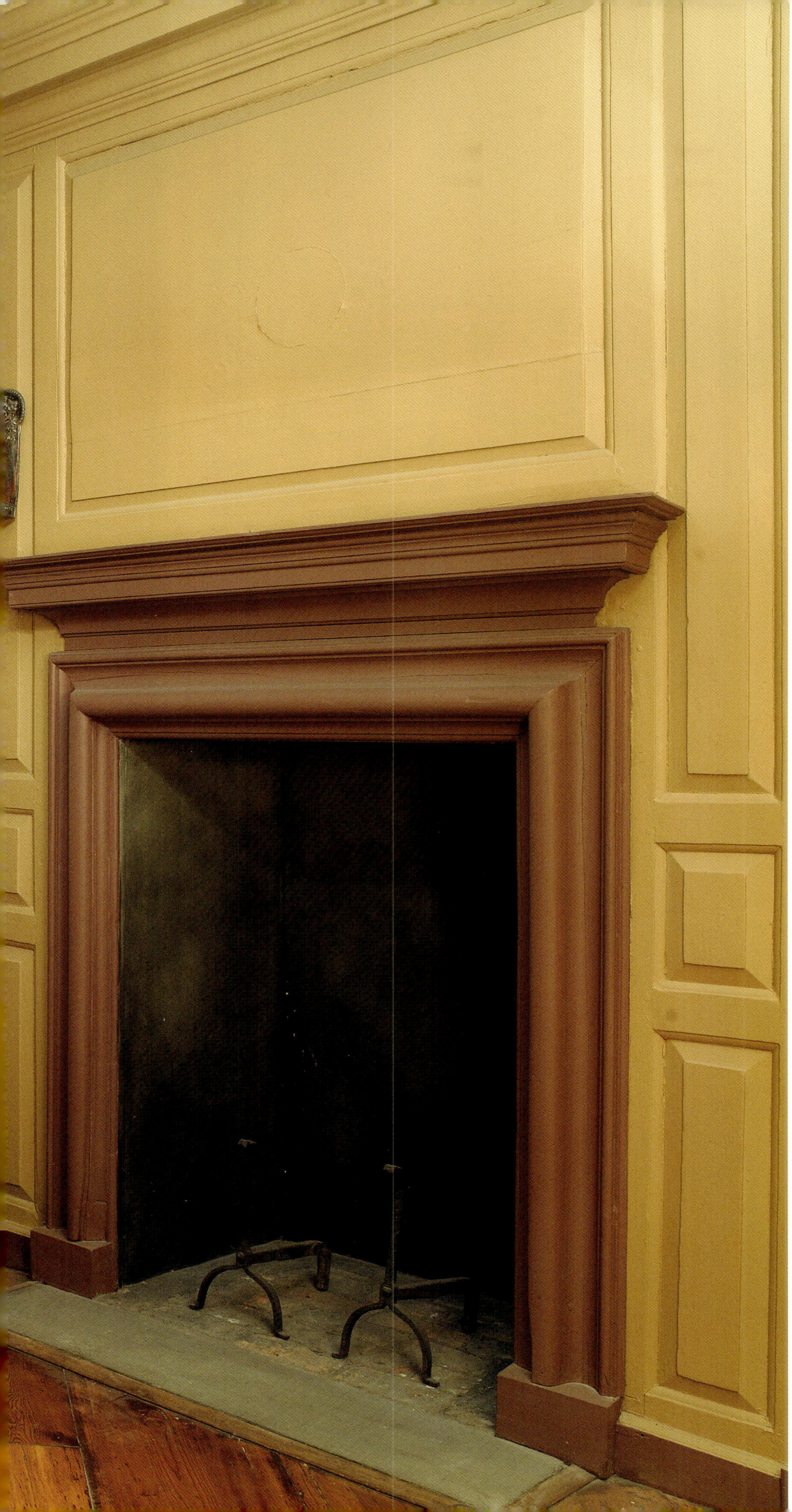

Seated Girl, 2009

Life-size mannequin, Dutch wax printed cotton, mixed media
73.7 x 45.1 x 73.7 cm
Private collection
Installation view, Brooklyn Museum, New York, 2009

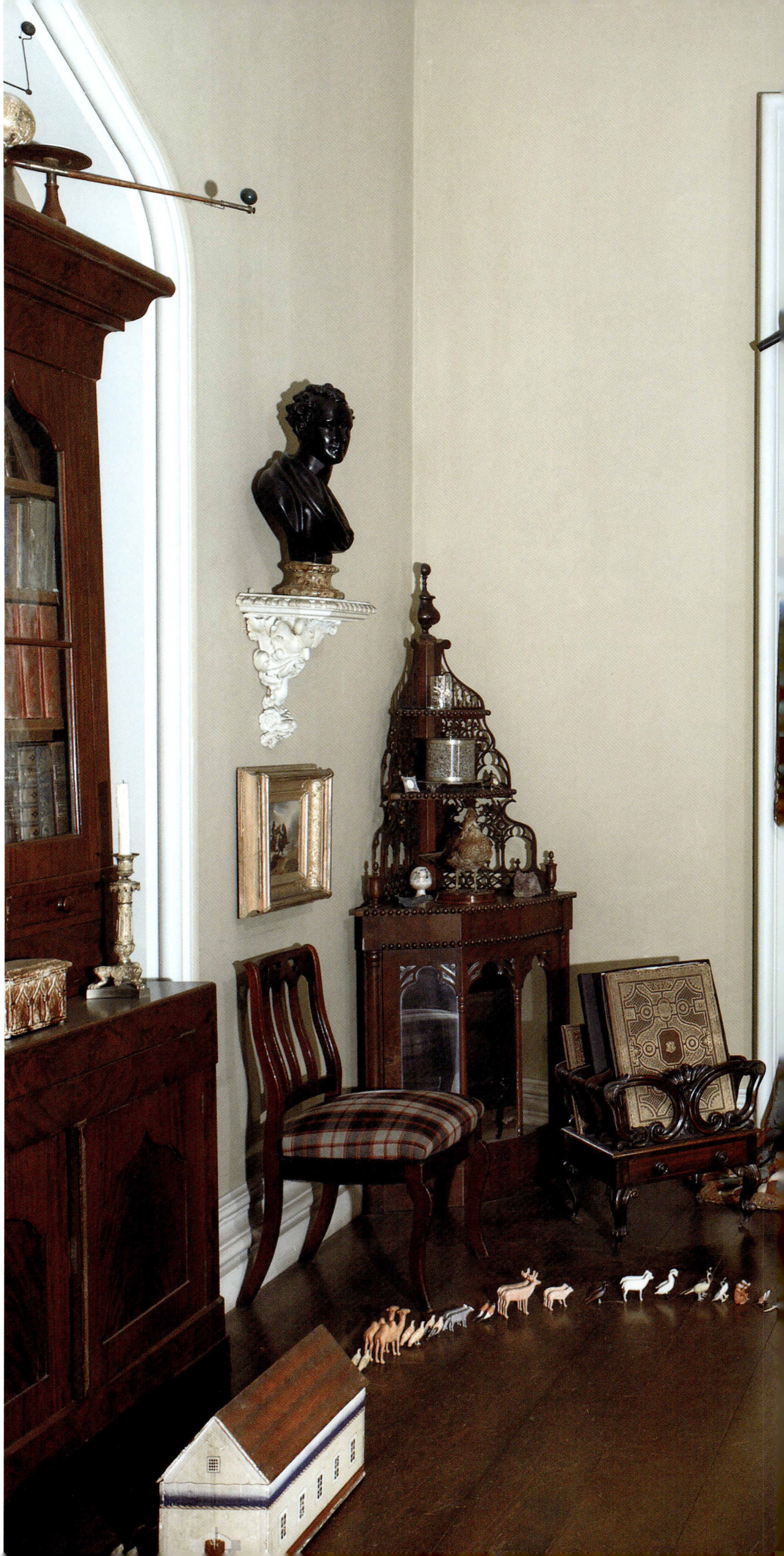

Boy Playing with Marbles, 2009

Life-size mannequin, Dutch wax printed cotton, mixed media
52.1 x 40.6 x 50.8 cm
Private collection
Installation view, Brooklyn Museum, New York, 2009

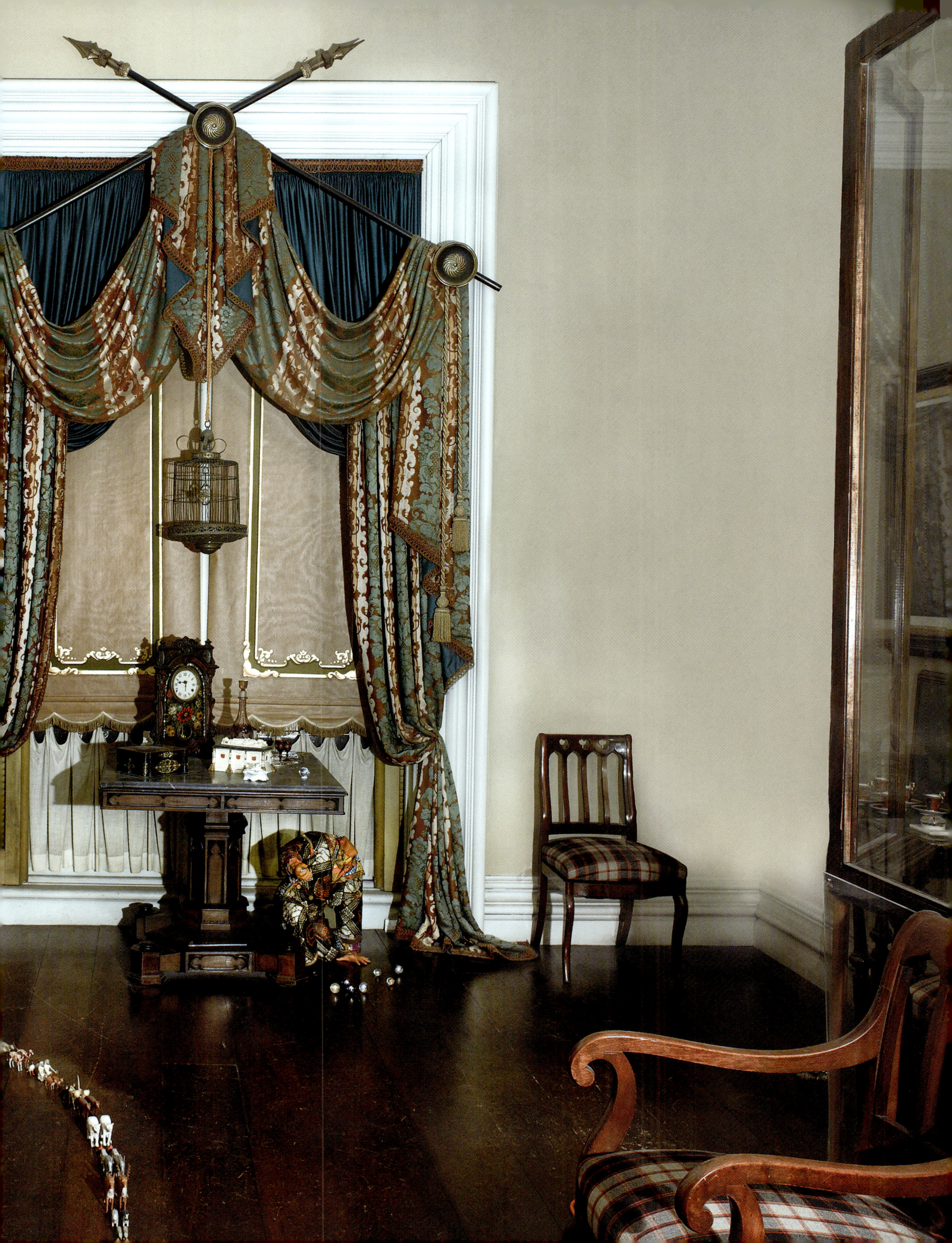

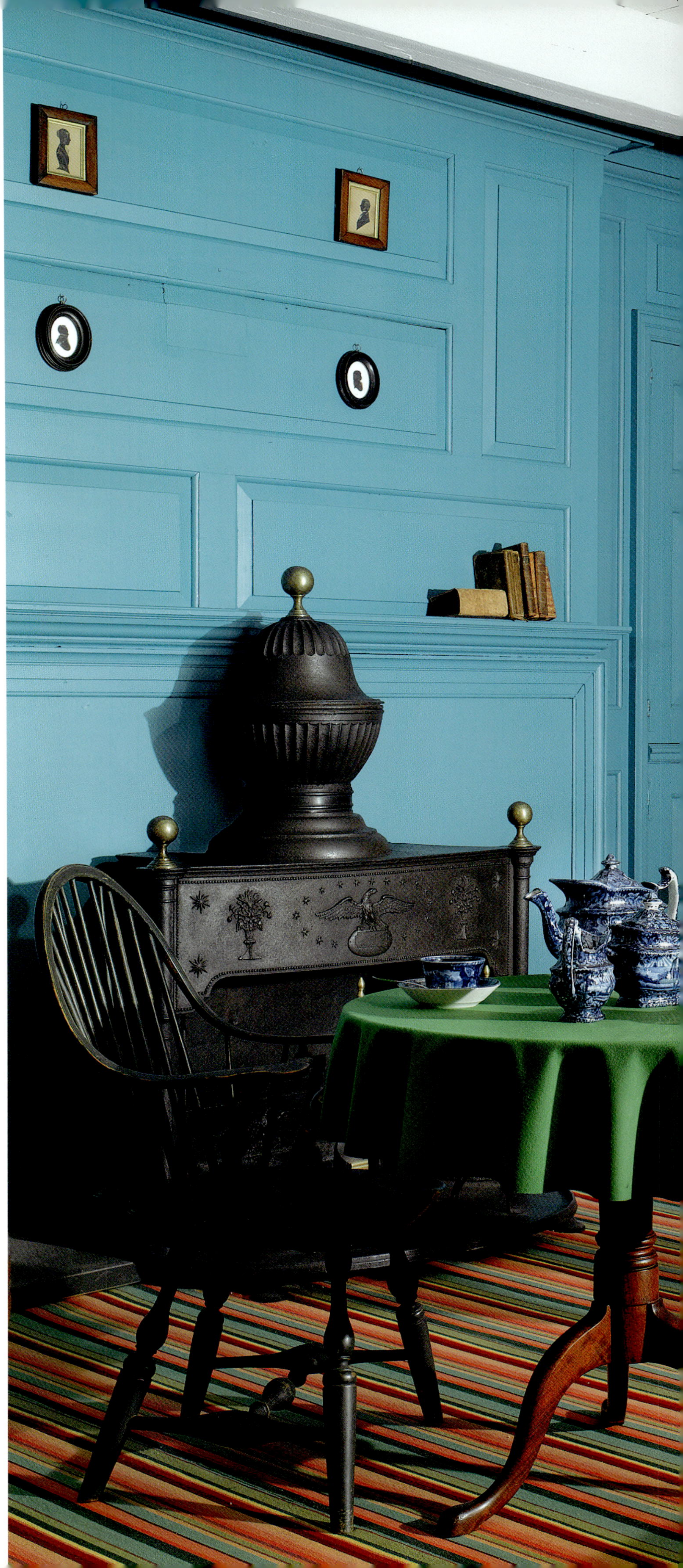

Boy Doing Headstand, 2009

Life-size mannequin, Dutch wax printed cotton, mixed media
69.9 x 83.8 x 77.5 cm
Collection of Jane and Leonard Korman
Installation view, Brooklyn Museum, New York, 2009

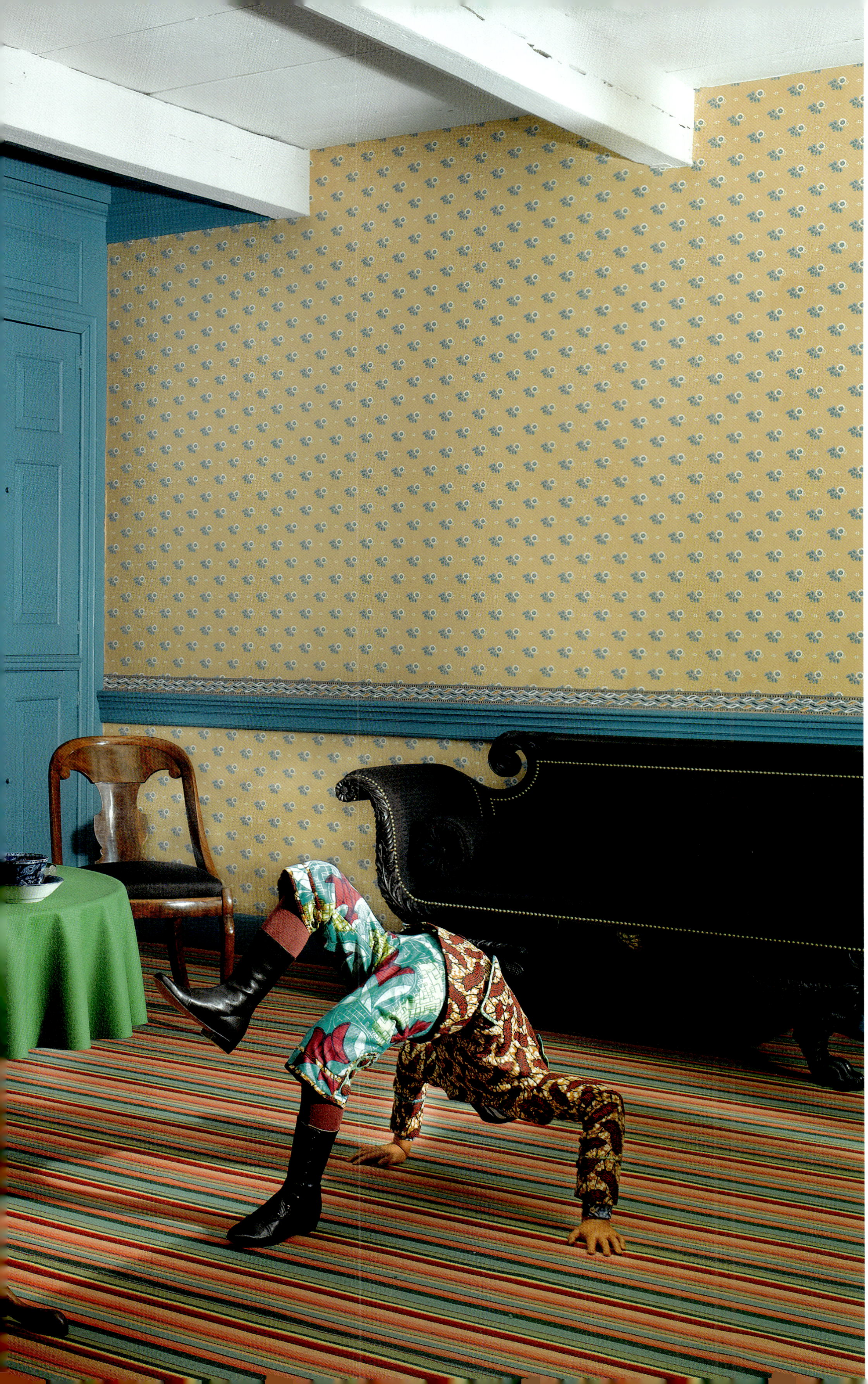

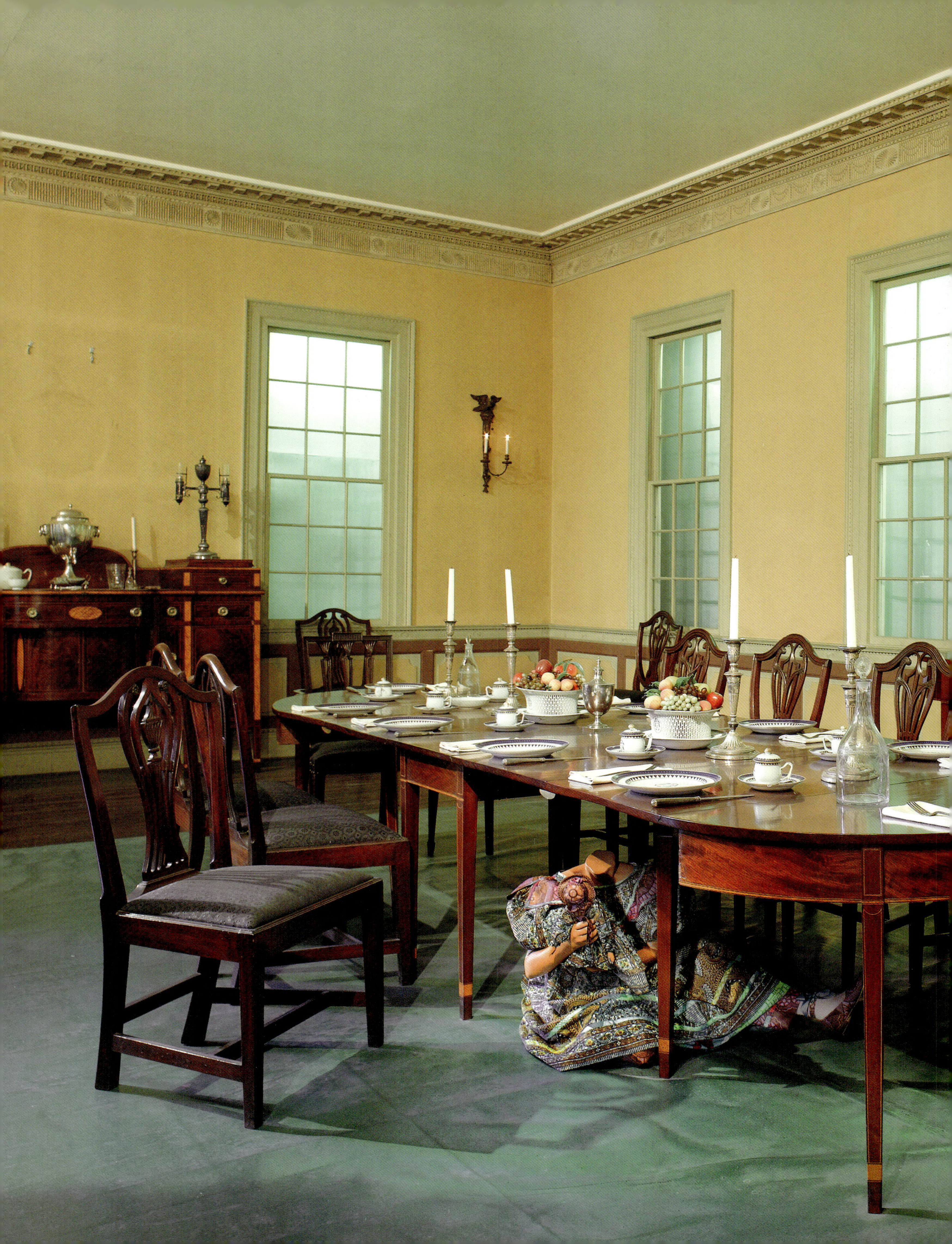

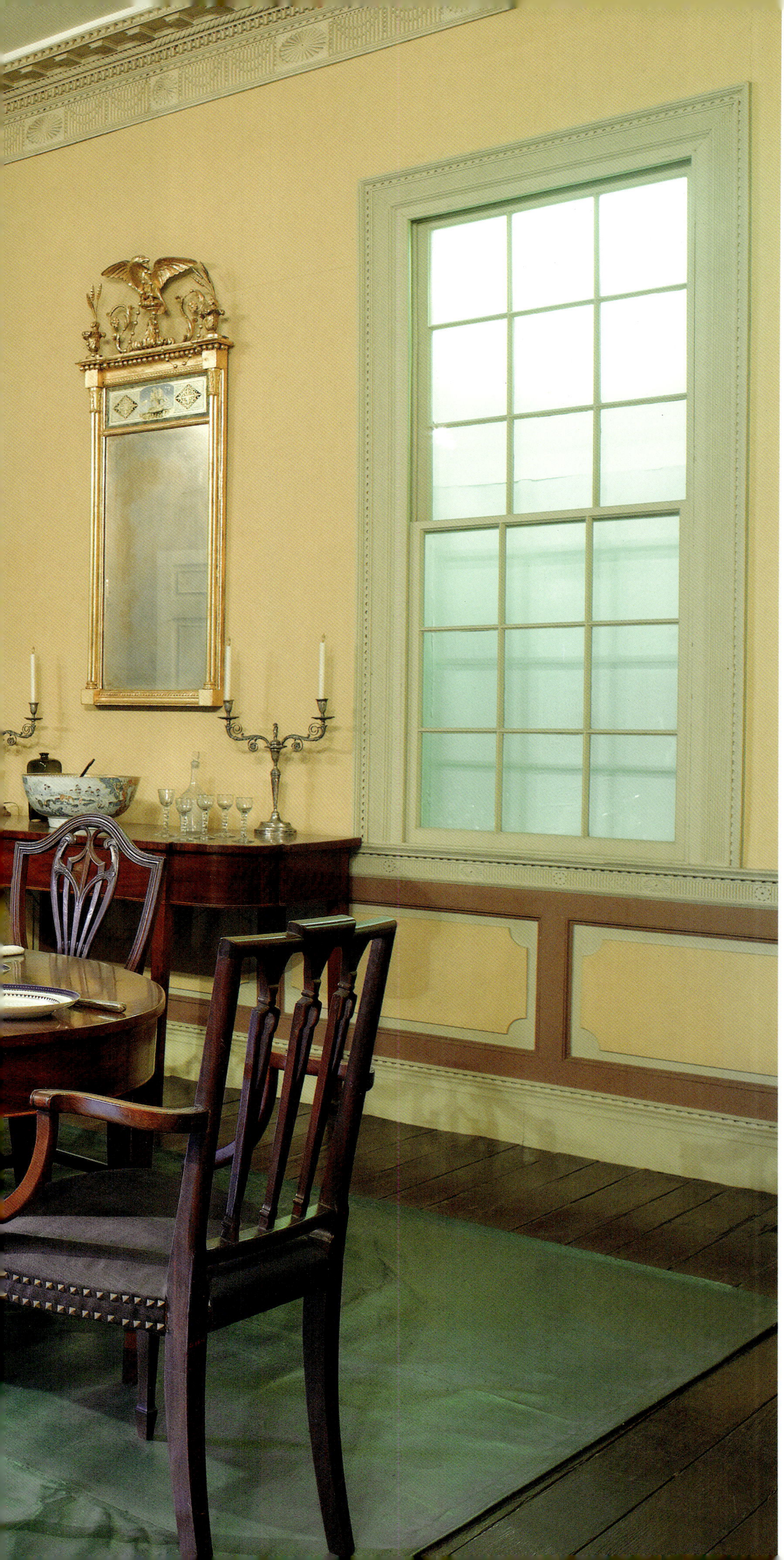

Girl Playing with Doll, 2009

Life-size mannequin, Dutch wax printed cotton, mixed media
45.1 x 68.6 x 91.4 cm
Private collection
Installation view, Brooklyn Museum, New York, 2009

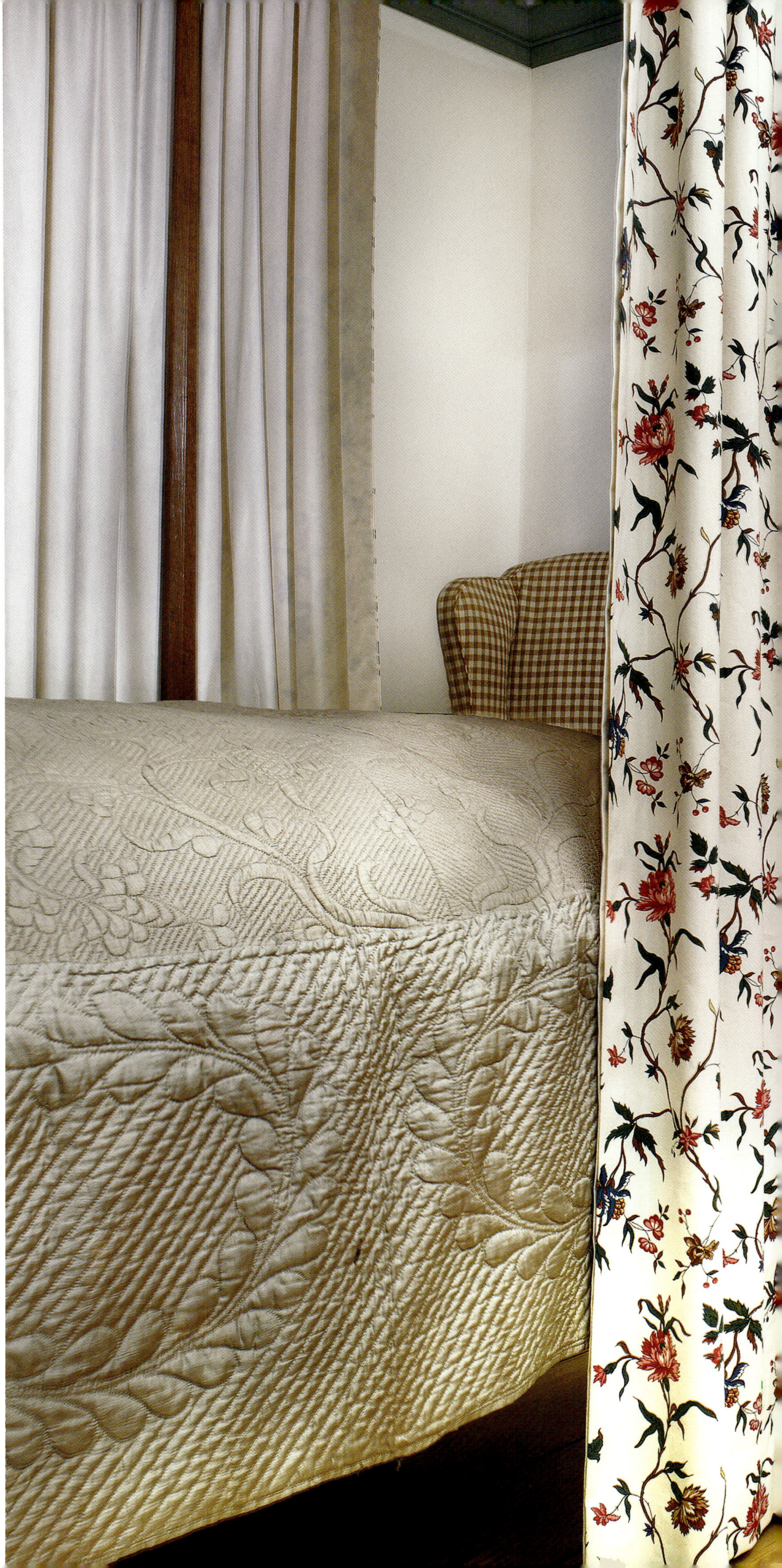

Girl on Scooter, 2009

Life-size mannequin, Dutch wax printed cotton, mixed media
76.2 x 61 x 95.3 cm
Ann and Mel Schaffer Family Collection
Installation view, Brooklyn Museum, New York, 2009

Overleaf:

Party Time: Re-imagine America, 2008–9

Nine life-size mannequins, Dutch wax printed cotton, leather boots, reproduction wood furniture, cutlery, glassware, taxidermy peacock
Dimensions variable
Newark Museum, New Jersey, Purchase 2010 Helen McMahon Brady Cutting Fund
Installation view, Newark Museum, New Jersey, 2009

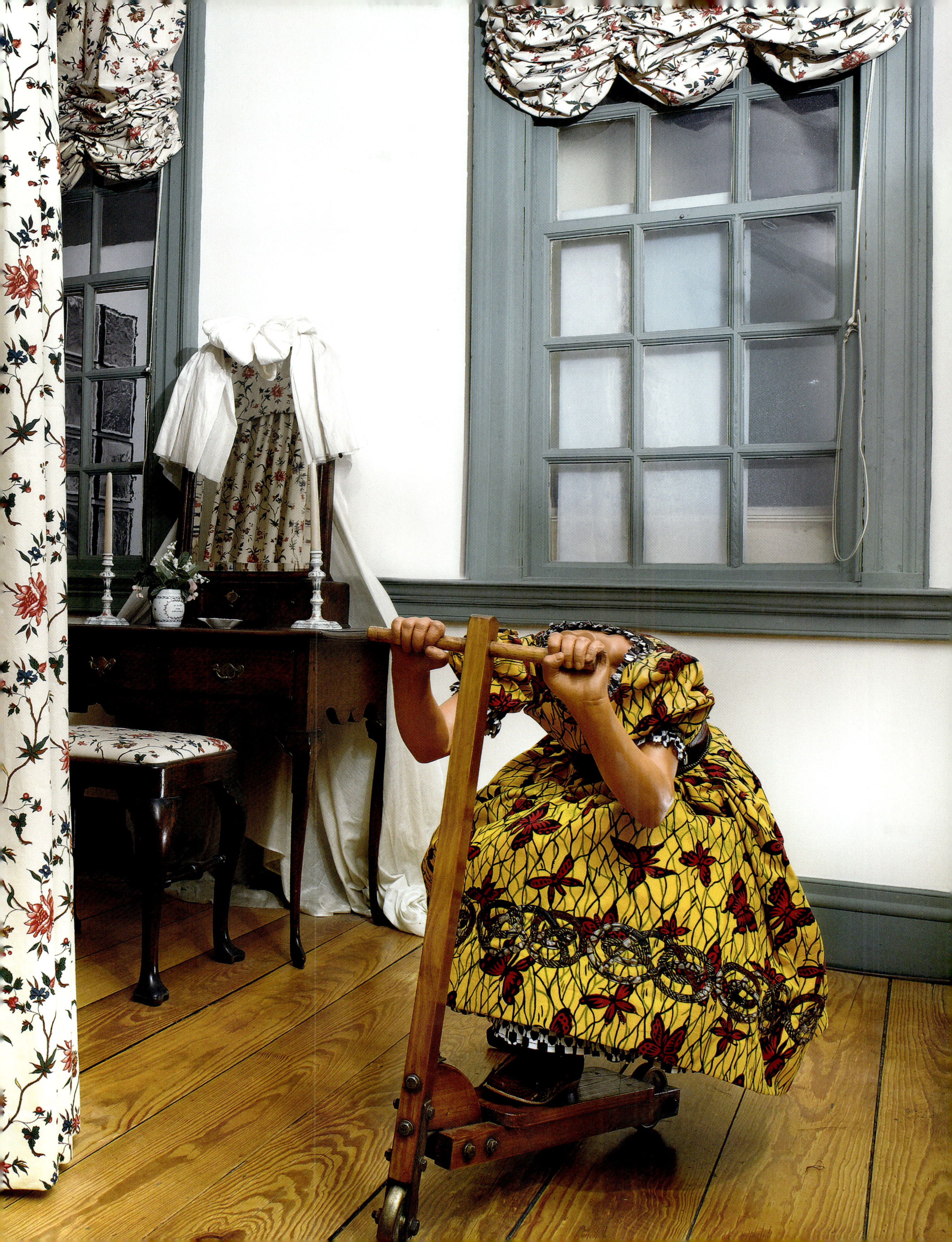

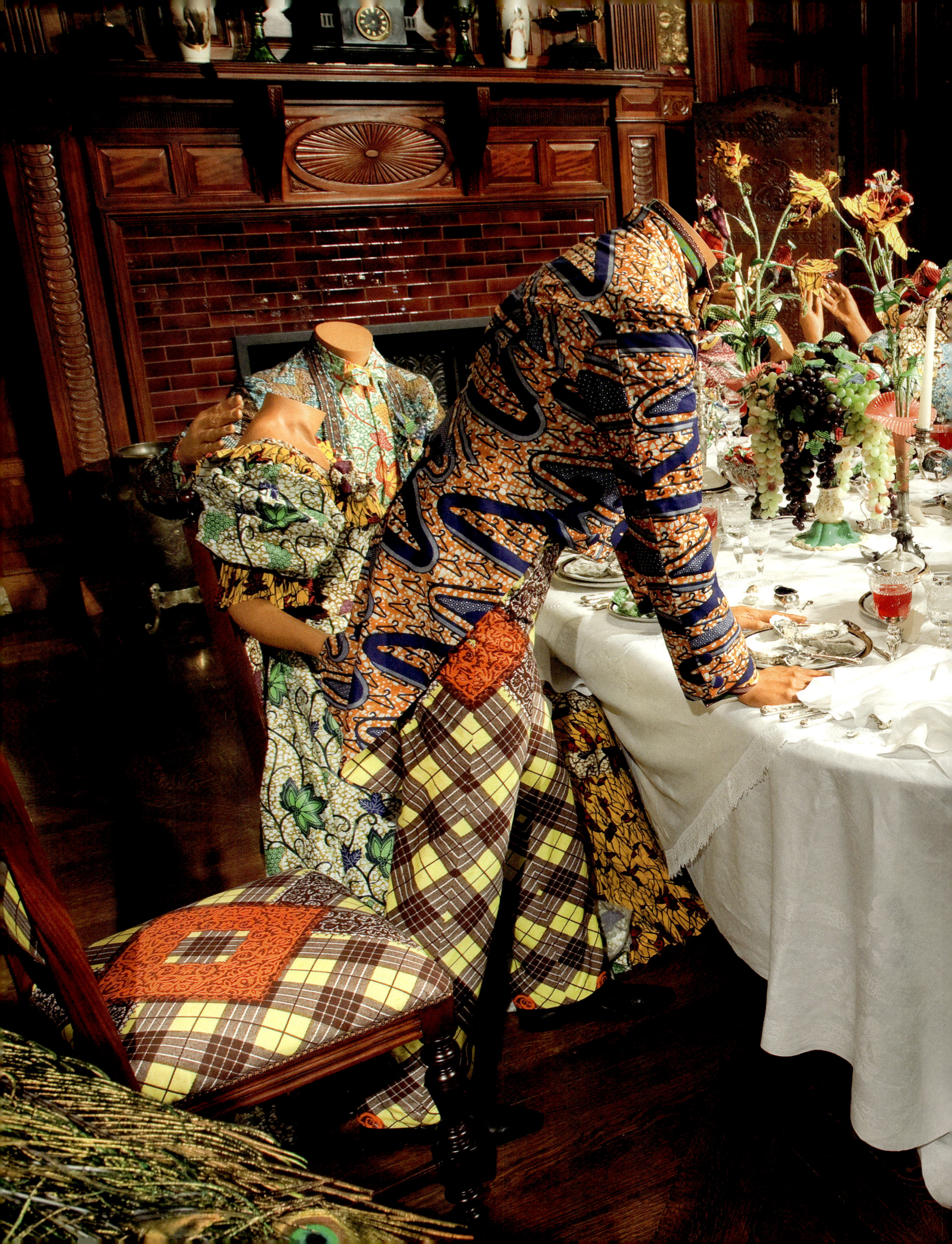

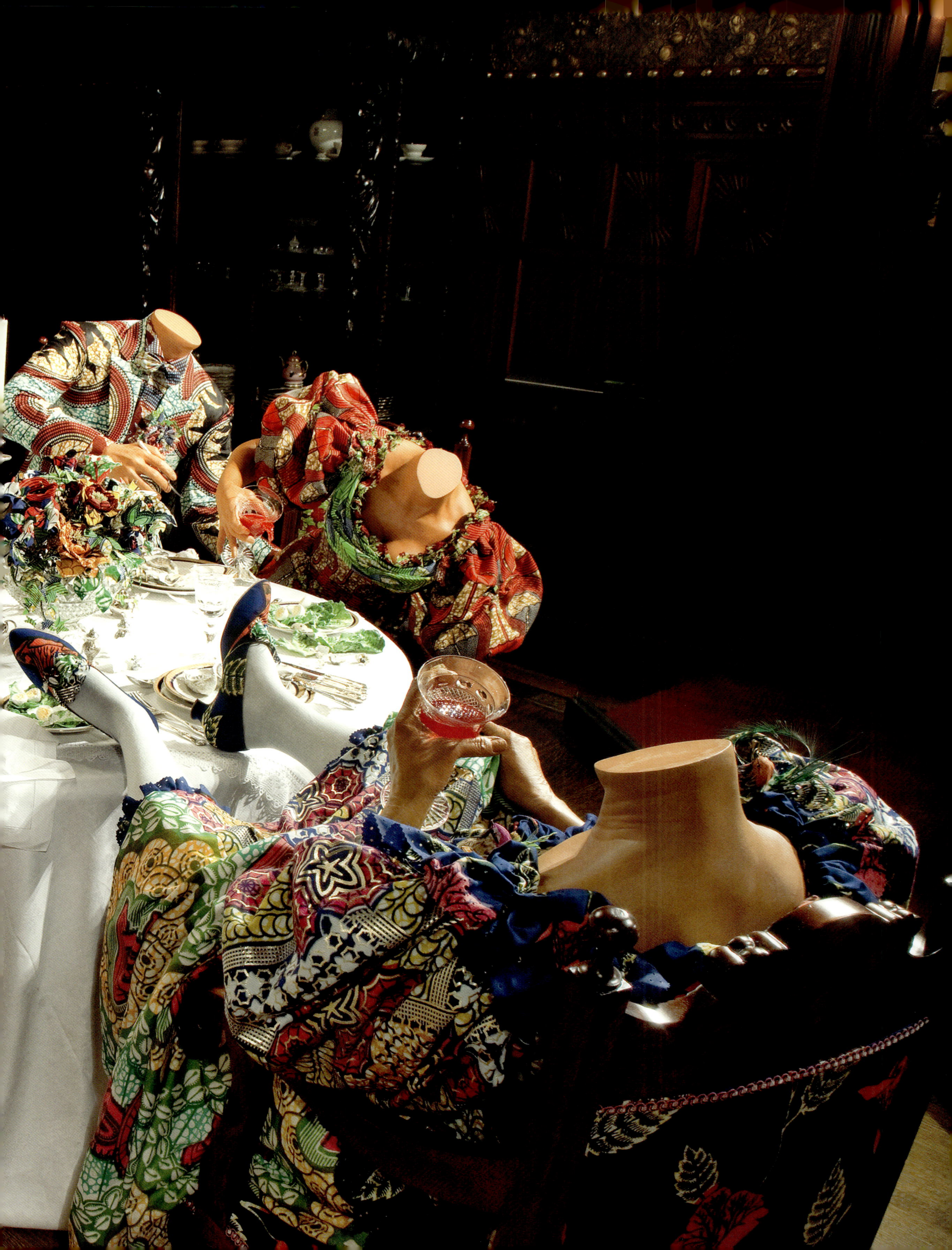

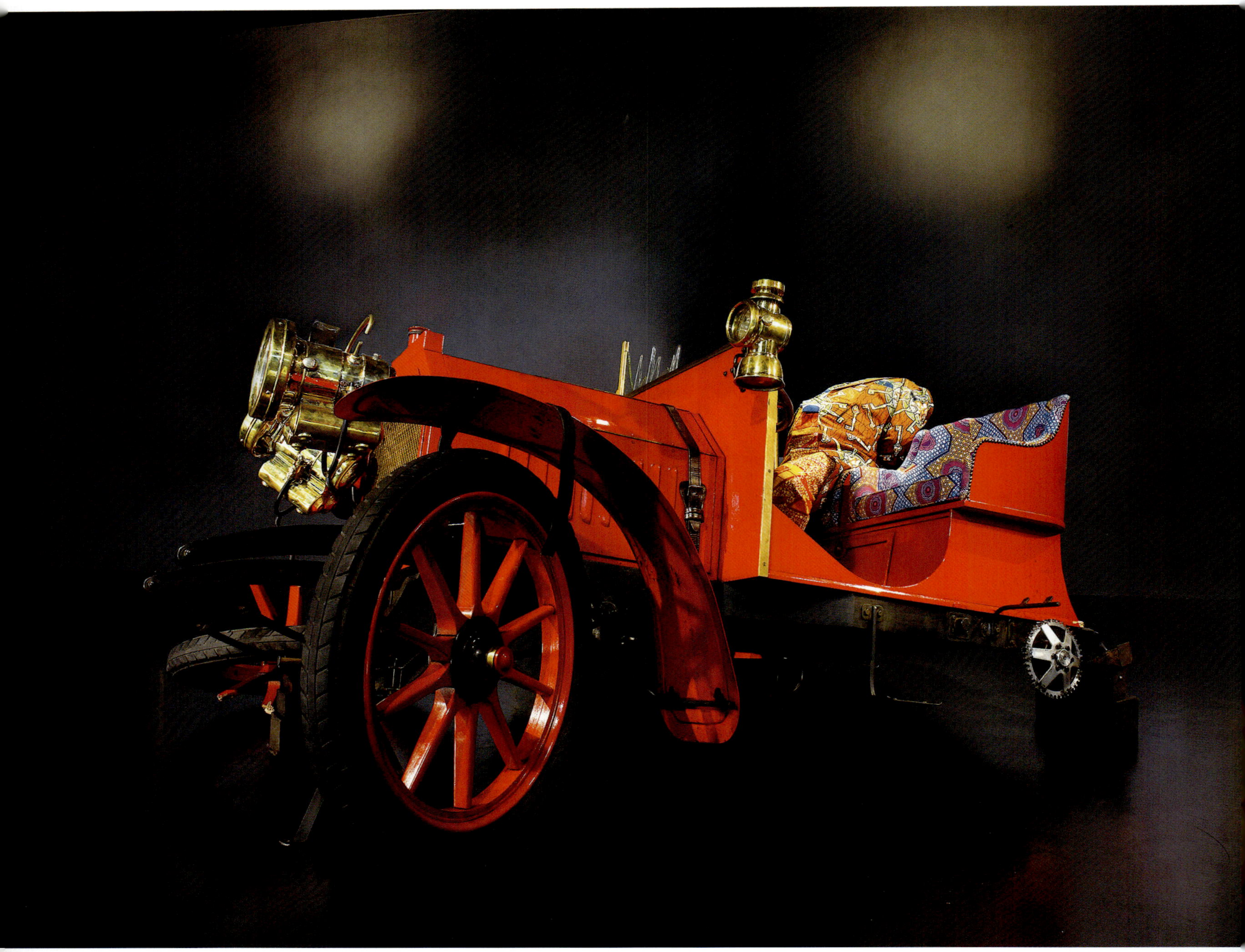

Crash Willy, 2009

Life-size mannequin, Dutch wax printed cotton, leather, fiberglass, metal
132 x 198 x 260 cm
Tiroche DeLeon Collection

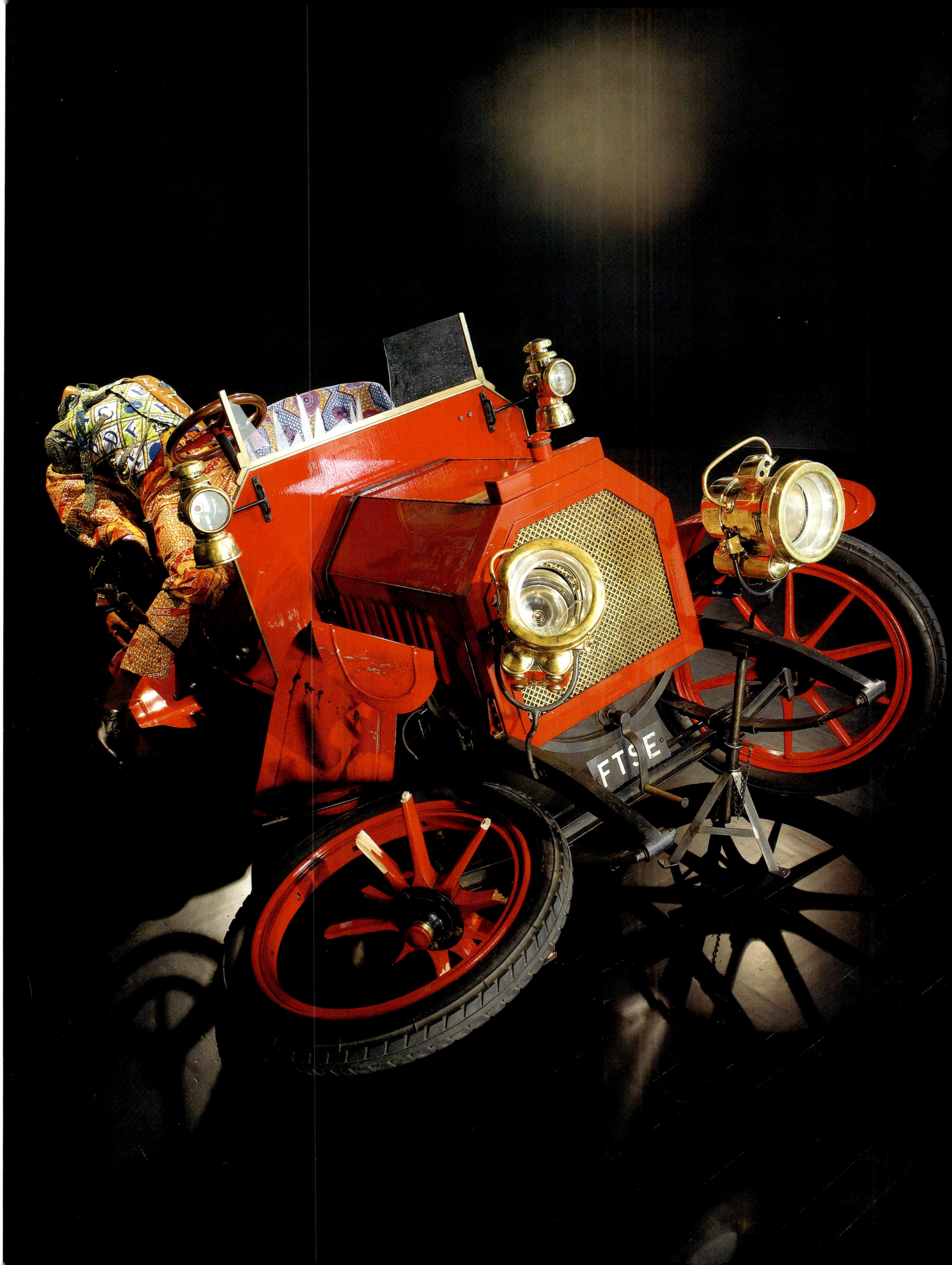
FTSE

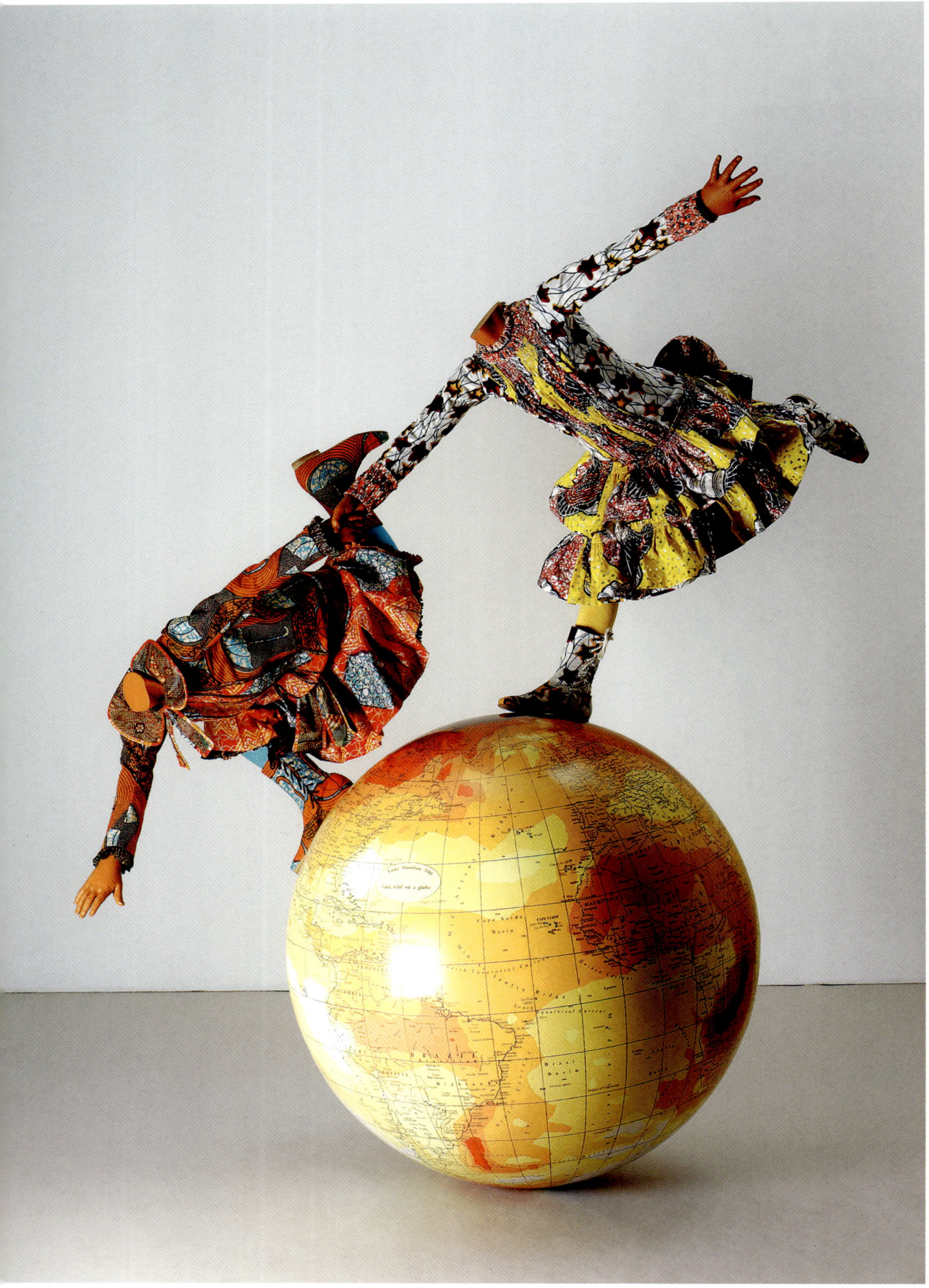

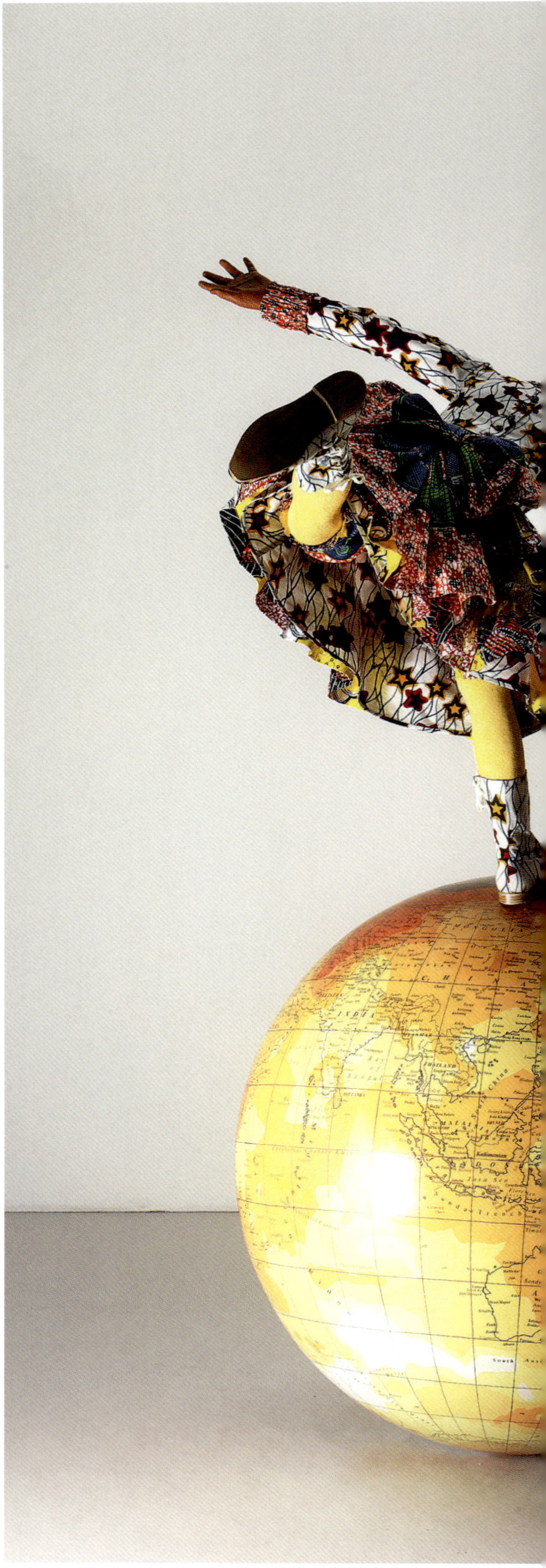

Girl, Girl on Globe, 2009

Two life-size mannequins, Dutch wax printed cotton, globe
98 x 109 x 50 cm, 50 x 115 x 33 cm (figures); 85 x 85 x 85 cm (globe)
Private collection

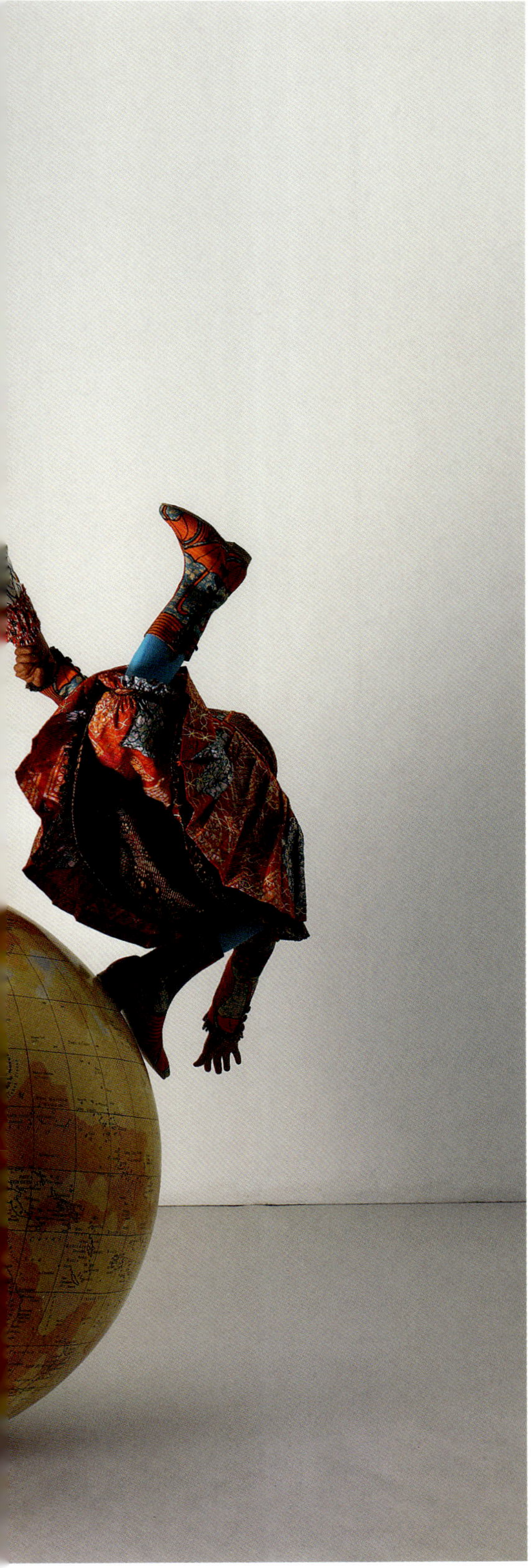

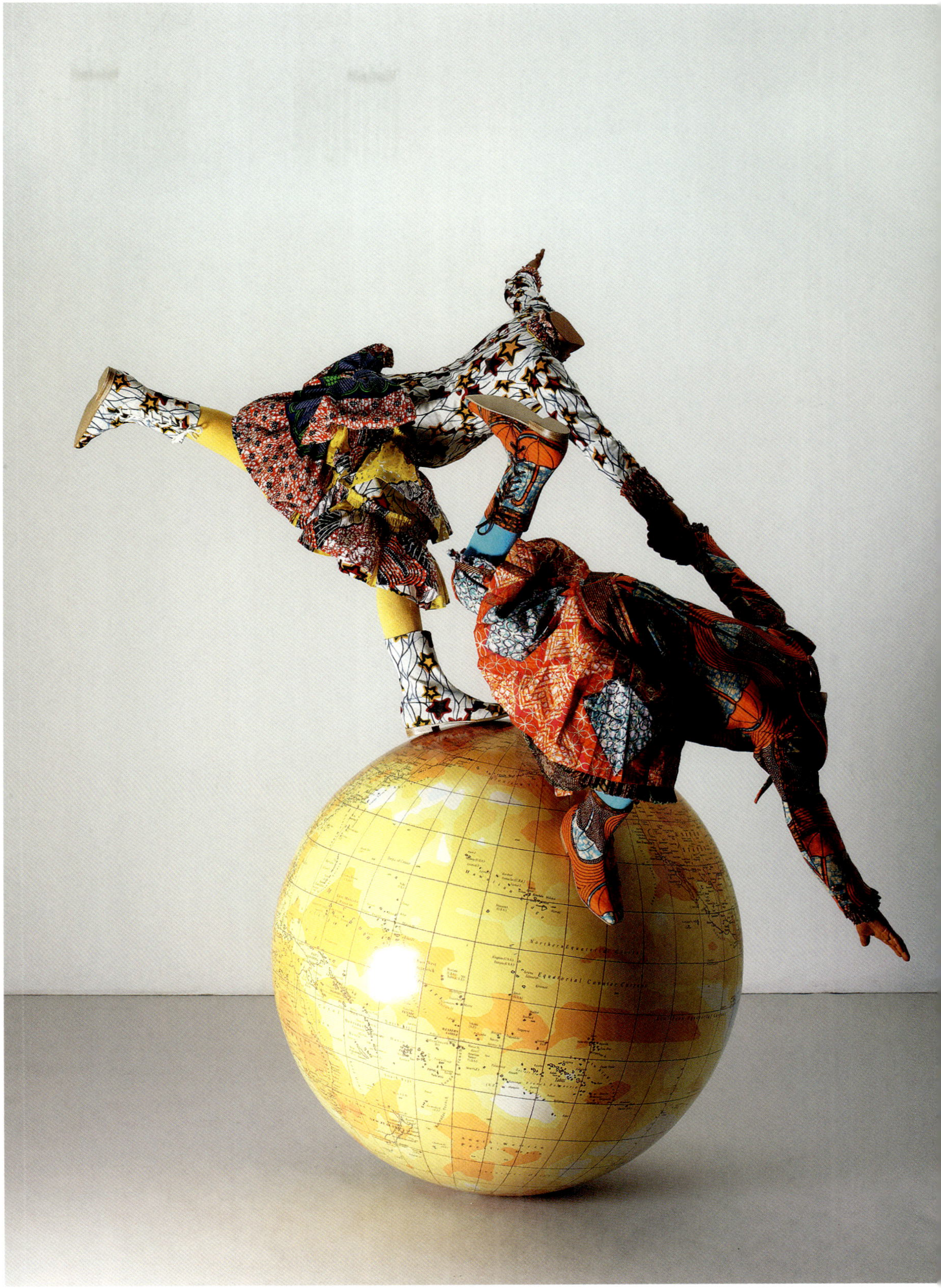

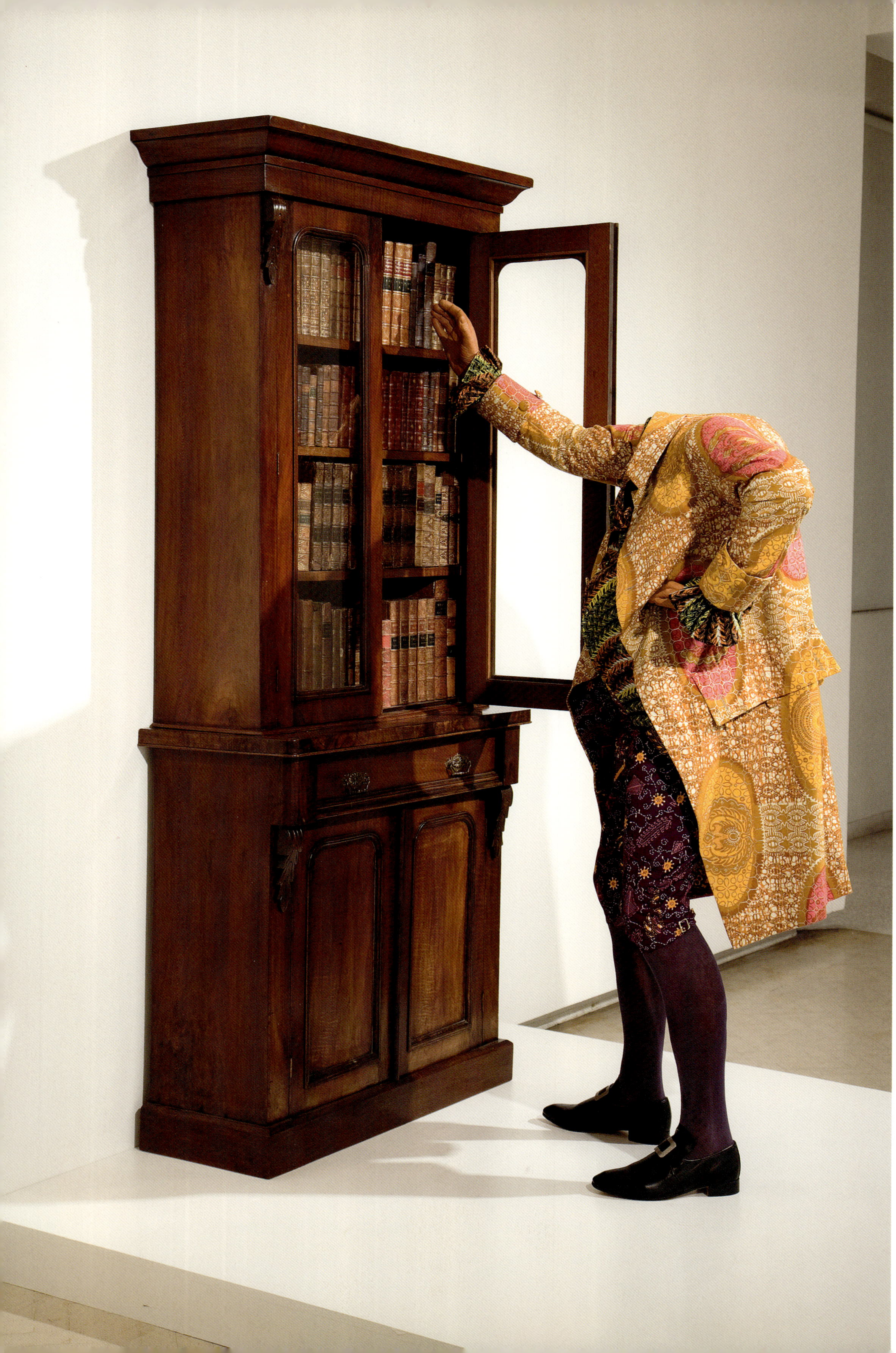

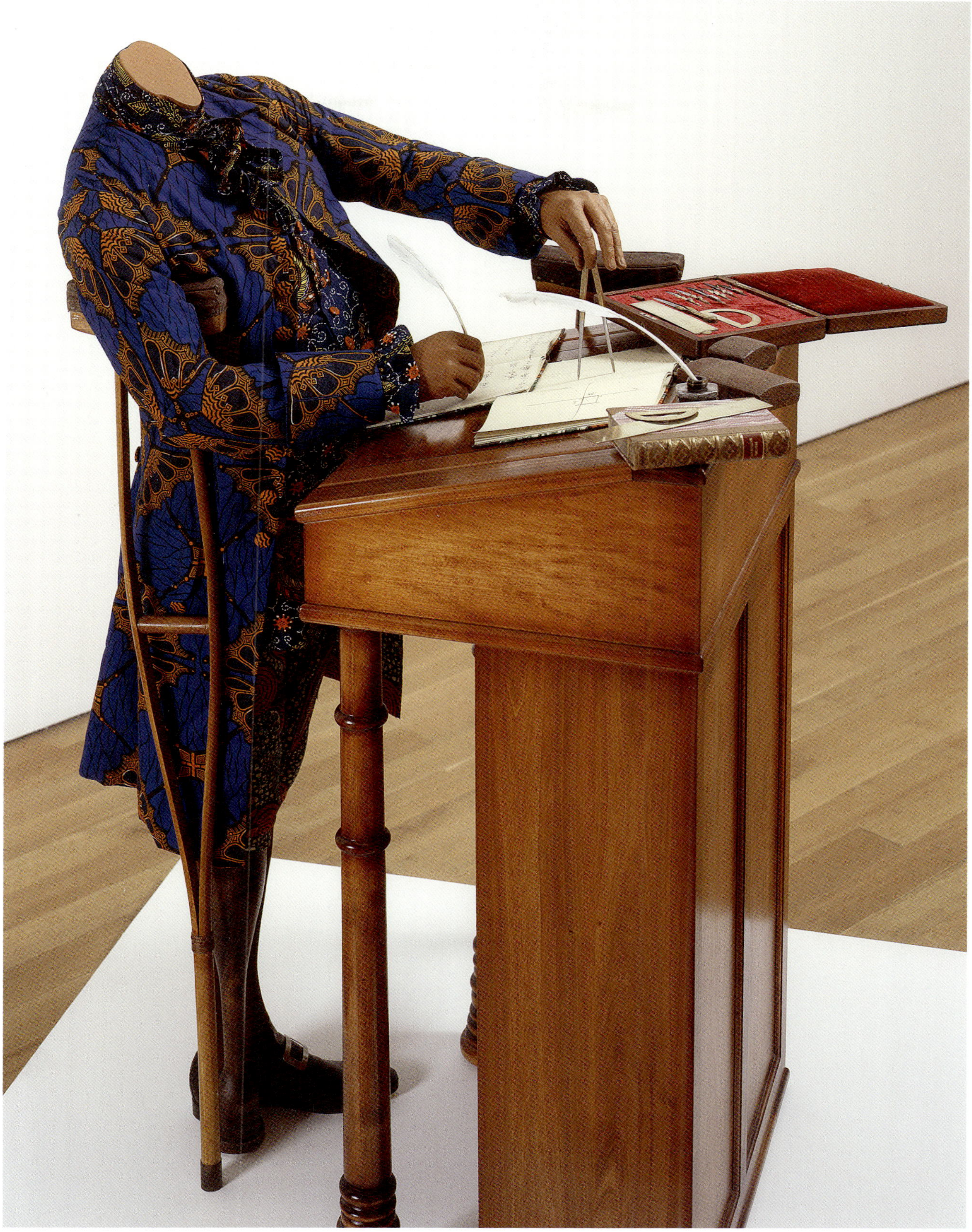

Opposite:

**The Age of Enlightenment—
Adam Smith**, 2008

Life-size mannequin, Dutch wax printed cotton, mixed media
170 x 110 x 85 cm
Private collection

**The Age of Enlightenment—
Jean le Rond d'Alembert**, 2008

Life-size mannequin, Dutch wax printed cotton, mixed media
166 x 65 x 75 cm
Berlingieri Collection

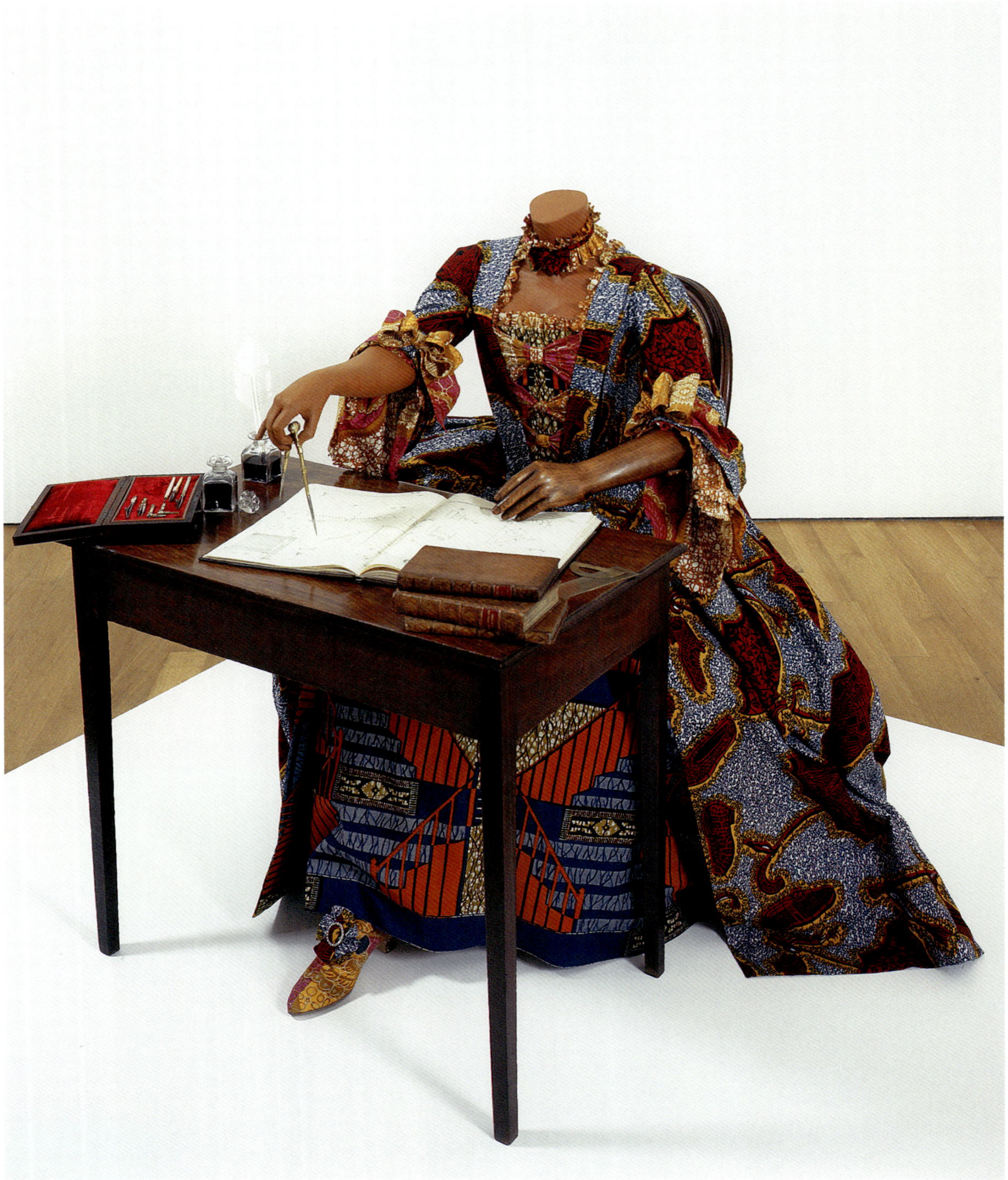

The Age of Enlightenment—Gabrielle Émilie Le Tonnelier de Breteuil, Marquise du Châtelet, 2008

Life-size mannequin, Dutch wax printed cotton, mixed media
118 x 65 x 85 cm
Private collection

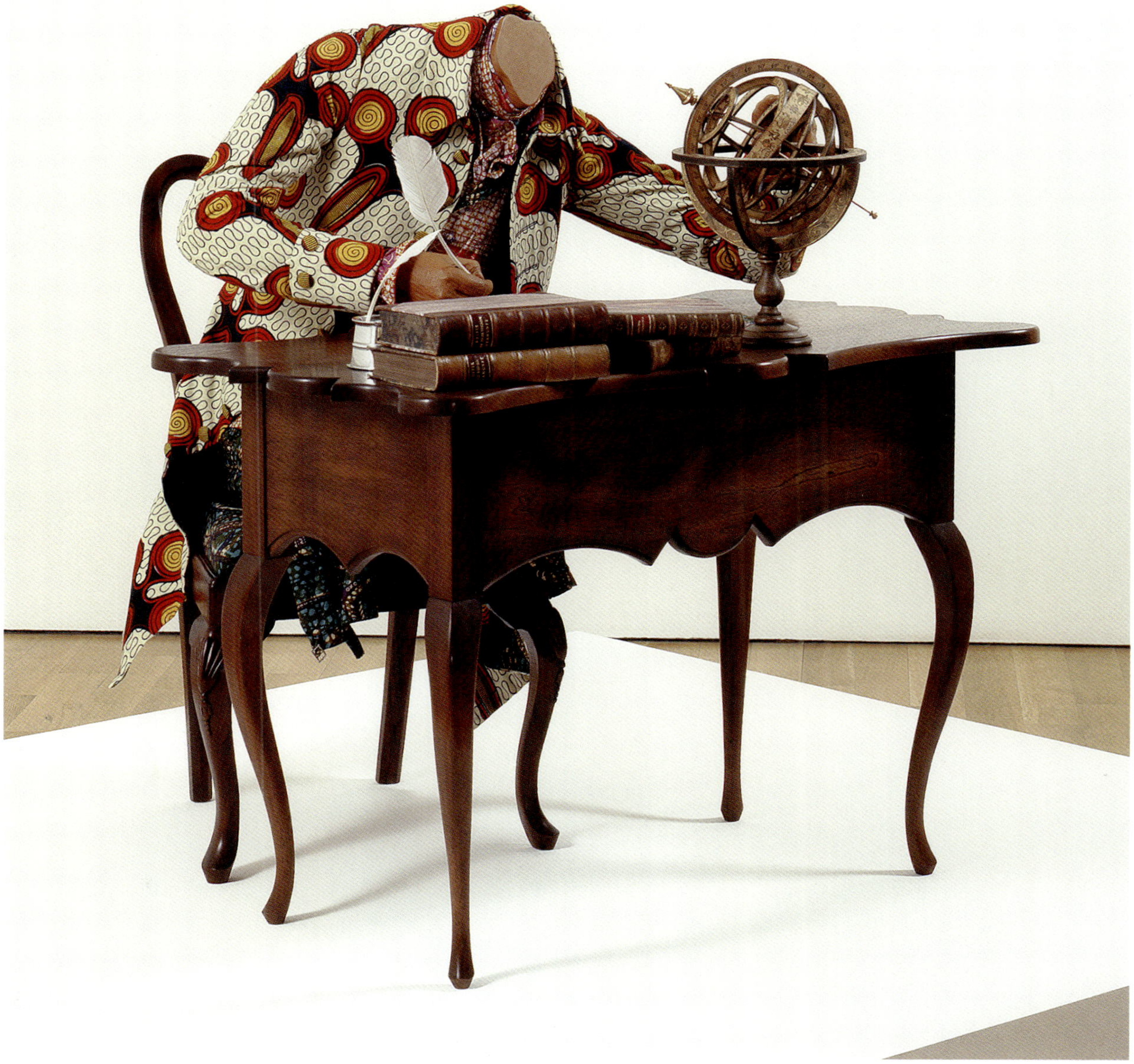

The Age of Enlightenment—Immanuel Kant, 2008

Life-size mannequin, Dutch wax printed cotton, mixed media
75 x 105 x 80 cm
Milwaukee Art Museum

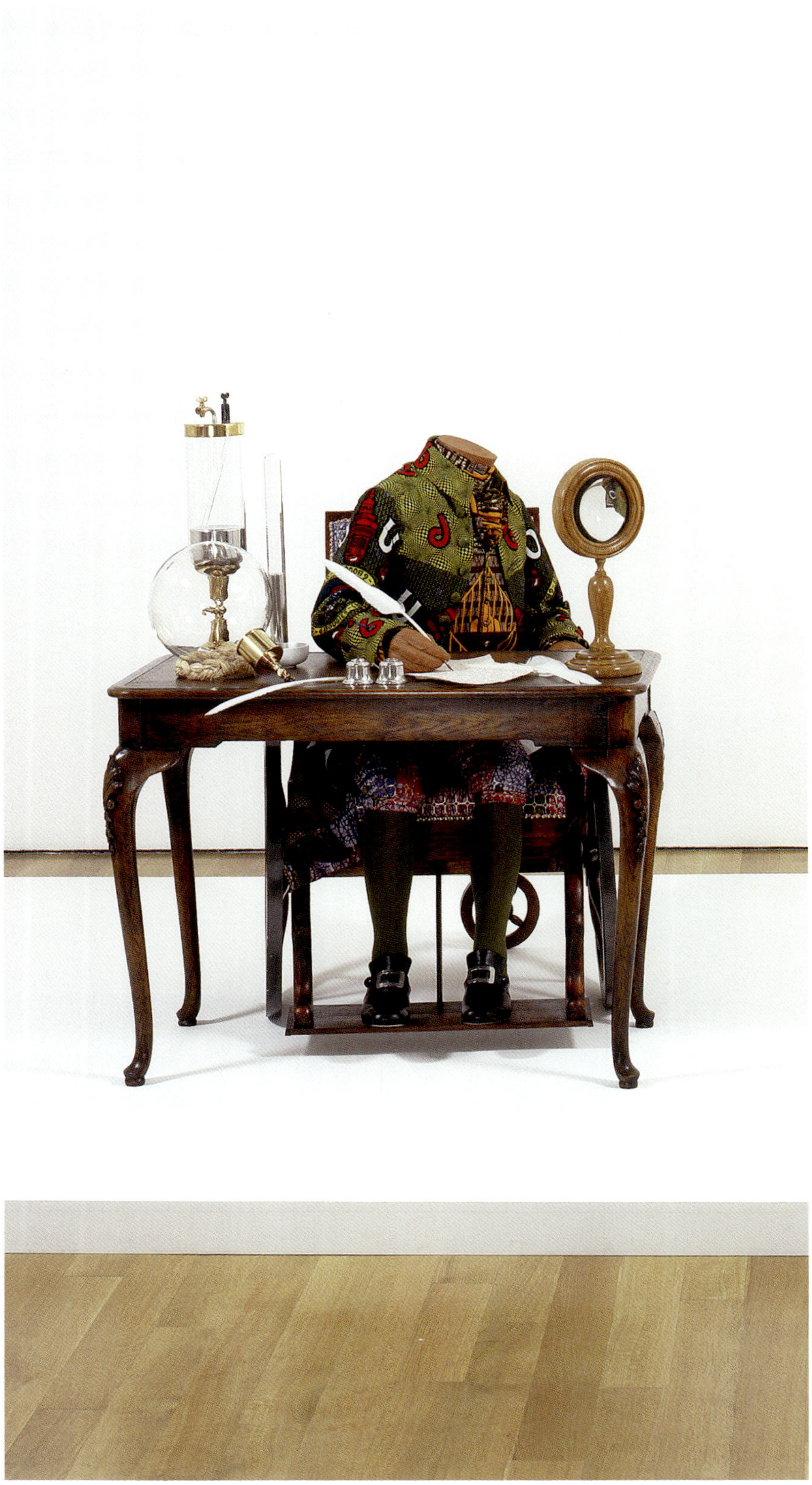

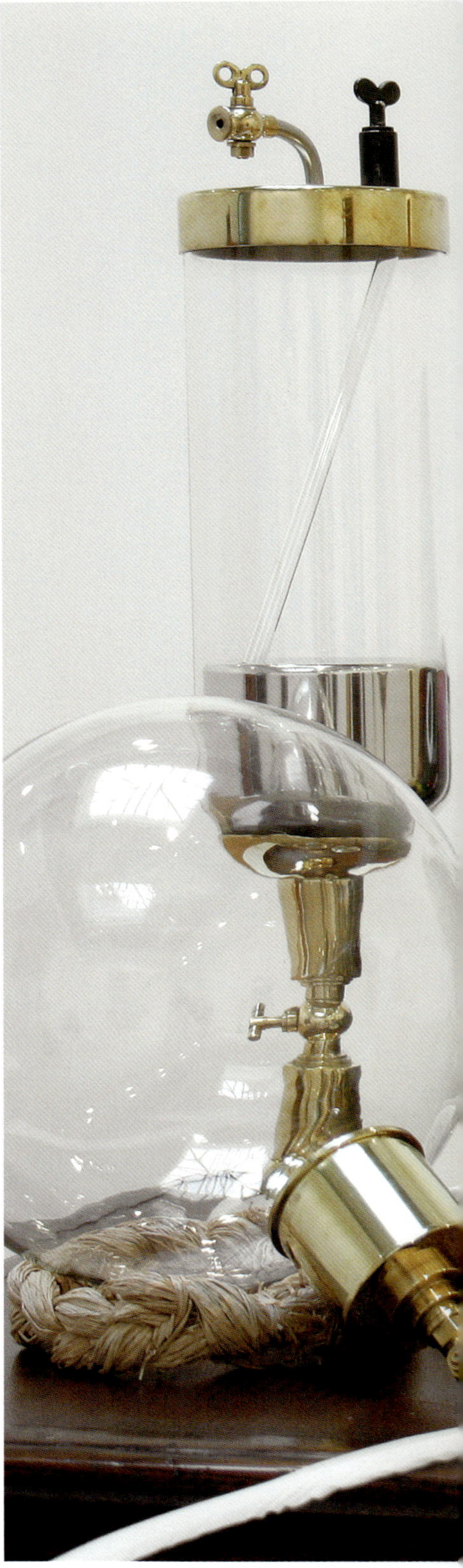

The Age of Enlightenment—Antoine Lavoisier, 2008

Life-size mannequin, Dutch wax printed cotton, mixed media
120 x 73 x 120 cm
Hirshhorn Museum and Sculpture Garden, Smithsonian Institution, Washington, DC, Joseph H. Hirshhorn Purchase Fund, 2008

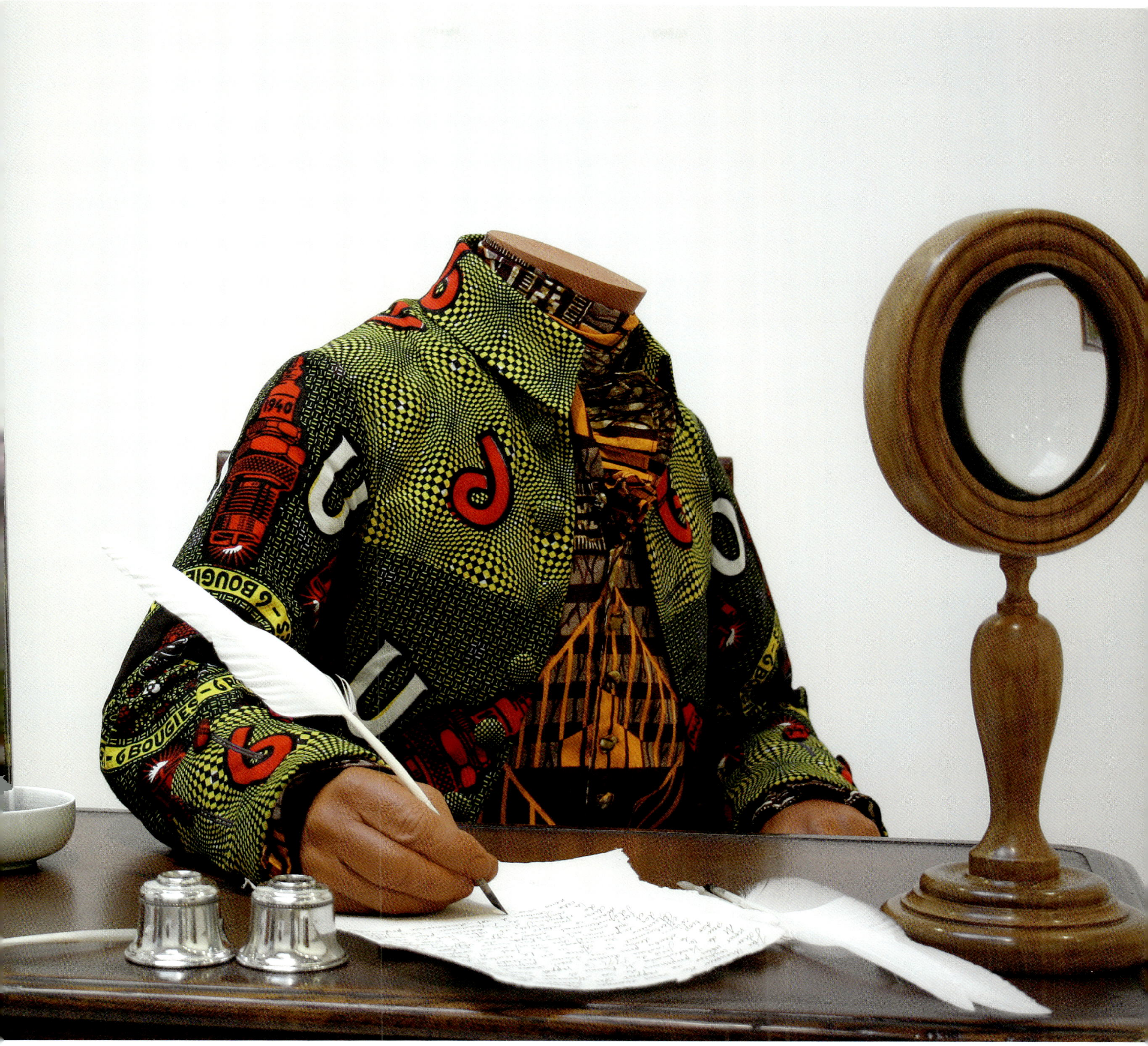
1940
BOUGIES

La Méduse, 2008

Wood, foam, Plexiglas, Dutch wax printed cotton, acrylic paint
212.1 x 167.6 x 137.2 cm
Nouveau Musée National de Monaco

Overleaf, left:

Man on Flying Machine, 2008

Life-size mannequin, Dutch wax printed cotton, steel, rubber, aluminum
155 x 60 x 70 cm (figure), 200 x 60 x 90 cm (flying machine), diam. 182 cm (blades)

Overleaf, right:

Girl on Flying Machine, 2008

Life-size mannequin, Dutch wax printed cotton, steel, rubber, aluminum
100 x 60 x 55 cm (figure), 165 x 56 x 80 cm (flying machine), diam. 170 cm (blades)

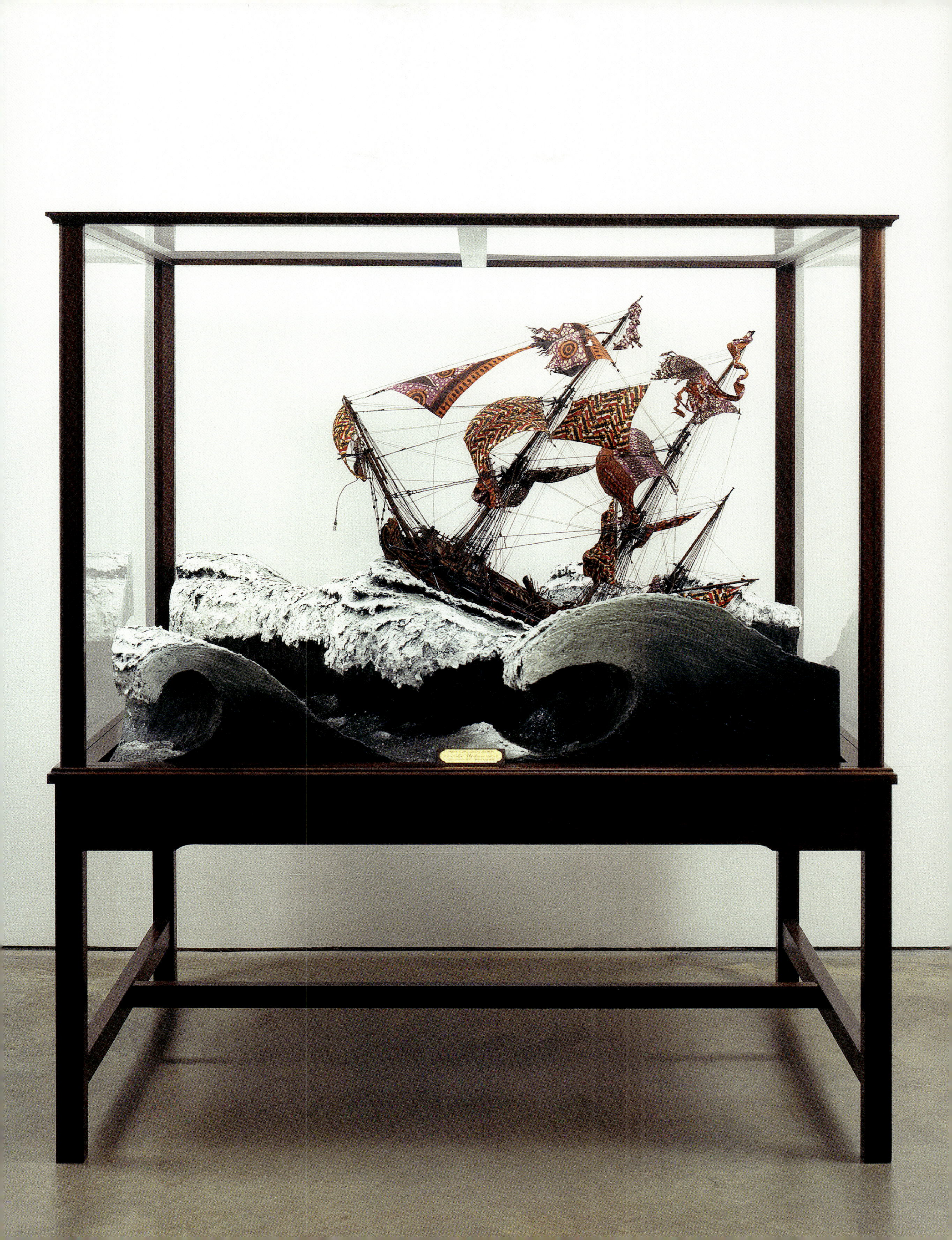

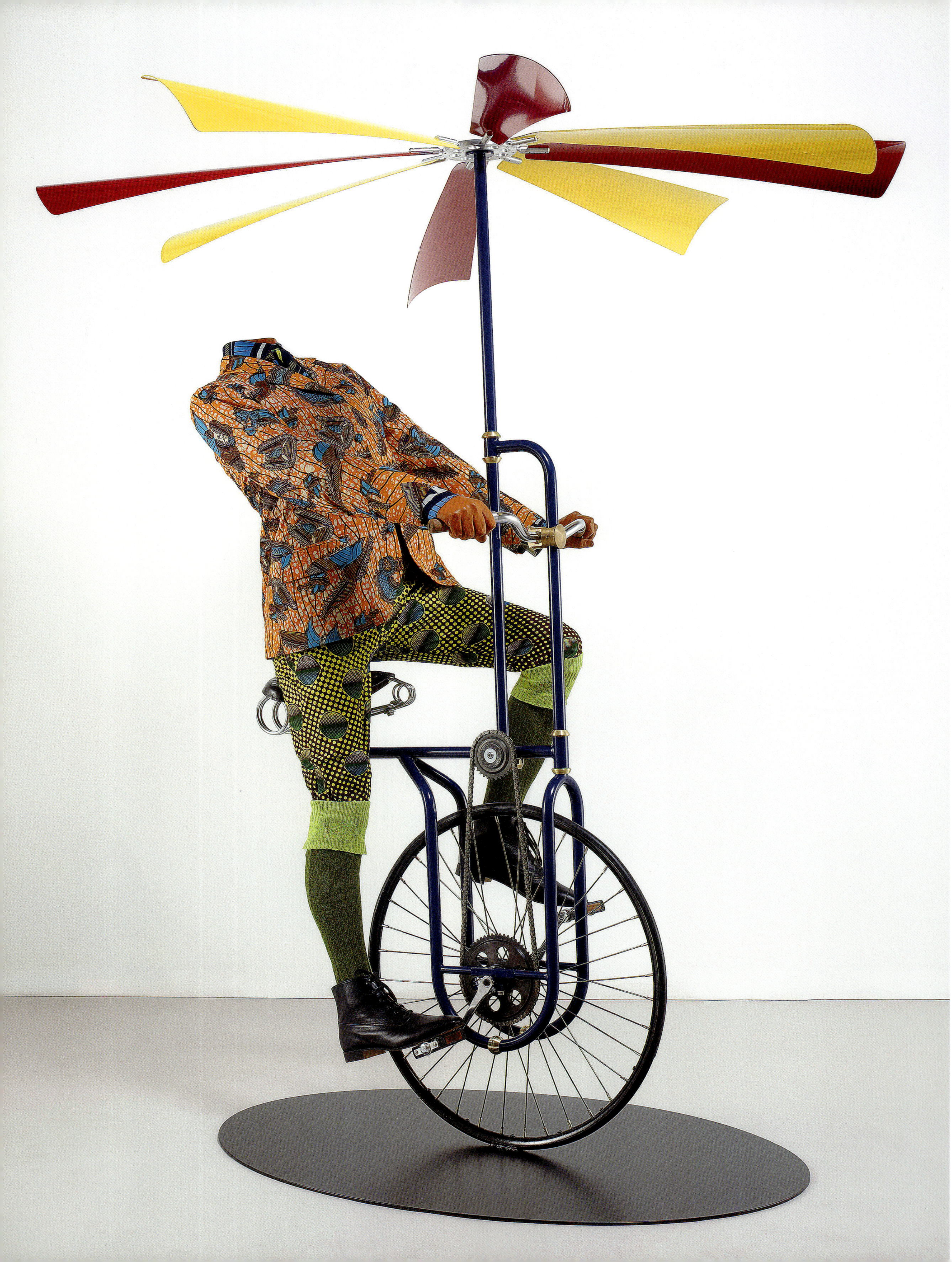

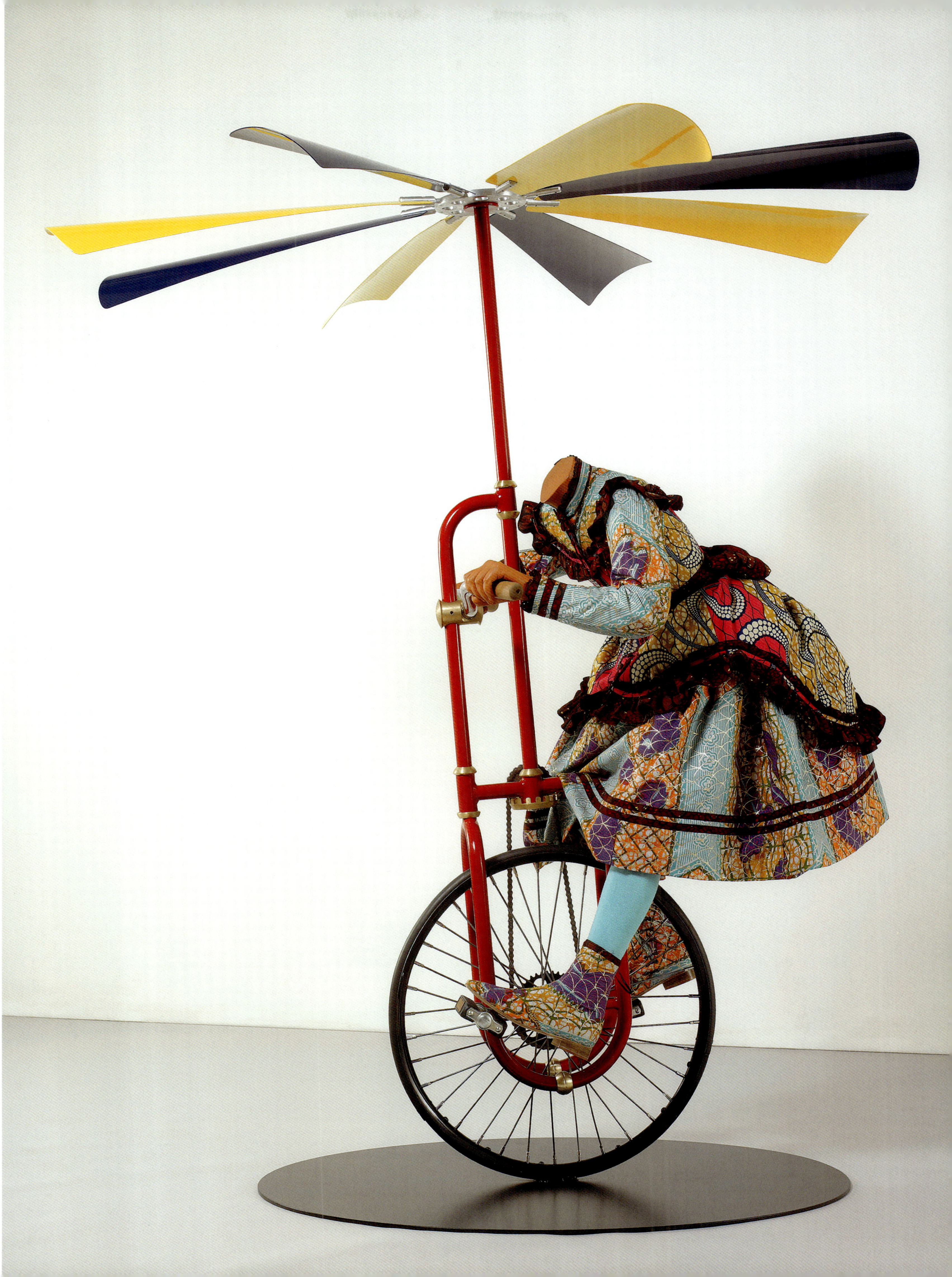

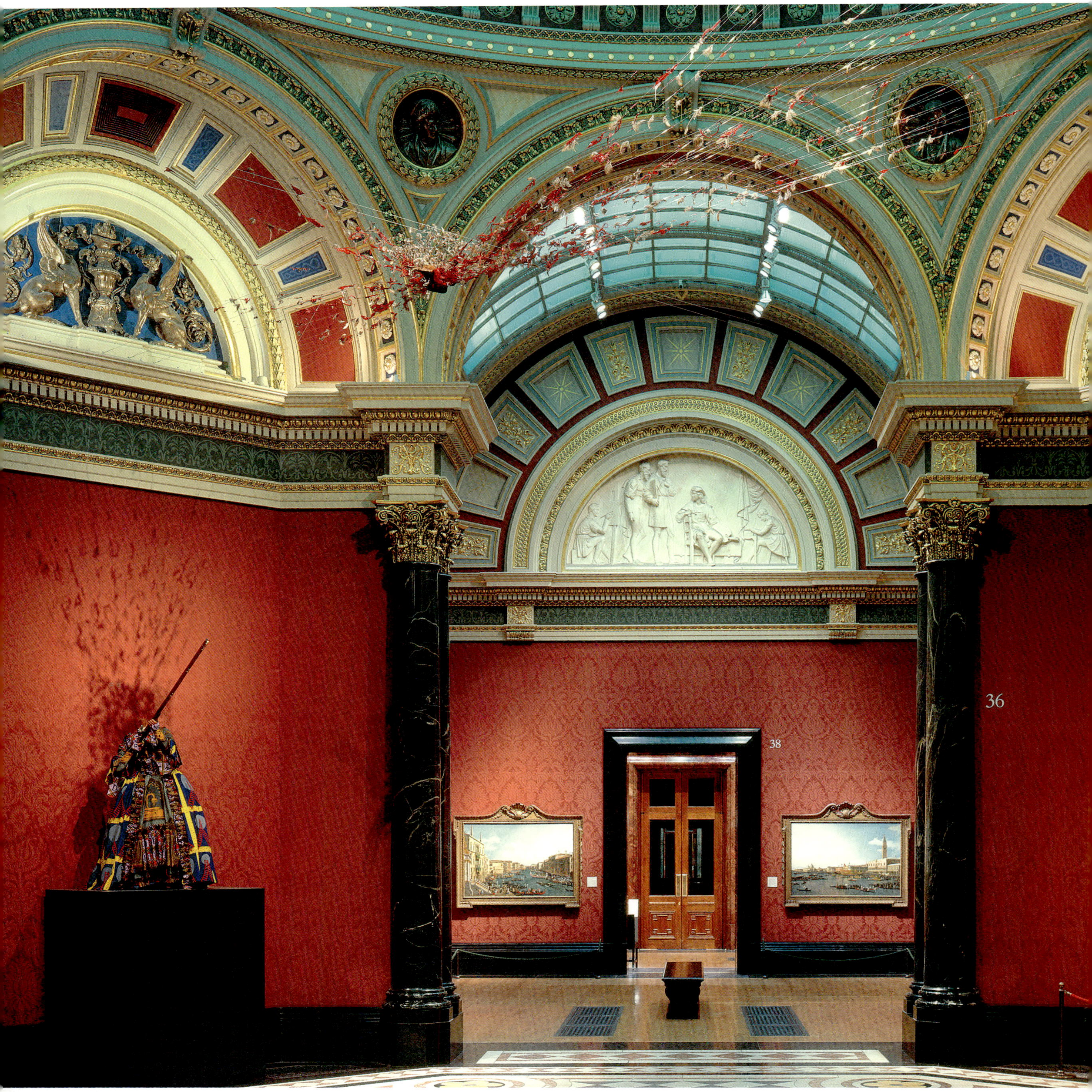
36
38

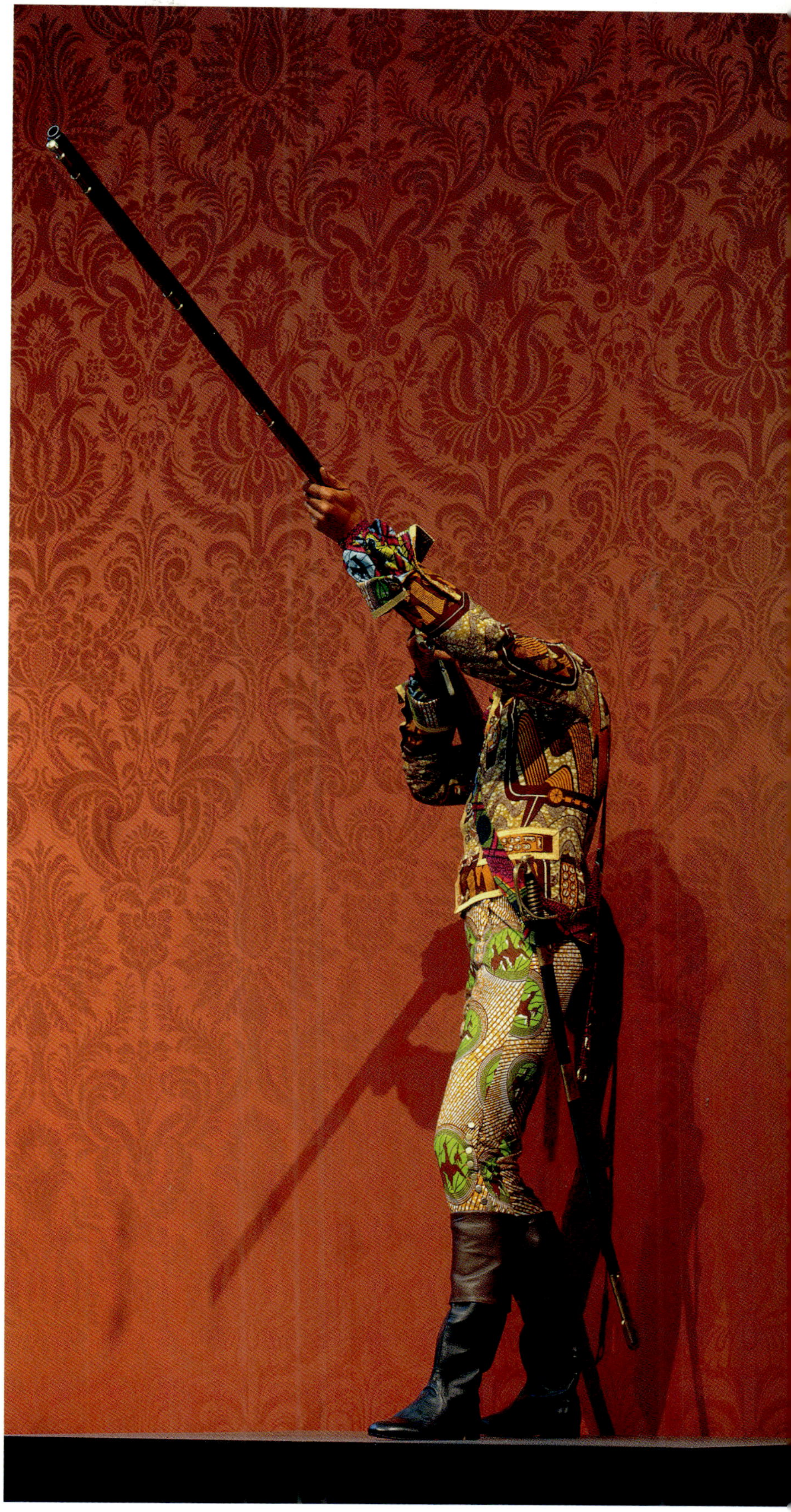

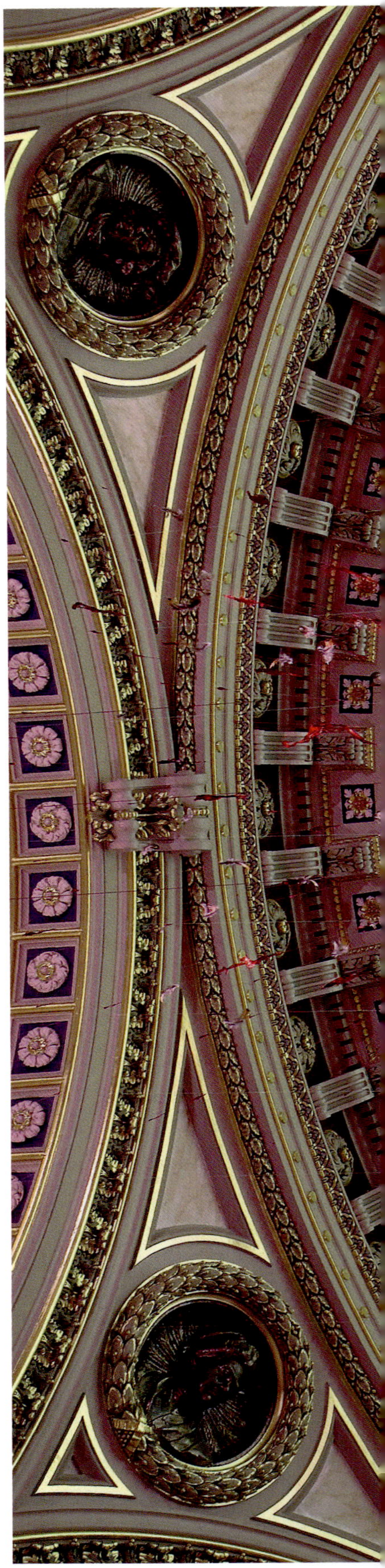

This and preceding spread:

Colonel Tarleton and Mrs. Oswald Shooting, 2007

Two life-size mannequins, Dutch wax printed cotton, guns, mixed media
389 x 192 x 152 cm (Tarleton on plinth), 393 x 192 x 152 cm (Oswald on plinth)
Courtesy gordonschachatcollection
Installation view, National Gallery, London, 2007

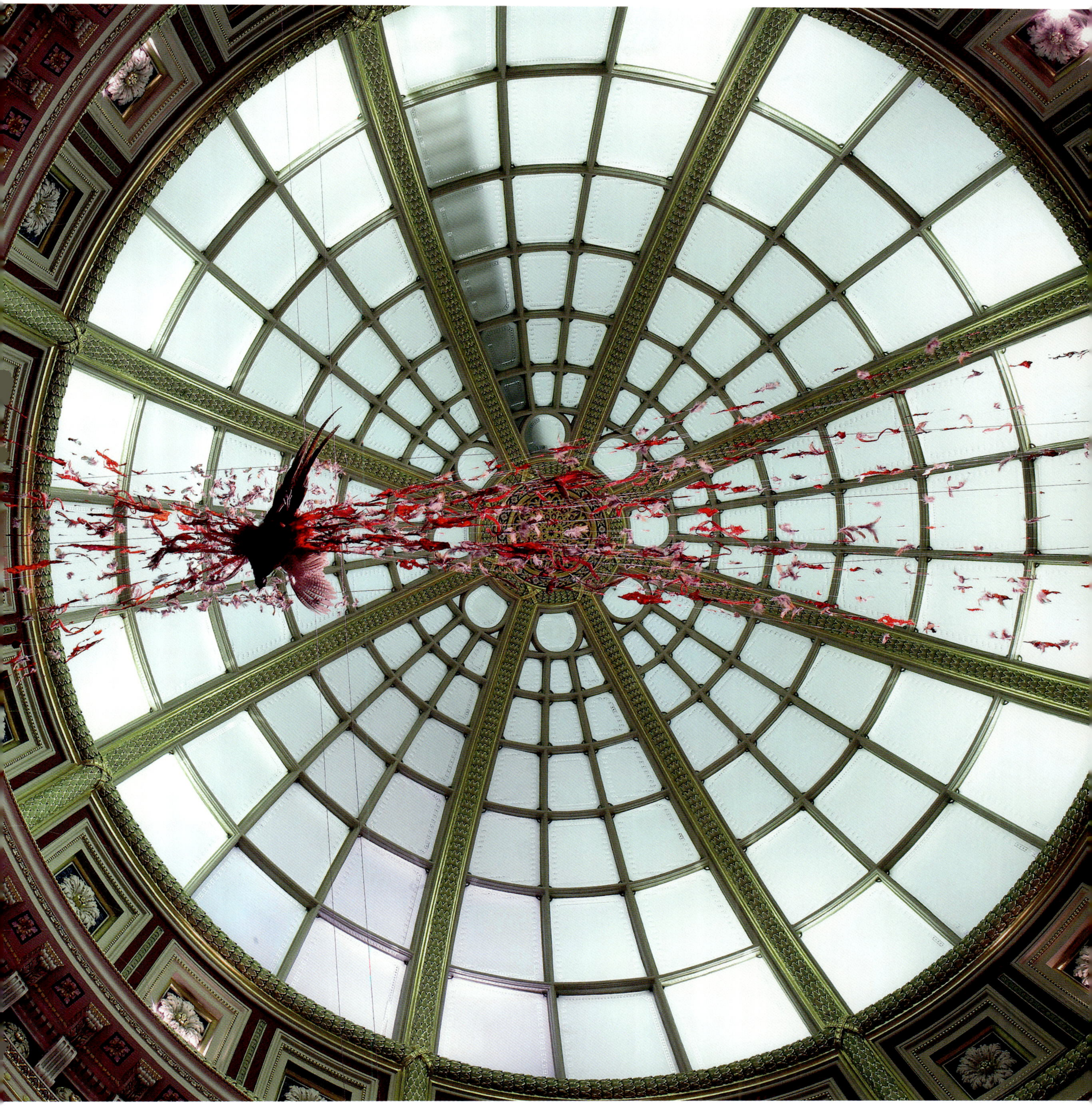

Girl Ballerina, 2007

Life-size mannequin, Dutch wax printed cotton, gun
120 x 50 x 60 cm
Collection of John and Amy Phelan

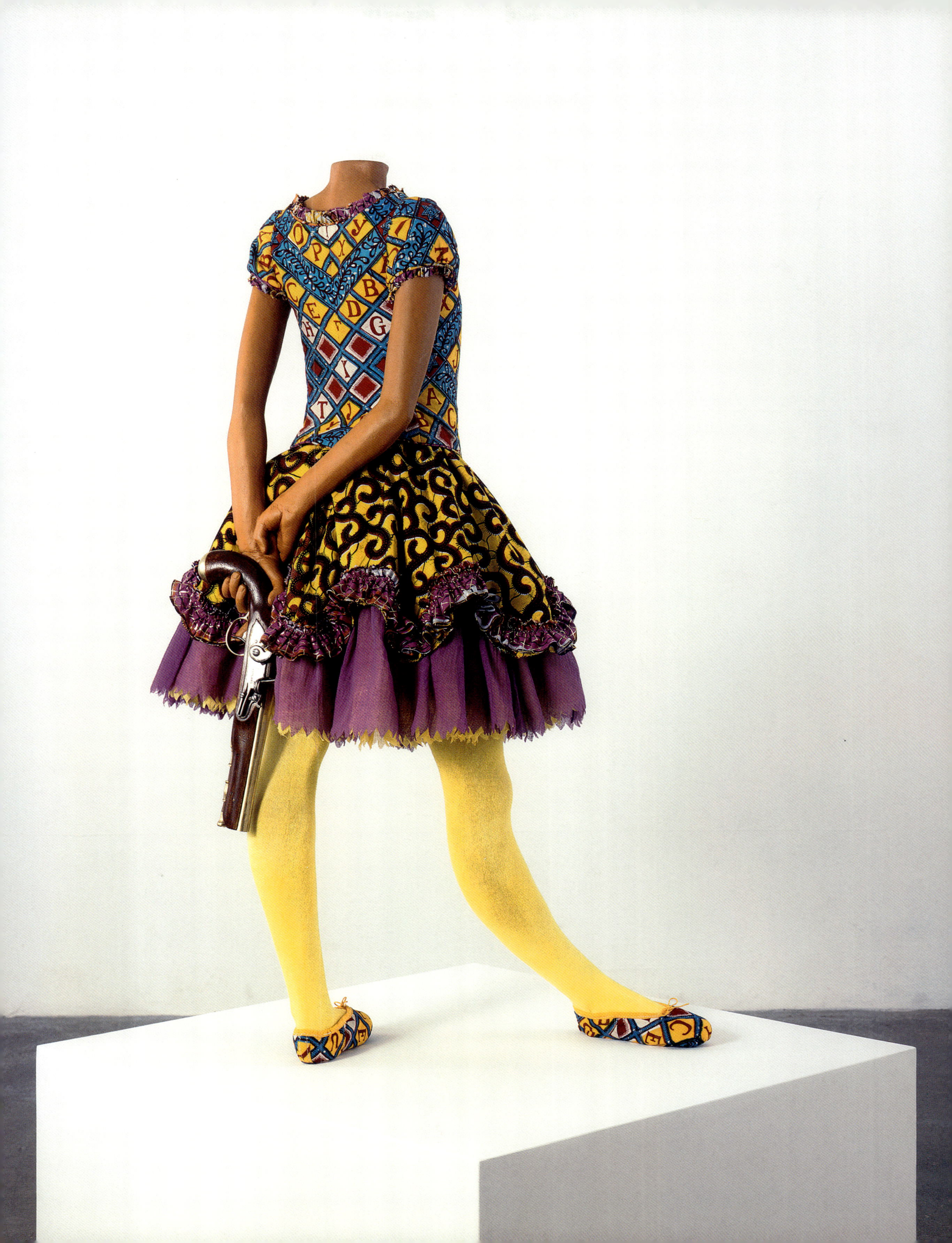

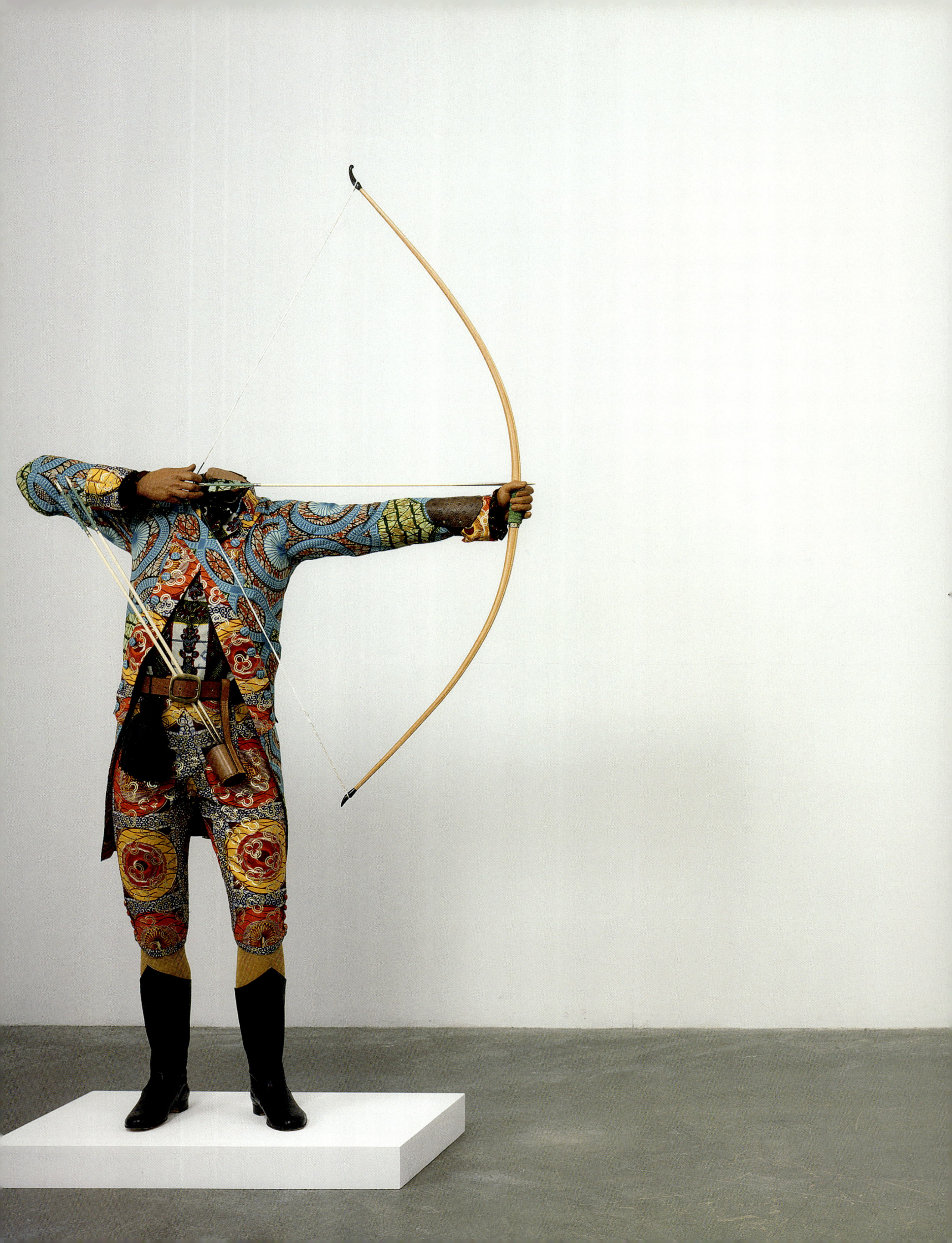

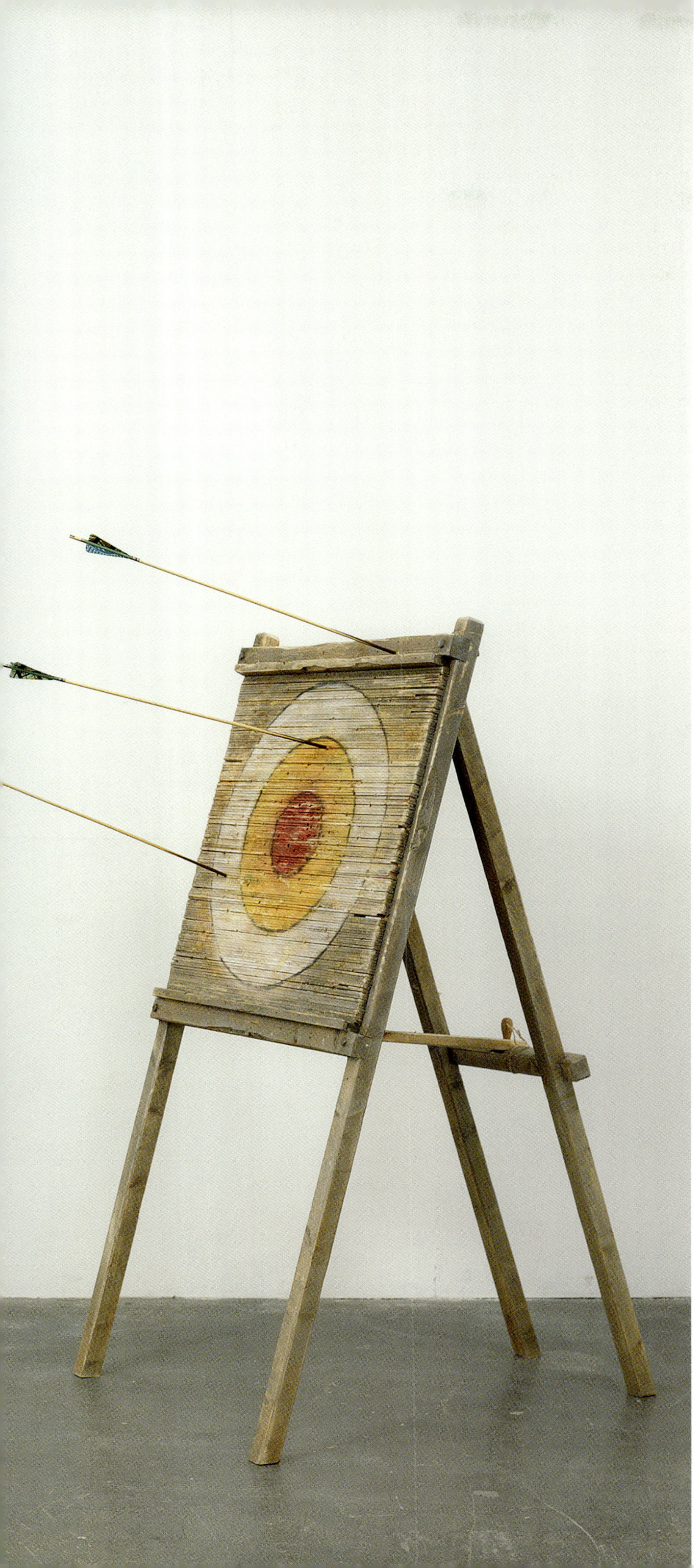

Sir Foster Cunliffe, Playing, 2007

Life-size mannequin, Dutch wax printed cotton, bow, arrows, target, mixed media
176 x 140 x 60 cm (figure), 150 x 100 x 30 cm (target)
Collection of Daniel E. and Rosy Levy; commissioned by the Victoria and Albert Museum, London, for the exhibition *Uncomfortable Truths*

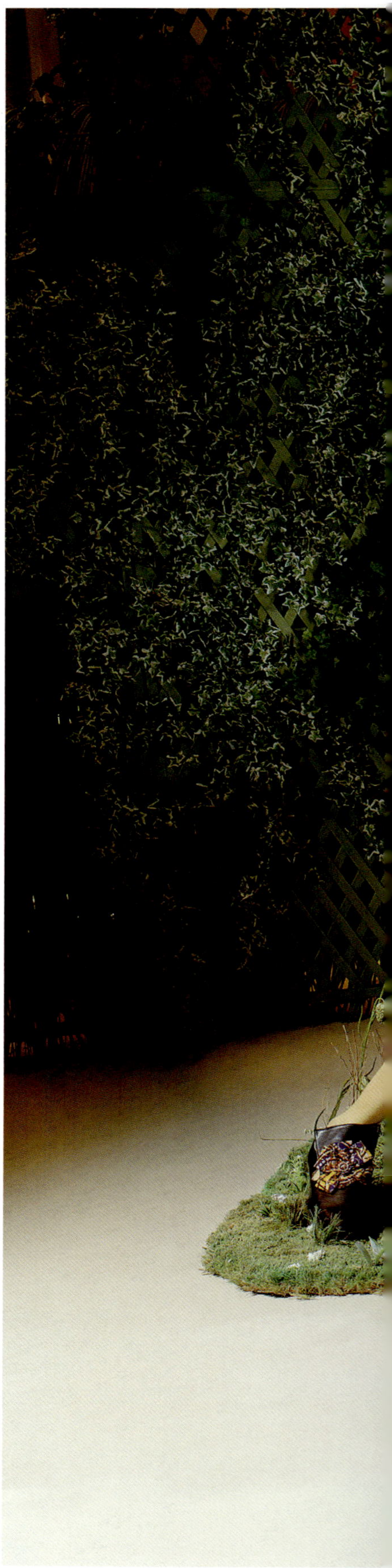

The Crowning, 2007

Two life-size mannequins, Dutch wax printed cotton, shoes, coir matting, artificial silk flowers, mixed media
160 x 280 x 210 cm
Installation view, Musée du quai Branly, 2007

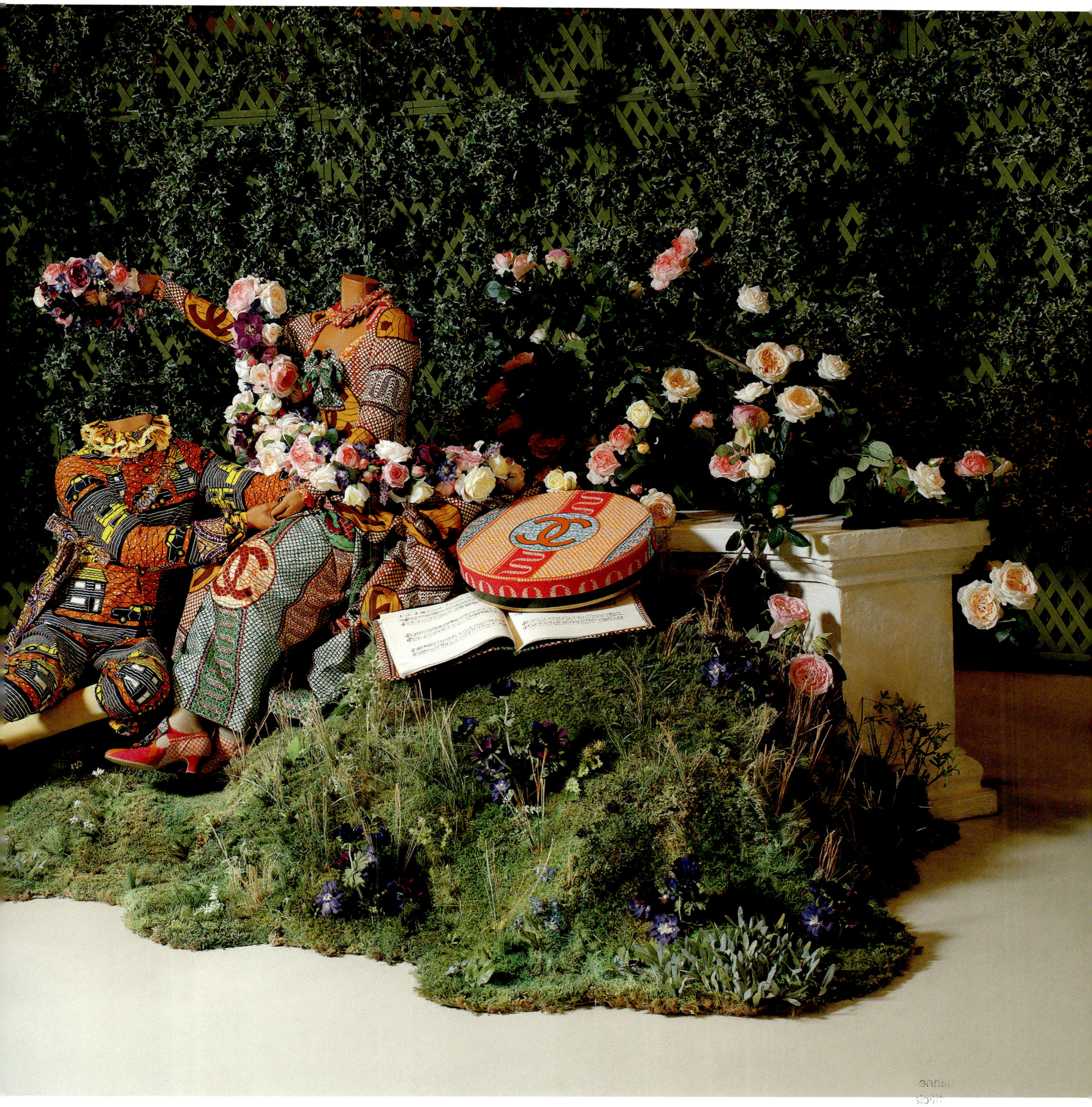

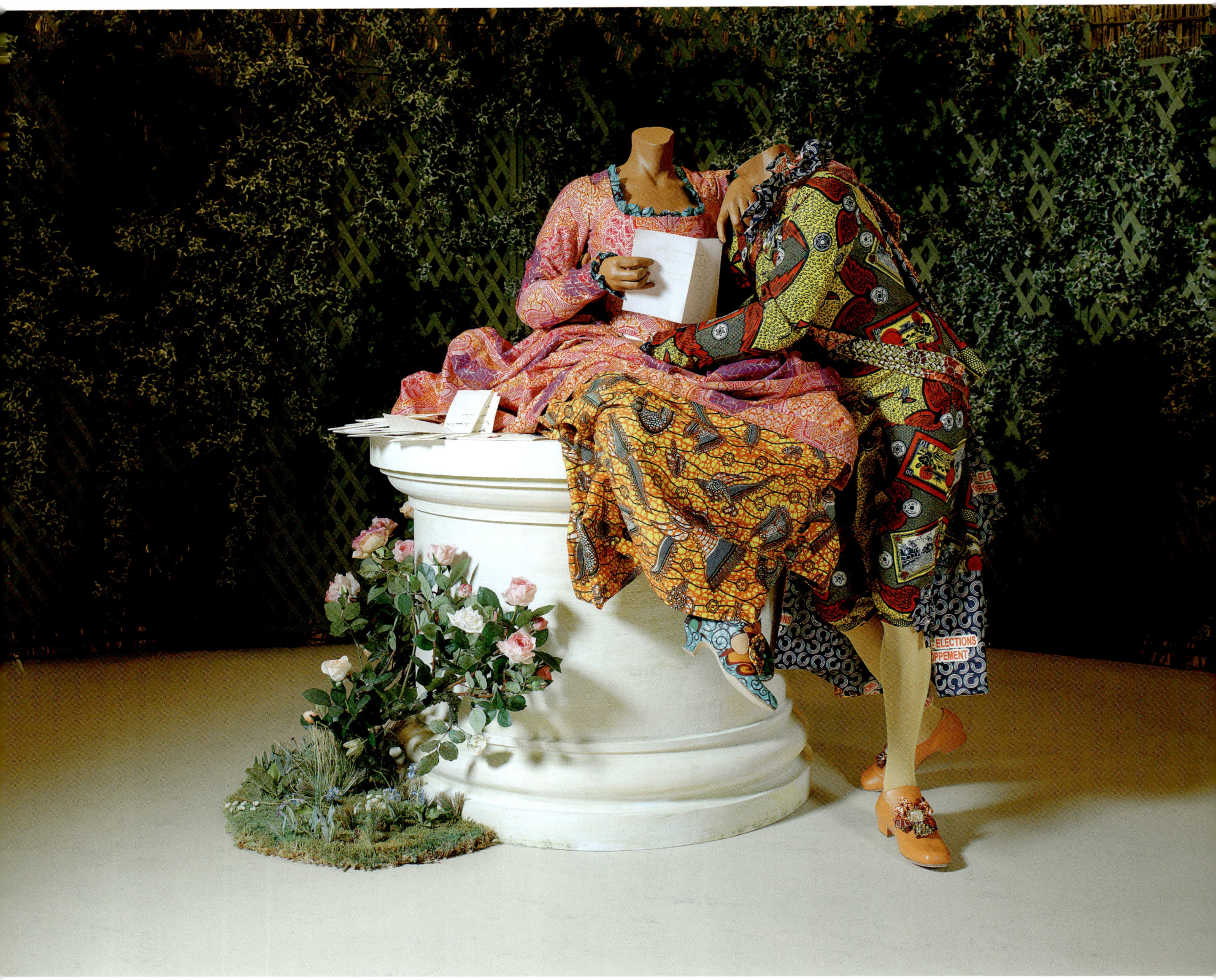

The Confession, 2007

Two life-size mannequins, Dutch wax printed cotton, shoes, coir matting, artificial silk flowers, mixed media
158 x 178 x 170 cm
Private collection, London; commissioned by the Musée du quai Branly, Paris, for the exhibition *Jardin d'Amour*
Installation view, Musée du quai Branly, 2007

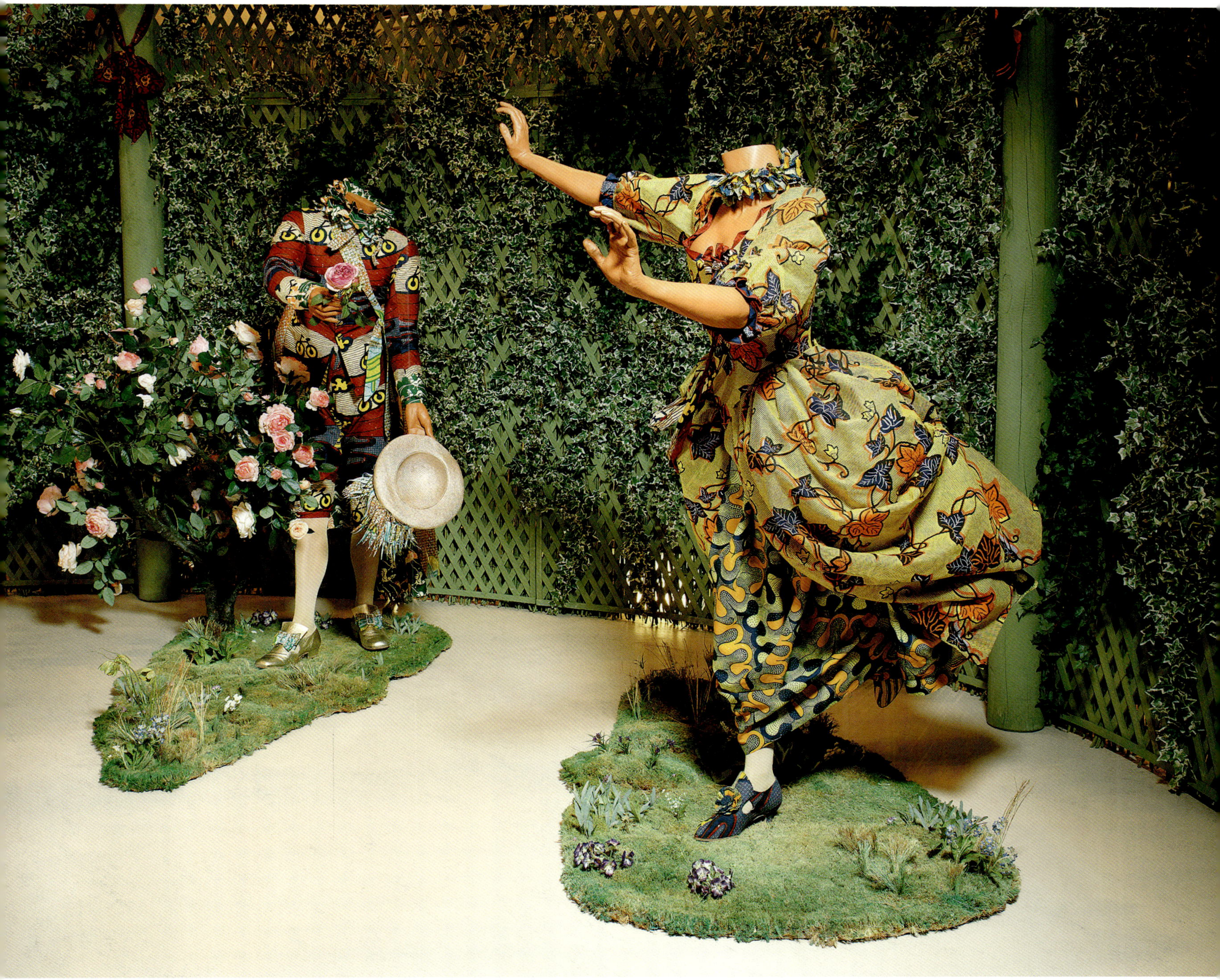

The Pursuit, 2007

Two life-size mannequins, Dutch wax printed cotton, shoes, coir matting, artificial silk flowers, mixed media
162 x 161 x 200 cm (male figure), 169 x 190 x 140 cm (female figure)
Rabo Art Collection; commissioned by the Musée du quai Branly, Paris, for the exhibition *Jardin d'Amour*
Installation view, Musée du quai Branly, 2007

How to Blow Up Two Heads at Once (Ladies), 2006

Two life-size mannequins, guns, Dutch wax printed cotton, shoes, leather riding boots, plinth
160 x 155 x 122 cm (each figure)
Davis Museum and Cultural Center, Wellesley College, Massachusetts, museum purchase, Wellesley College Friends of Art

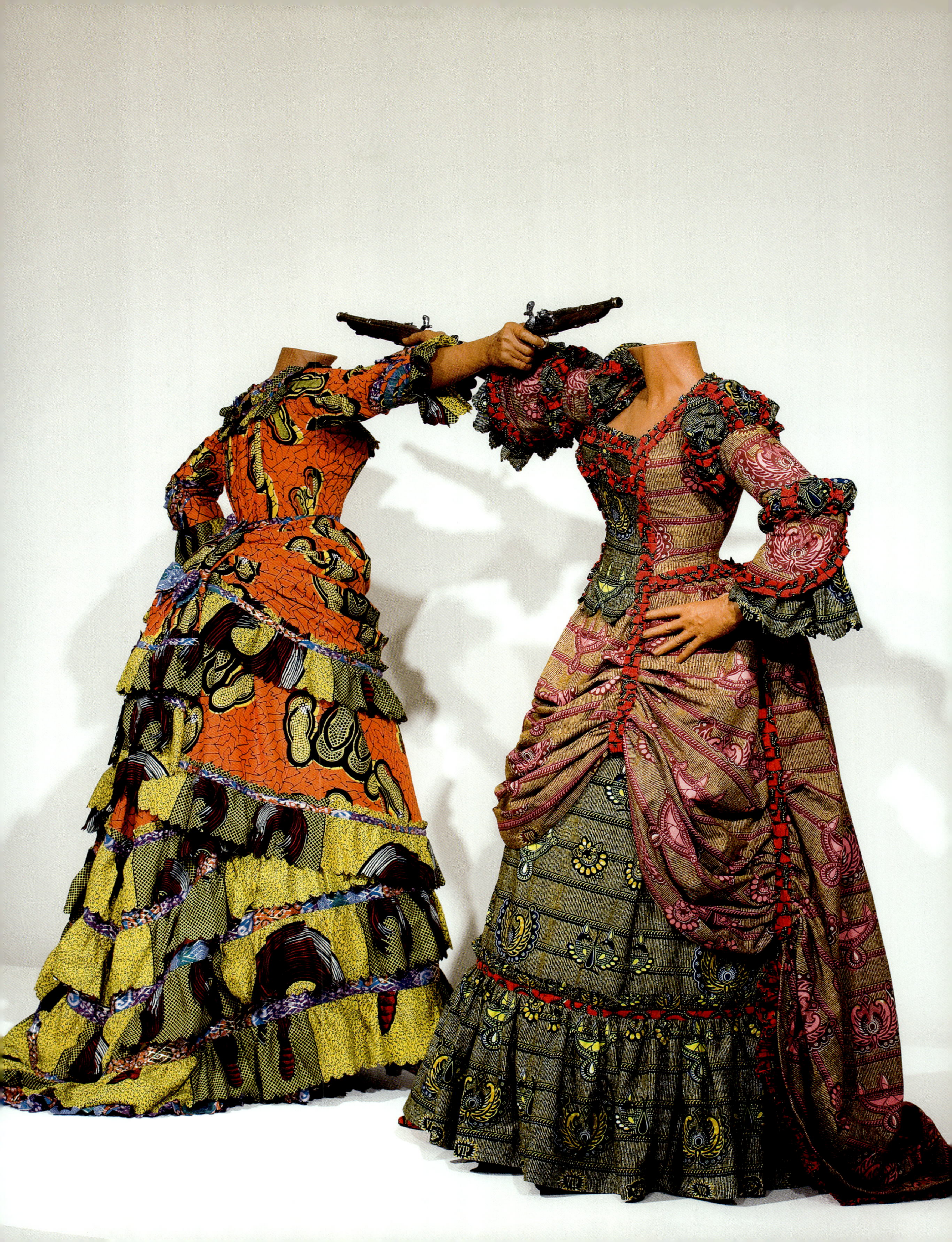

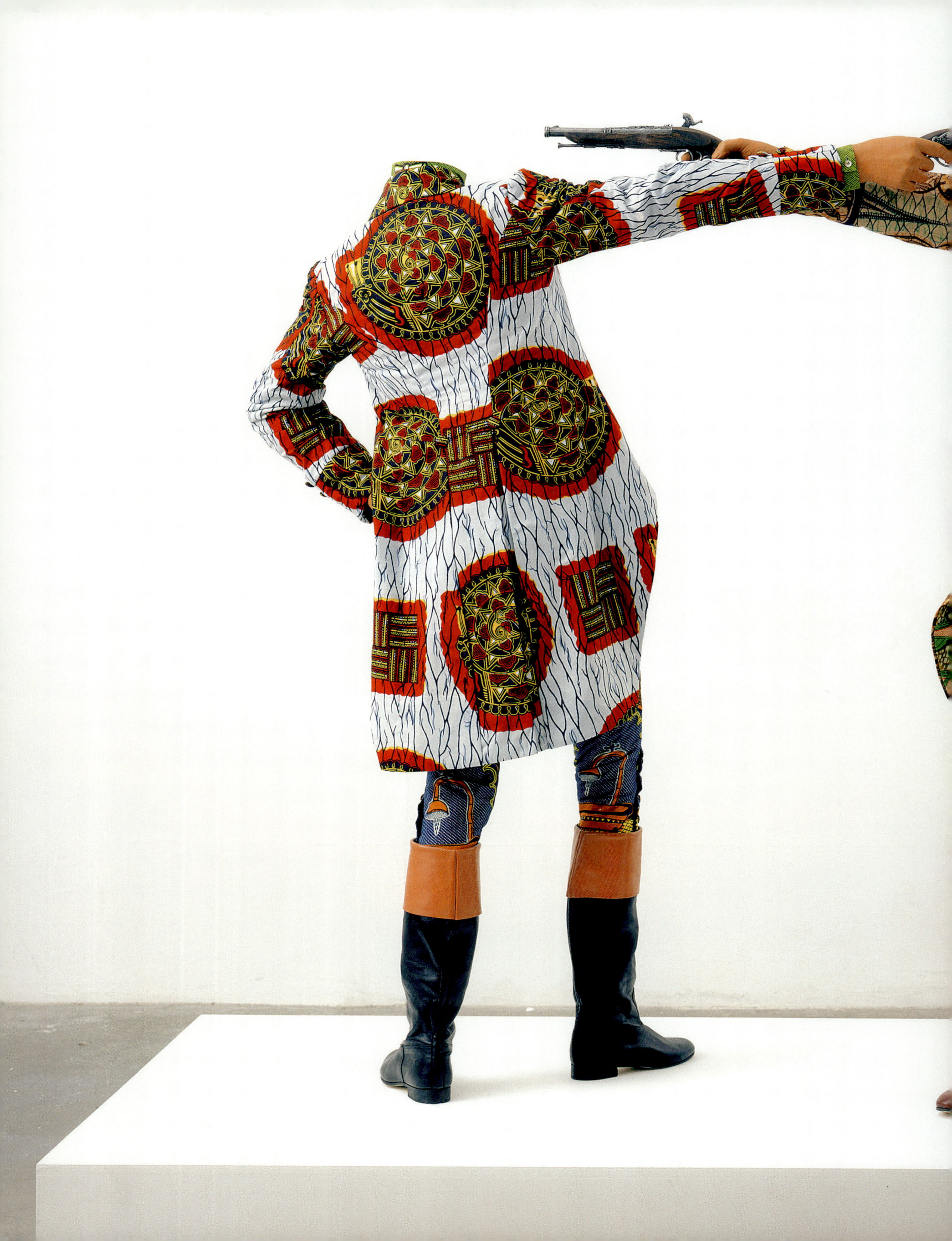

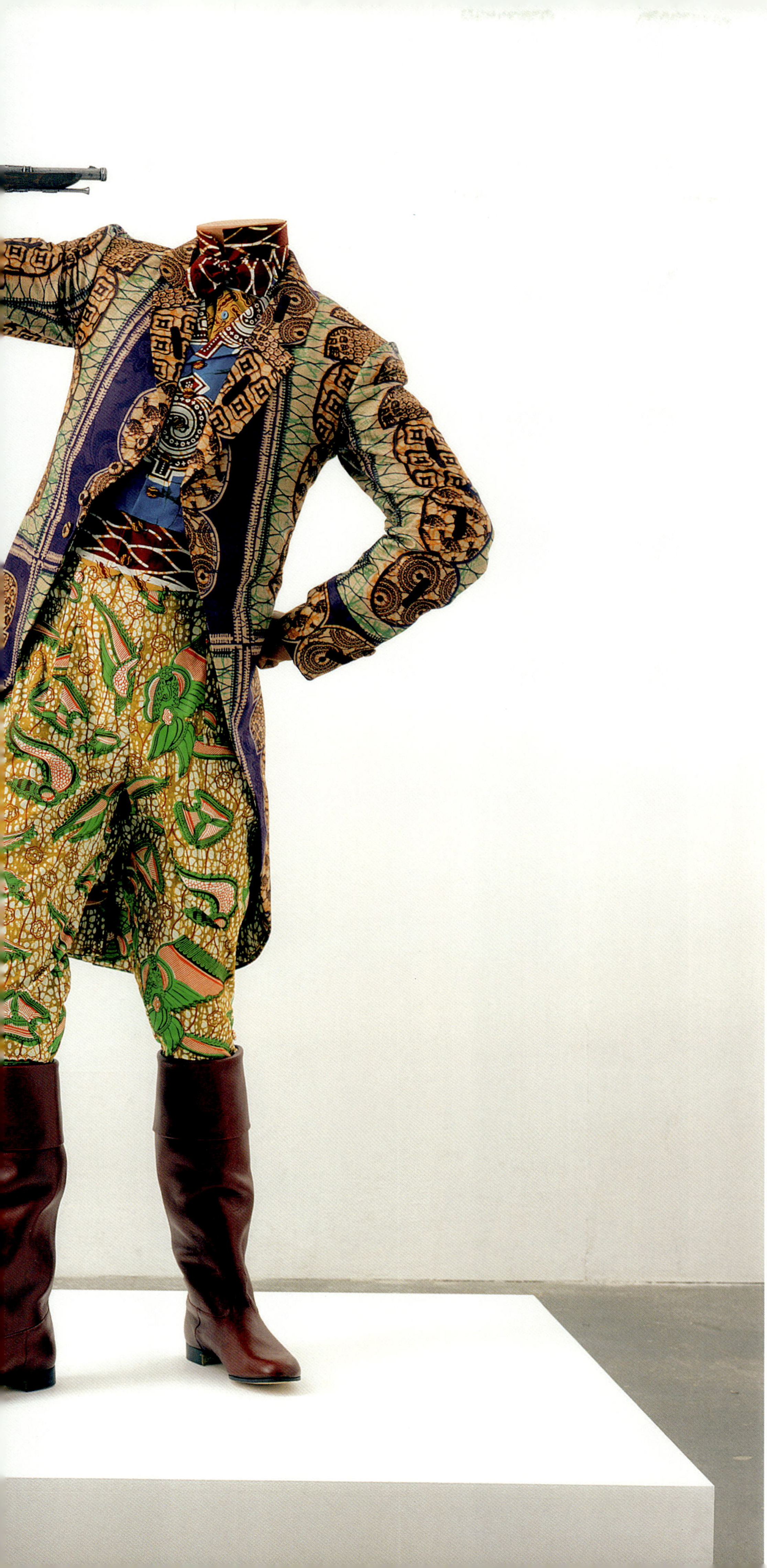

How to Blow Up Two Heads at Once (Gentlemen), 2006

Two life-size mannequins, guns, Dutch wax printed cotton, leather riding boots
175 x 160 x 40 cm (each figure)
Sindika Dokolo African Collection of Contemporary Art

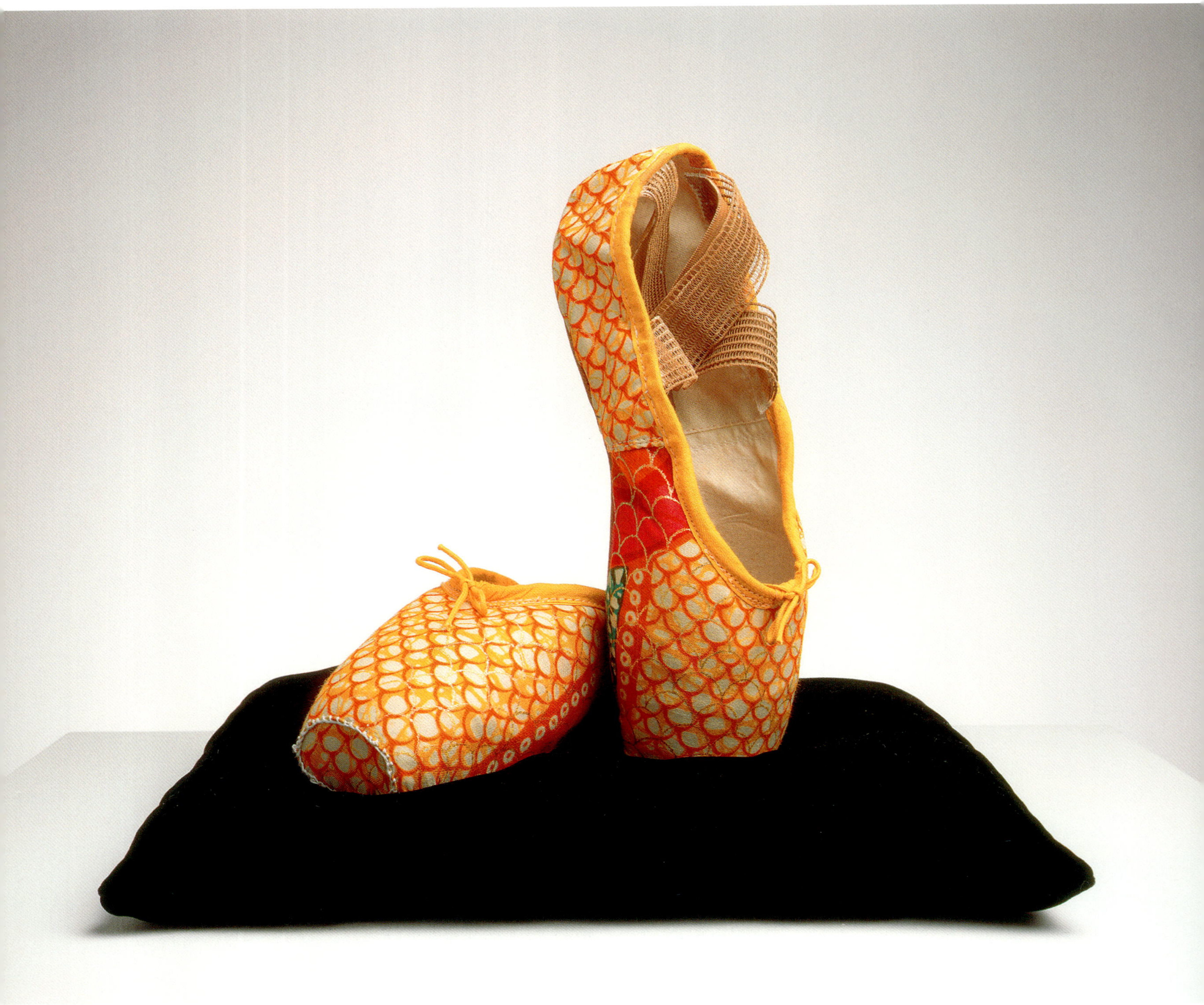

Pointe Shoe (Odile) II, 2006

Dutch wax printed cotton, black cushion
25 x 30 x 30 cm
Private collection

Opposite:

Flower Cloud II, 2006

Life-size mannequin, Dutch wax printed cotton, cast resin
306 x 170 x 150 cm
Collezione Sandro Manuli, Milan

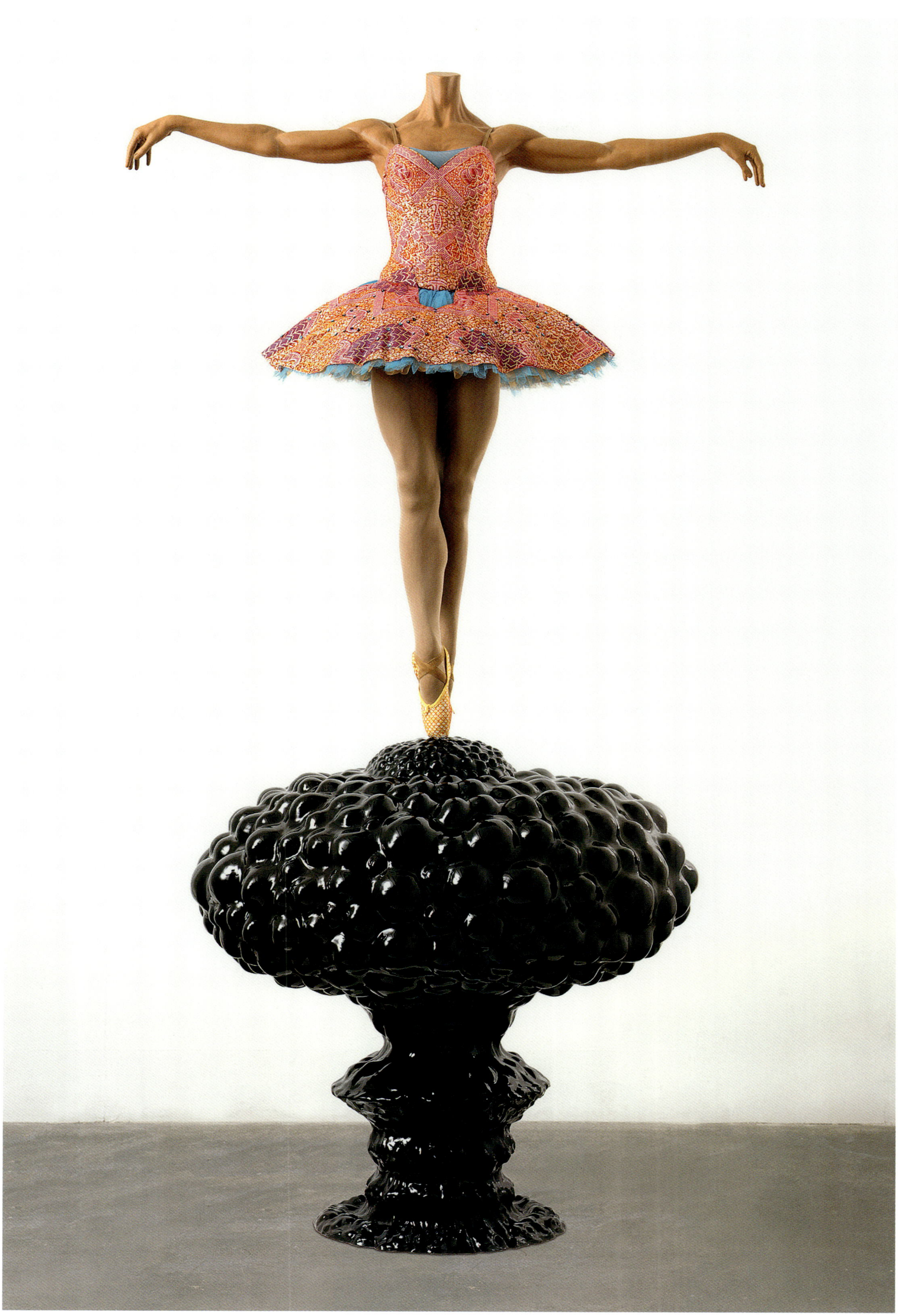

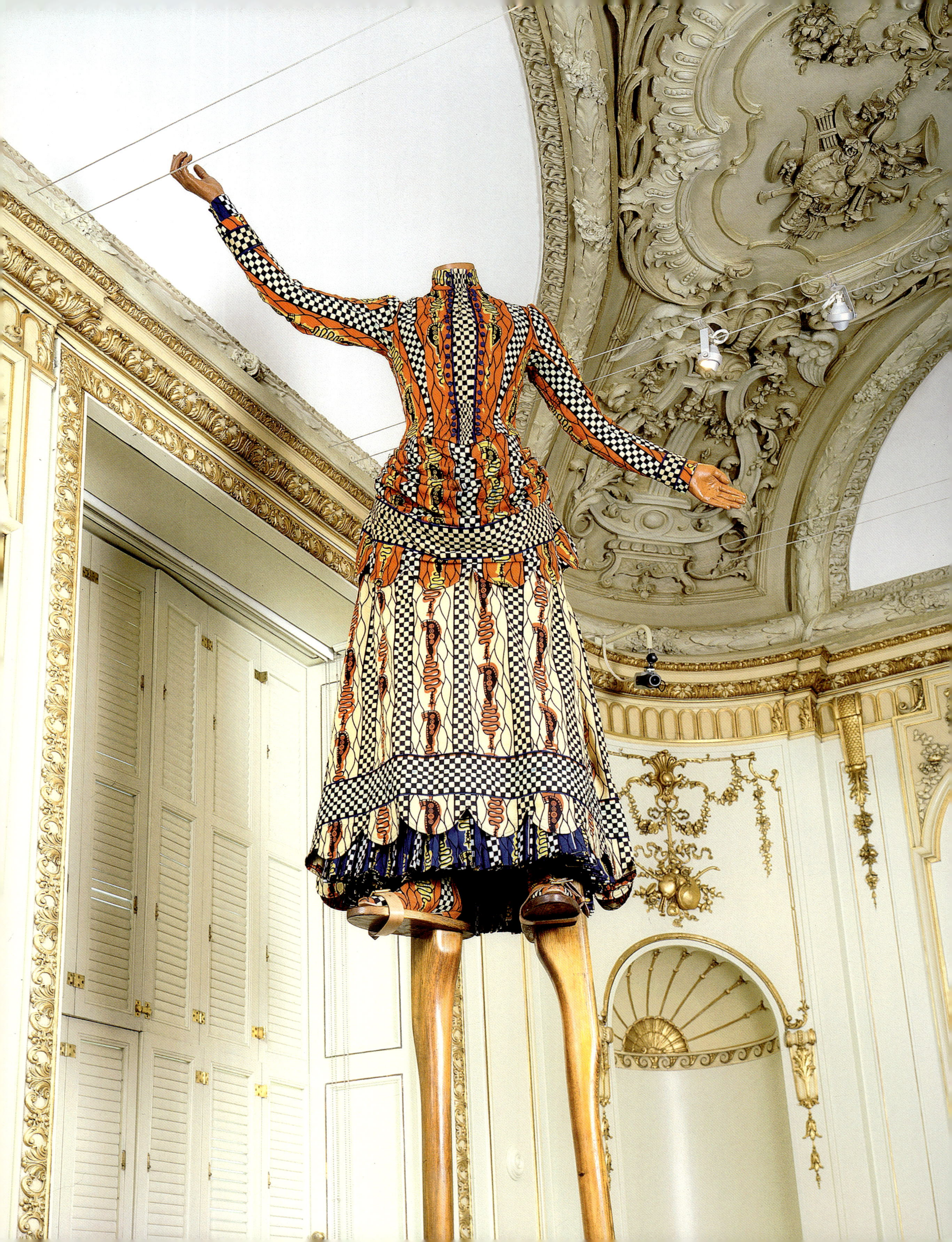

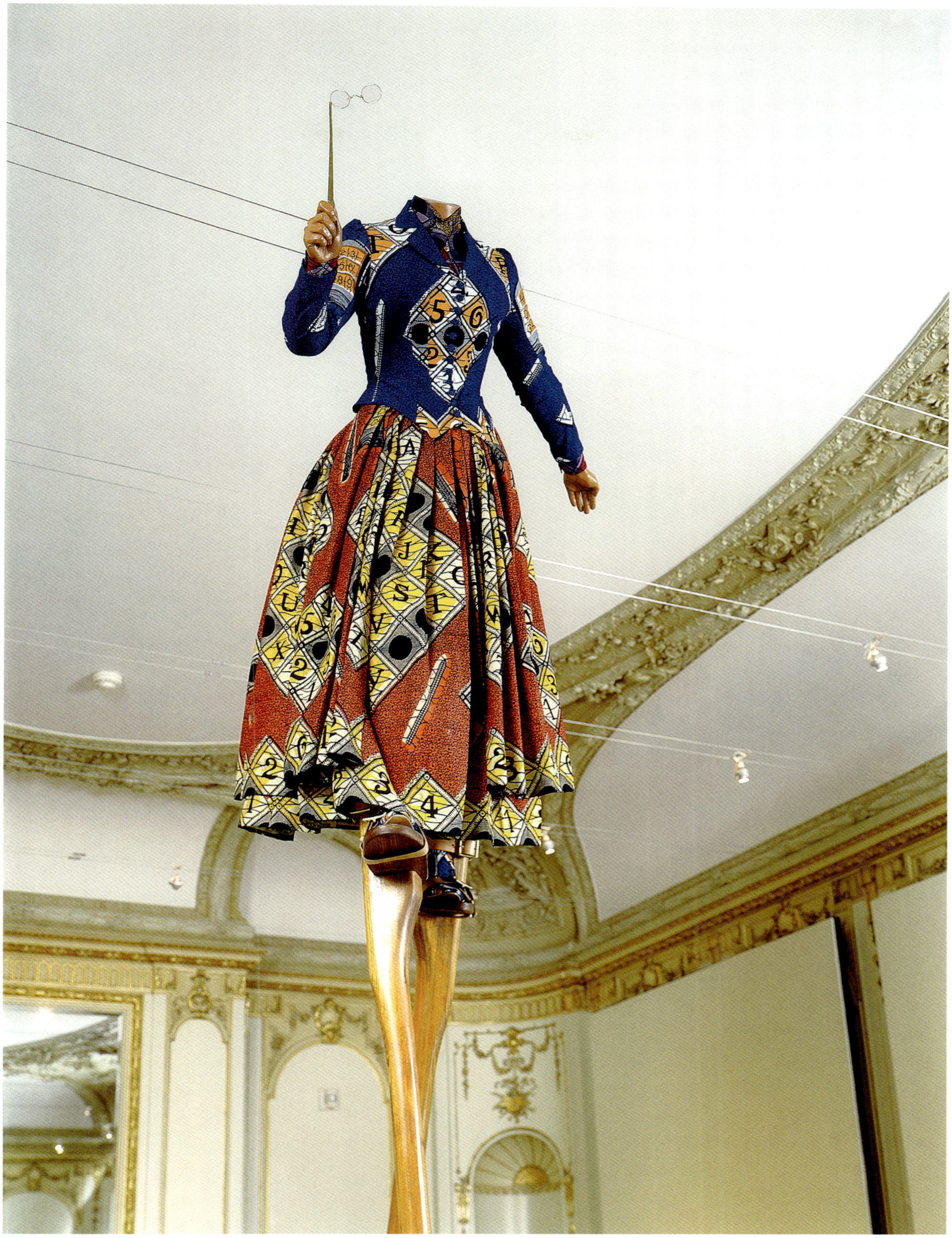

Opposite:

Eleanor Hewitt, 2005

Life-size mannequin, Dutch wax printed cotton, steel stands, stilts
150 x 50 x 58 cm (figure), 253 x 7.6 x 7.6 cm (stilts)
North Carolina Museum of Art
Installation view, Cooper-Hewitt, National Design Museum, New York, 2005

Sarah Hewitt, 2005

Life-size mannequin, Dutch wax printed cotton, steel stands, stilts
150 x 50 x 58 cm (figure), 253 x 7.6 x 7.6 cm (stilts)
Detroit Institute of Arts, museum purchase, W. Hawkins Ferry Fund, Friends of Modern Art Acquisition Fund, Janis and William Wetsman Foundation Fund, and funds from Lila and Gilbert B. Silverman, and Andrew L. and Gayle Shaw Camden Contemporary and Decorative Arts Fund 2006
Installation view, Cooper-Hewitt, National Design Museum, New York, 2005

Reverend on Ice, 2005

Life-size mannequin, semi-opaque synthetic polymer resin, Dutch wax printed cotton, wool, leather, wood, steel
160 x 402.3 x 601.5 cm
National Gallery of Victoria, Melbourne, purchased with the assistance of NGV Contemporary, 2006

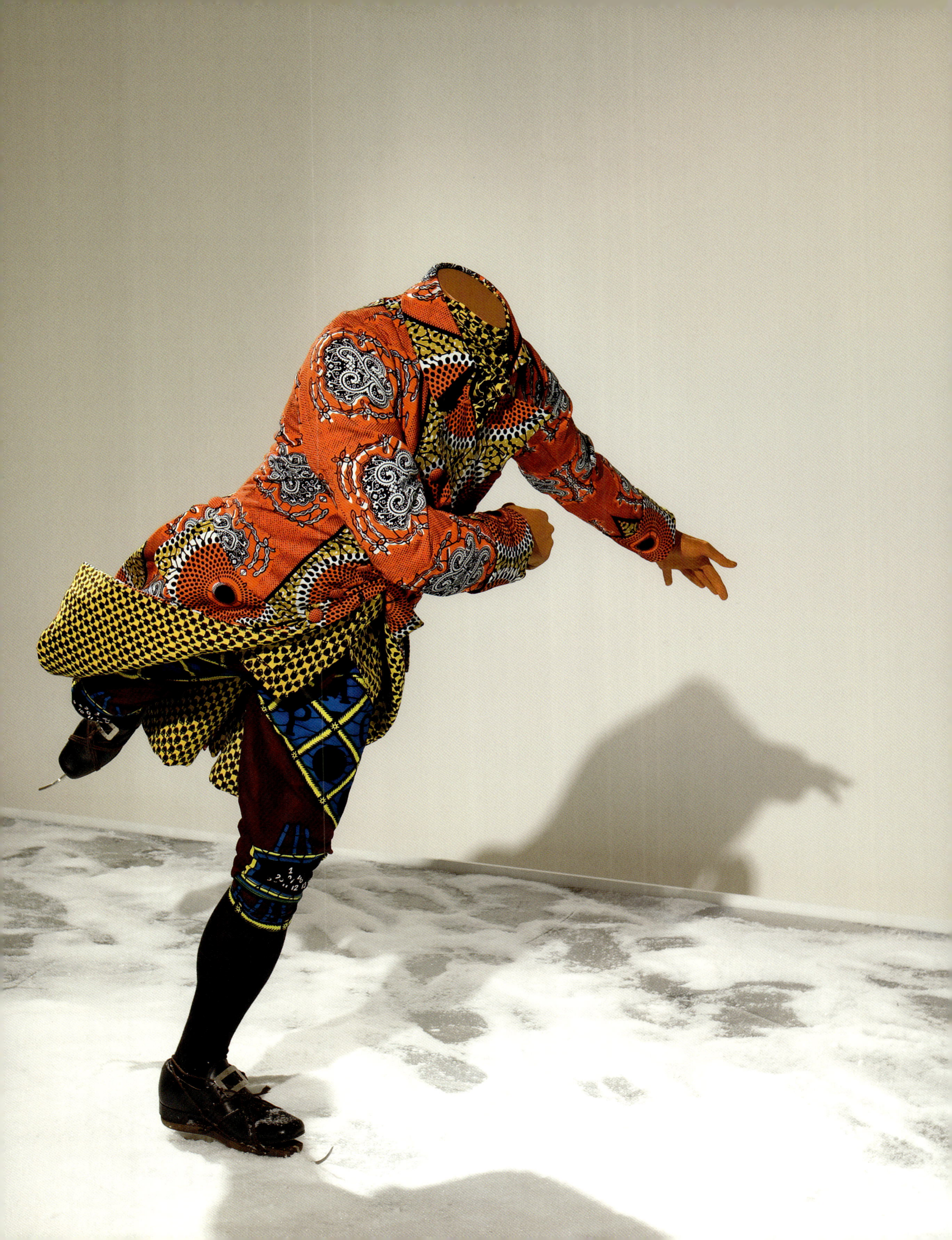

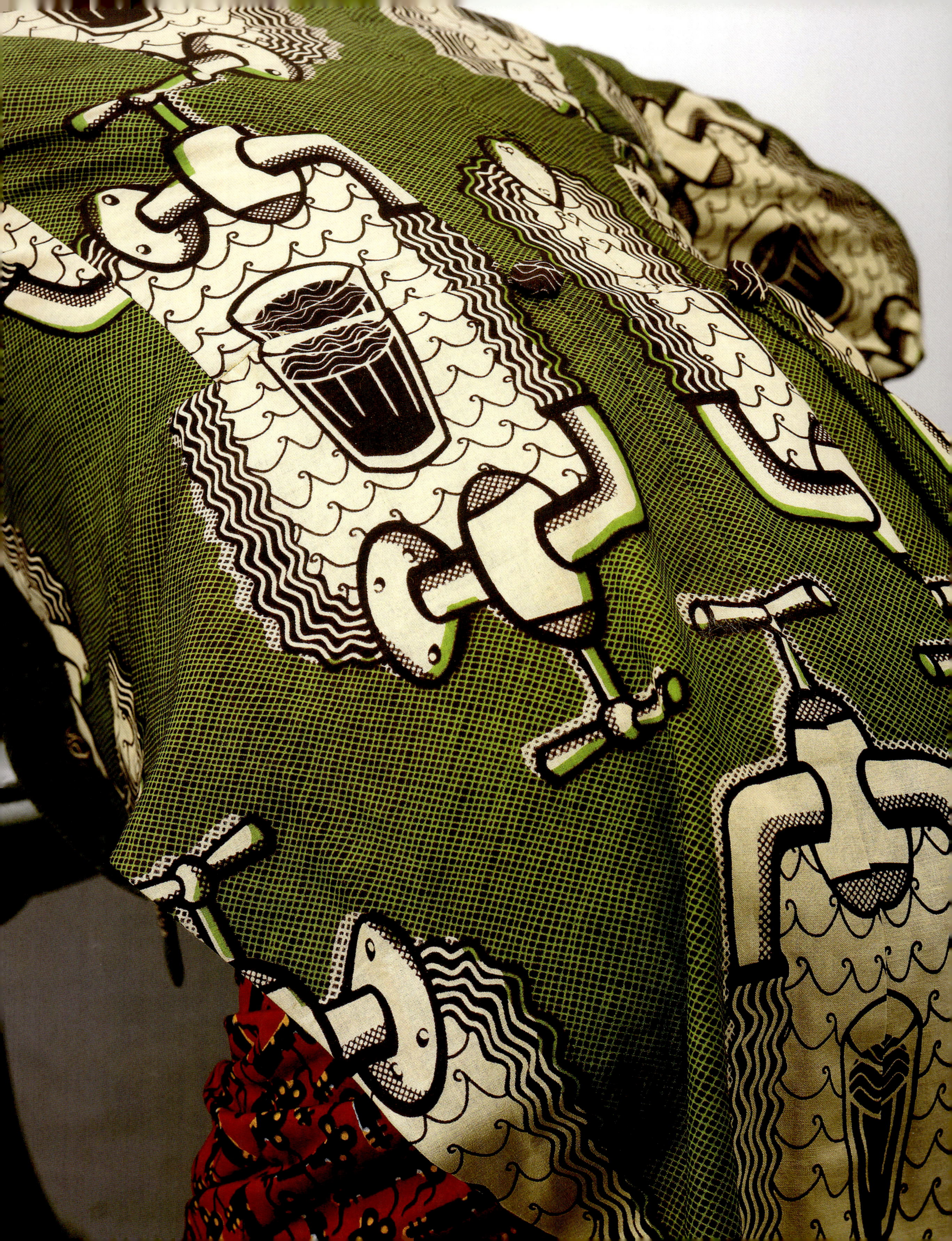

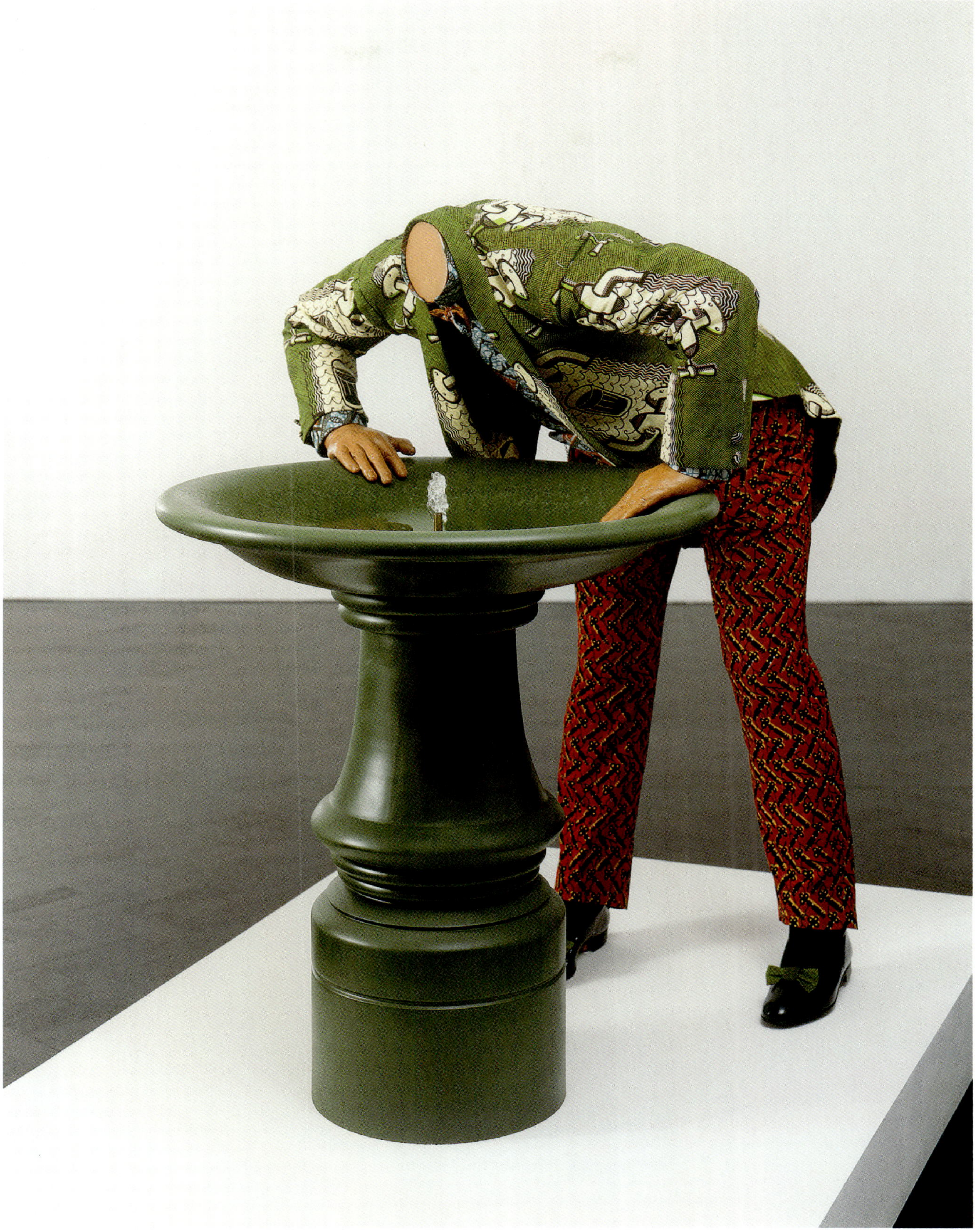

Headless Man Trying to Drink, 2005

Life-size mannequin, fountain, Dutch wax printed cotton,
polymer-gypsum fountain, water pump
130 x 110 x 140 cm
Collection of Melva Bucksbaum and Raymond Learsy

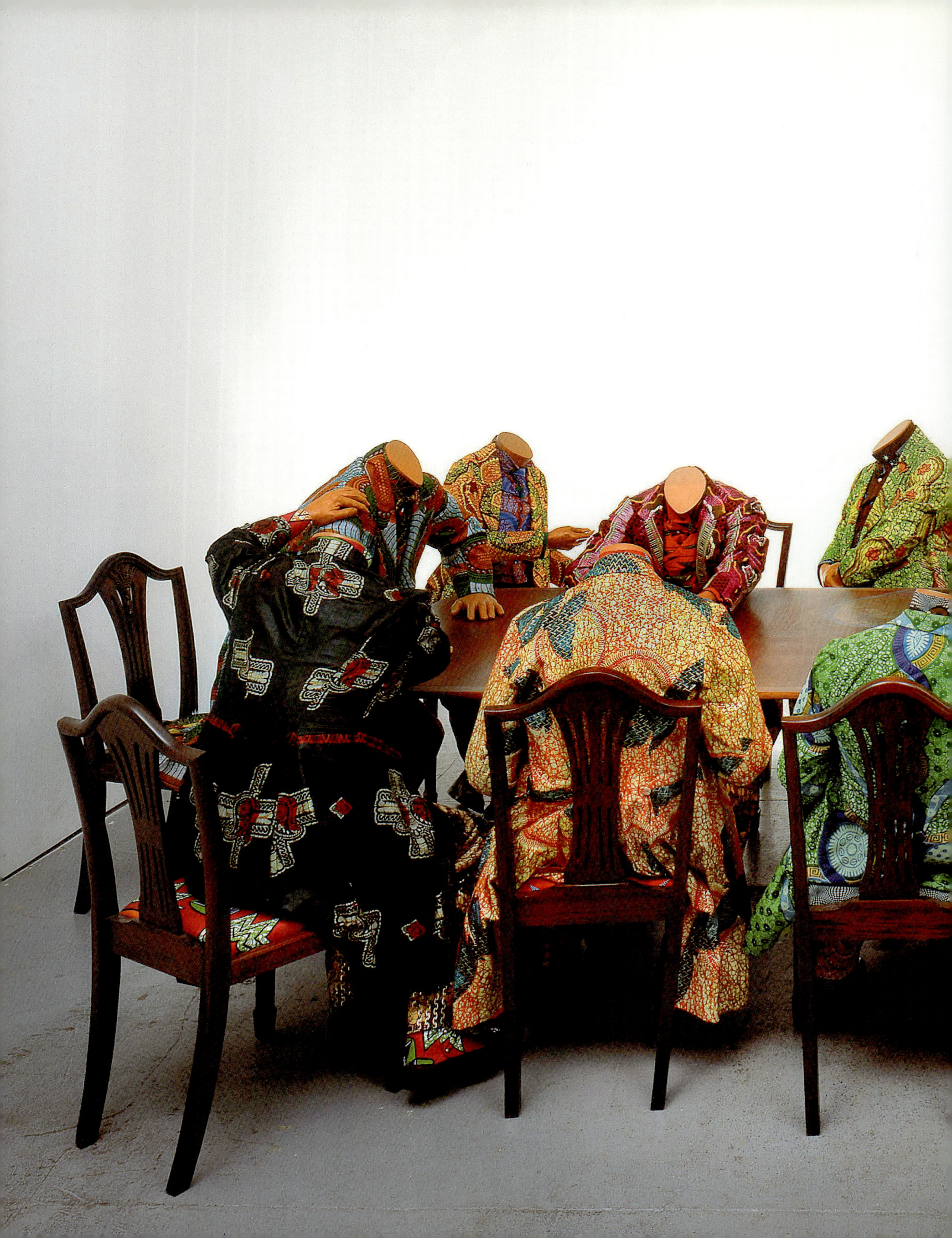

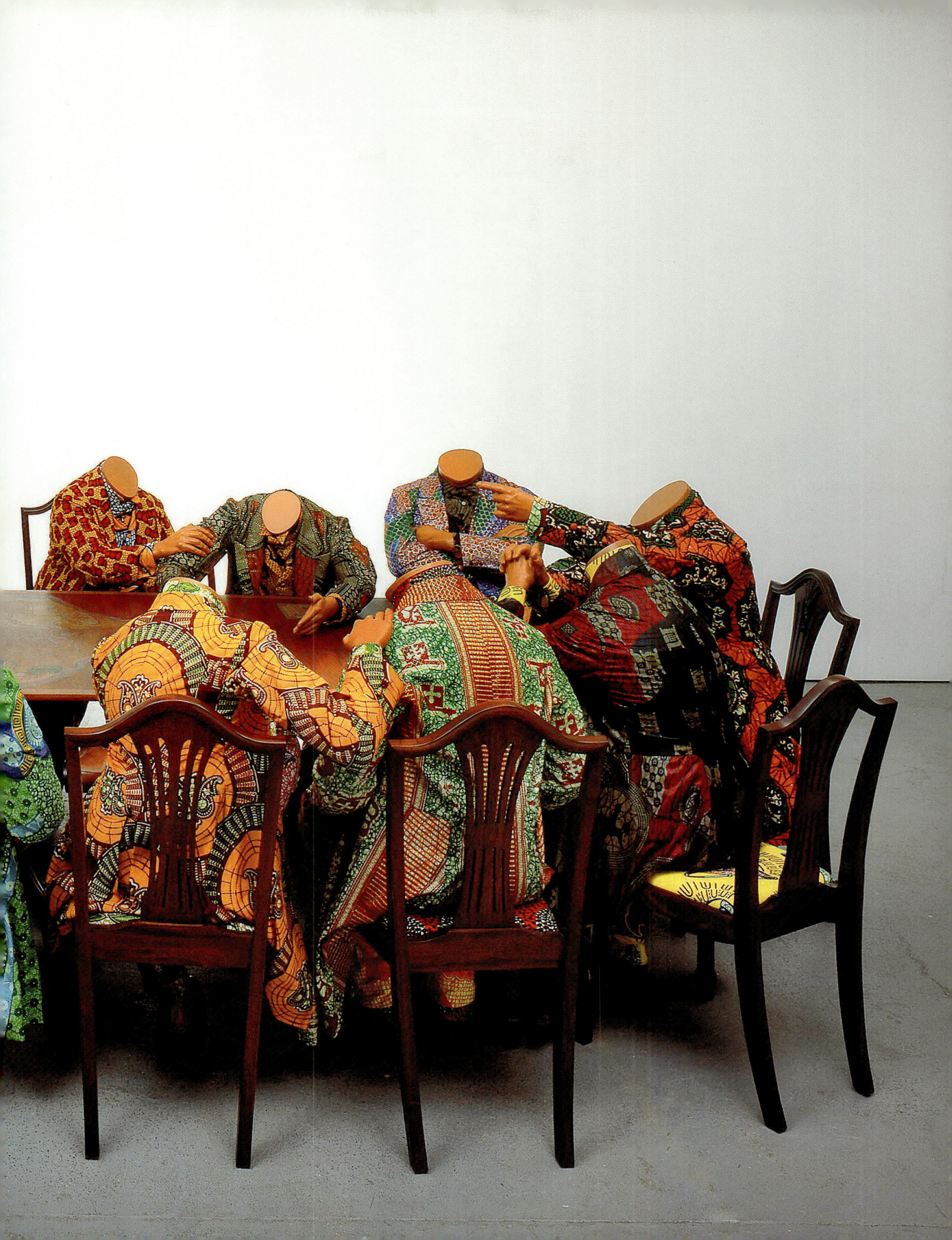

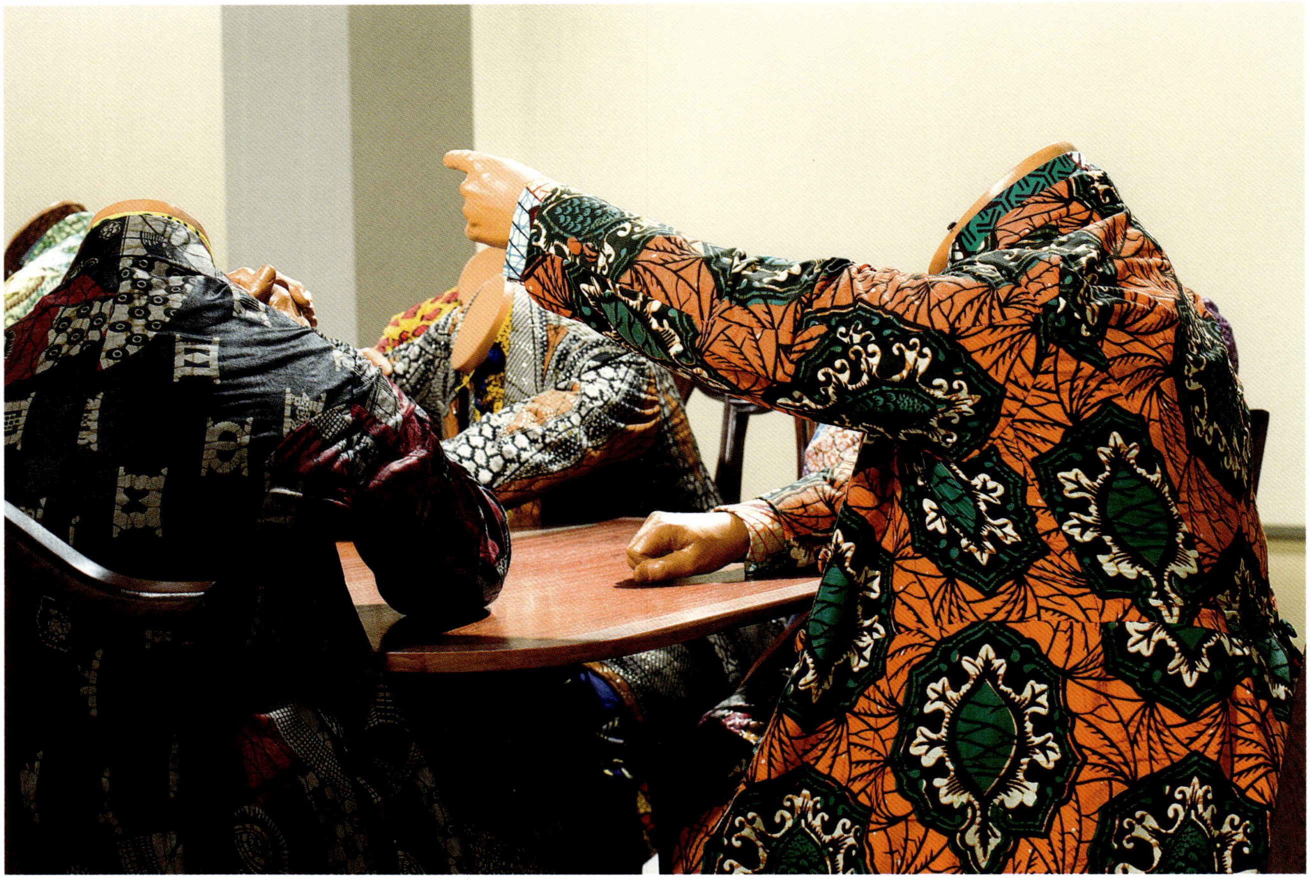

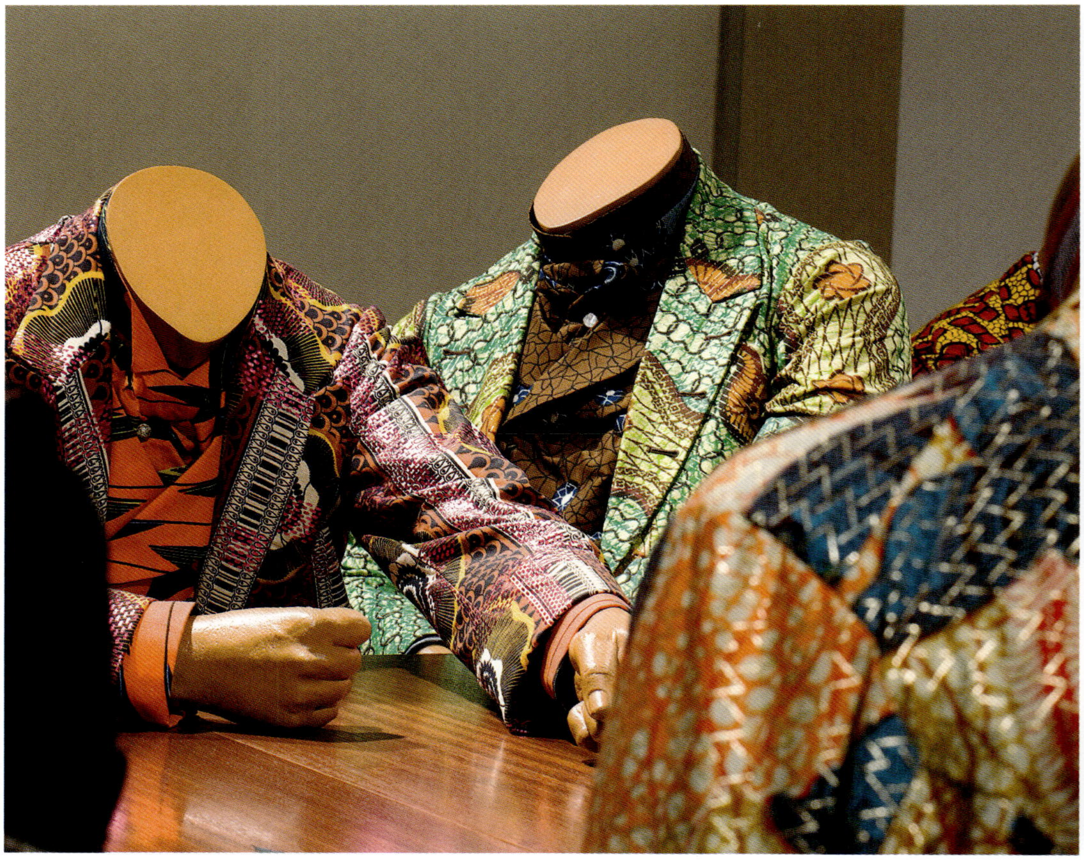

This and preceding spread:

Scramble for Africa, 2003

Fourteen life-size mannequins, fourteen chairs, table, Dutch wax printed cotton
132 x 488 x 280 cm
The Pinnell Collection, Dallas; commissioned by the Museum for African Art, New York

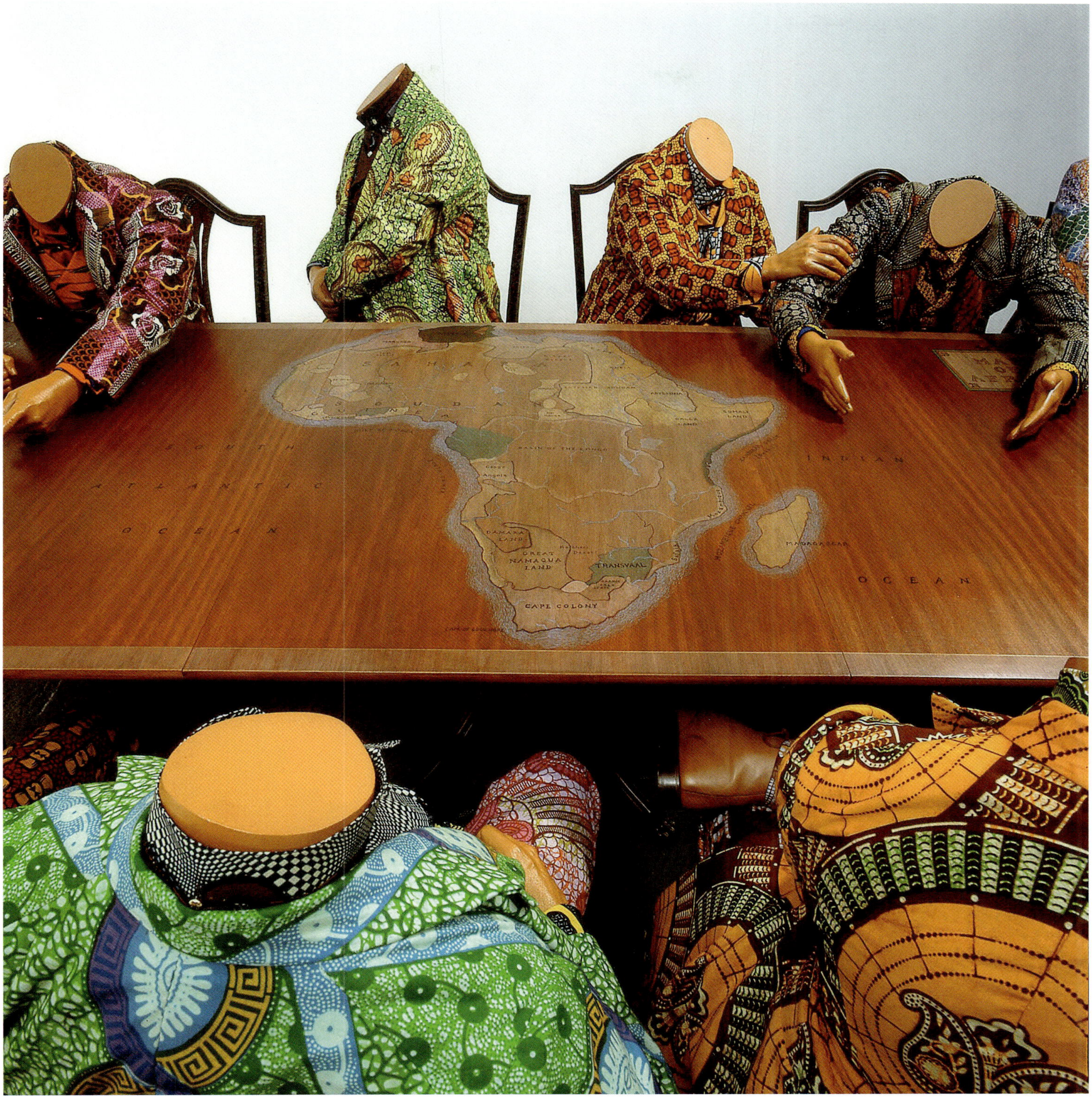
DAMARA LAND
GREAT NAMAQUA LAND
TRANSVAAL
CAPE COLONY
MADAGASCAR
INDIAN
OCEAN
OCEAN

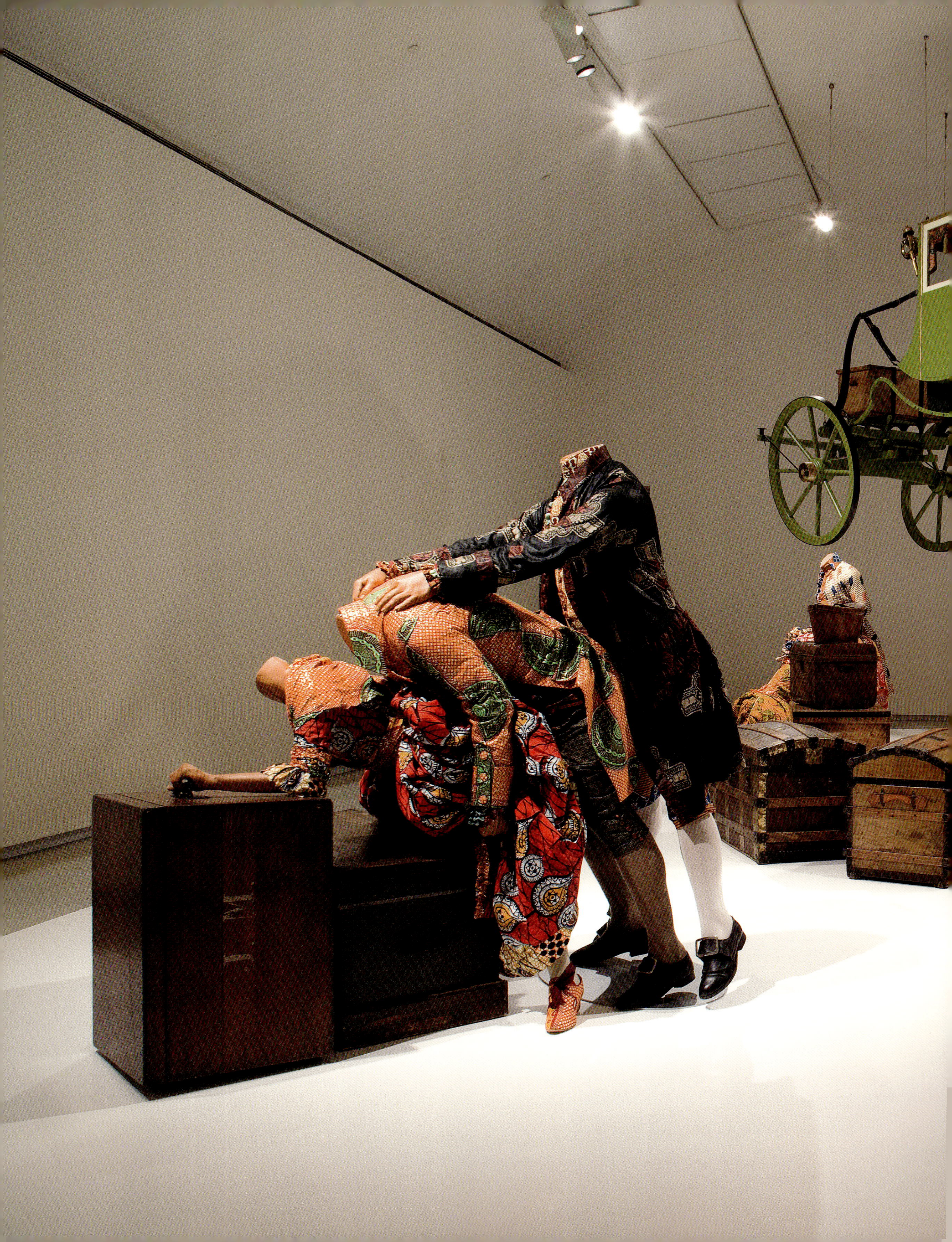
J.M.

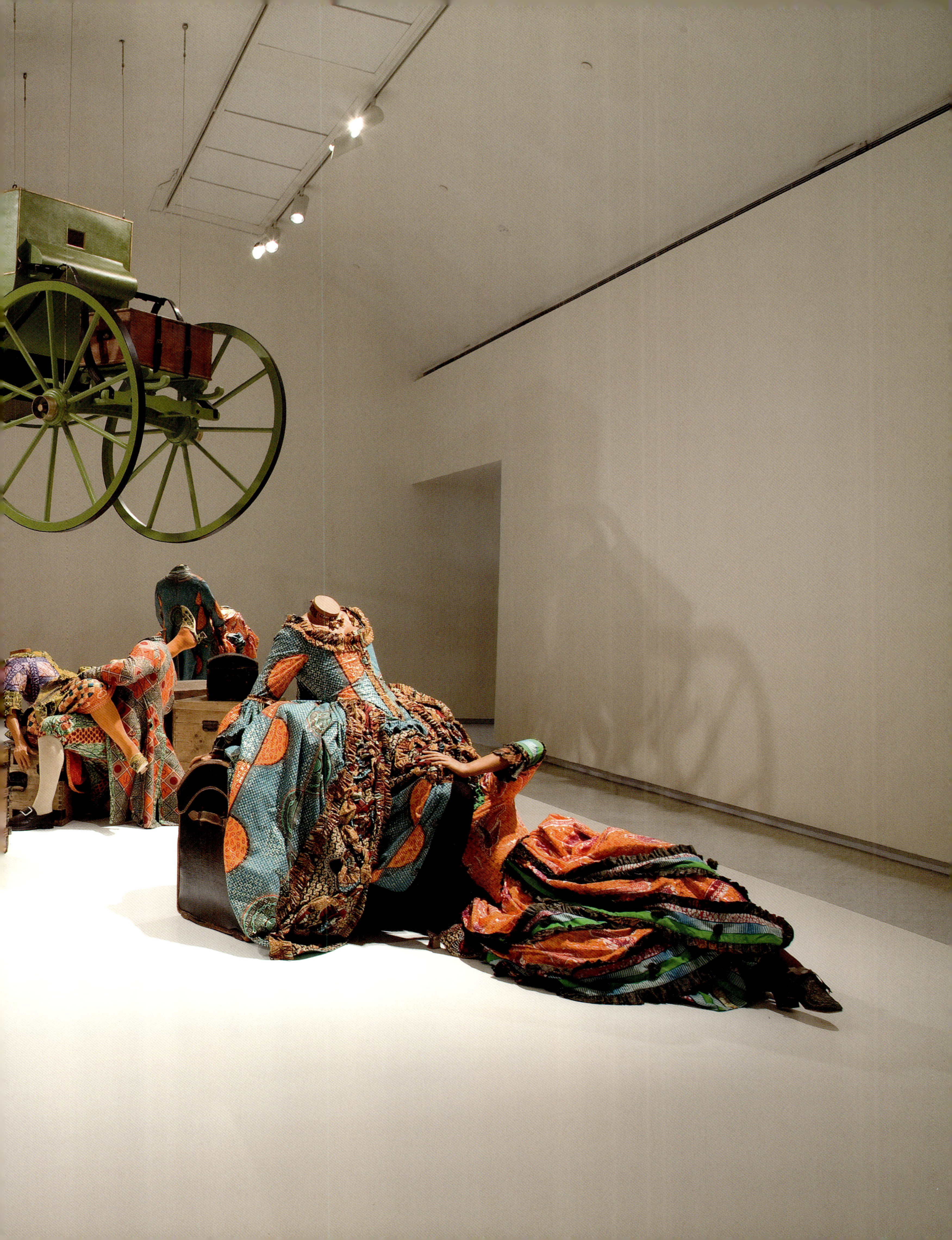

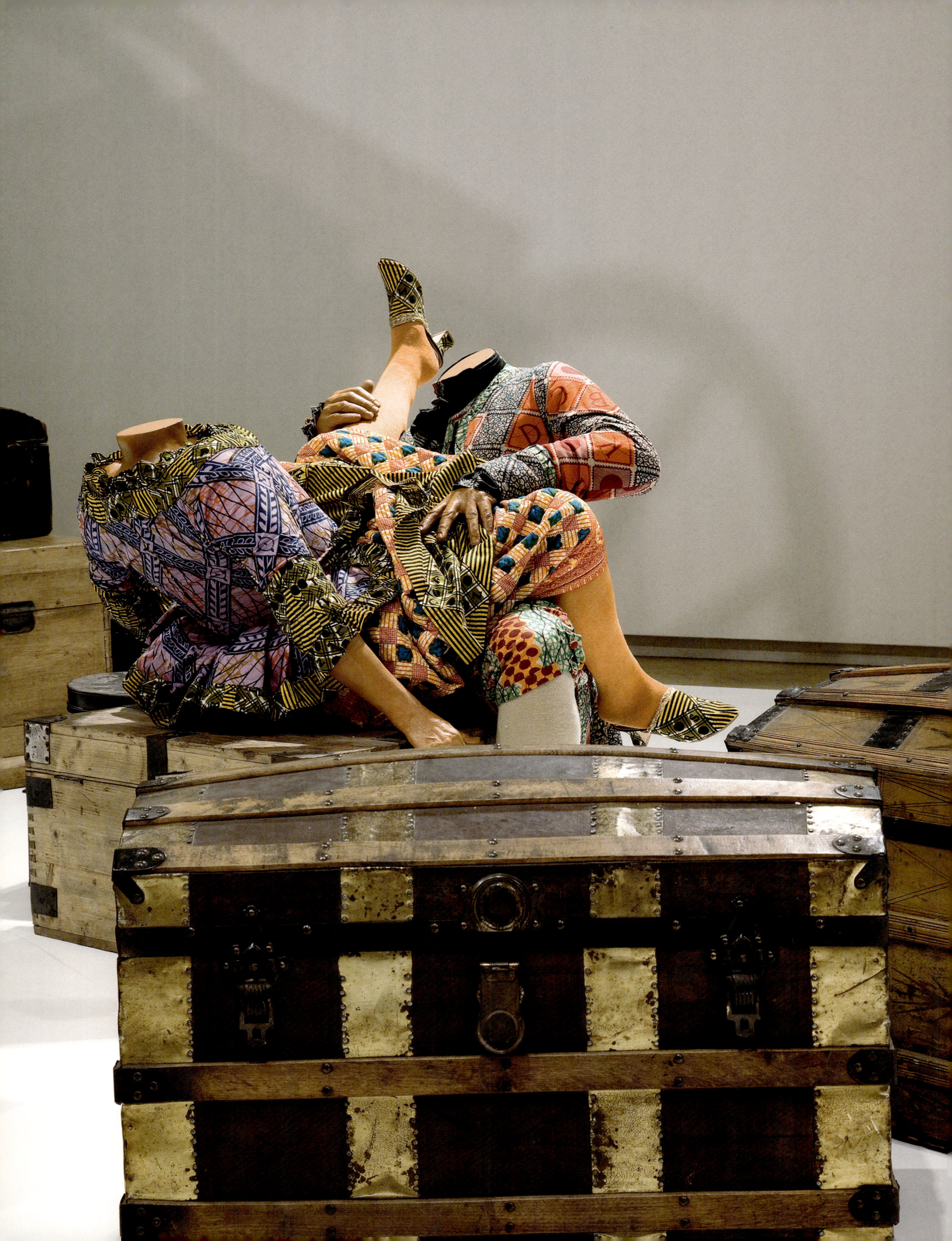

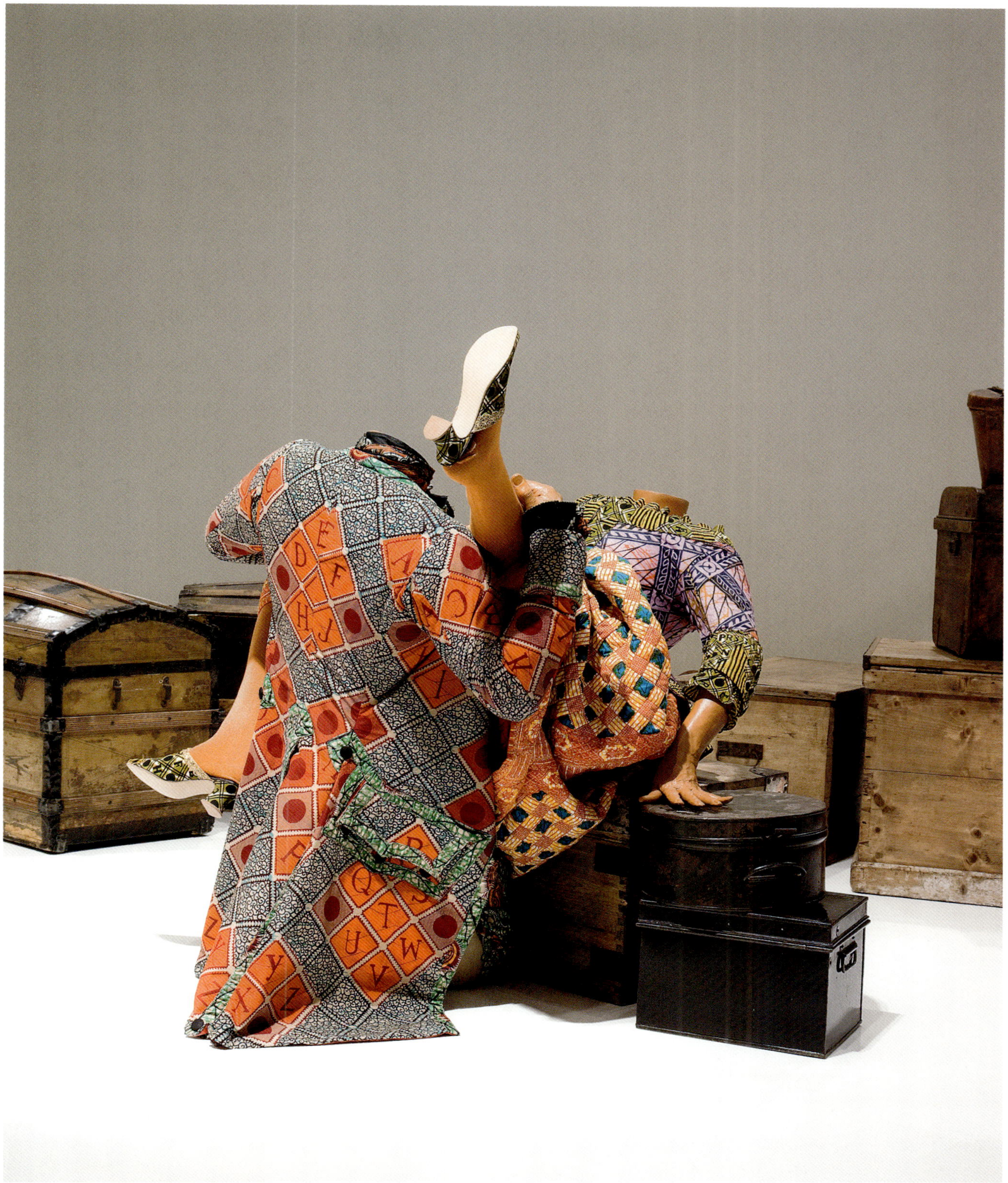

This and preceding spread, overleaf:

Gallantry and Criminal Conversation, 2002

Eleven life-size mannequins, metal and wood cases, Dutch wax printed cotton, leather, wood, steel
200 x 260 x 470 cm (carriage), overall dimensions variable
Commissioned by Okwui Enwezor for Documenta 11, 2002
Installation view, Museum of Contemporary Art Australia, 2008

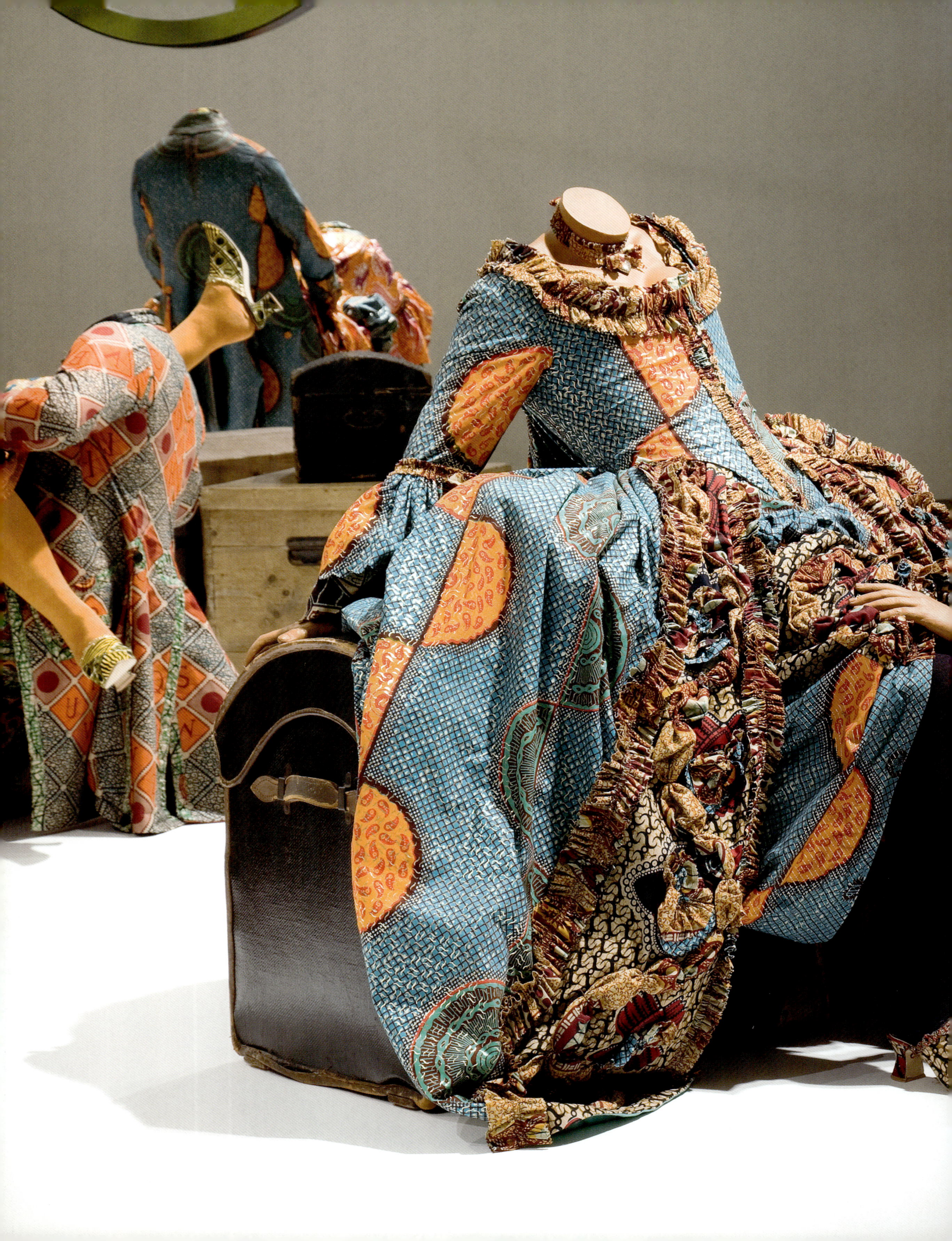

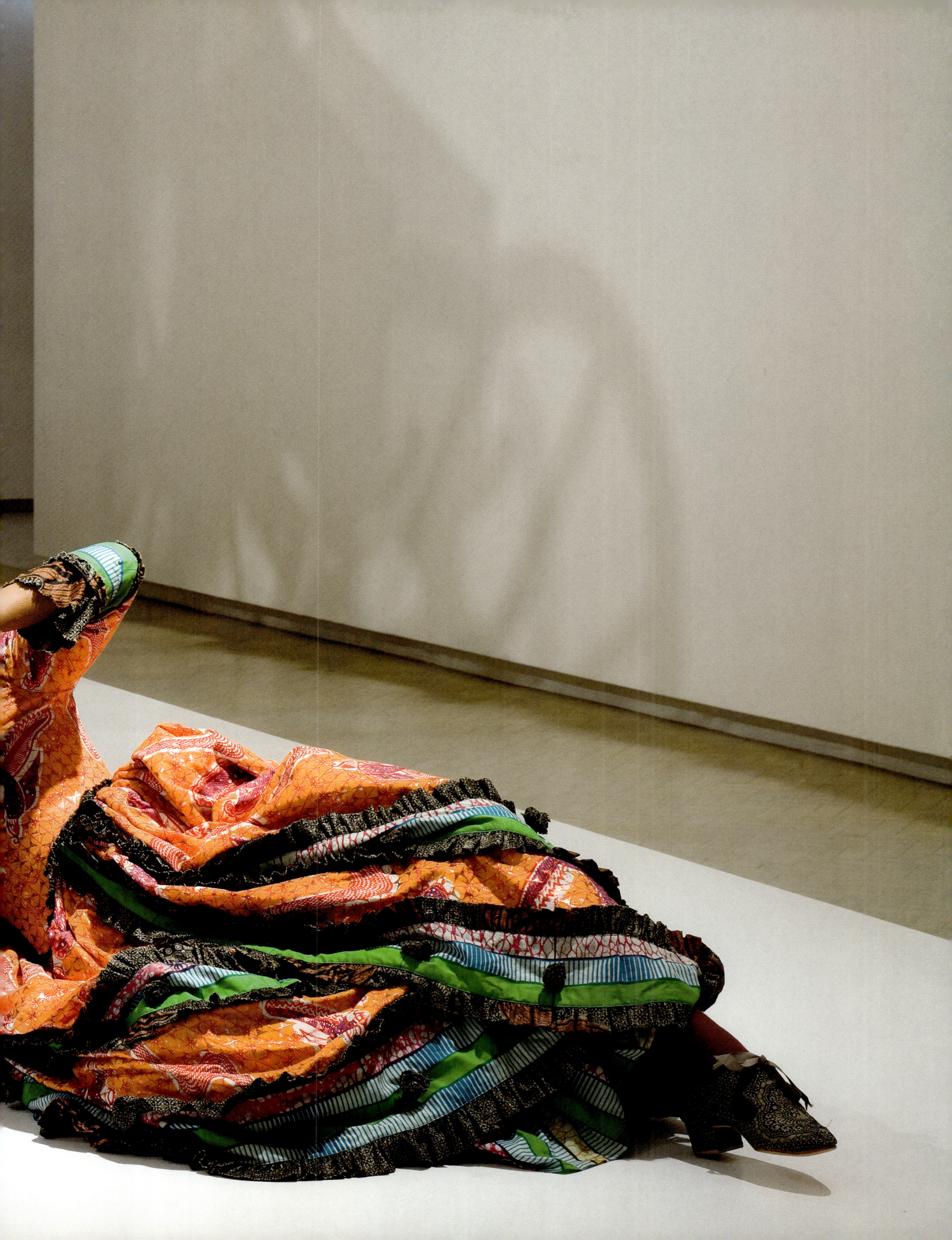

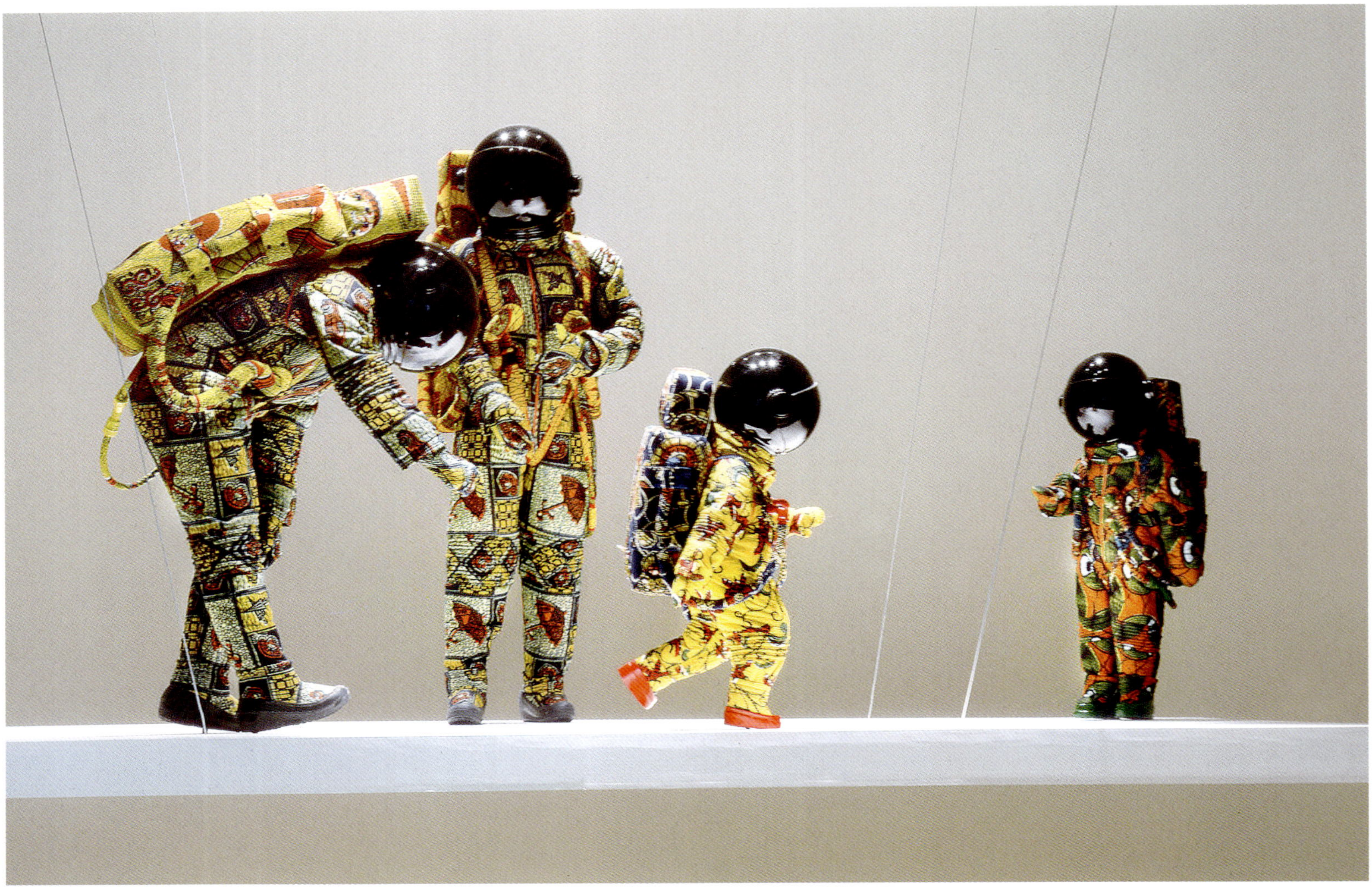

Vacation, 2000

Four mannequins, plastic, Dutch wax printed cotton
152.5 x 61 x 61 cm (each of two figures), 101.6 x 61 x 61 cm (each of two figures)
The Israel Museum, Jerusalem, gift of the New York Contemporary Art Acquisitions Committee of American Friends of the Israel Museum

Opposite:

Space Walk, 2002

Screen-printed cotton, fiberglass, plywood, vinyl, plastic, steel
212 x 63 x 56 cm (each figure), 370 x 153 x 153 cm (spaceship)
Installation view, Art Basel, 2003

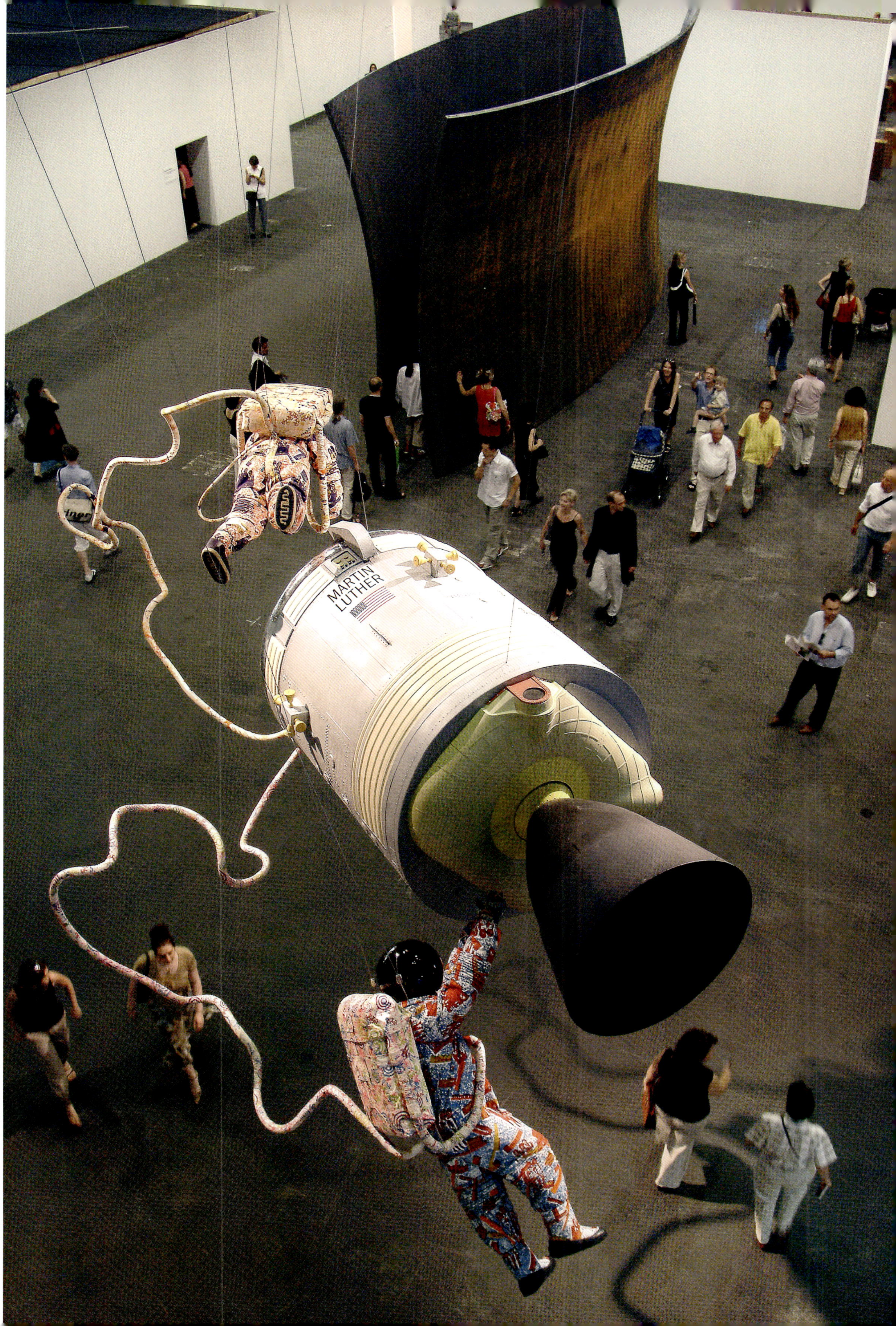
MARTIN
LUTHER

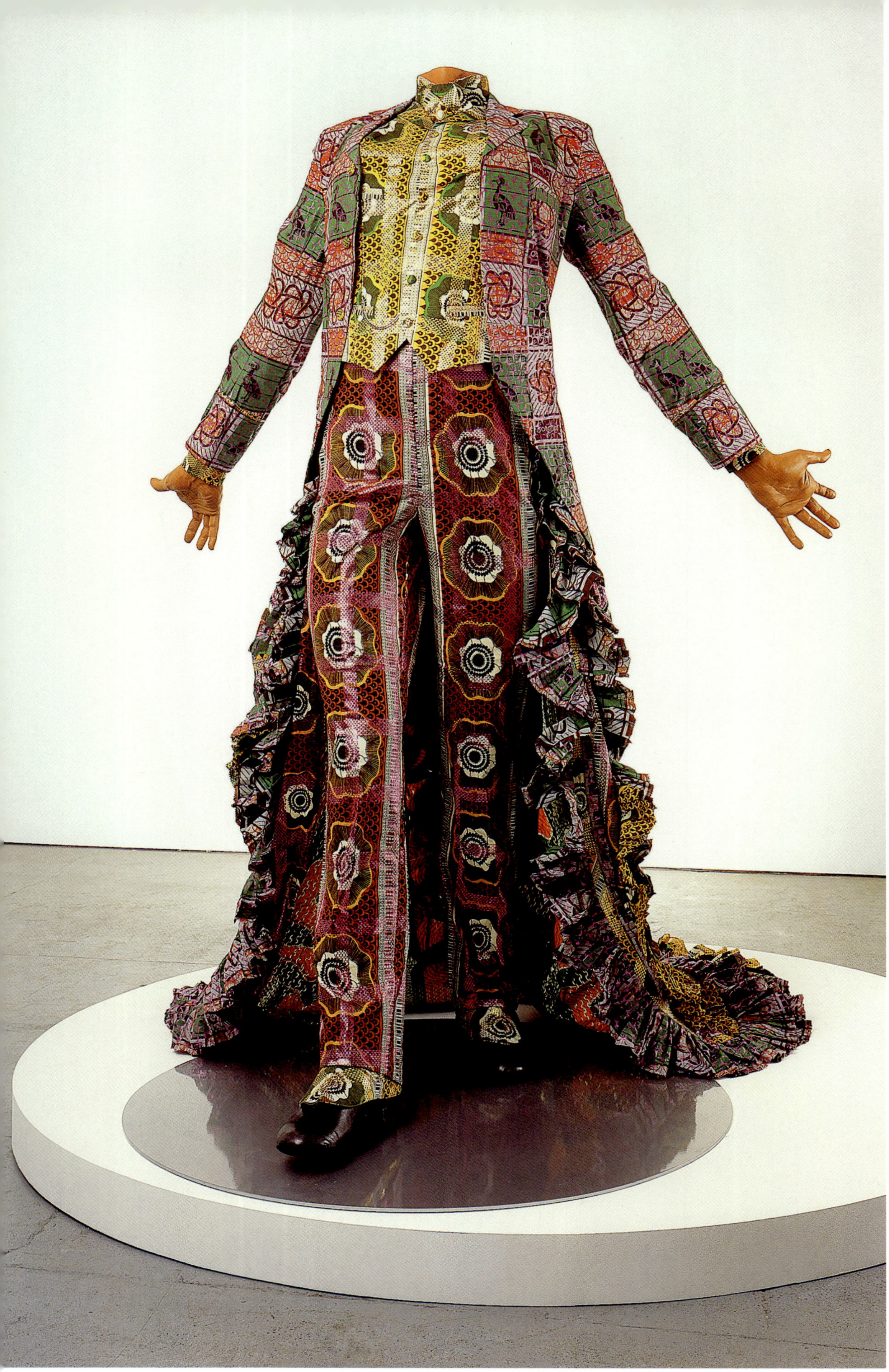

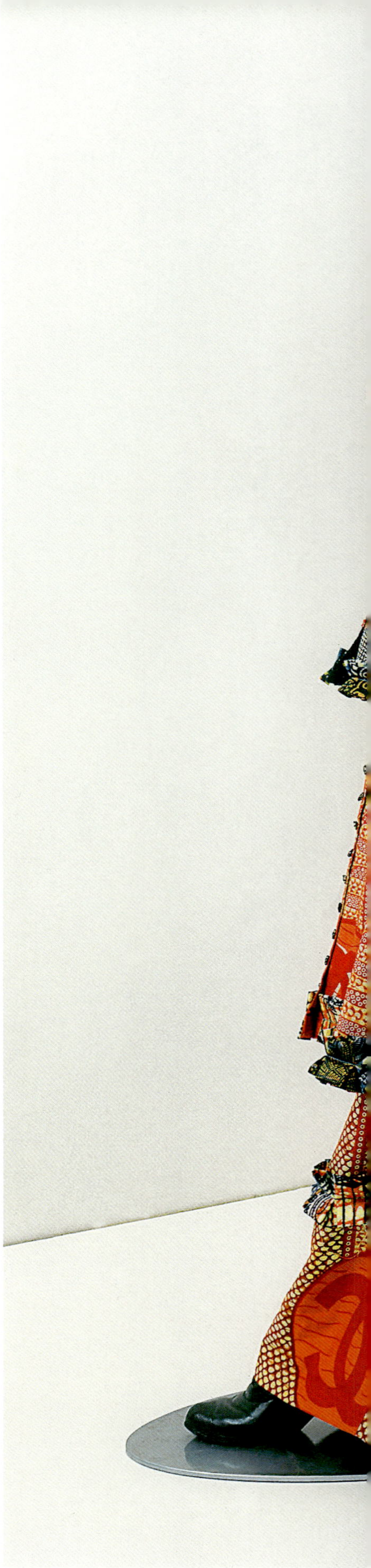

Big Boy, 2002

Life-size mannequin, Dutch wax printed cotton
215 x 170 x 140 cm
Art Institute of Chicago, gift of Susan and Lewis Manilow, 2004

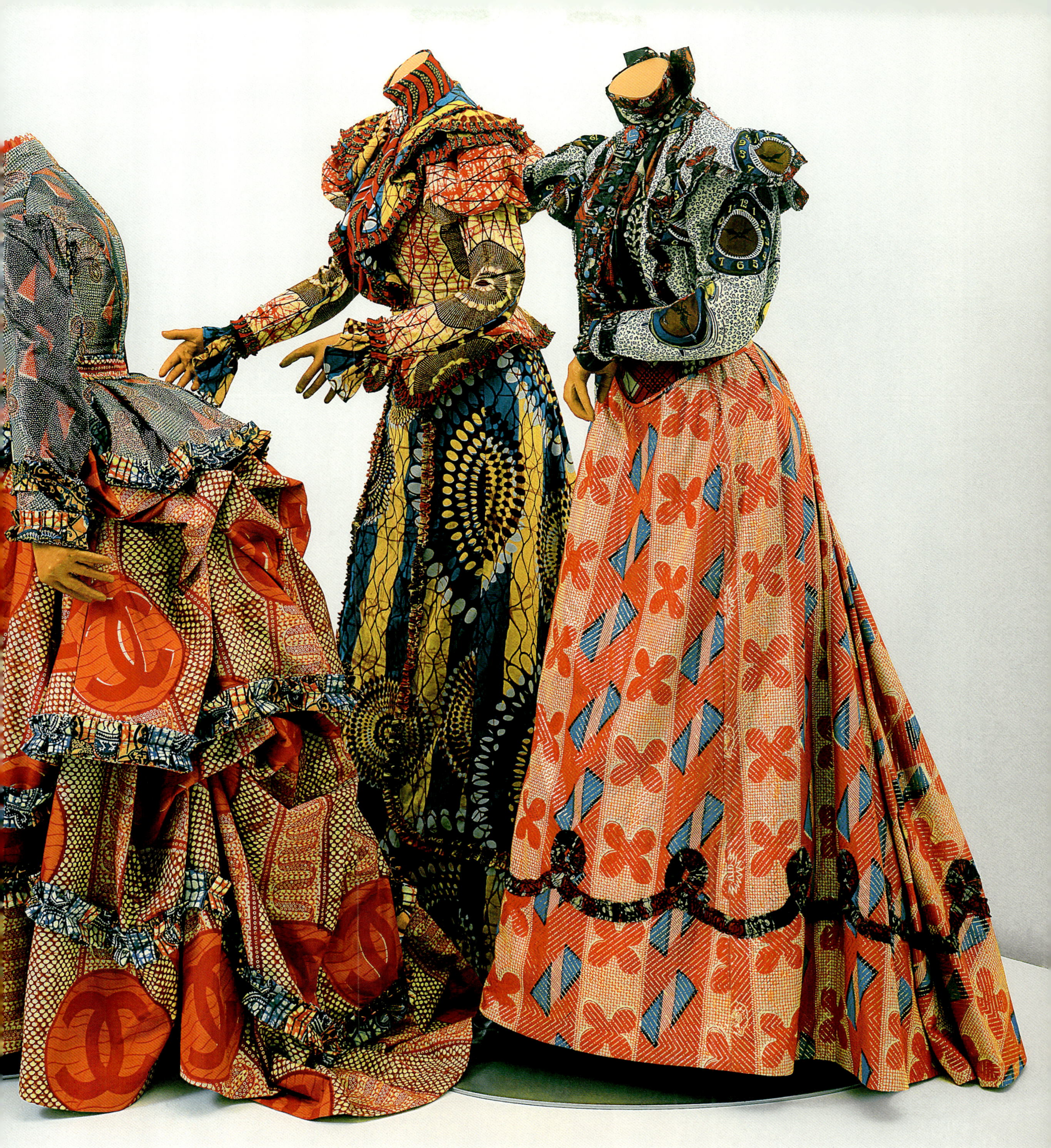

Three Graces, 2001

Three life-size mannequins, Dutch wax printed cotton
Dimensions variable
Speed Art Museum, Louisville, Kentucky, purchased with funds from the Alice Speed Stoll Accessions Trust

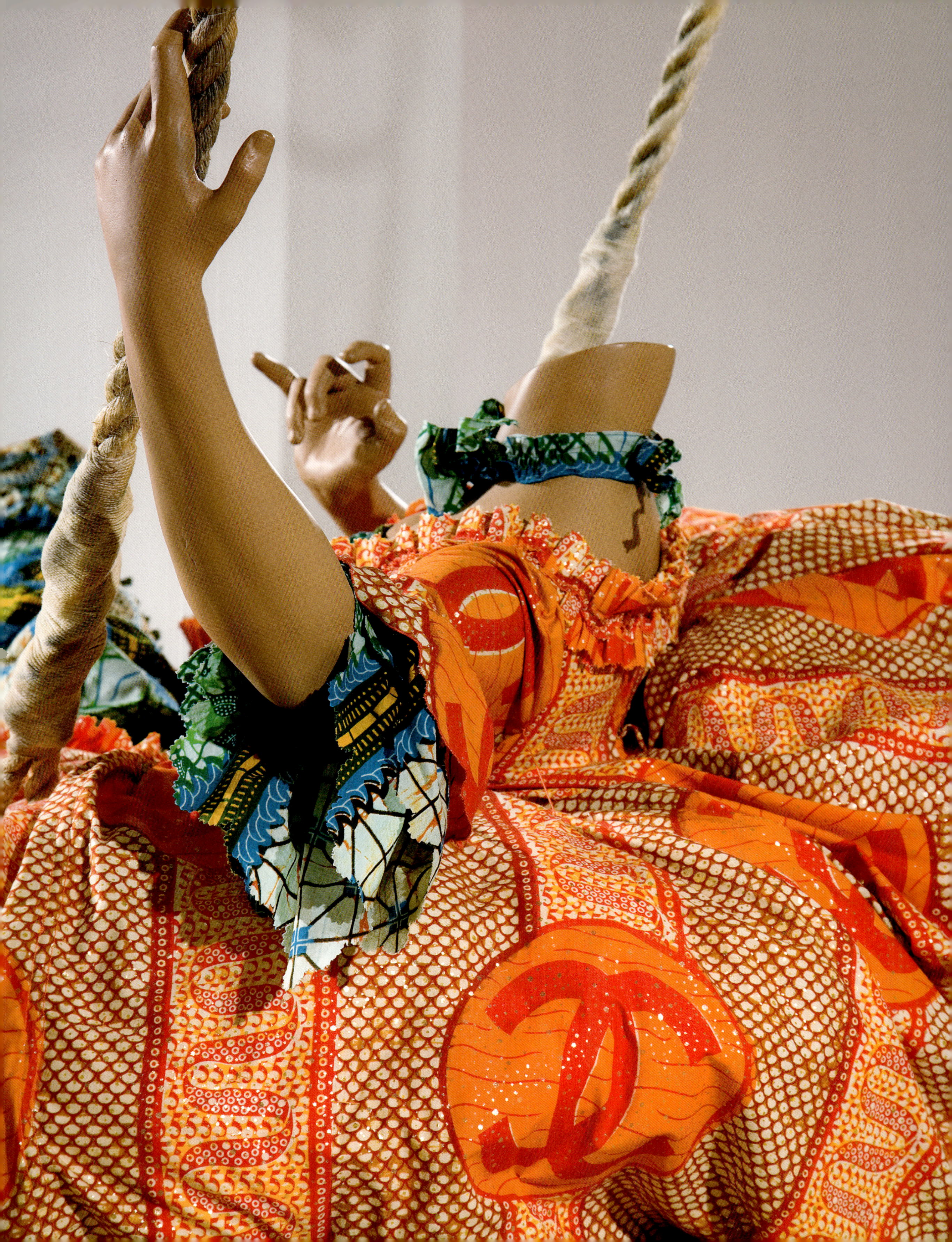

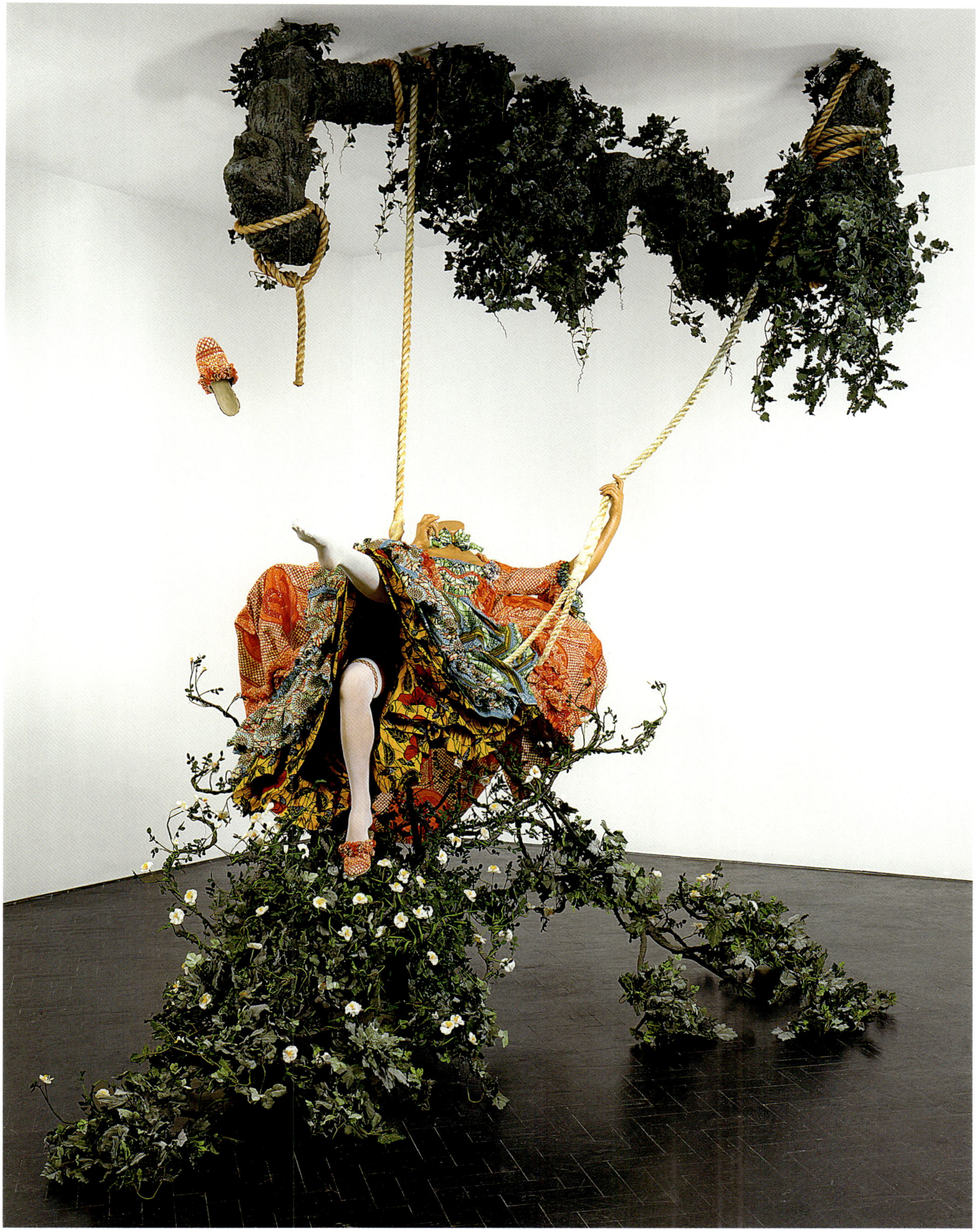

The Swing (after Fragonard), 2001

Dutch wax printed cotton, life-size mannequin, swing, artificial foliage
330 x 350 x 220 cm
Tate, purchased 2001

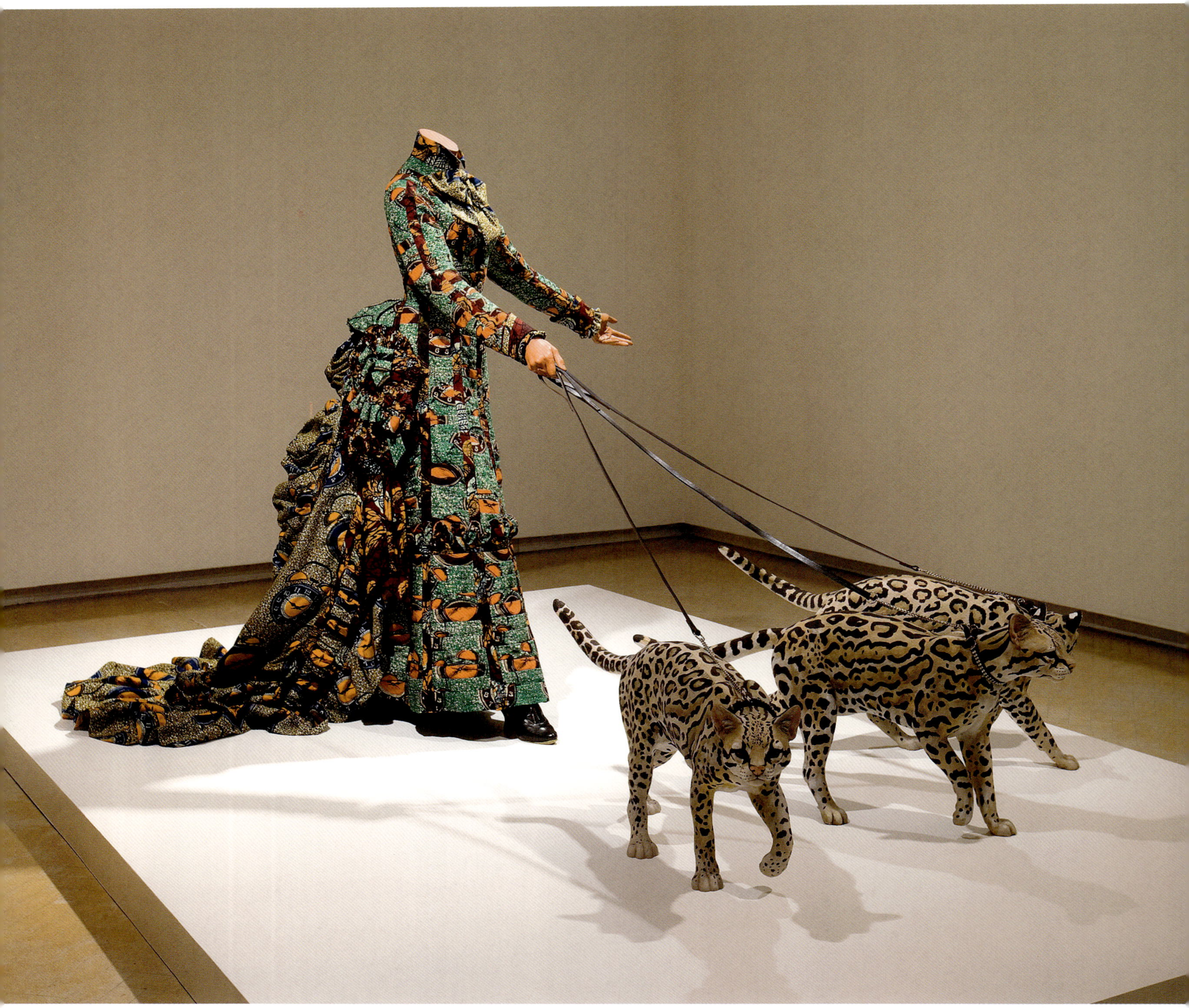

Leisure Lady (with Ocelots), 2001

Life-size mannequin, three fiberglass ocelots, Dutch wax printed cotton, leather, glass
160 x 80 x 80 cm (figure), 40 x 60 x 20 cm (each ocelot), overall dimensions variable
Vanhaerents Art Collection, Brussels

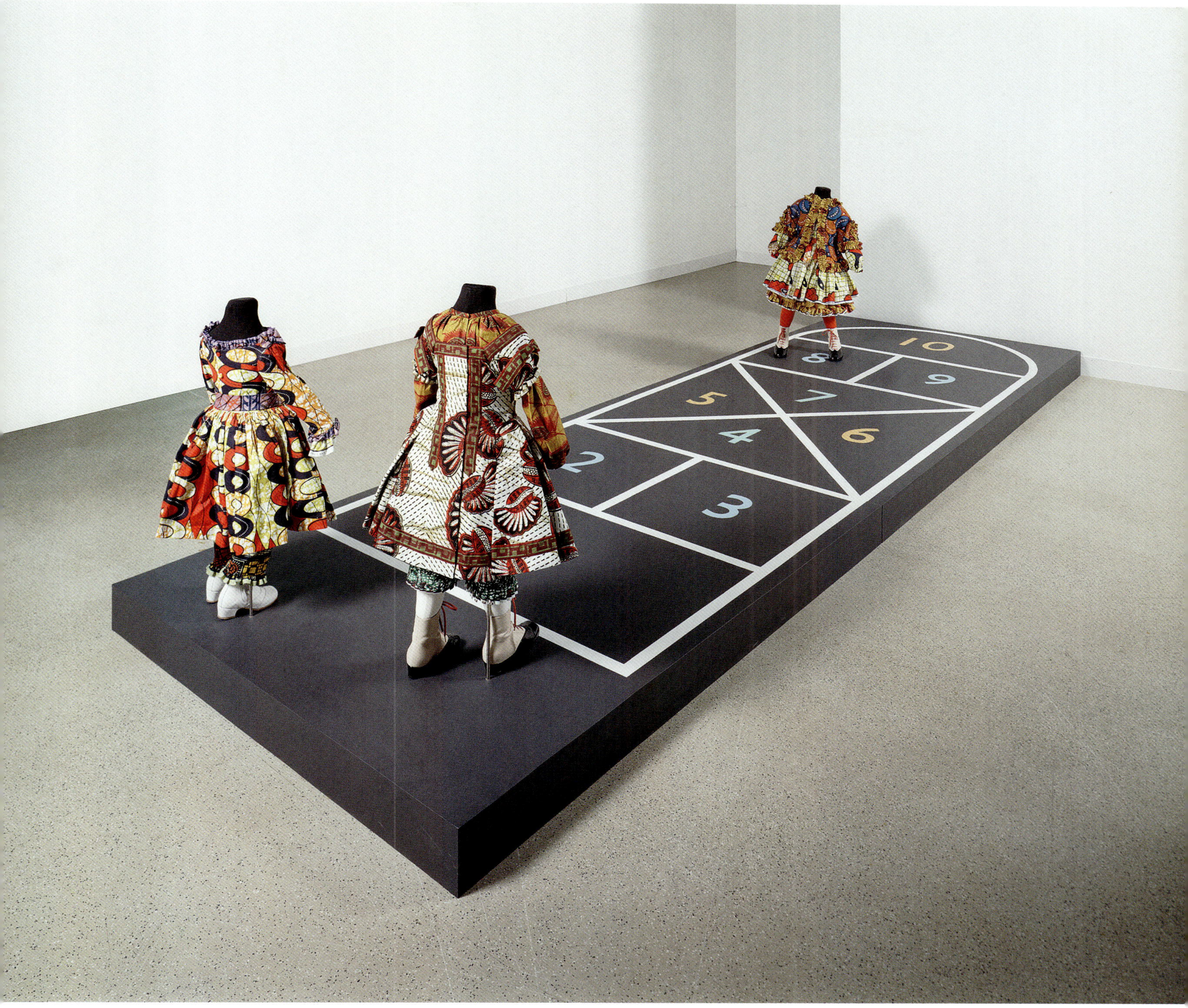

Hopscotch, 2000

Three life-size mannequins, mixed media, Dutch wax printed cotton, wood plinth
110 x 50 x 50 cm (each figure), 12.6 x 453 x 139.4 cm (plinth)
Collection of Ninah and Michael Lynne

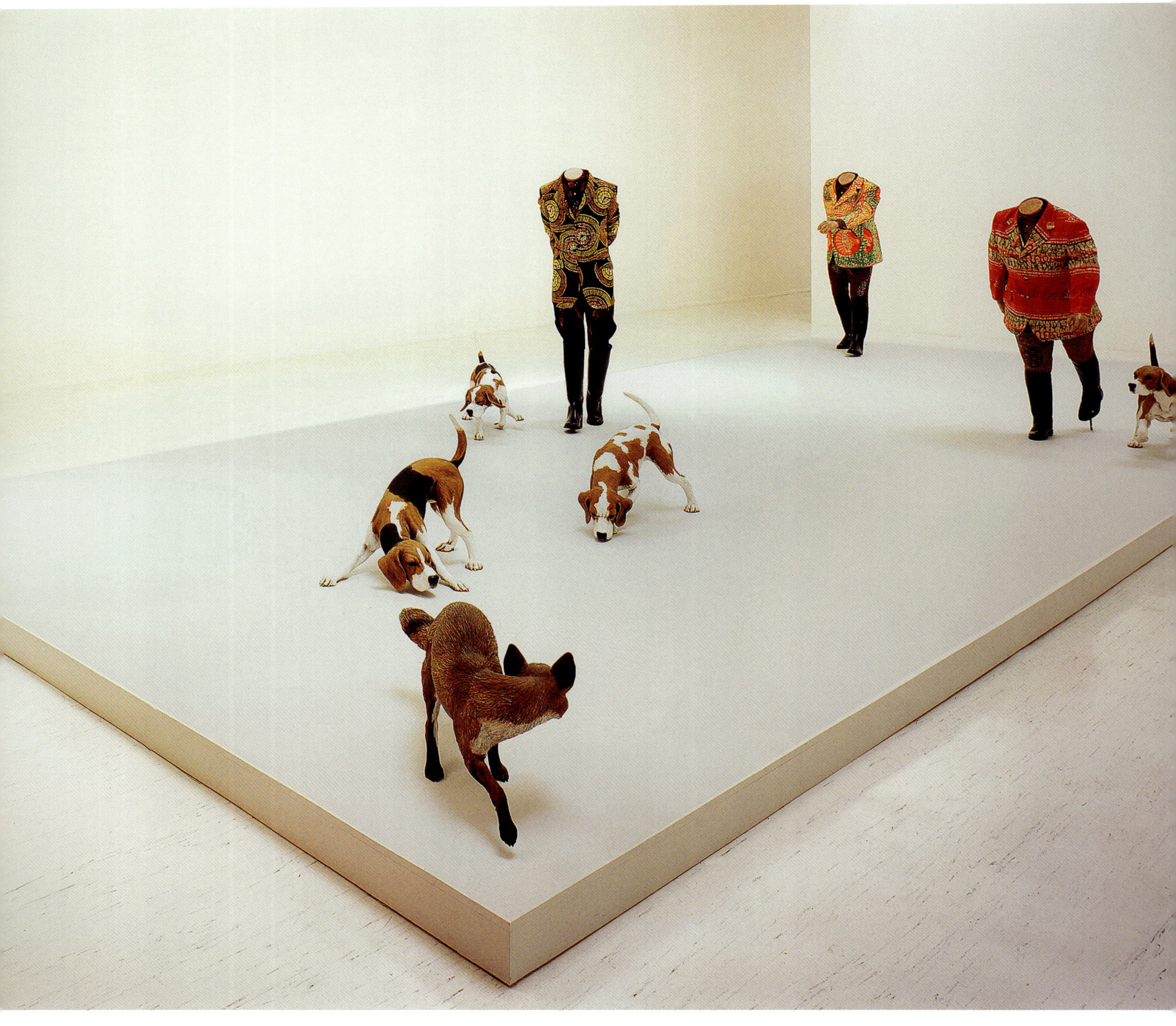

Hound, 2000

Three life-size mannequins, four fiberglass dogs, fiberglass fox,
Dutch wax printed cotton
960 x 397 x 170 cm
Collections of Peter Norton and Eileen Harris Norton,
Santa Monica, California

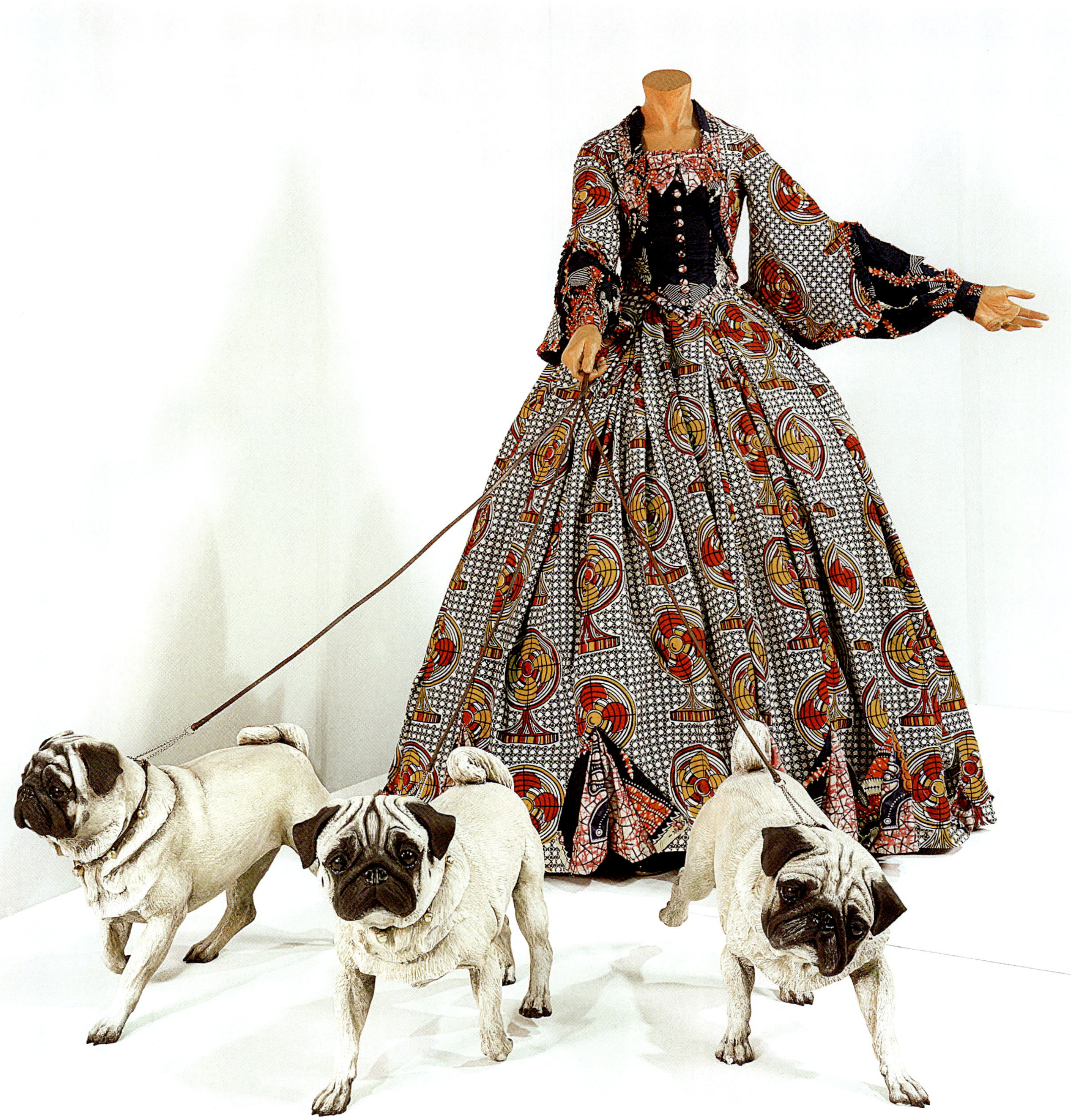

Leisure Lady (with Pugs), 2001

Life-size mannequin, three fiberglass dogs, Dutch wax printed cotton leather
160 x 80 x 80 cm (figure), 40 x 60 x 20 cm (each dog), overall dimensions variable
Collection of Jerome L. and Ellen Stern

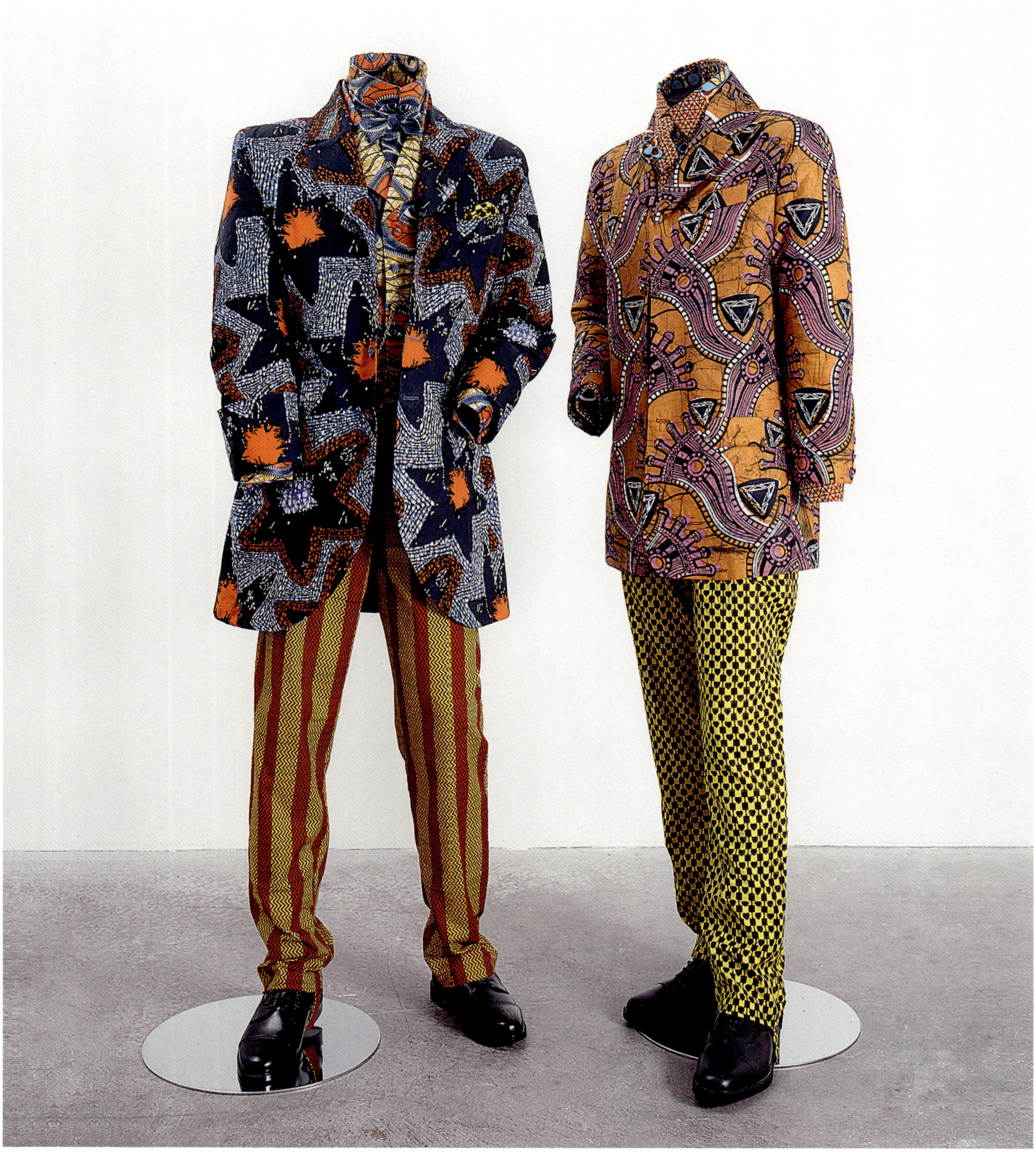

Affectionate Men, 1999

Two life-size mannequins, Dutch wax printed cotton, mixed media
152.5 x 61 x 61 cm (each figure)
Fondazione Sandretto re Rebaudengo per l'Arte, Italy

Opposite:

Victorian Couple, 1999

Two life-size mannequins, Dutch wax printed cotton, mixed media
165.1 x 53.3 x 30.5 cm (male figure), 156.2 x 49.5 x 45.7 cm (female figure)
Norton Museum of Art, West Palm Beach, Florida, purchase, through the generosity of the Contemporary and Modern Art Council and the R. H. Norton Trust, 2006

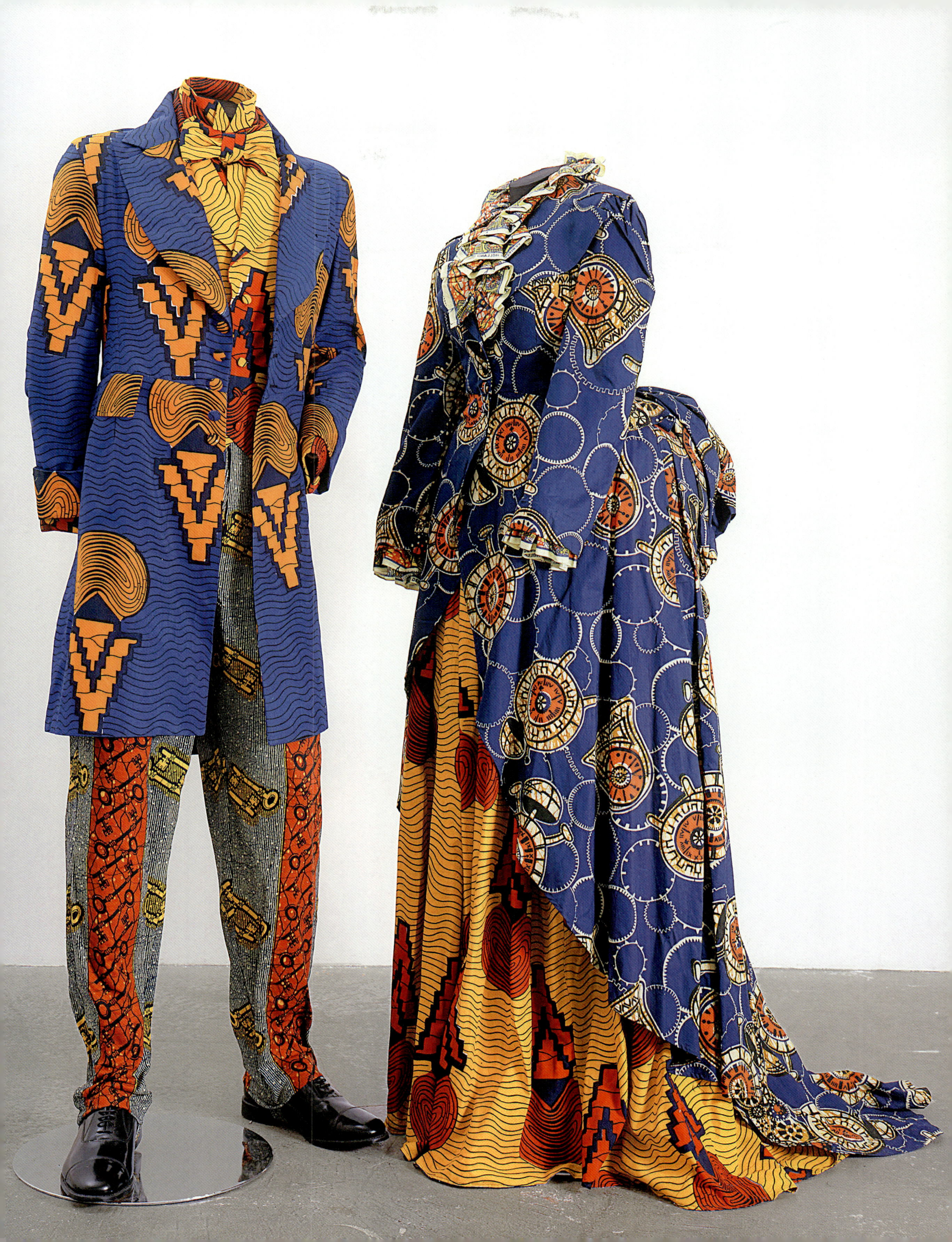

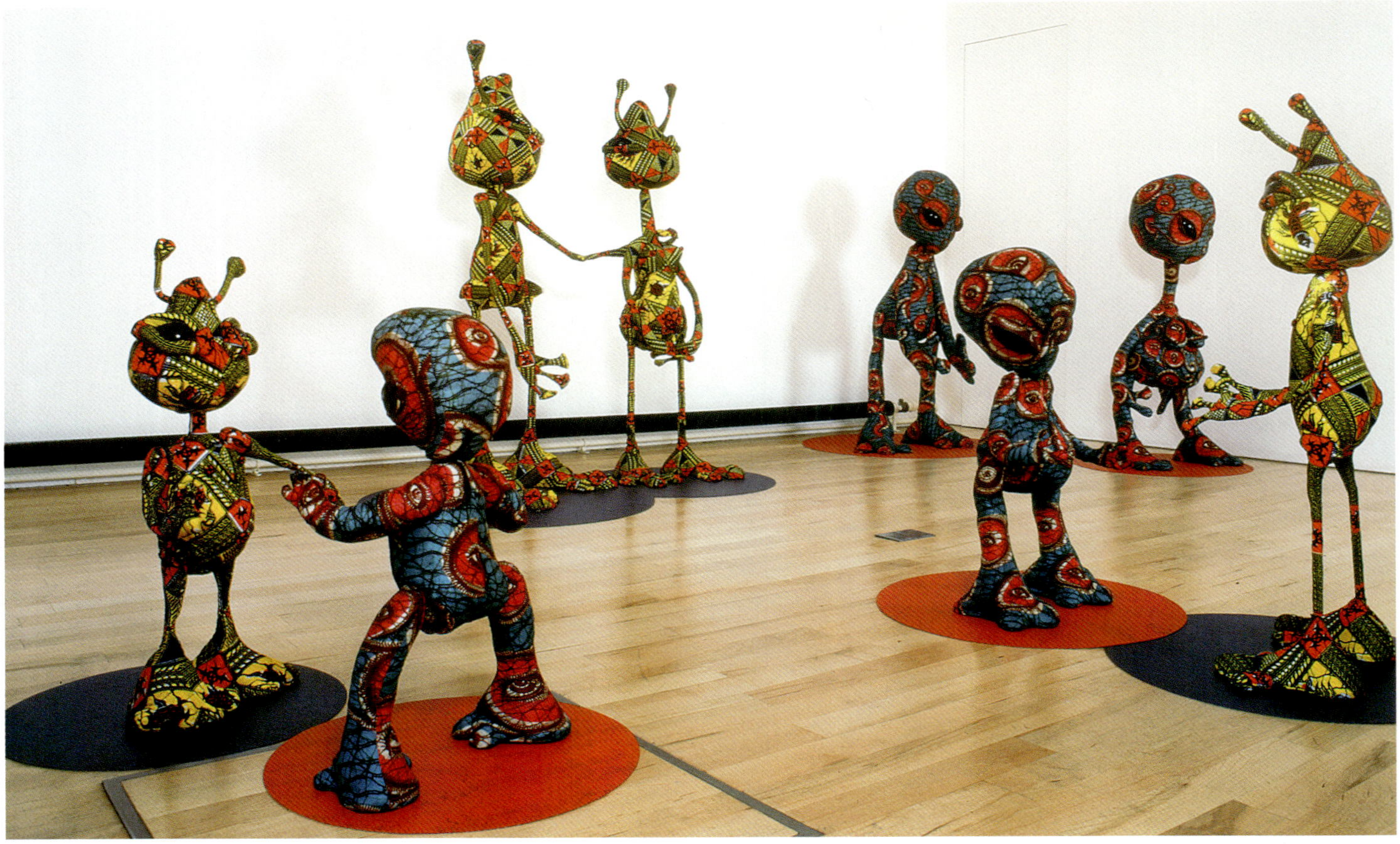

Alien Obsessives, Mum, Dad, and the Kids, 1998

Dutch wax printed cotton, plastic, polyester fiberfill on plastic
and metal armatures
Dimensions variable
Museum of Contemporary Art, Chicago, restricted gift of Howard
and Donna Stone

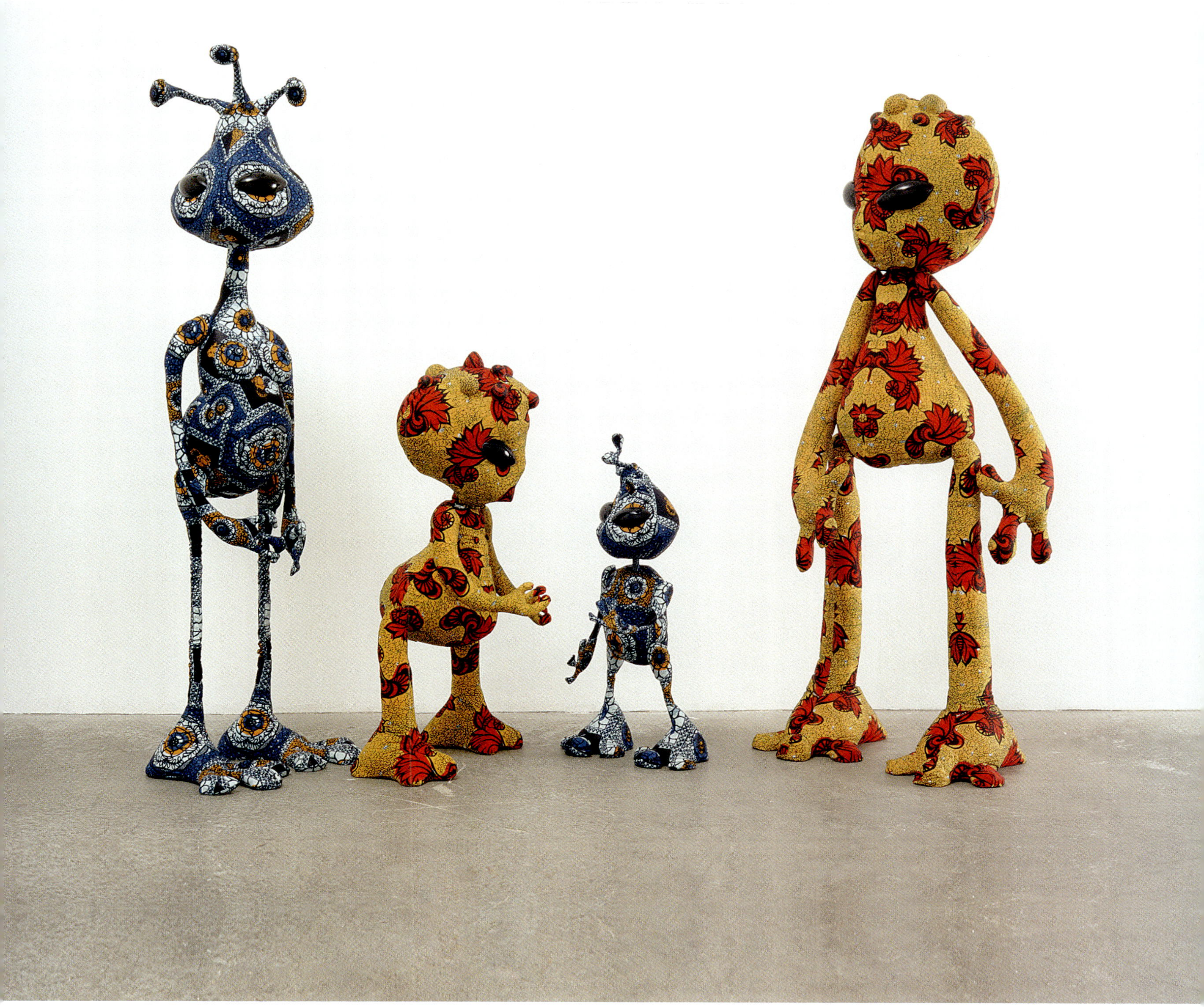

Dysfunctional Family, 1999

Dutch wax printed cotton, plastic, polyester fiberfill on plastic
and metal armatures
52 x 148 x 37 cm (father), 40 x 150 x 36 cm (mother),
54 x 89 x 46 cm (boy), 36 x 69 x 30 cm (girl)
Walker Art Center, Minneapolis

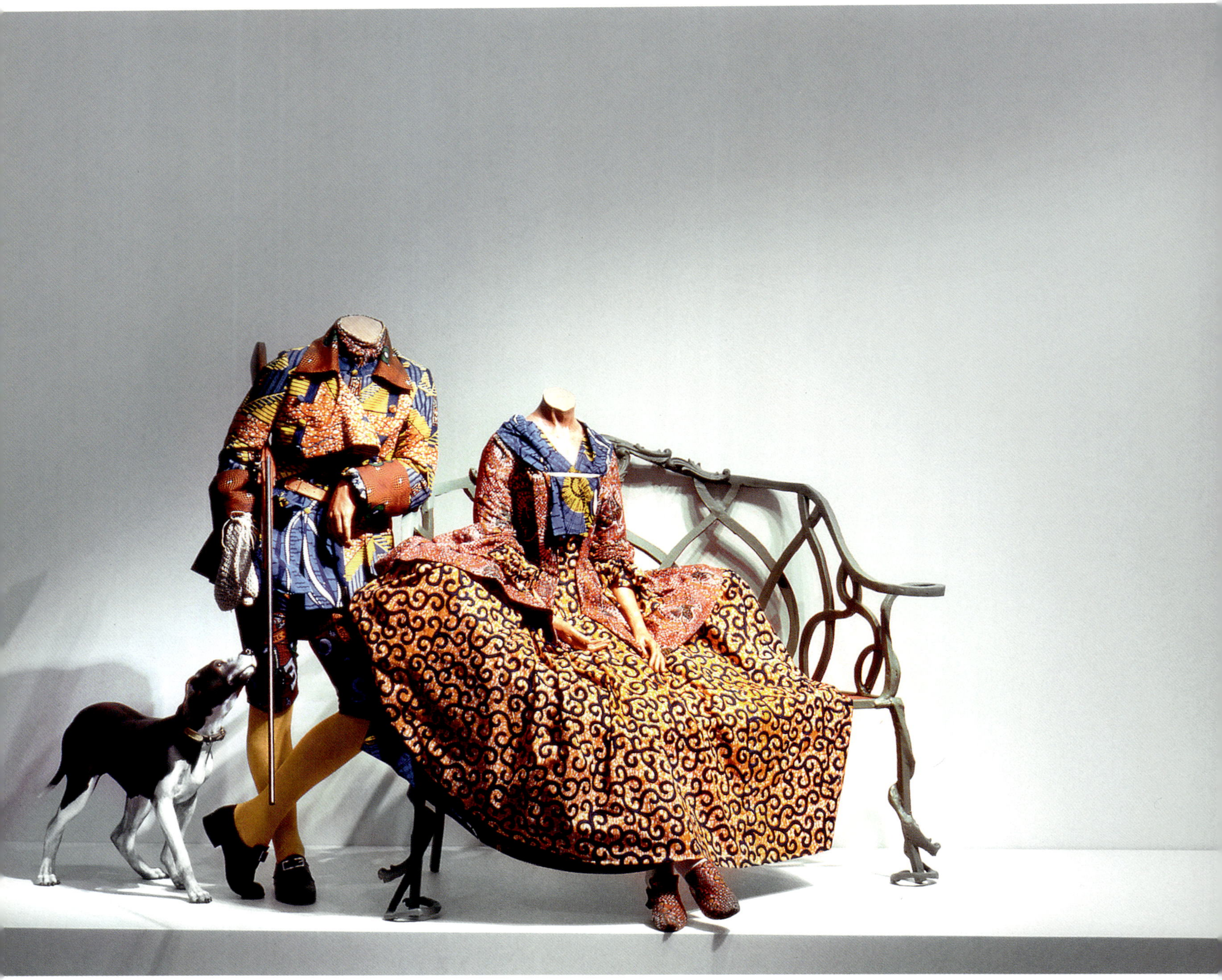

Mr. and Mrs. Andrews without Their Heads, 1998

Two life-size mannequins, bench, gun, dog, Dutch wax printed cotton
165 x 570 x 254 cm
National Gallery of Canada, Ottawa, purchased 1999

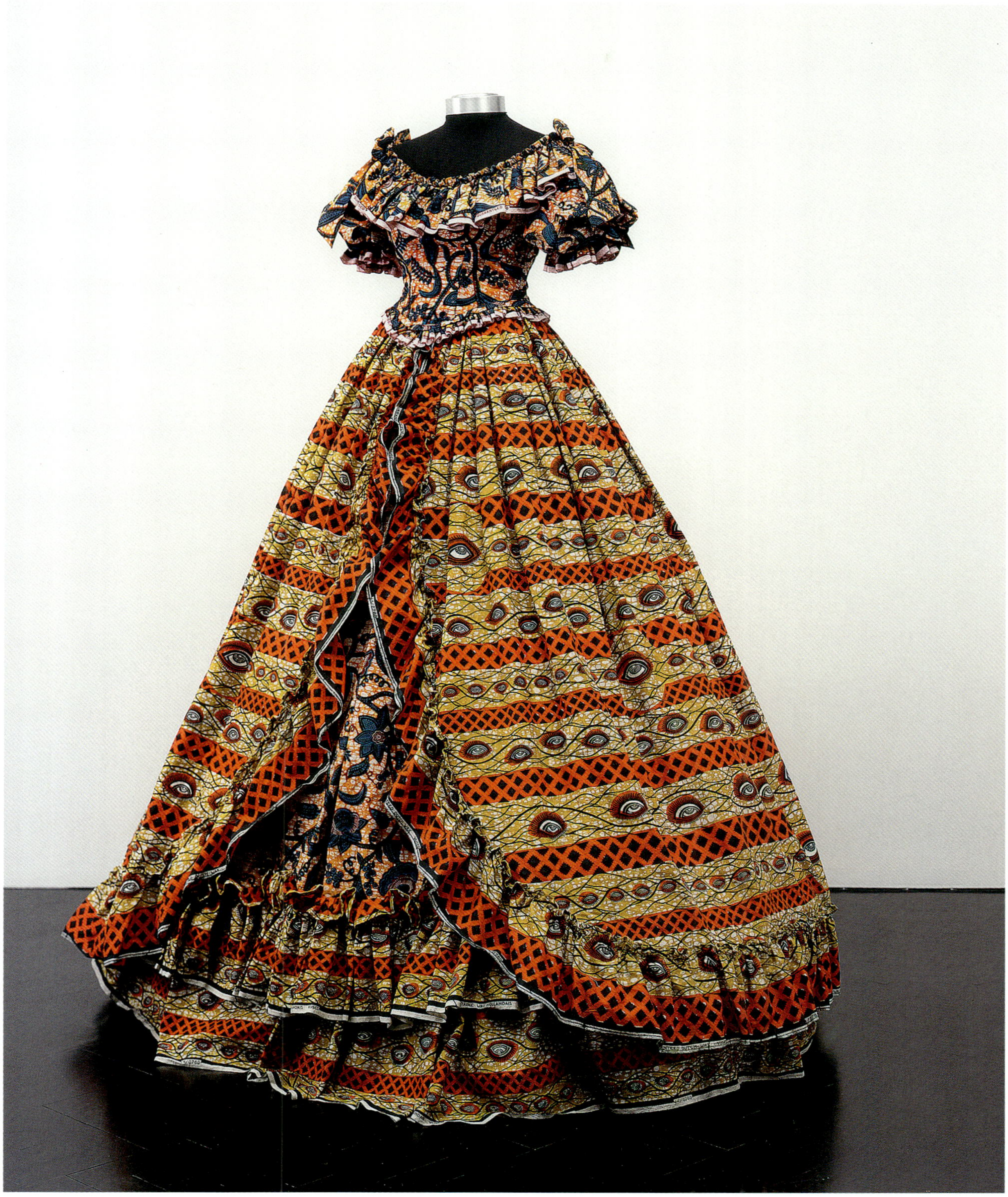

Dressing Down, 1997

Life-size mannequin, Dutch wax printed cotton, crinoline, aluminum, plastic, felt
150 x 150 x 175 cm
Private collection

Opposite and overleaf:

The Victorian Philanthropist's Parlour, 1996–97

Reproduction furniture, fire screen, carpet, props, Dutch wax printed cotton
Dimensions variable, approx. 260 x 488 x 530 cm

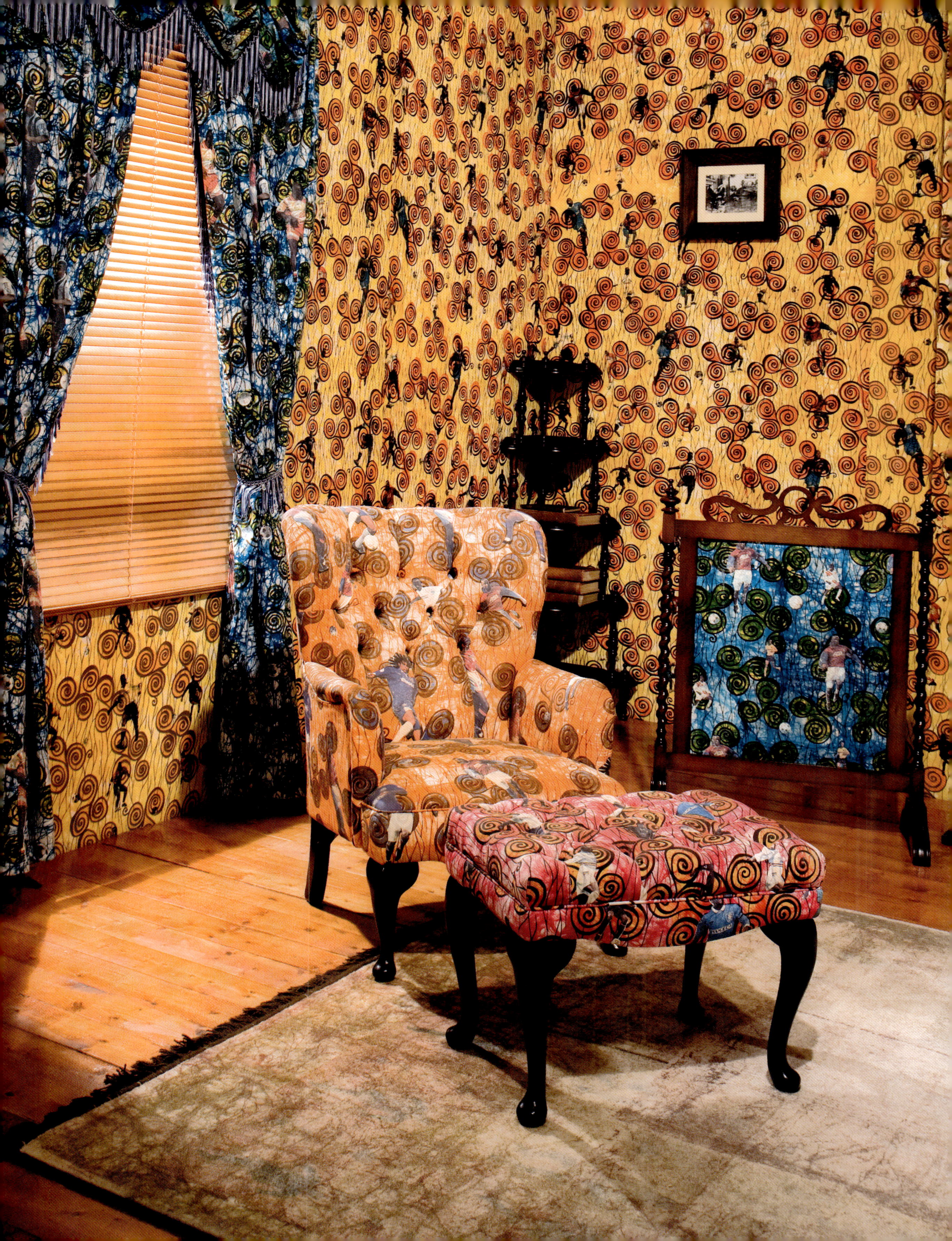

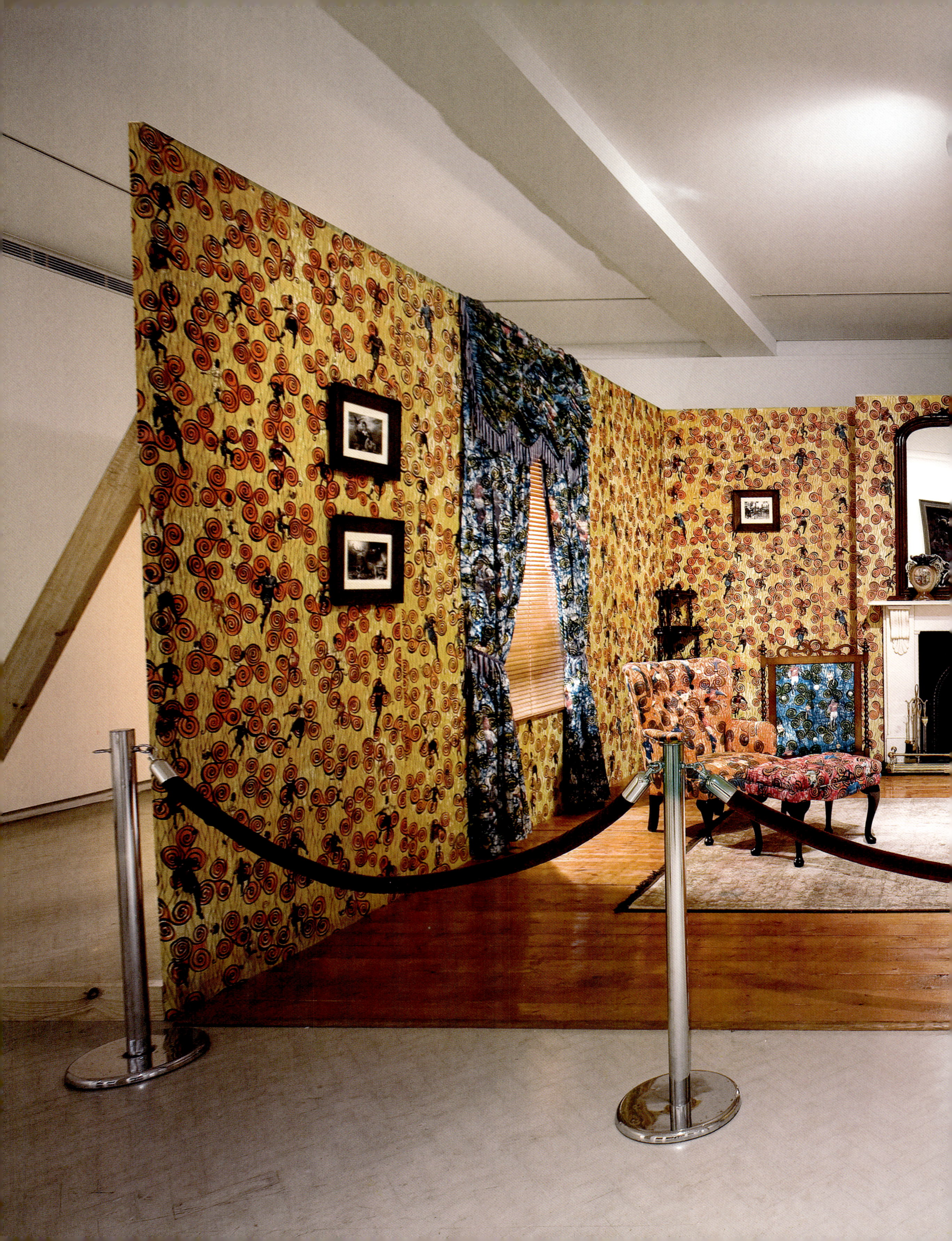

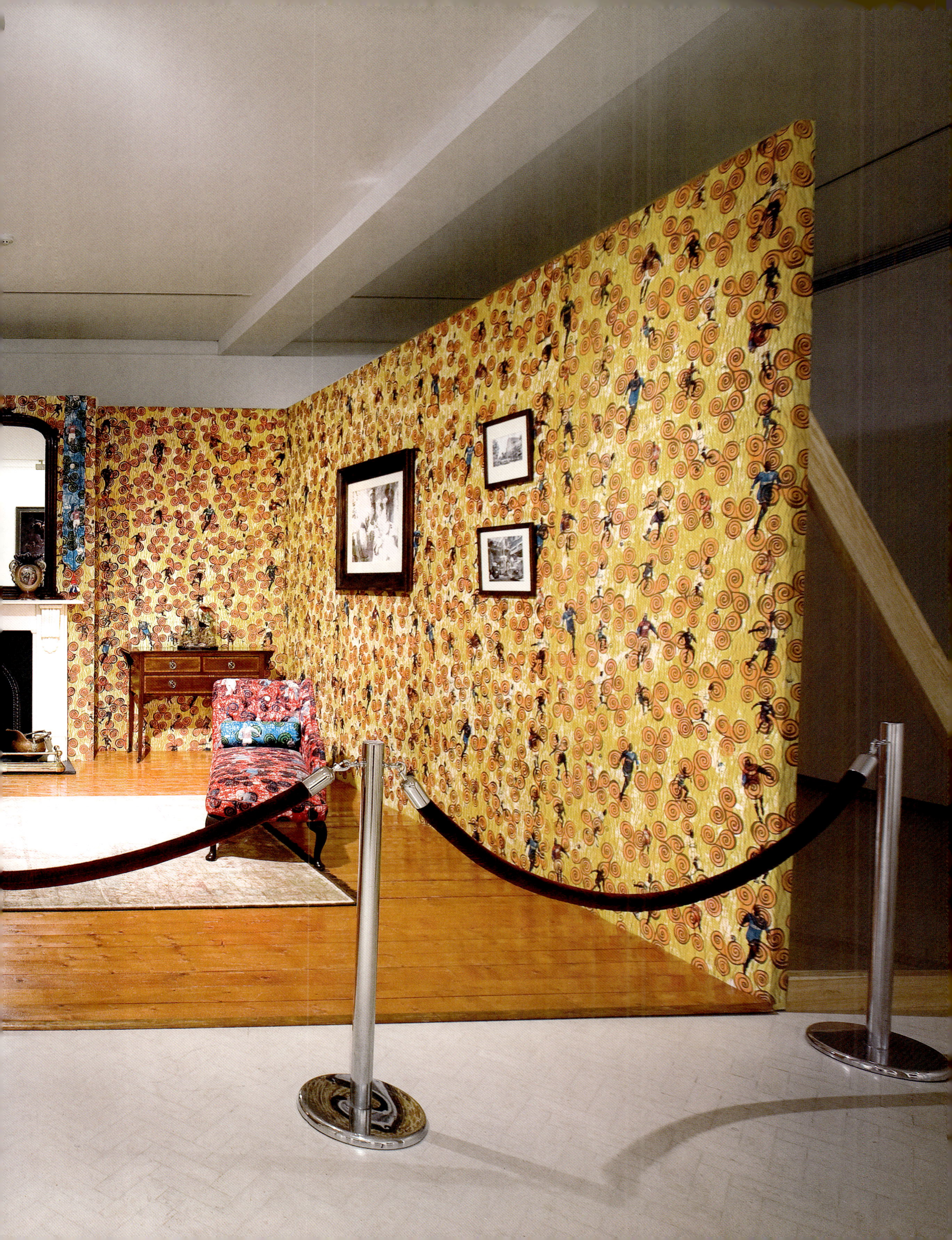

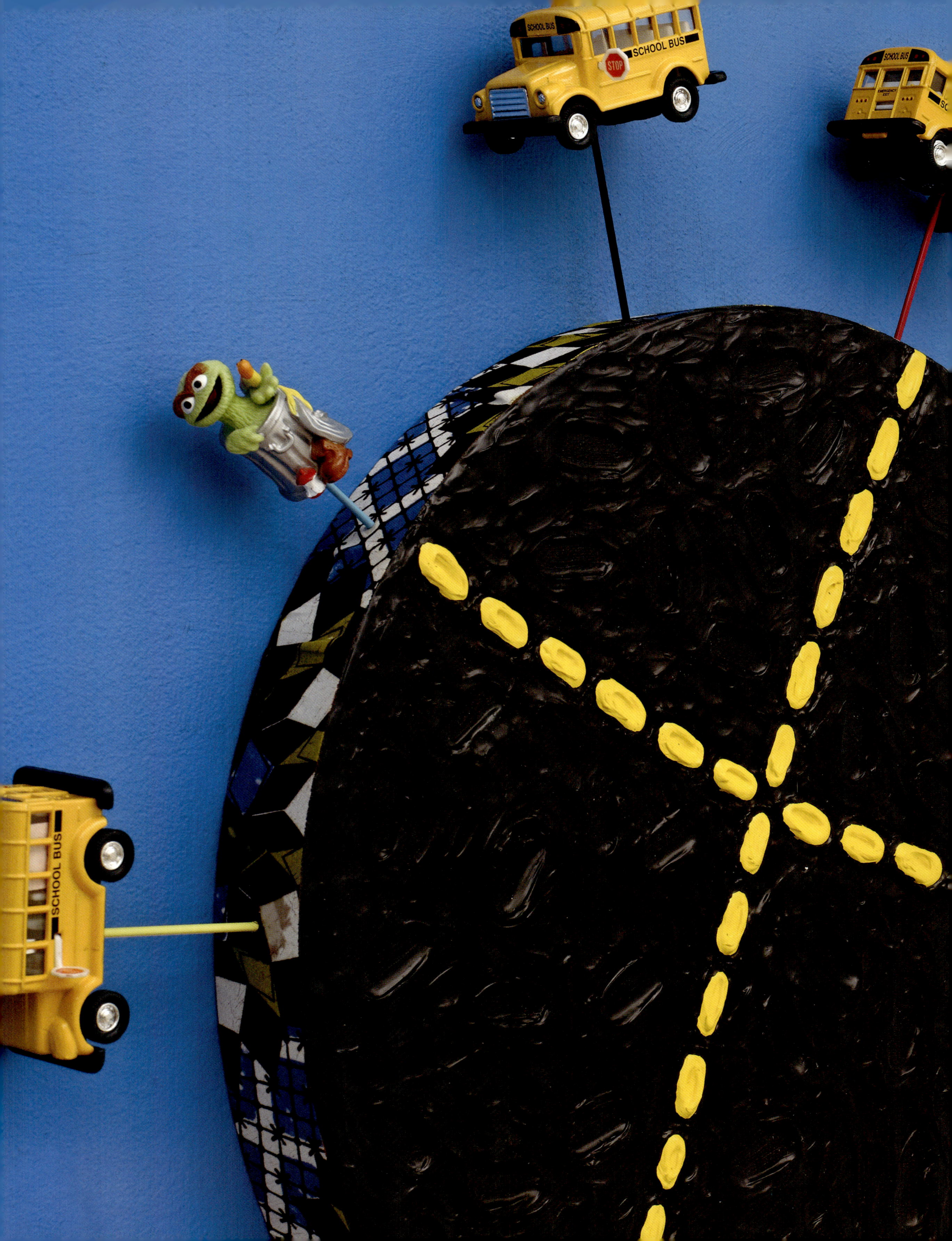
SCHOOL BUS
STOP
SCHOOL BUS
SCHOOL BUS
SCHOOL BUS

PAINTING AND WORKS ON PAPER

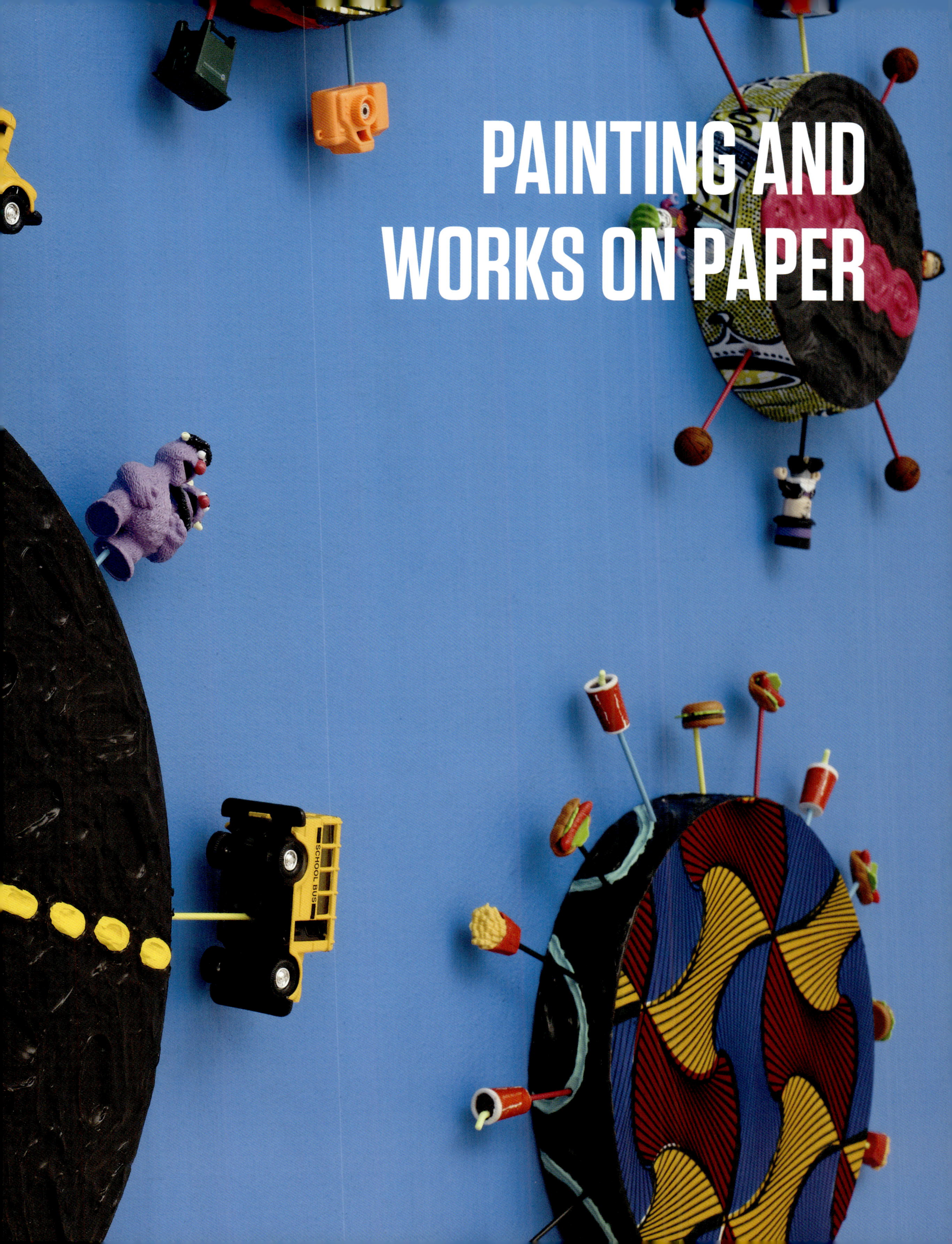

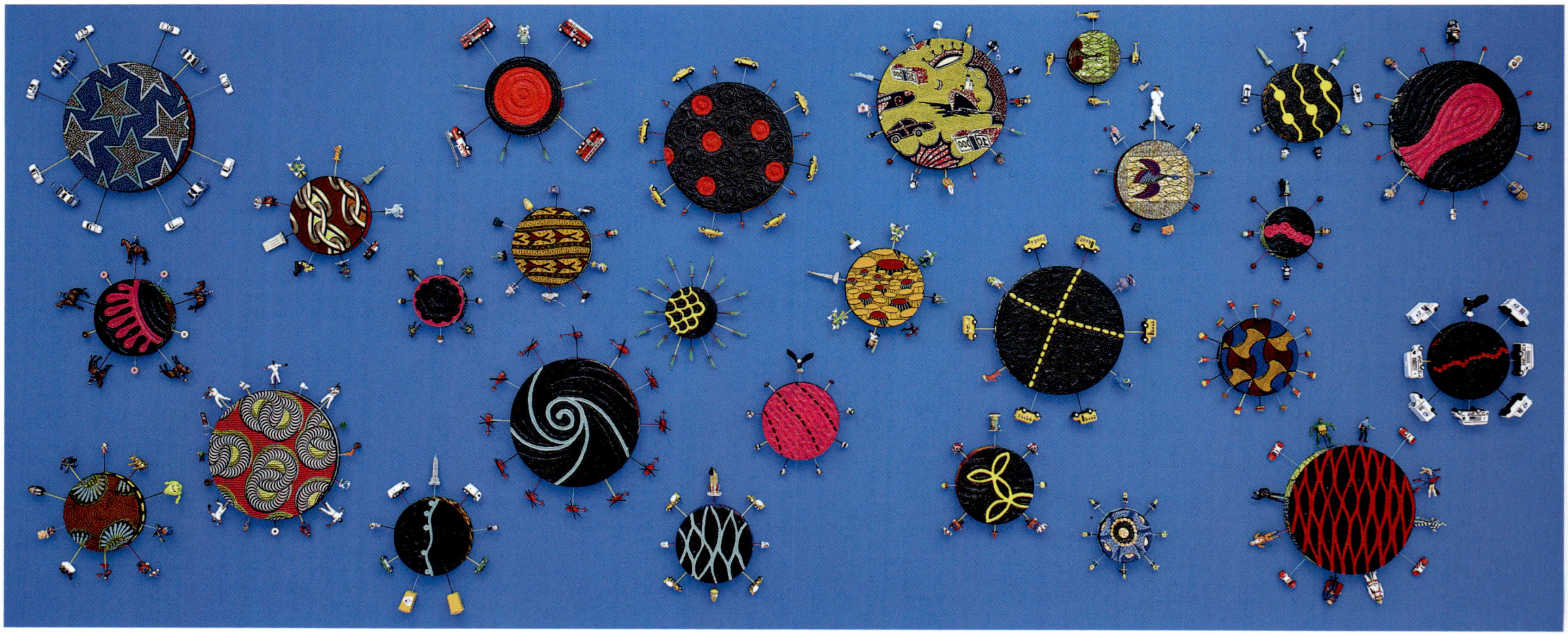

Preceding spread and above:

New York Toy Painting, 2012

Emulsion and acrylic on twenty-seven Dutch wax printed cotton canvases, wire, toys, acrylic on wall
250 x 620 x 16 cm

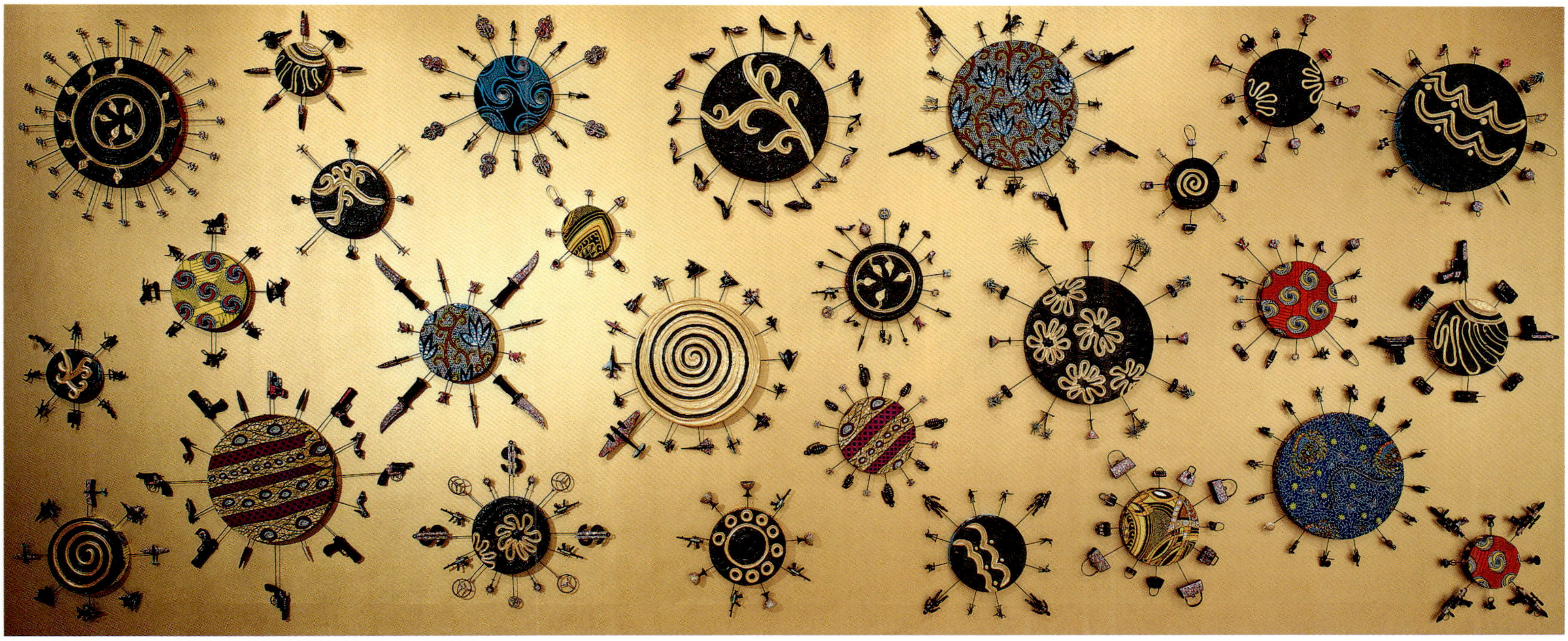

Bling Painting, 2013

Emulsion and acrylic on twenty-seven Dutch wax printed cotton canvases, toys adorned with diamanté, acrylic on wall
250 x 620 x 7 cm

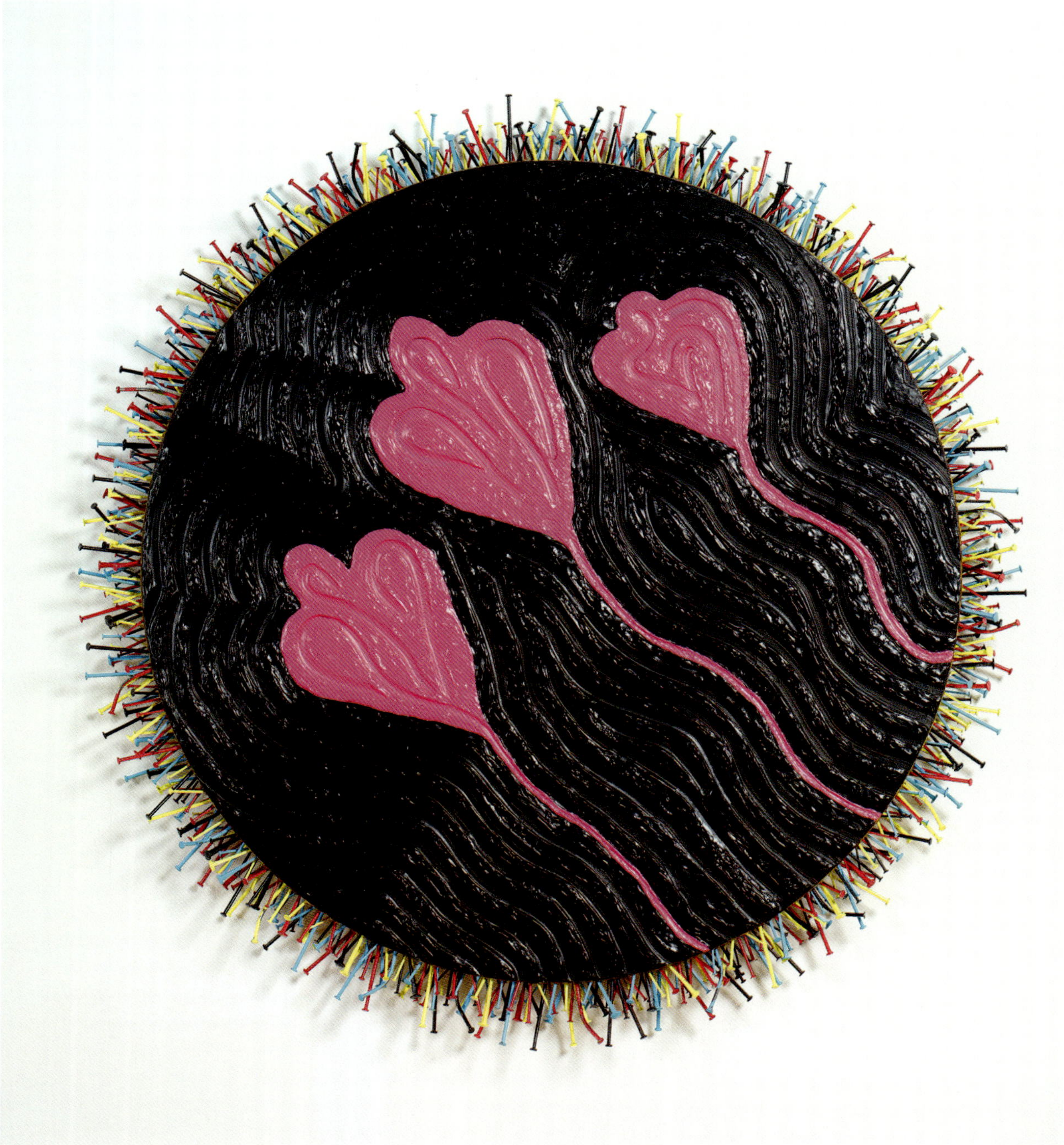

Circular Fetish Painting with Nails 6, 2012

Acrylic and acrylic aerosol spray paint on Dutch wax printed cotton, steel and aluminum nails, Medite MDF
118 x 118 x 10 cm

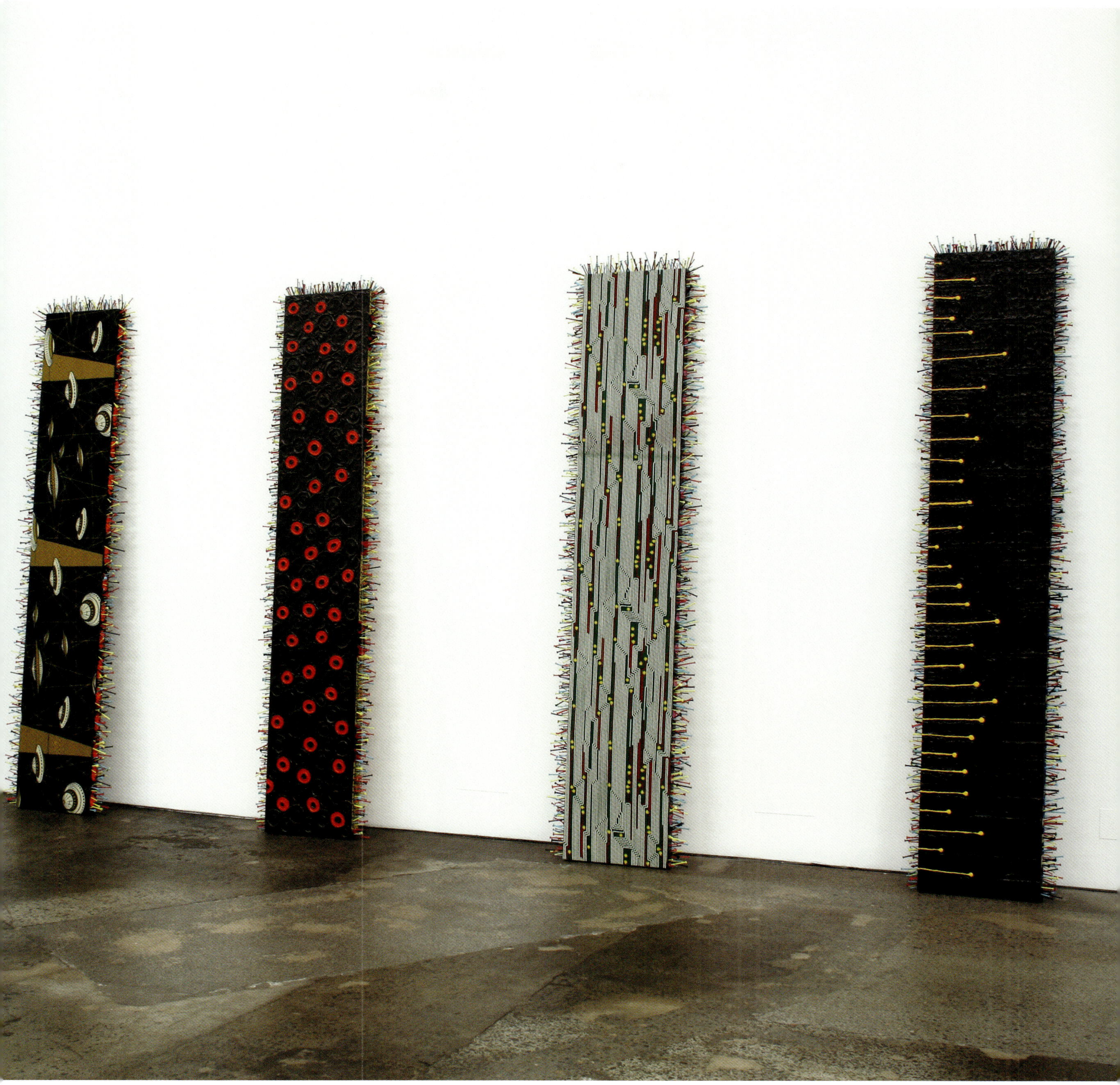

Totem Paintings, 2011 (from left: *5*, *1*, *4*, *2*)

Paint on Dutch wax printed cotton, steel nails, spray paint, MDF
Four panels, each 250 x 60 x 10 cm

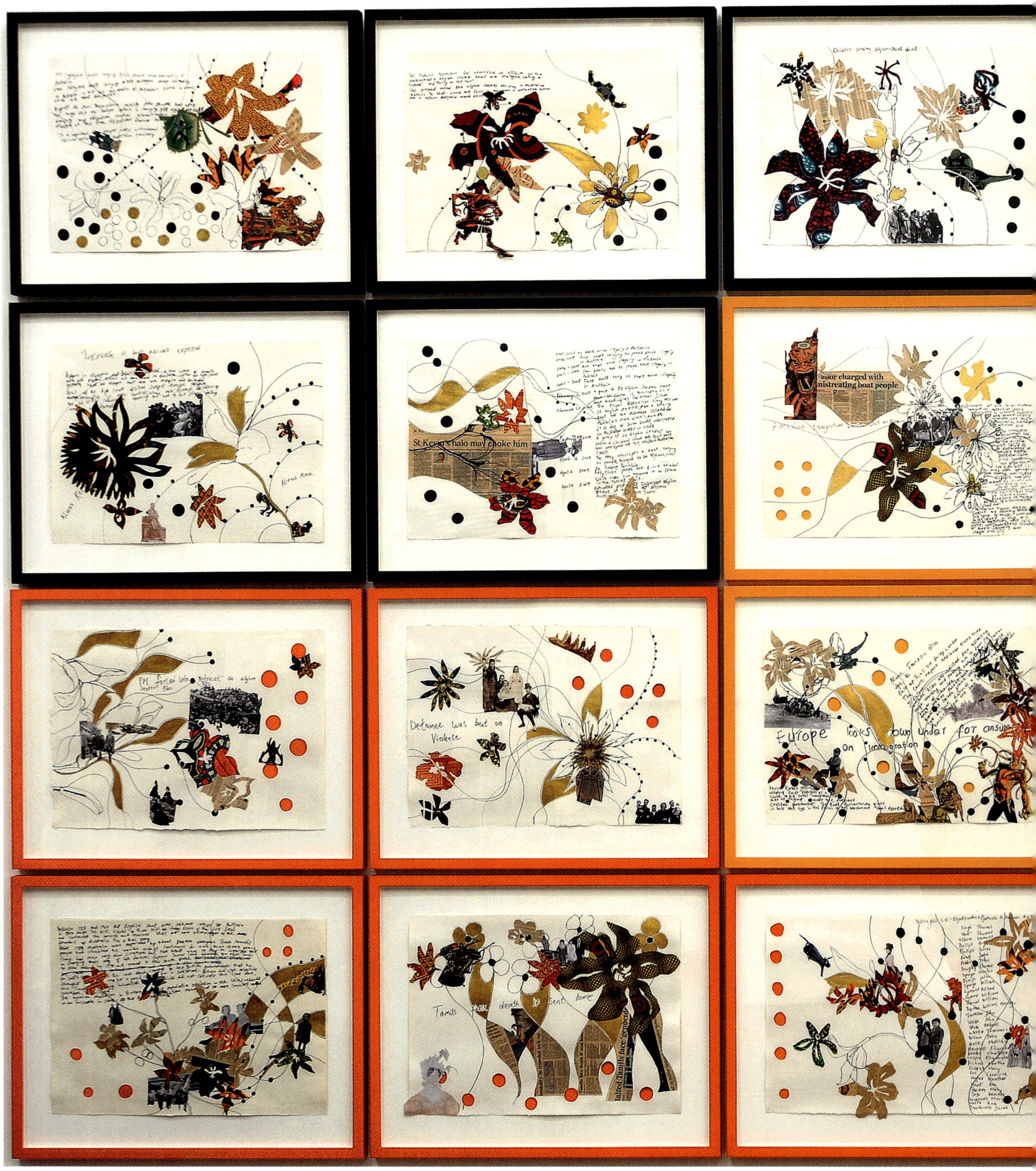

Alien Flag Drawings, 2011

Paper, ink, Dutch wax printed cotton, found paper, 22-carat gold leaf
Twenty-four drawings, each 76.5 x 95 cm (framed)

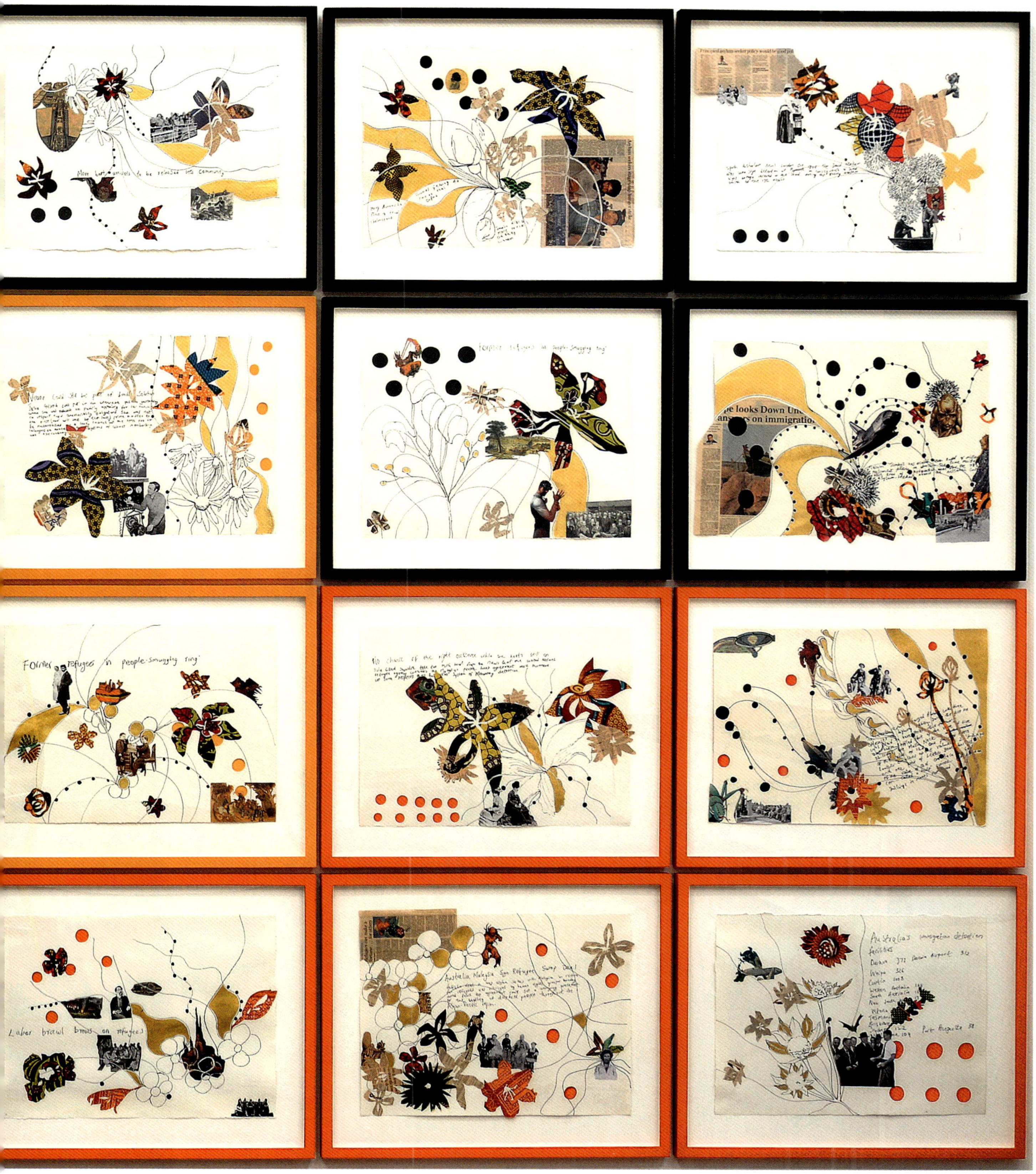
Former refugees in people-smuggling ring
Labor brawl brews on refugees

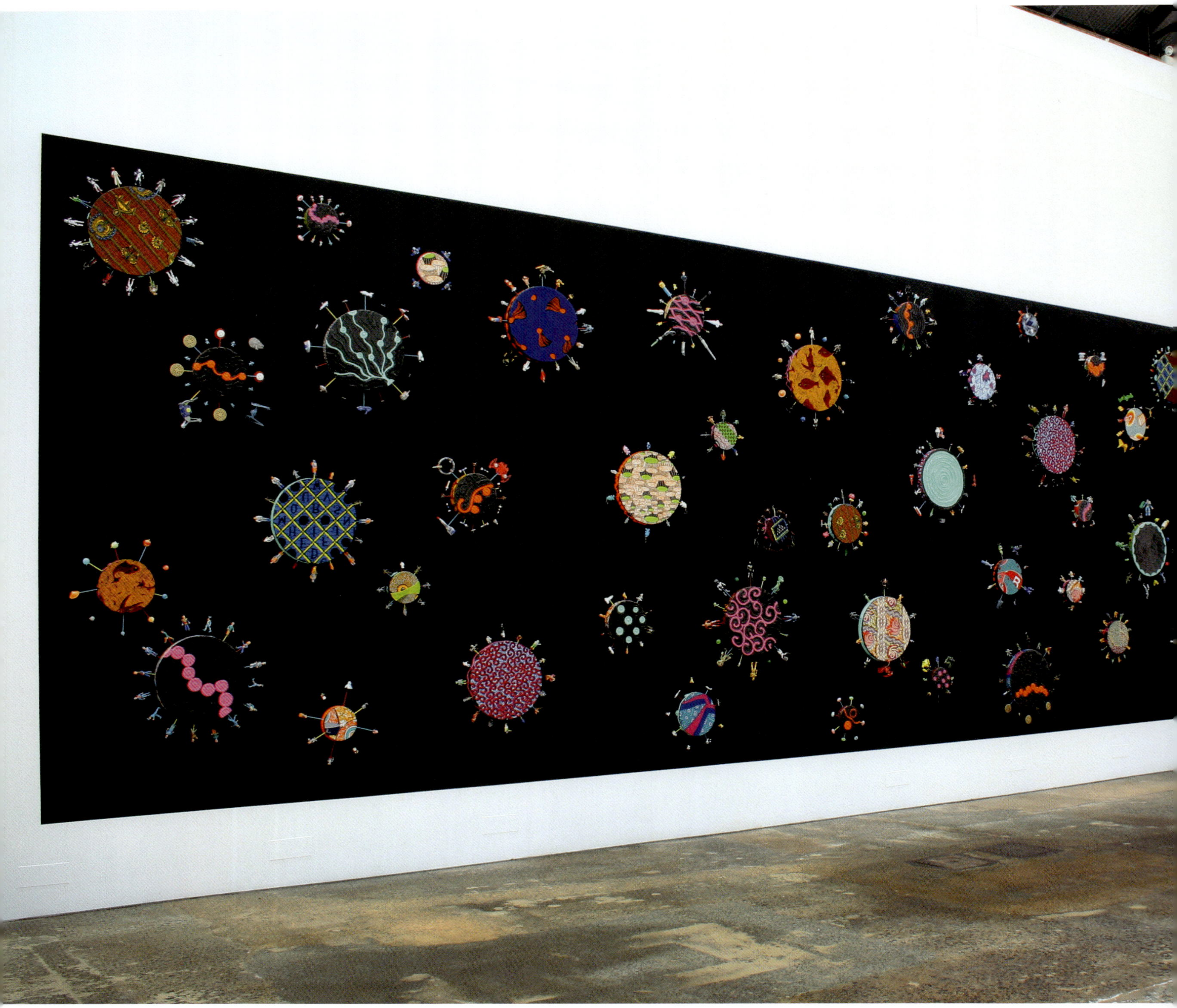

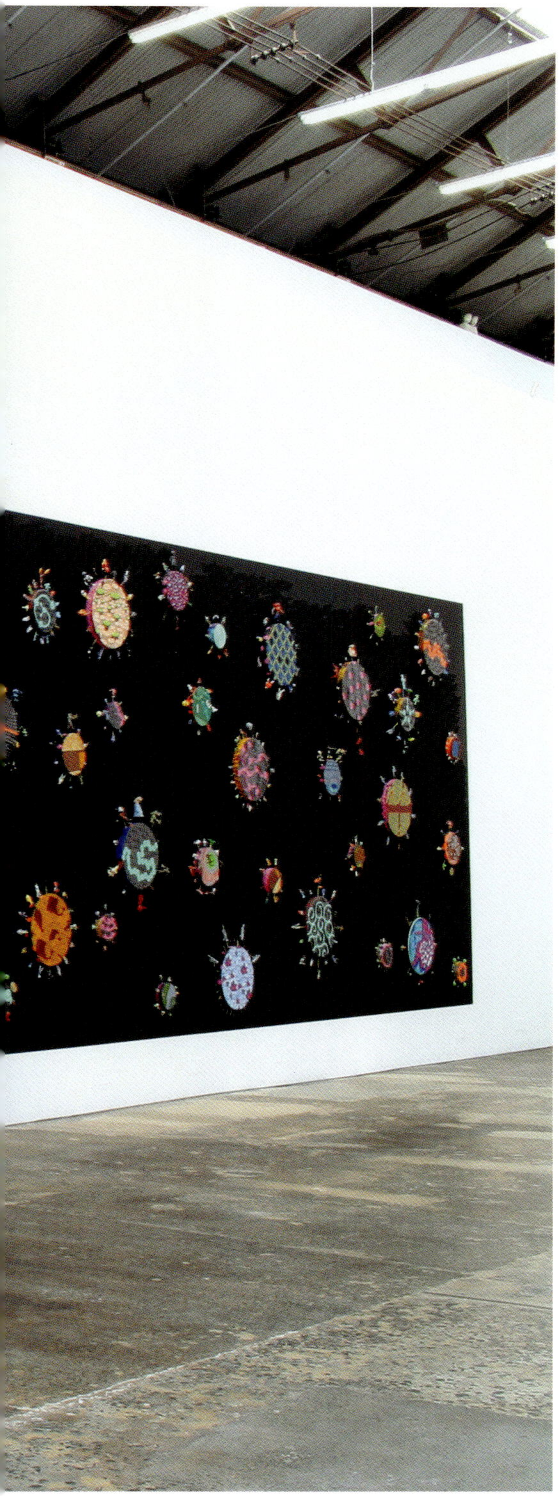

Alien Toy Painting, 2011

Acrylic paint on seventy-five Dutch wax printed cotton canvases, steel, spray paint, MDF, acrylic on wall
375 x 1860 x 16 cm
Art Gallery of New South Wales, Tony Gilbert Bequest Fund 2012

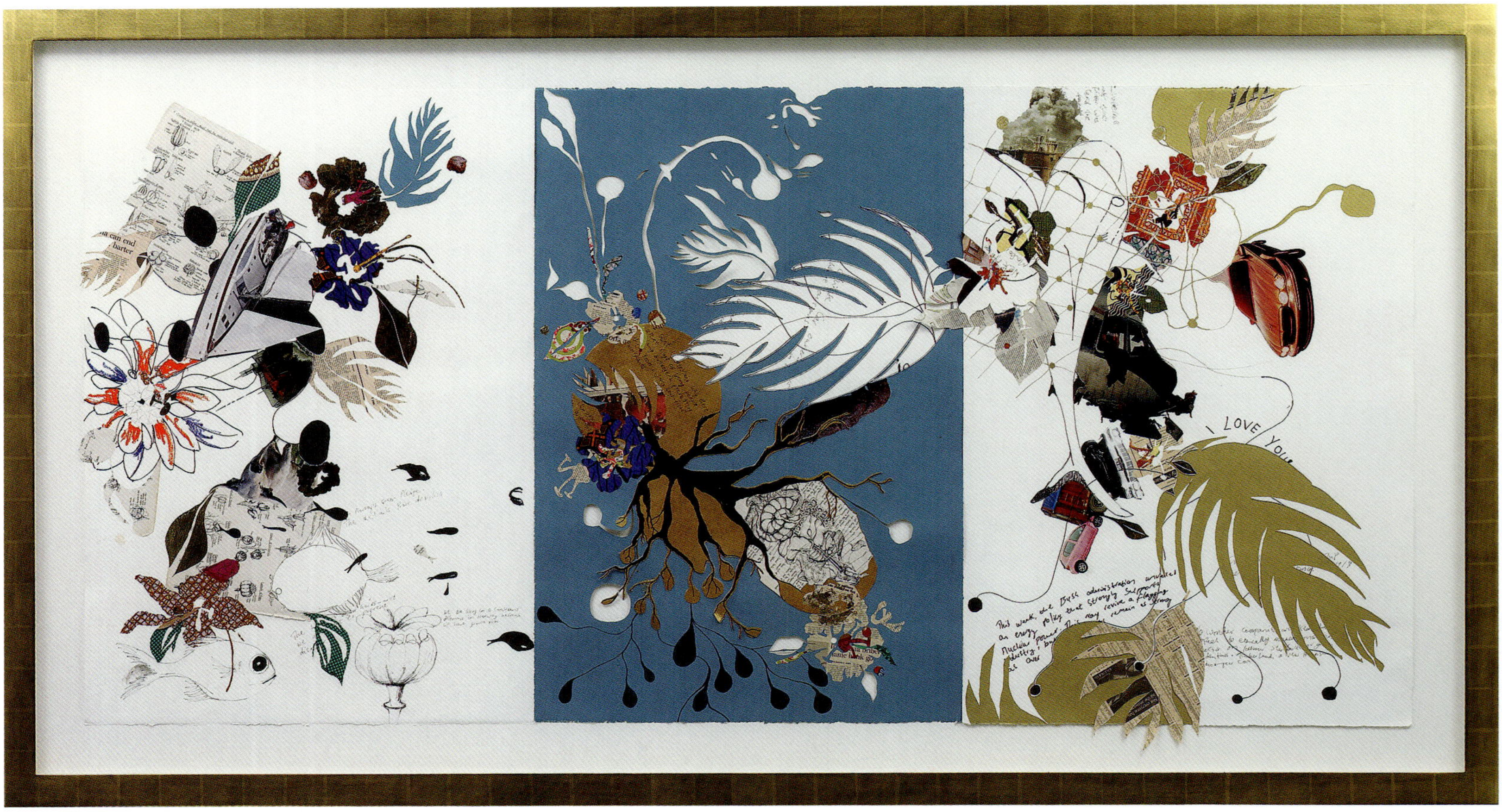

Climate Shit Drawing 6 (Triptych), 2009

Ink, Dutch wax printed cotton, newsprint, gold foil on paper
142.5 x 266.5 cm

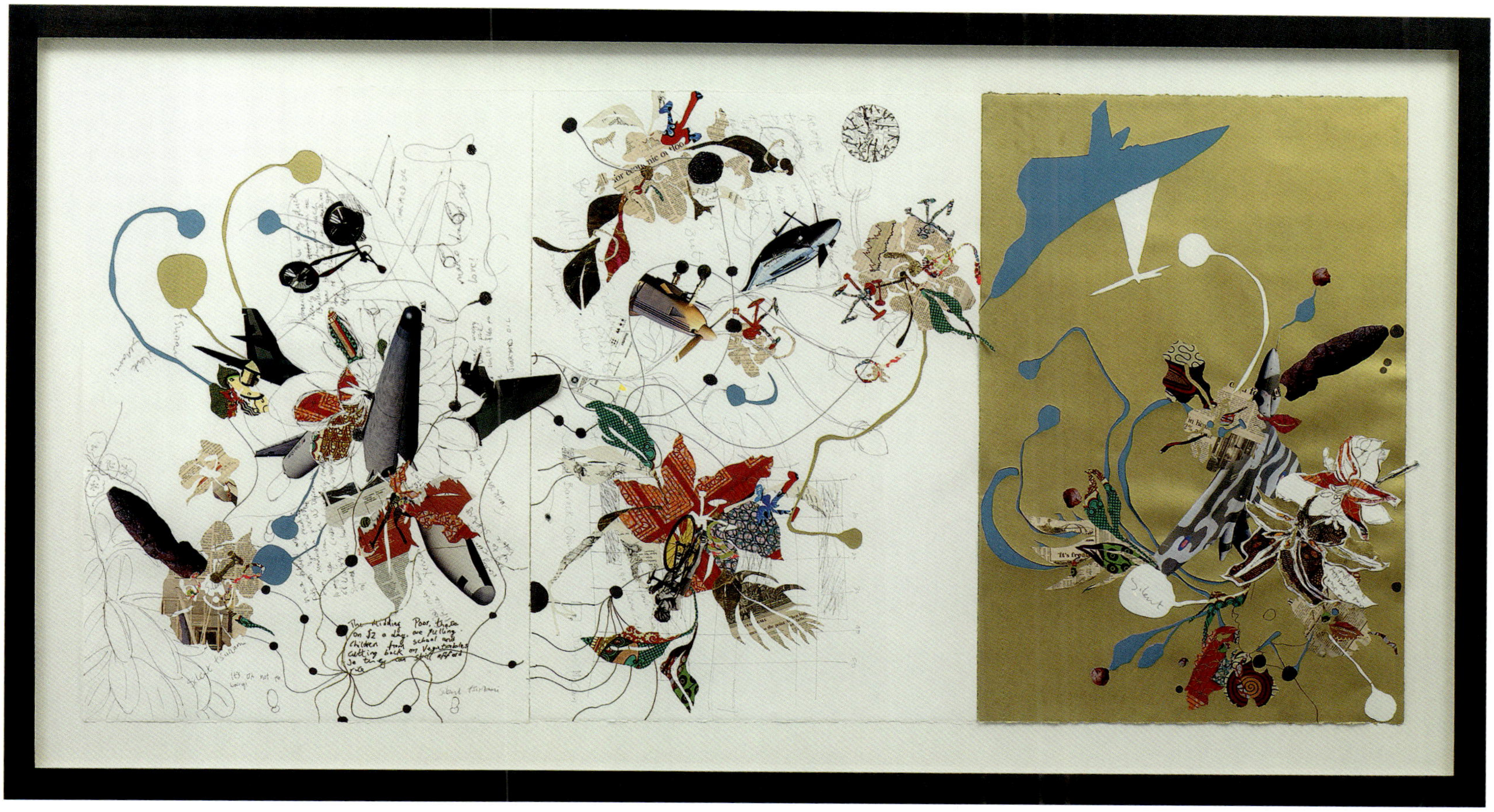

Climate Shit Drawing 7 (Triptych), 2009

Ink, Dutch wax printed cotton, newsprint, gold foil on paper
142.5 x 266.5 cm

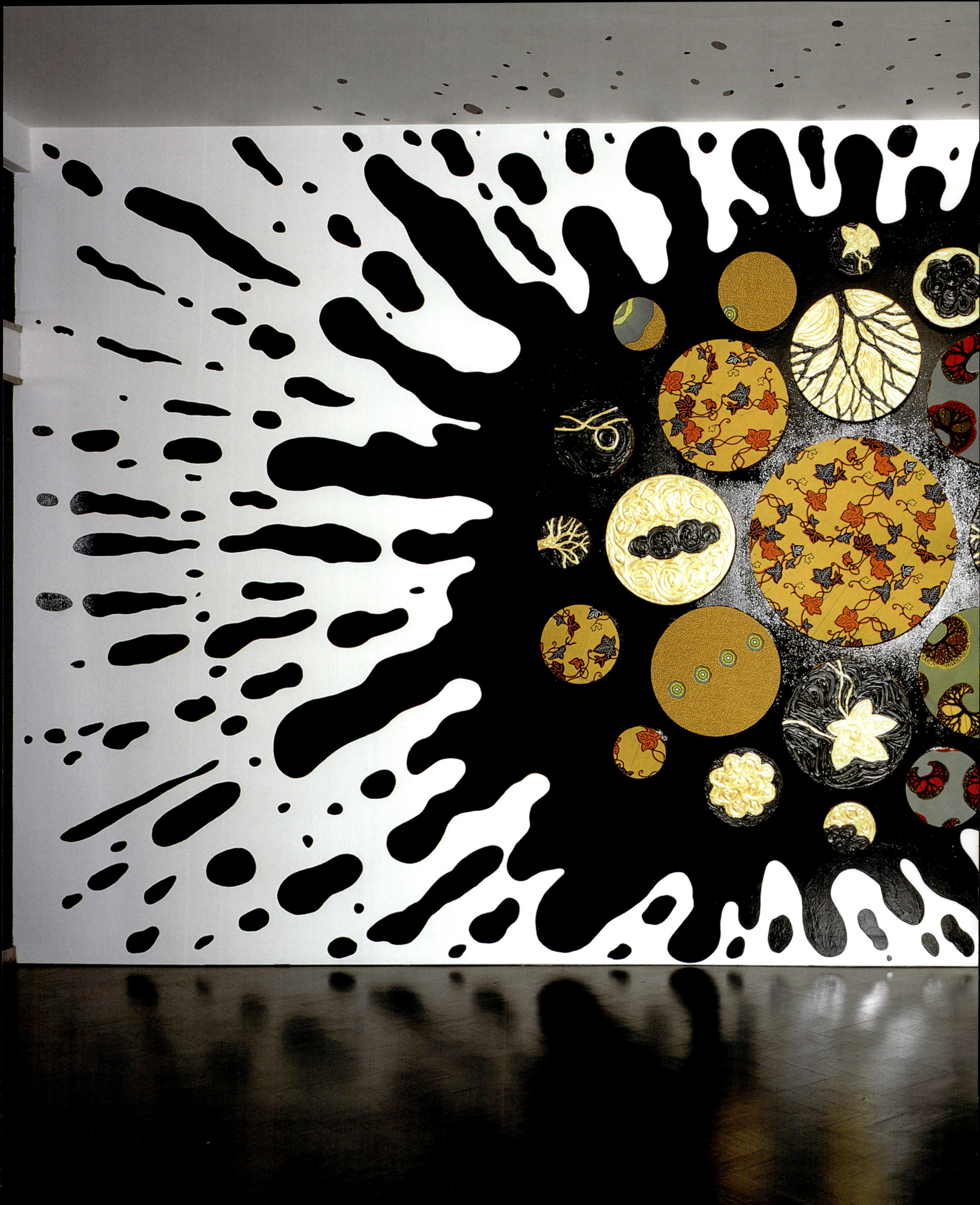

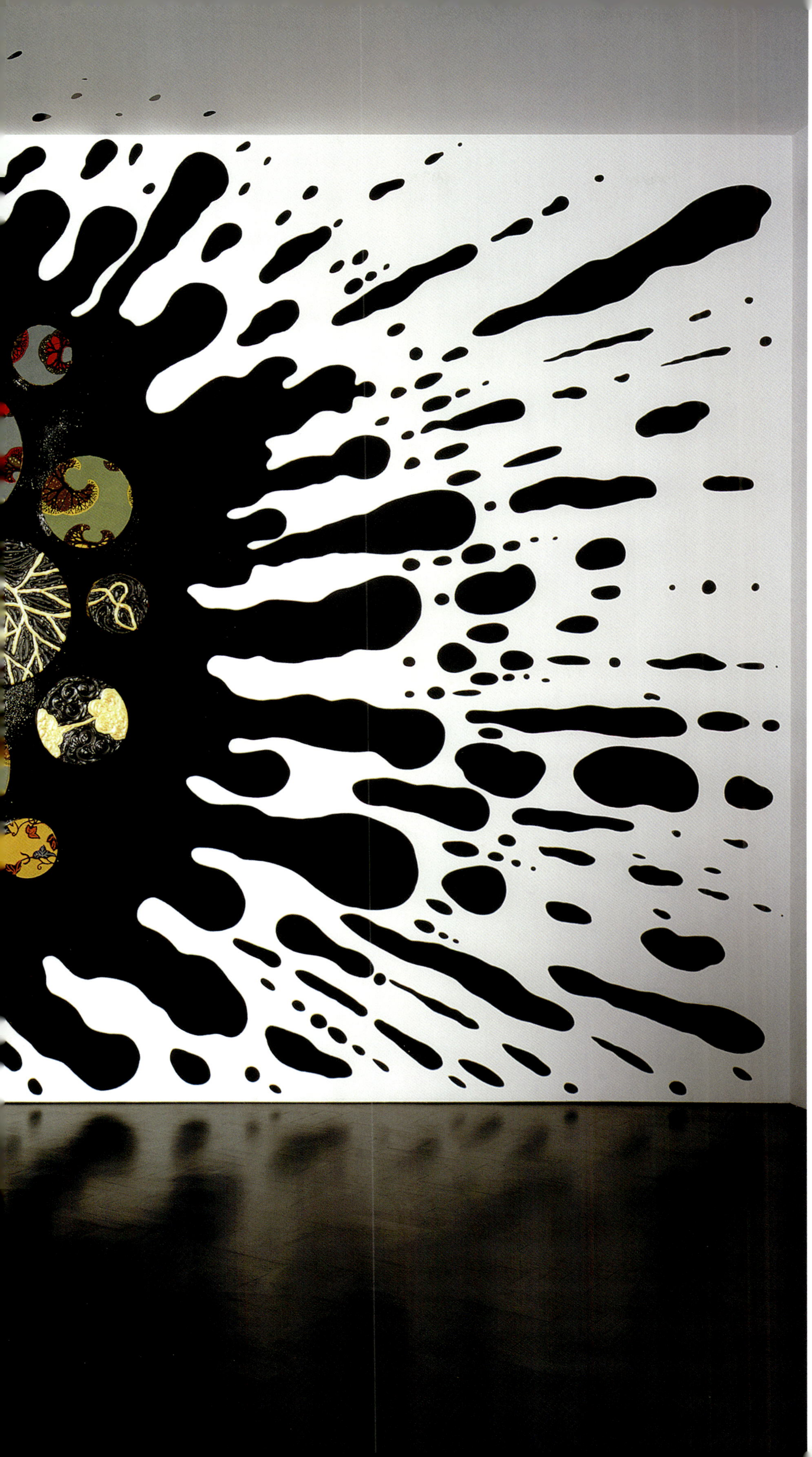

Black Gold I, 2006

Acrylic on twenty-five Dutch wax printed cotton canvases
330 x 673 cm
Smithsonian Institution, National Museum of African Art, Museum Purchase 2008

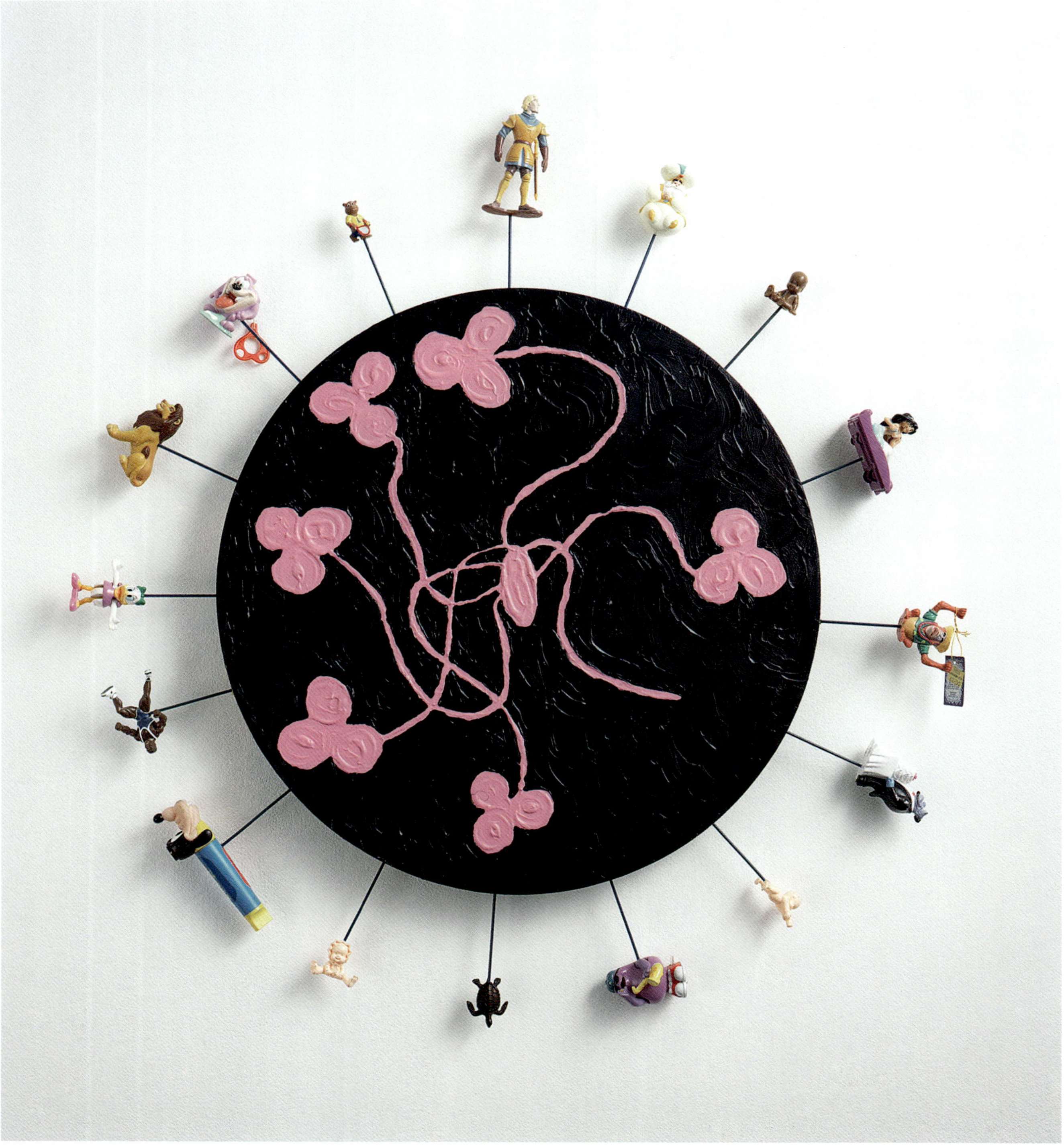

Toy Painting 1, 2003

Acrylic and emulsion on Dutch wax printed cotton, wire, toys
94 x 94 x 5 cm
Collection of Vicki and Kent Logan

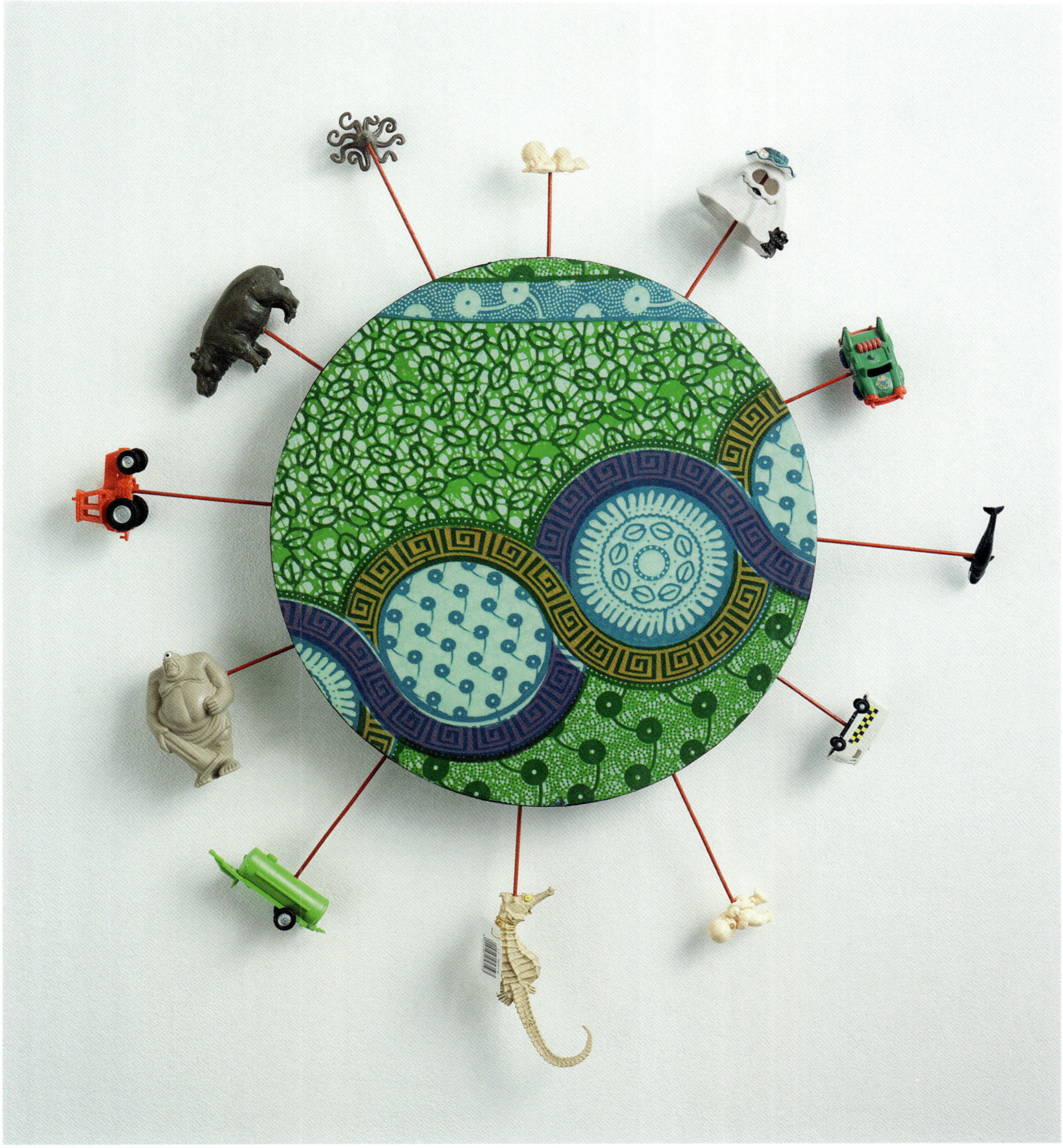

Toy Painting 11, 2003

Acrylic and emulsion on thirty Dutch wax printed cotton canvases, wire, toys
75 x 75 x 5 cm
Collection of Anne and Joel Ehrenkranz

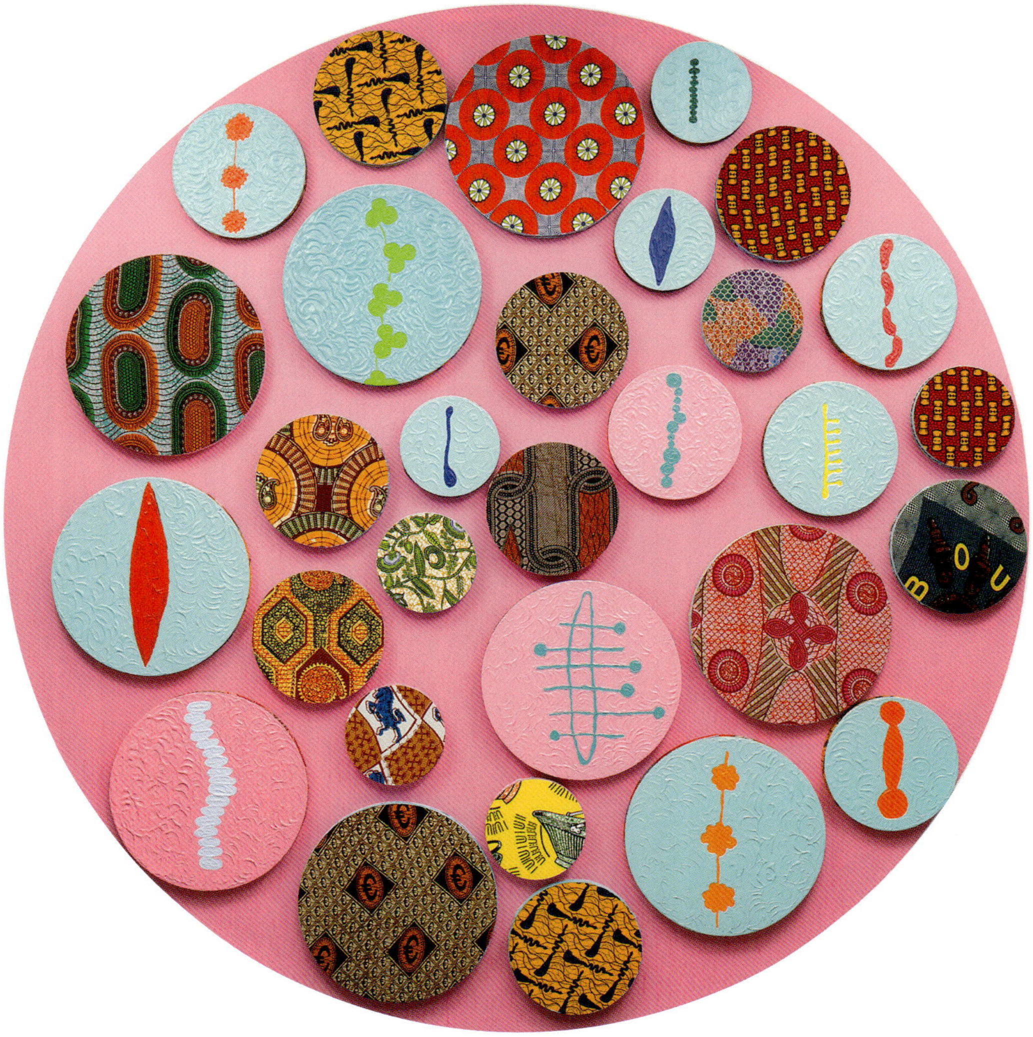

Line Painting, 2003

Emulsion and acrylic on Dutch wax printed cotton, acrylic on wall
312 x 312 x 5 cm
Arts Council Collection, London

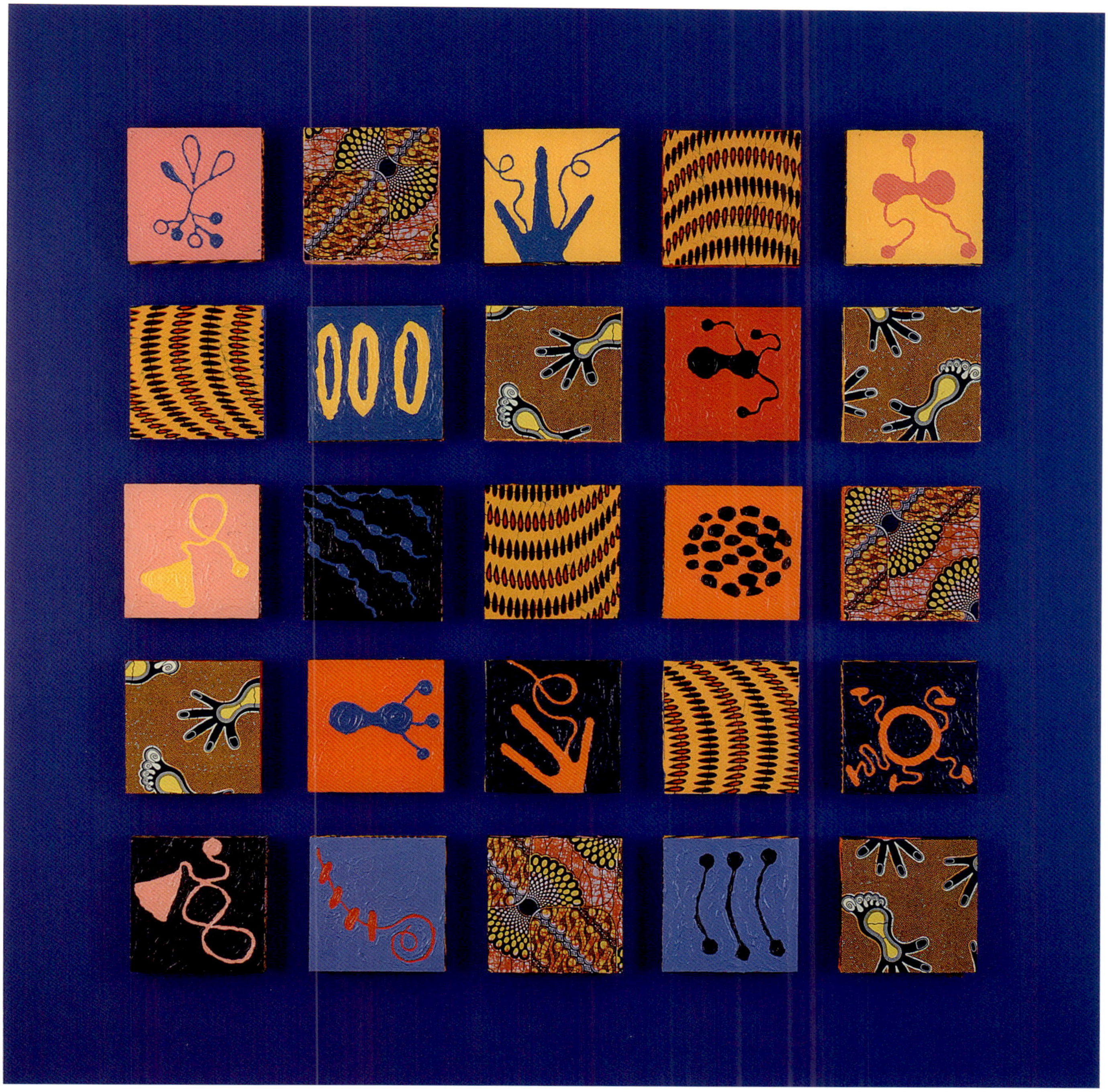

Deep Blue, 1997

Emulsion and acrylic on twenty-five Dutch wax printed cotton canvases, acrylic on wall
250 x 250 x 5 cm
Worcester Art Museum, Massachusetts, purchased with the assistance of the Charlotte E. W. Buffington Fund, 1998

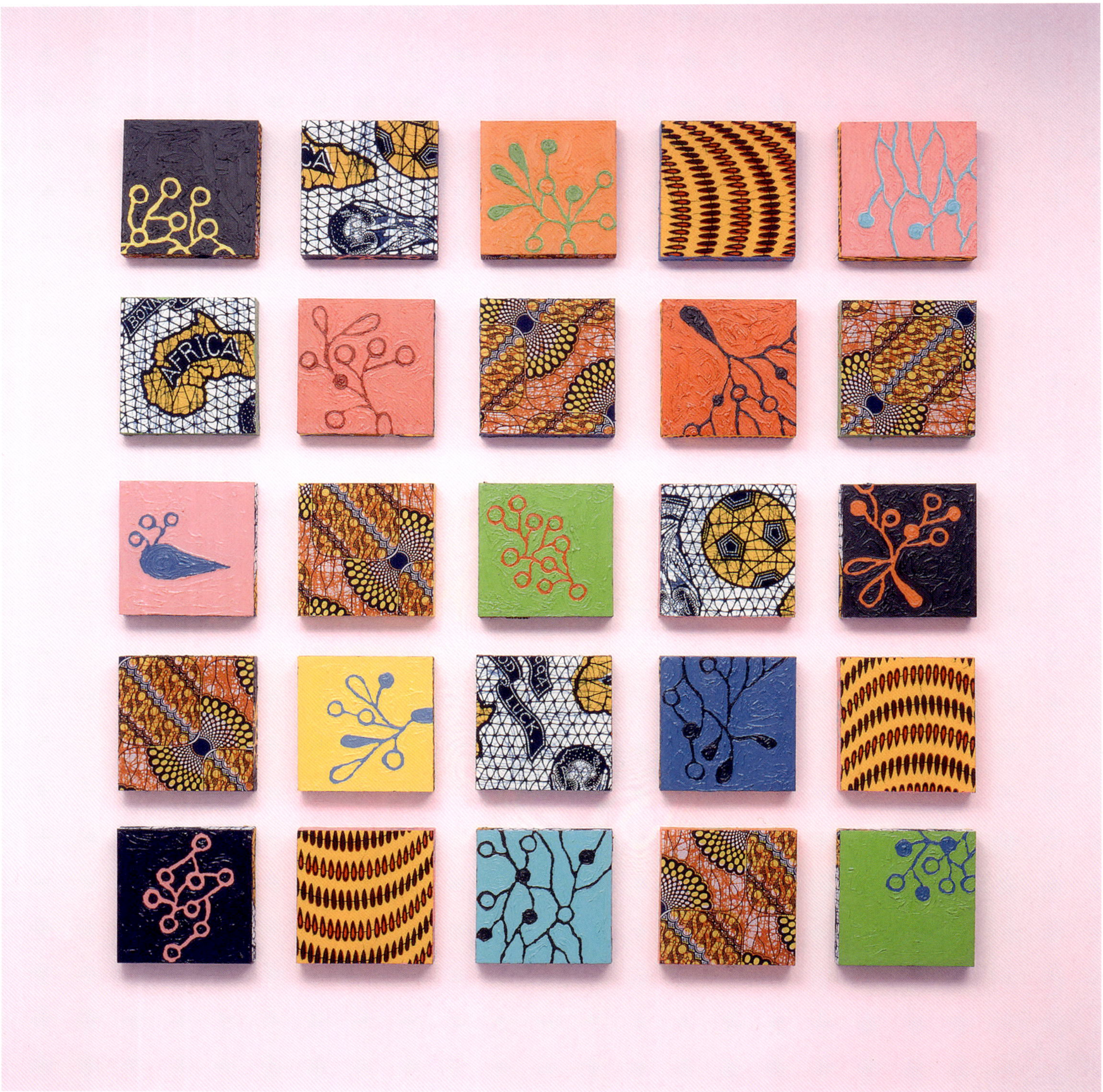

Feather Pink, 1997

Emulsion and acrylic on twenty-five Dutch wax printed cotton canvases, acrylic on wall
250 x 250 x 5 cm
Art Institute of Chicago, gifts of The Peter Norton Foundation, 1998

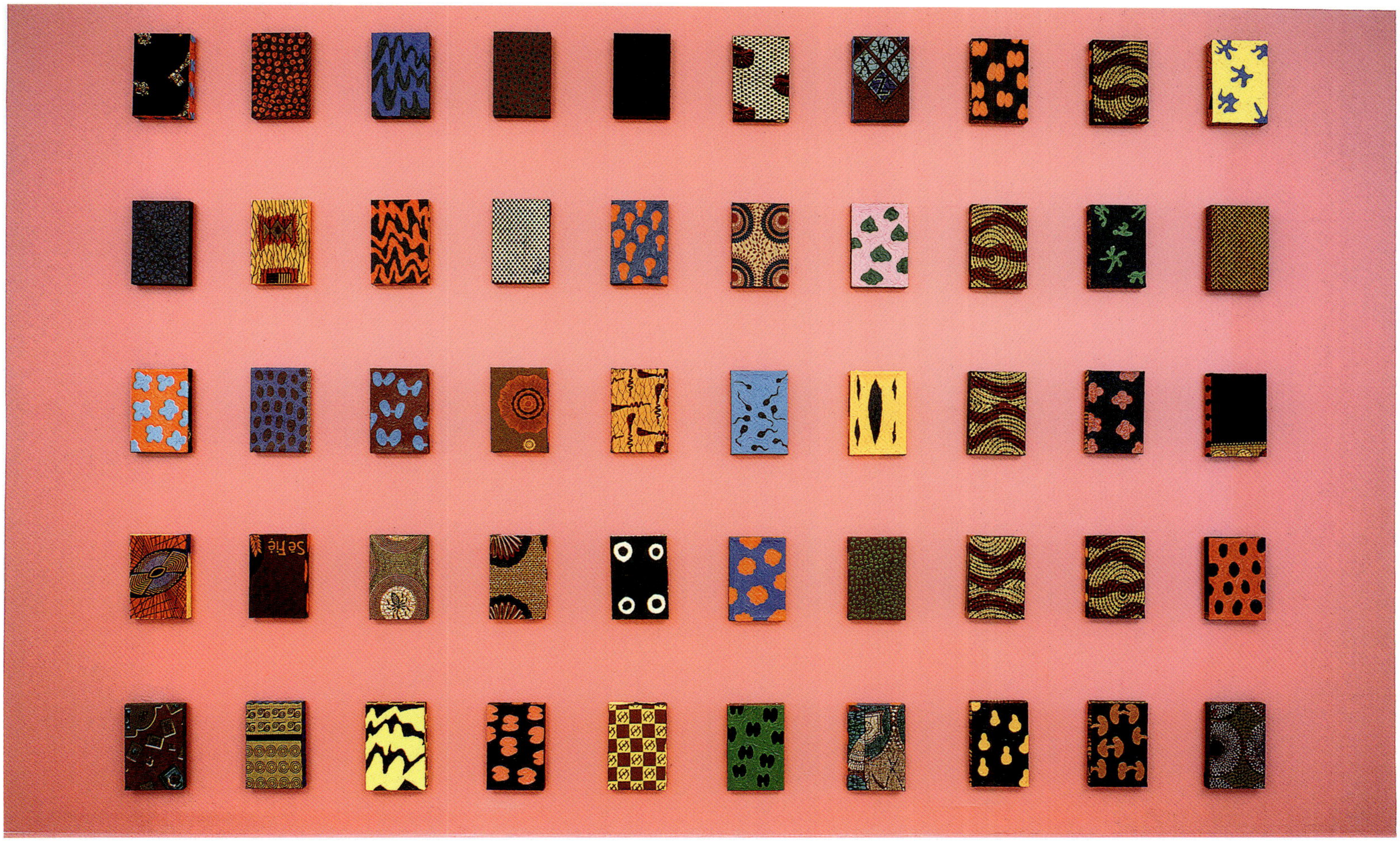

Double Dutch, 1994

Emulsion and acrylic on fifty Dutch wax printed cotton canvases,
acrylic on wall
332 x 588 x 4.5 cm
Private collection, USA

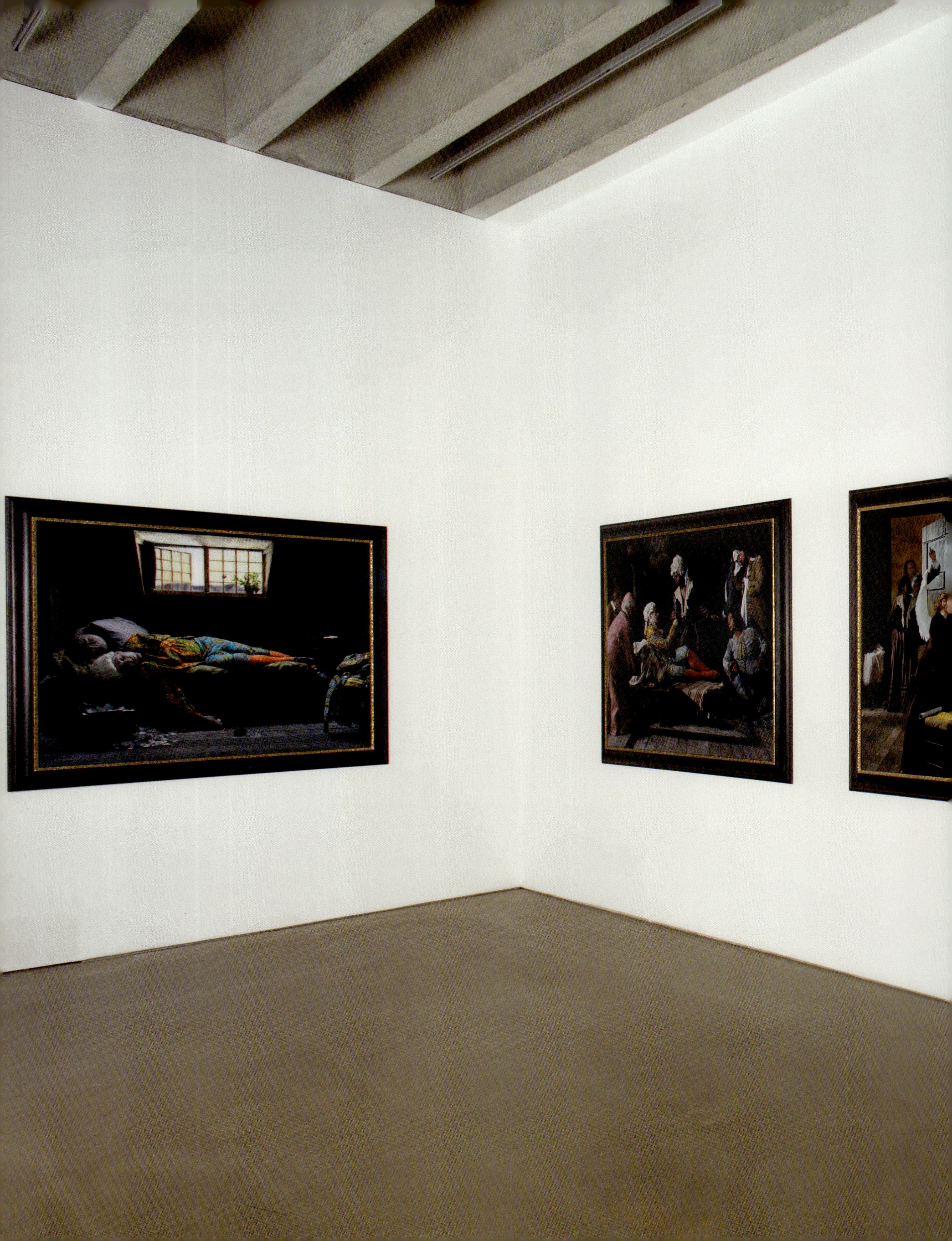

PHOTOGRAPHY

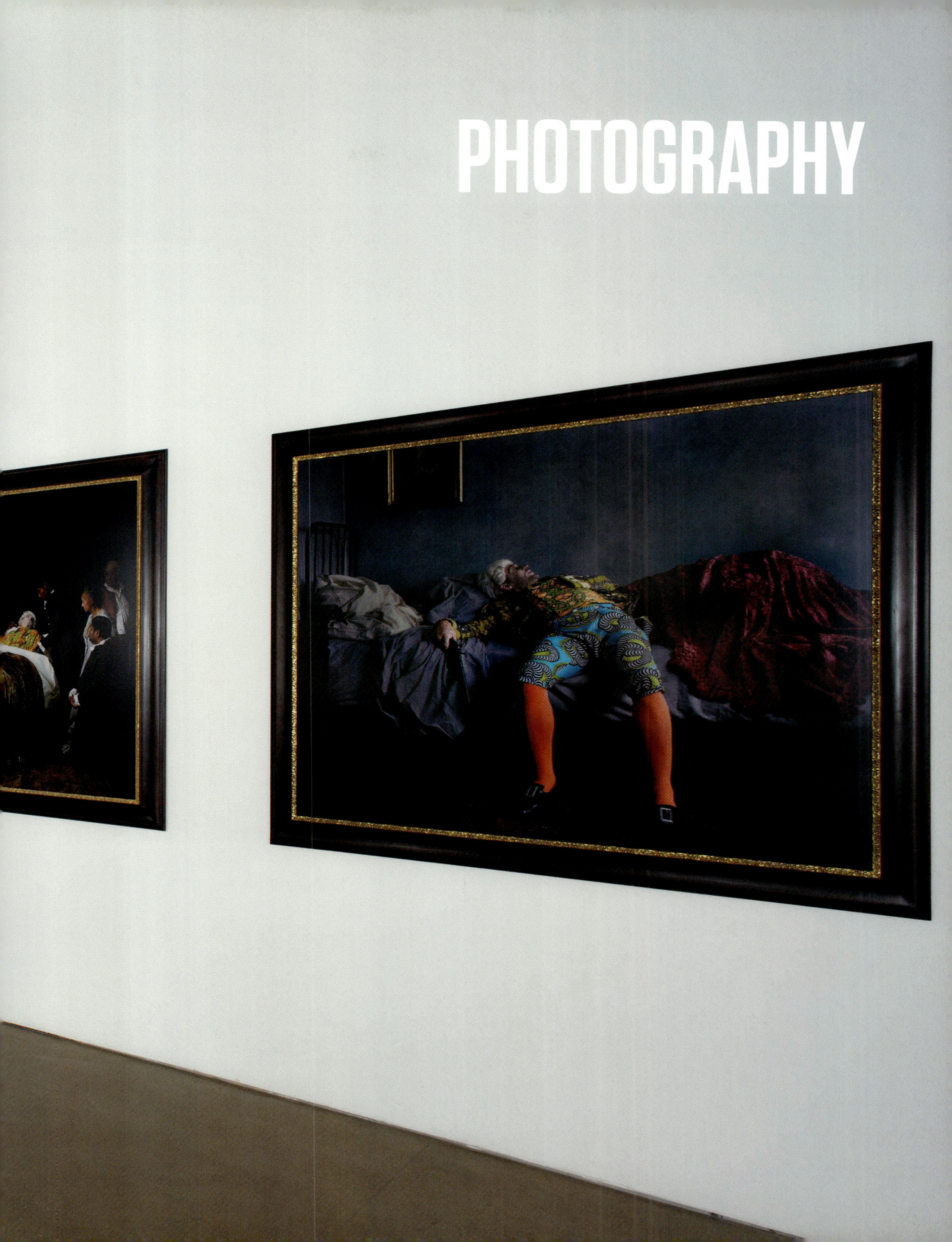

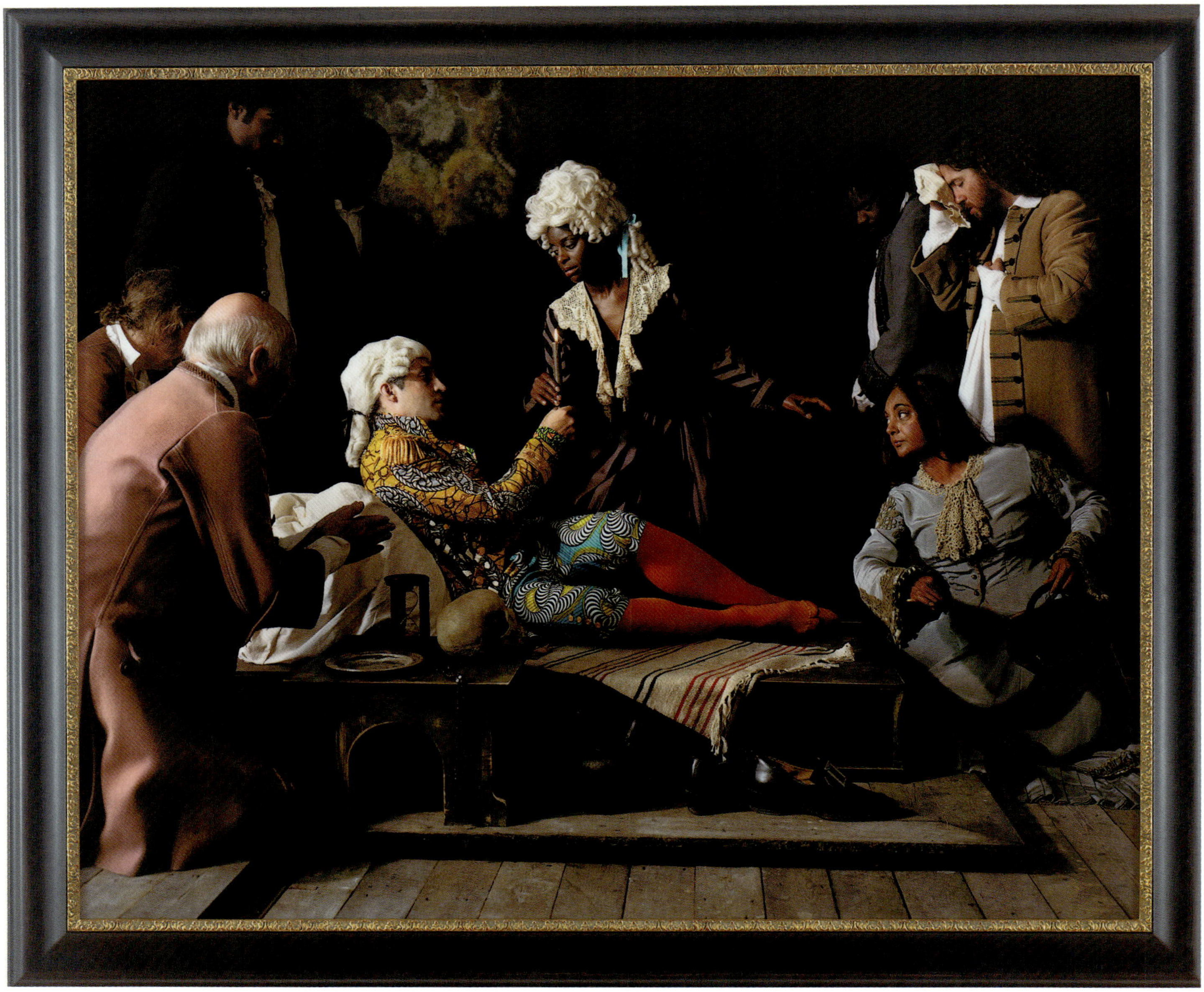

Preceding spread:

Fake Death Pictures, 2011 (from left: *The Death of Chatterton—Henry Wallis, The Death of St. Francis—Bartolomé Carducho, The Death of Leonardo da Vinci in the Arms of Francis I—François-Guillaume Ménageot, The Suicide—Manet*)

Digital chromogenic prints, ed. of 5
Four prints, each 148.9 x 194 cm (framed)
Installation view, Yorkshire Sculpture Park, Wakefield, UK, 2013

Fake Death Picture (The Death of St. Francis—Bartolomé Carducho), 2011

Digital chromogenic print, ed. of 5
194 x 148.9 cm (framed)

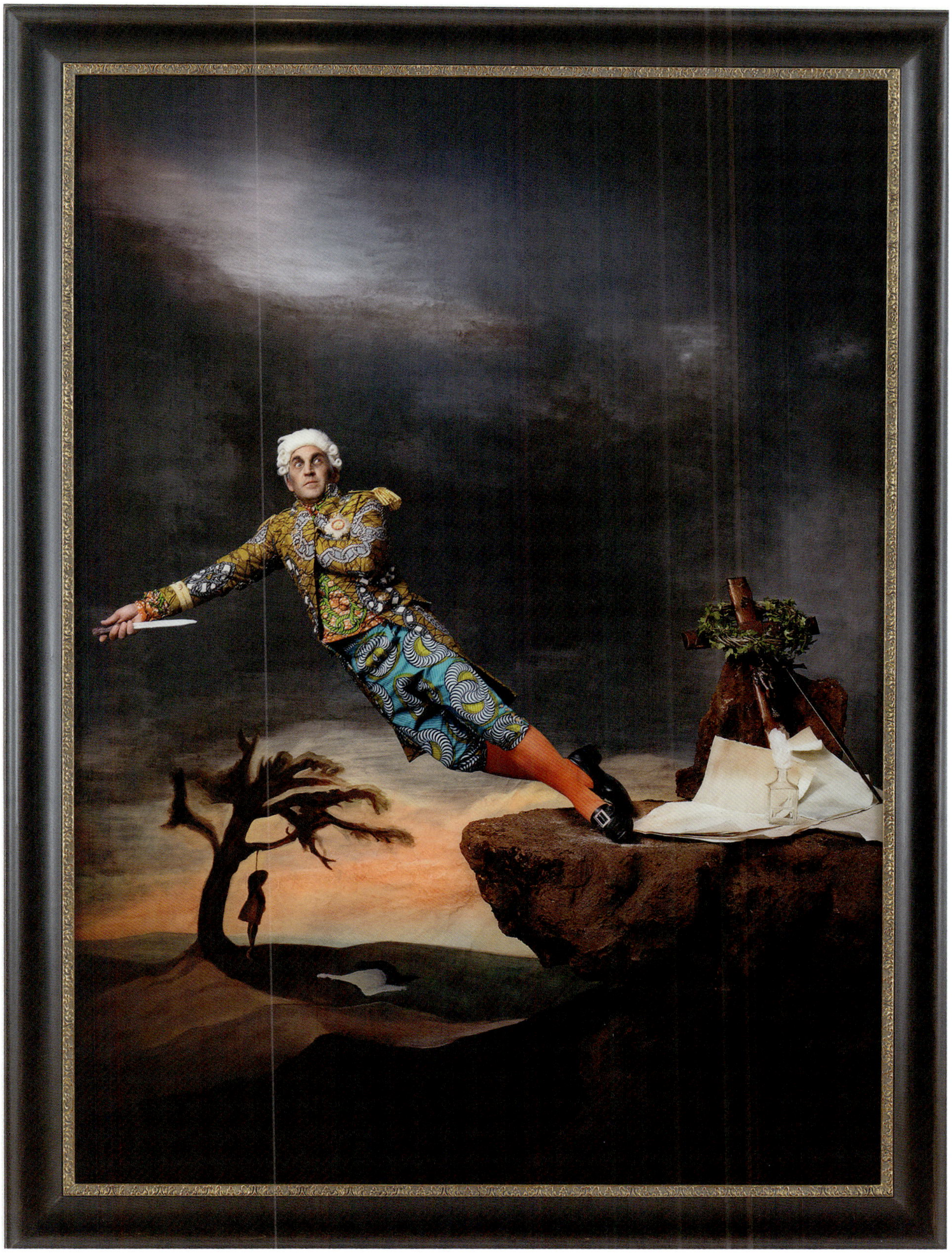

Fake Death Picture (The Suicide—Leonardo Alenza),
2011

Digital chromogenic print, ed. of 5
194 x 148.9 cm (framed)

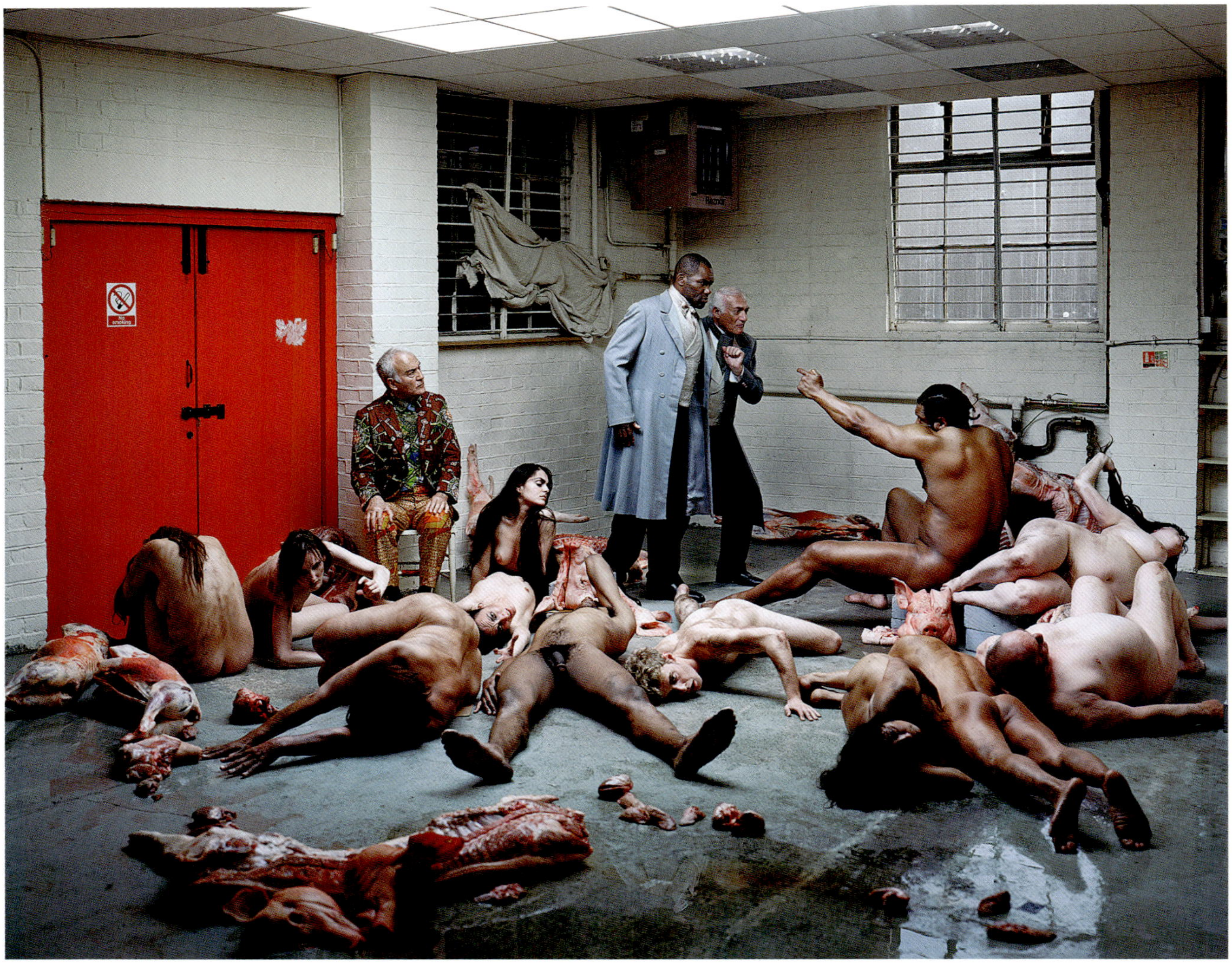

Willy Loman: The Rise and Fall, 2009
(from left: *Gluttons, Paradise*)

Four C-type prints, ed. of 5
Each 199.5 x 250 cm (framed)

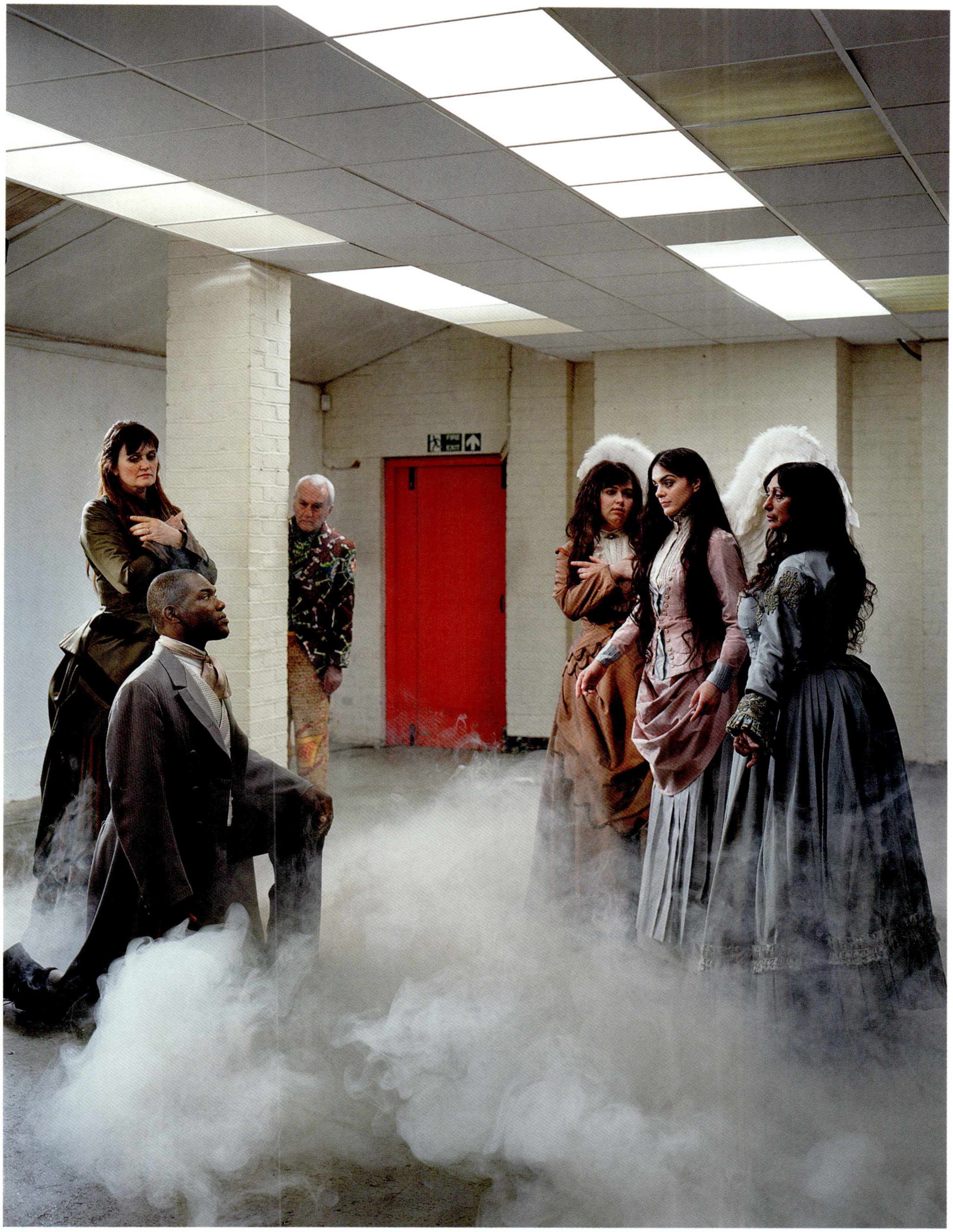

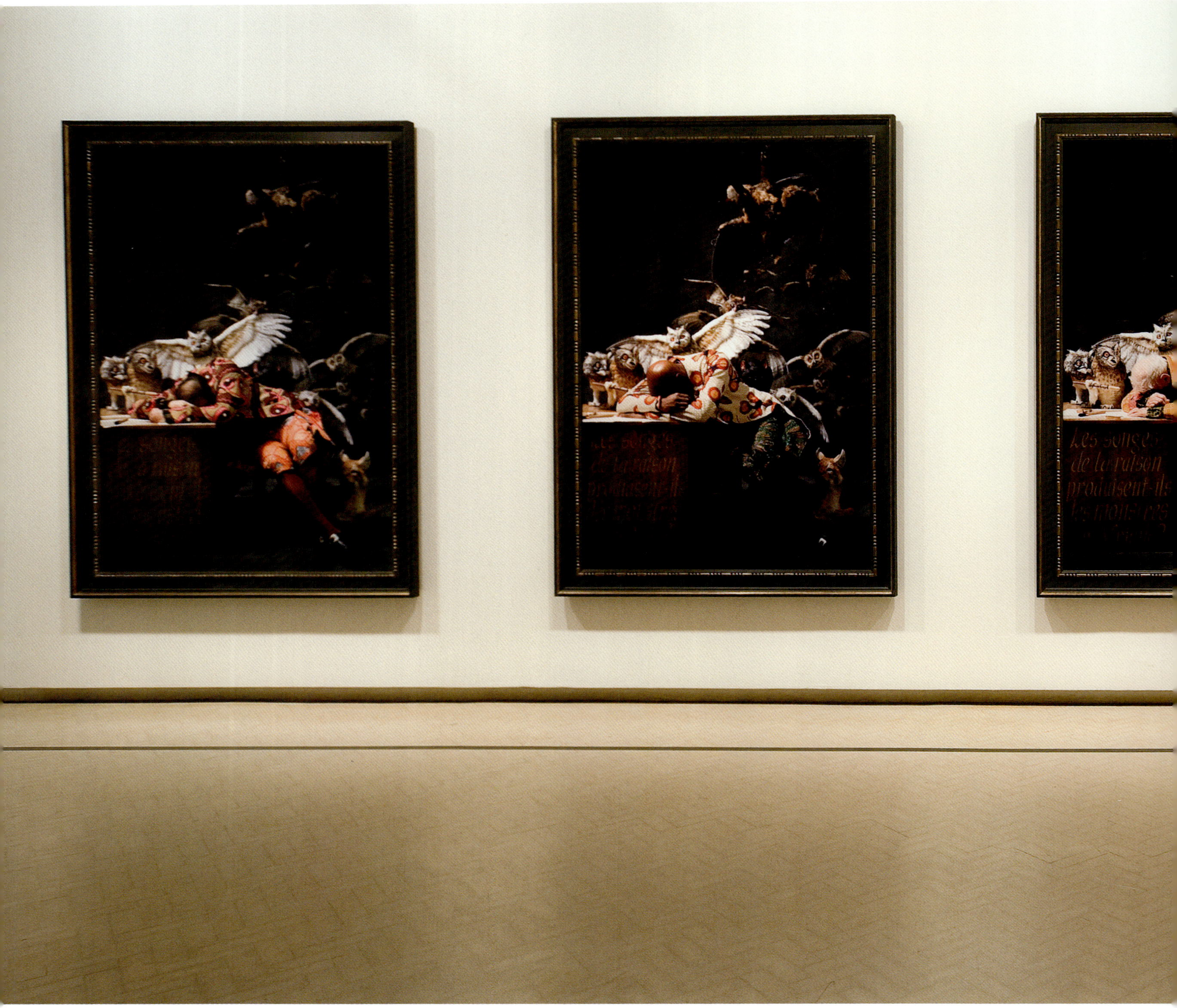

The Sleep of Reason Produces Monsters, 2008
(from left: *Australia*, *Asia*, *Africa*, *Europe*, *America*)

Five chromogenic prints mounted on aluminum, ed. of 5
Each 207 x 147.3 cm (framed)
Installation view, Museum of Contemporary Art Australia, 2008

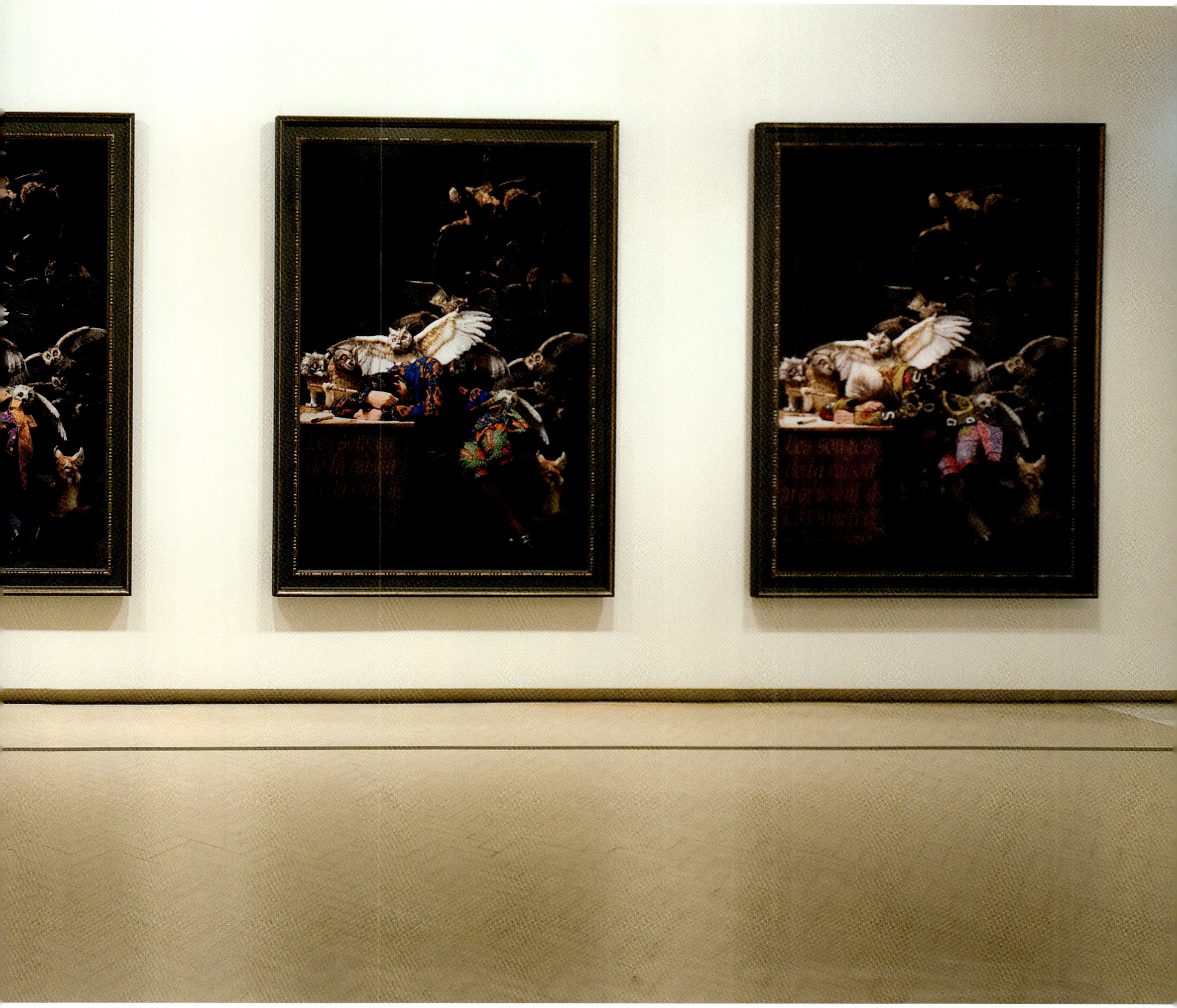

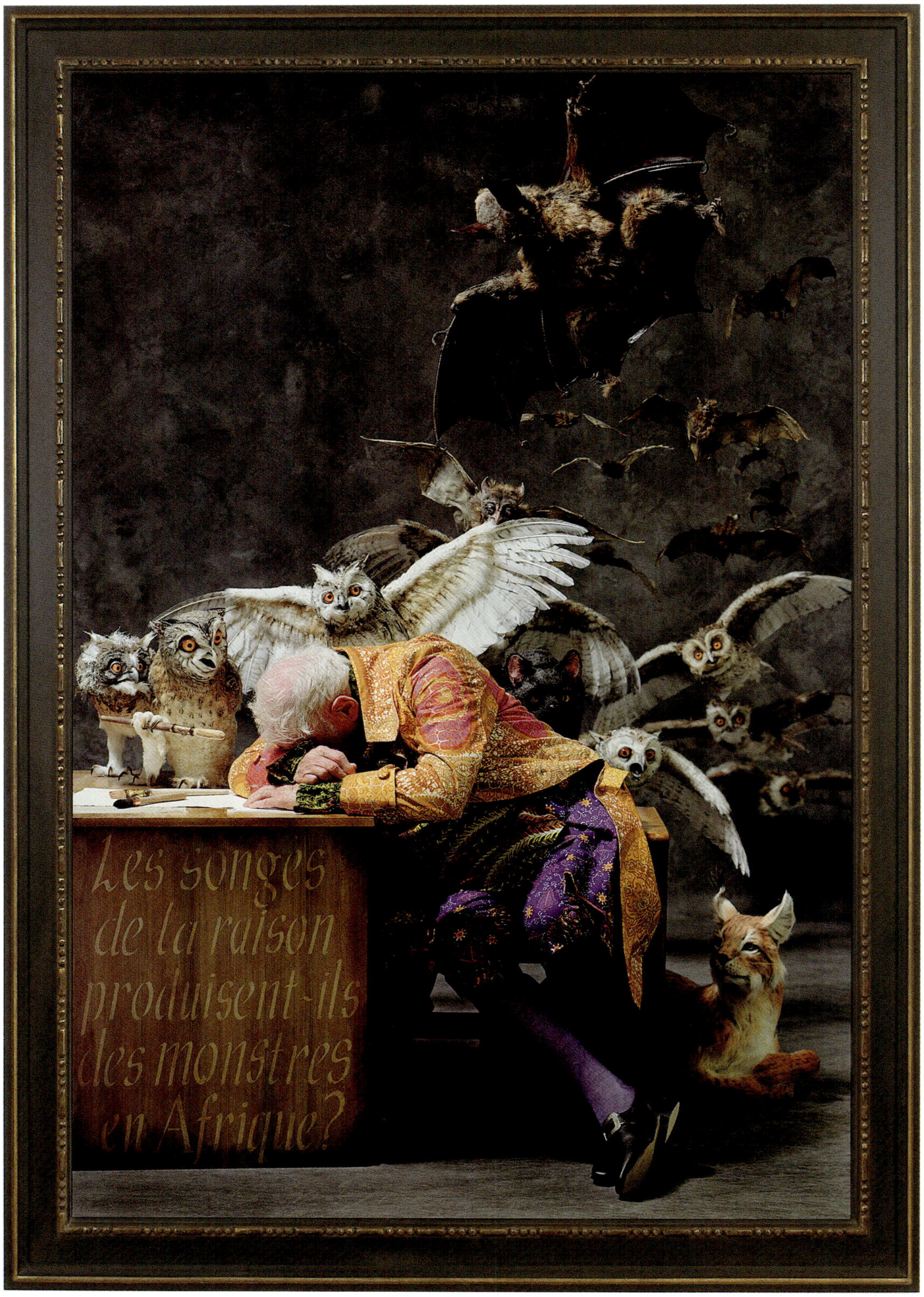

The Sleep of Reason Produces Monsters (Africa), 2008

Chromogenic print mounted on aluminum, ed. of 5
207 x 147.3 cm (framed)

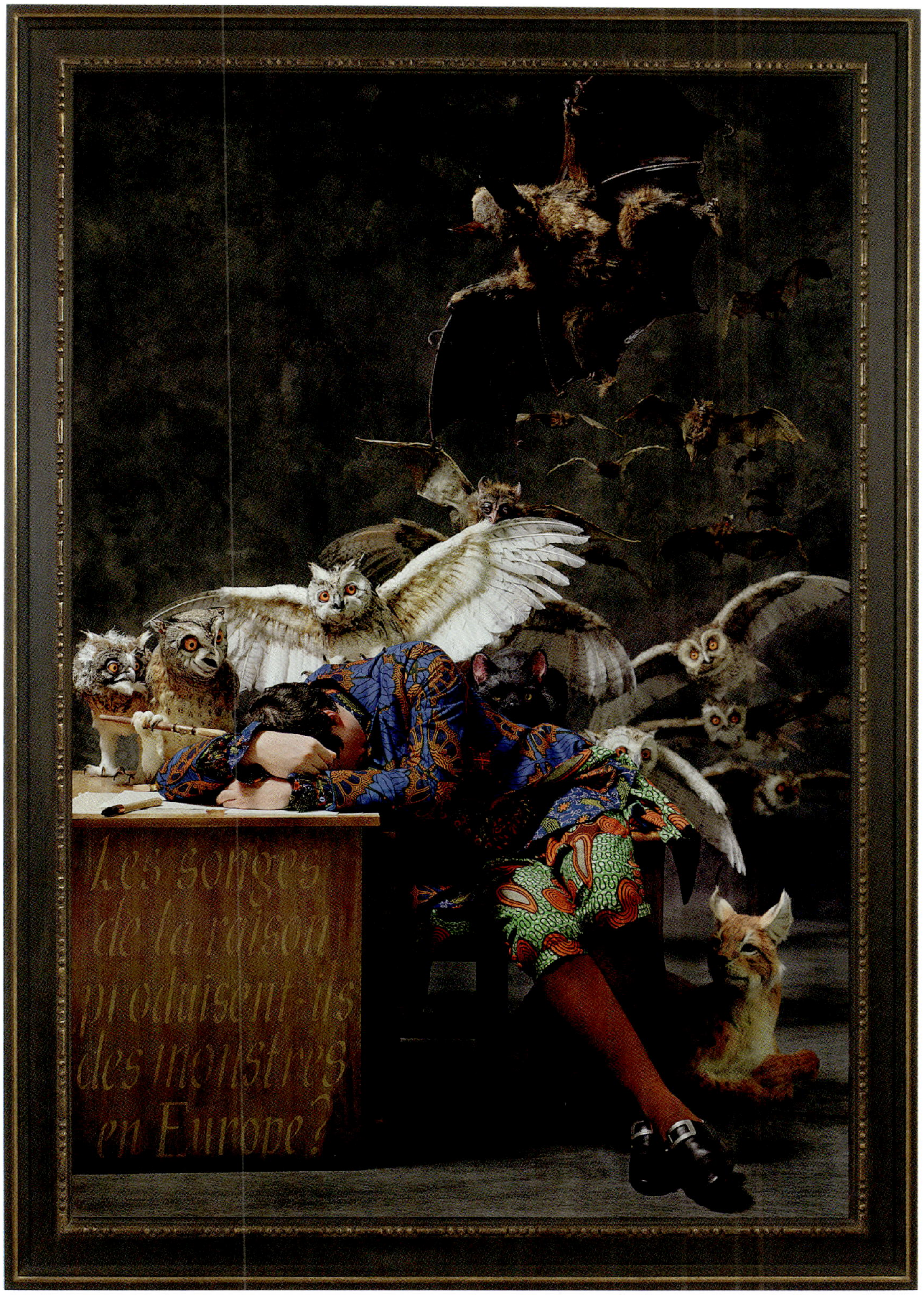

The Sleep of Reason Produces Monsters (Europe), 2008

Chromogenic print mounted on aluminum, ed. of 5
207 x 147.3 cm (framed)

La Méduse, 2008

Chromogenic print mounted on sintra board, ed. of 10
124.5 x 155 cm (framed)

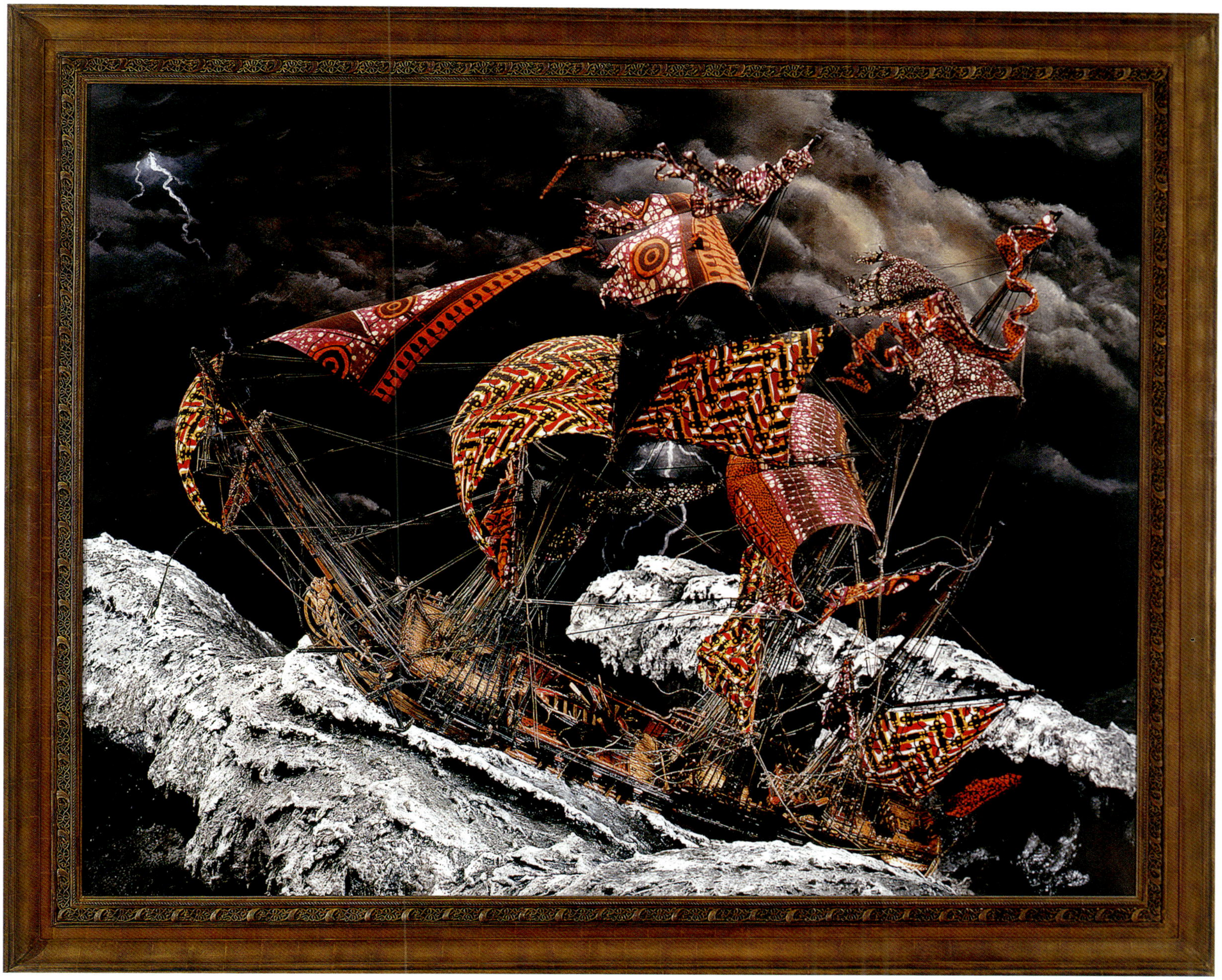

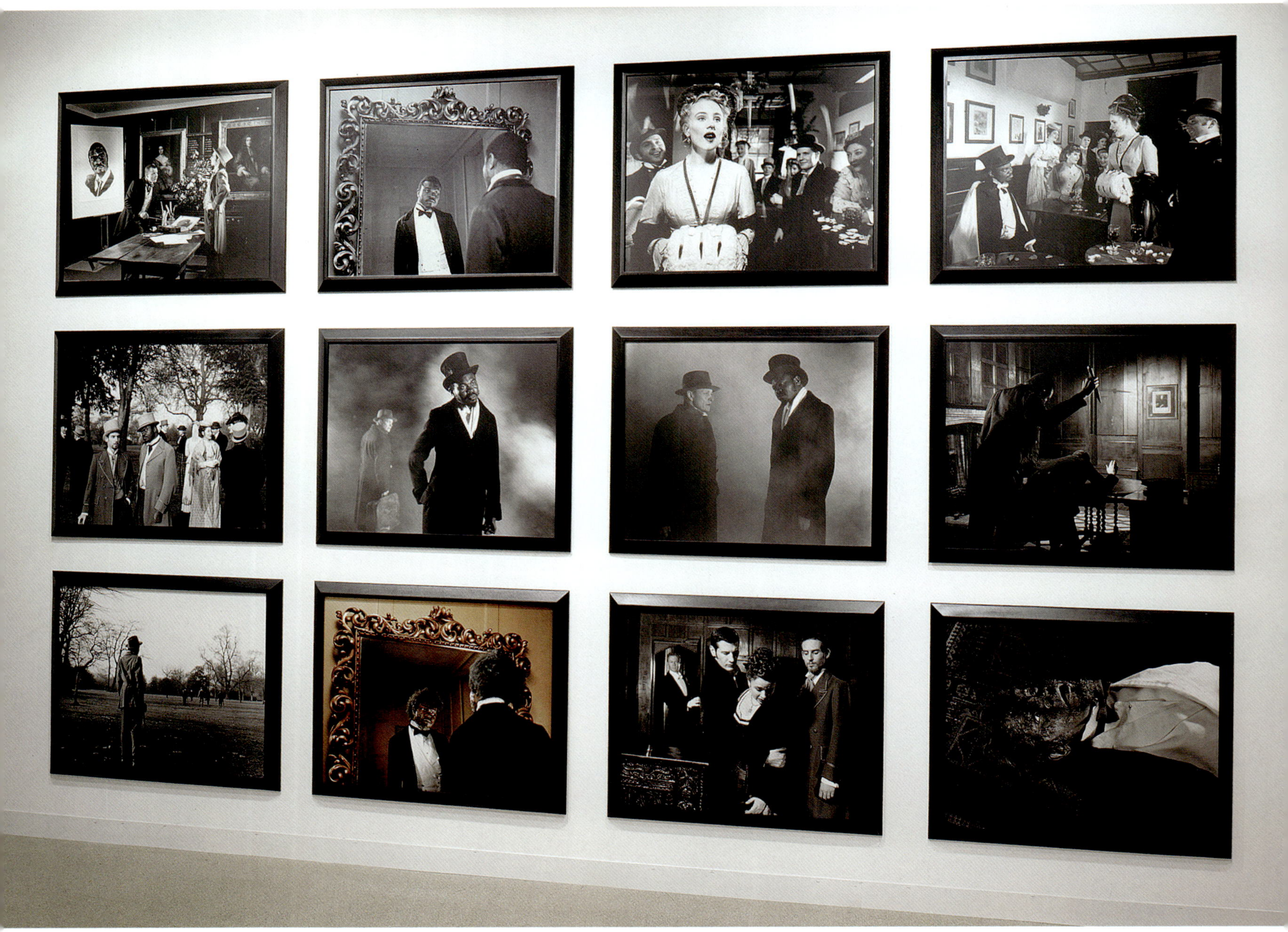

Dorian Gray, 2001

Eleven black-and-white resin prints, one digital lambda print,
ed. 4/5
Each 134 x 165 cm (framed)
Fisher Landau Center for Art
Installation view, Art Basel, 2003

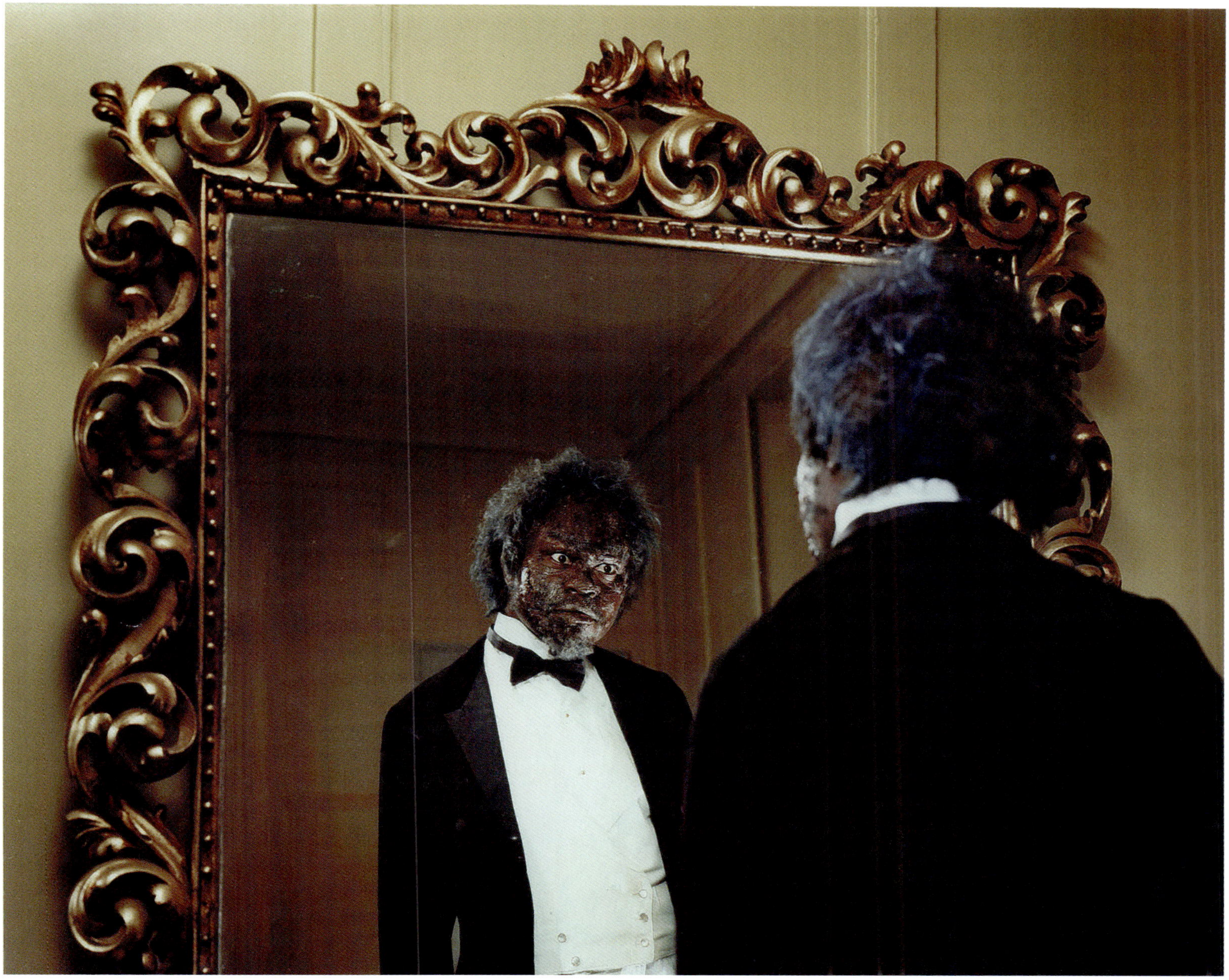

Dorian Gray (Scene 10), 2001

Digital lambda print, ed. 4/5
134 x 165 cm (framed)
Fisher Landau Center for Art

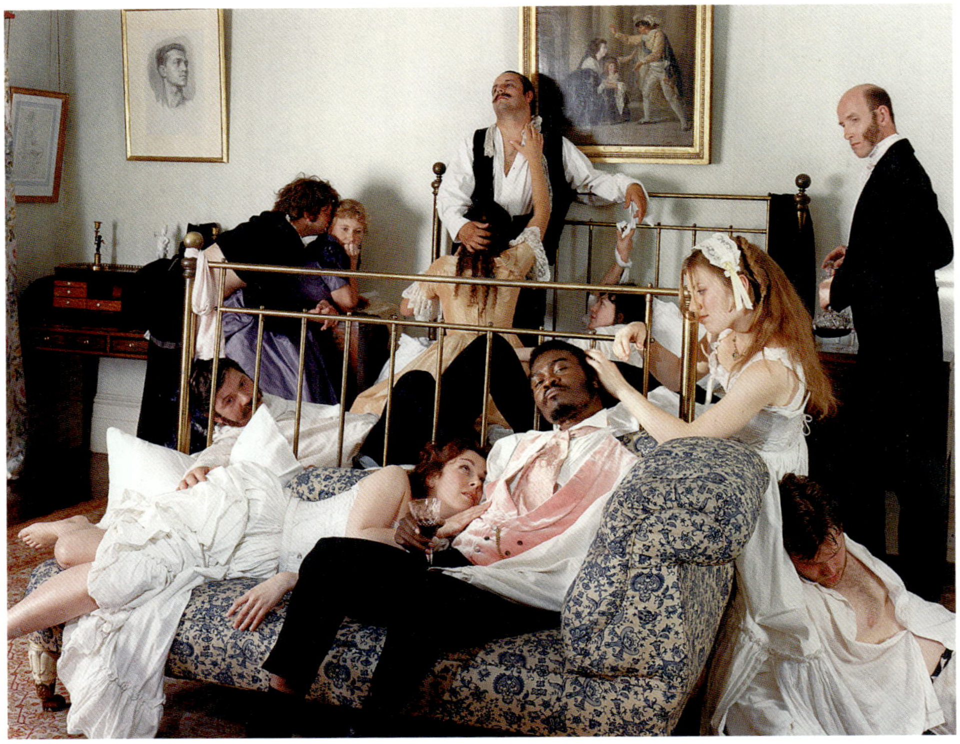

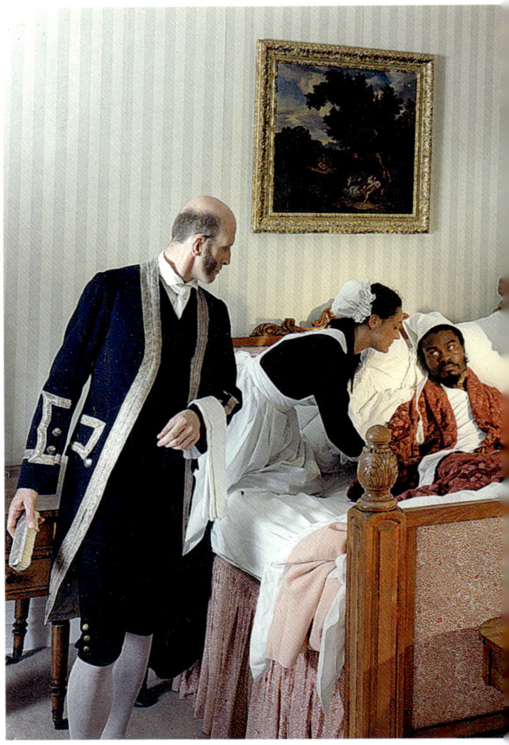

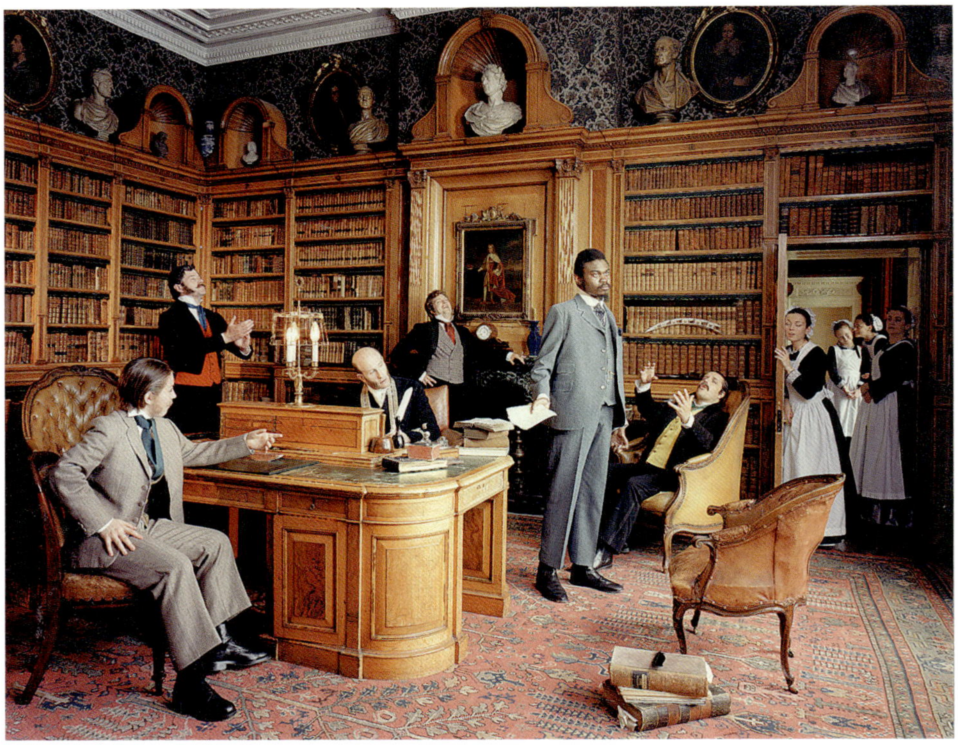

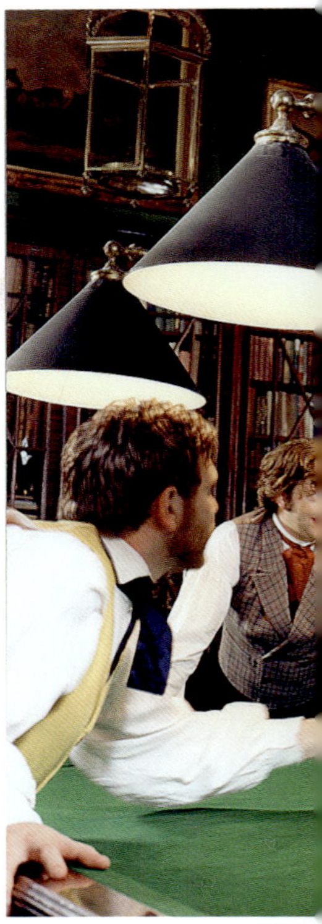

Diary of a Victorian Dandy, 1998

(from top left: *03.00 Hours*, *11.00 Hours*, *14.00 Hours*, *17.00 Hours*, *19.00 Hours*)
Five chromogenic prints
Each 183 x 228.6 cm (framed)

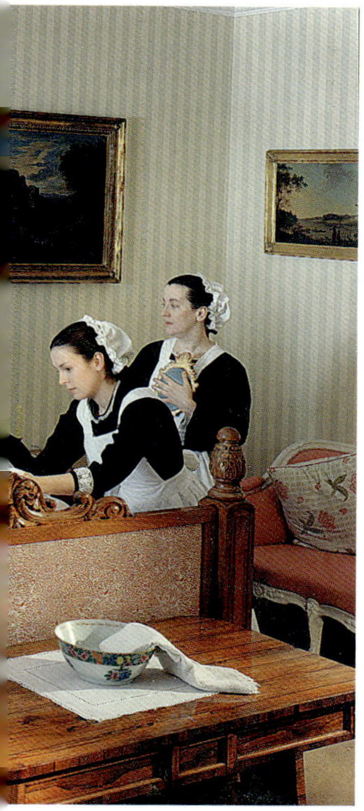

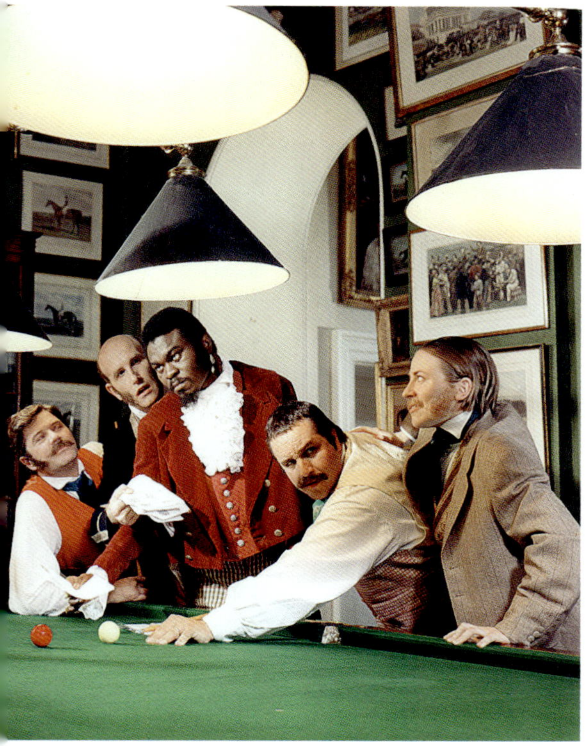

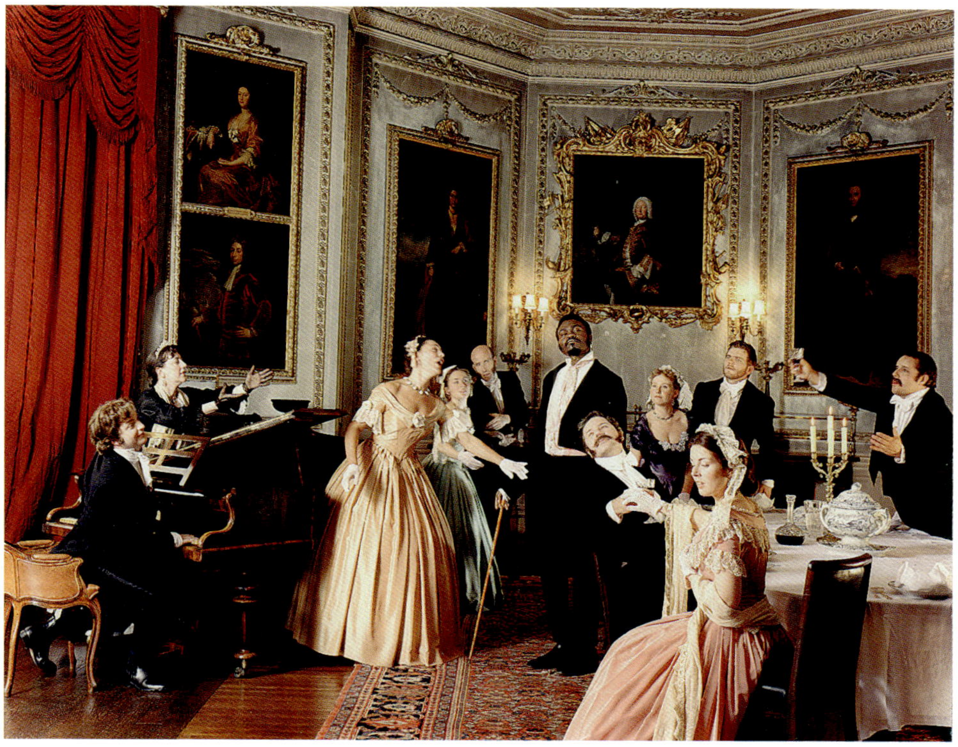

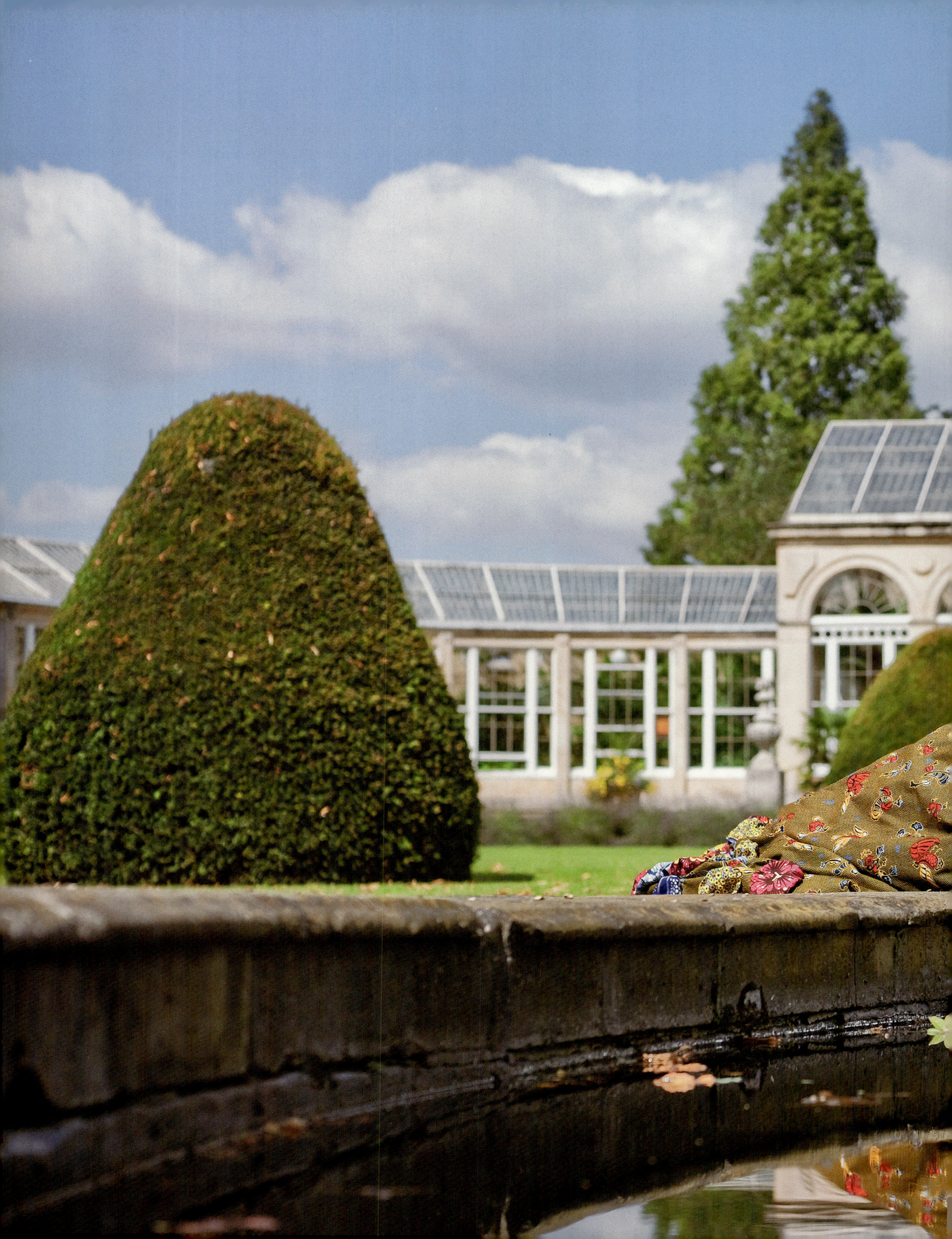

FILM

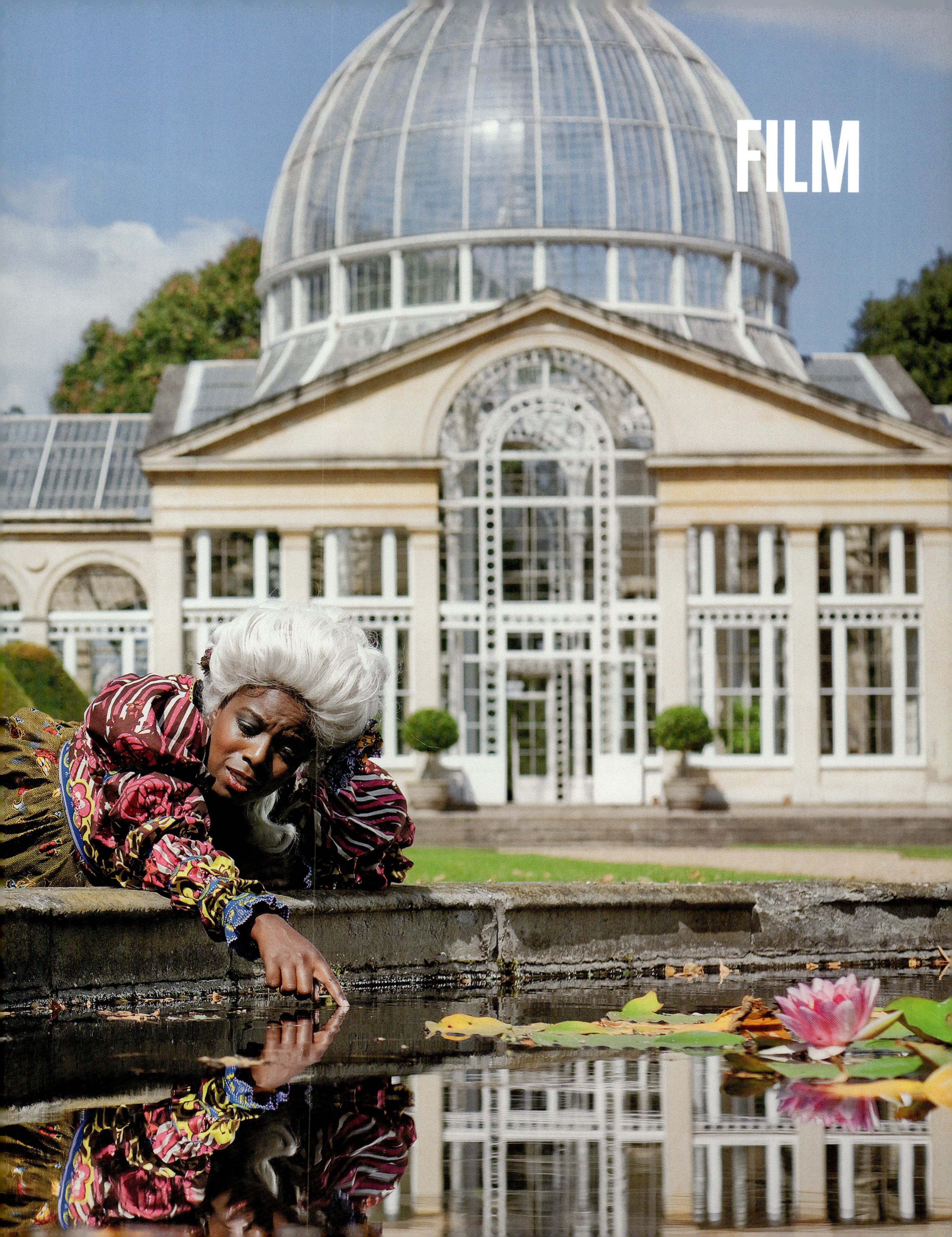

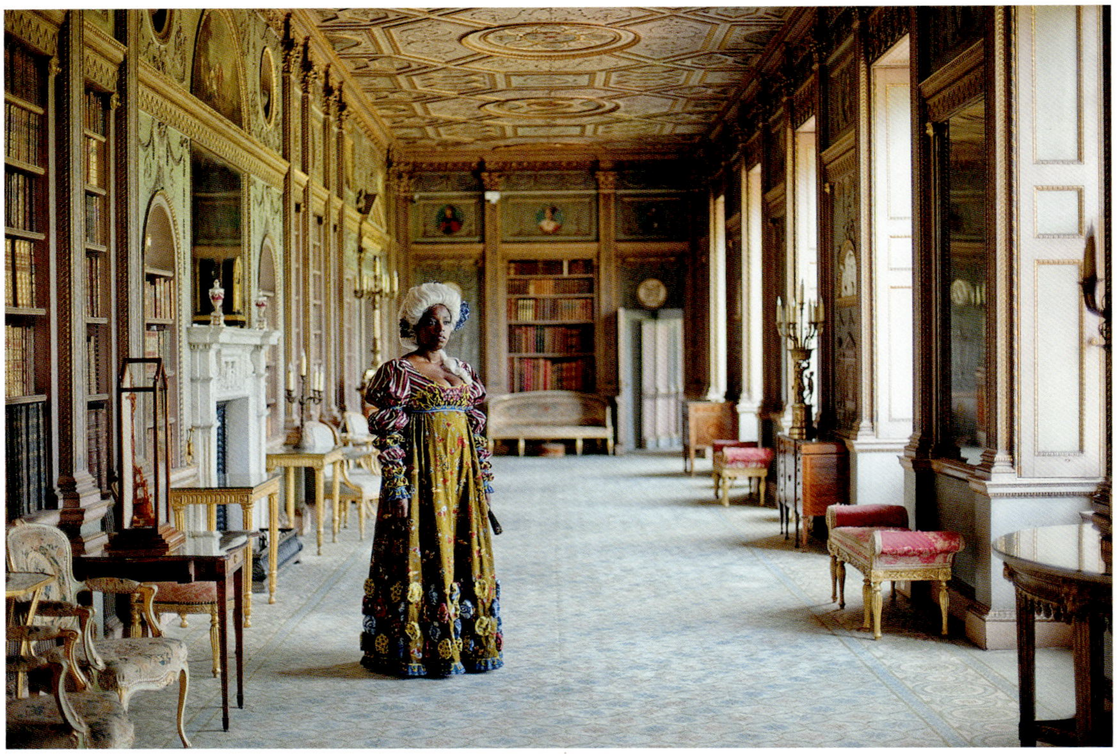

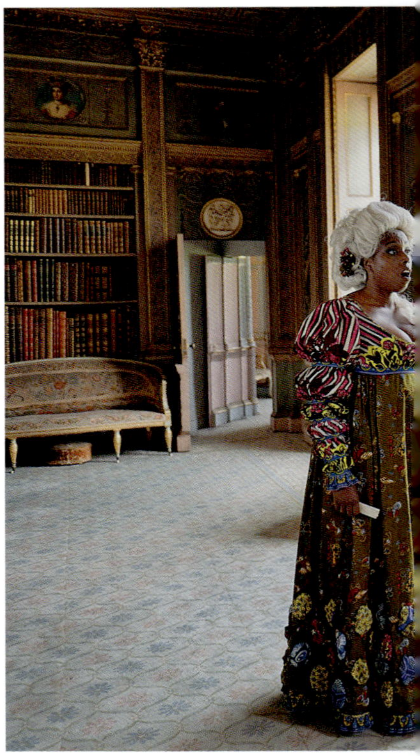

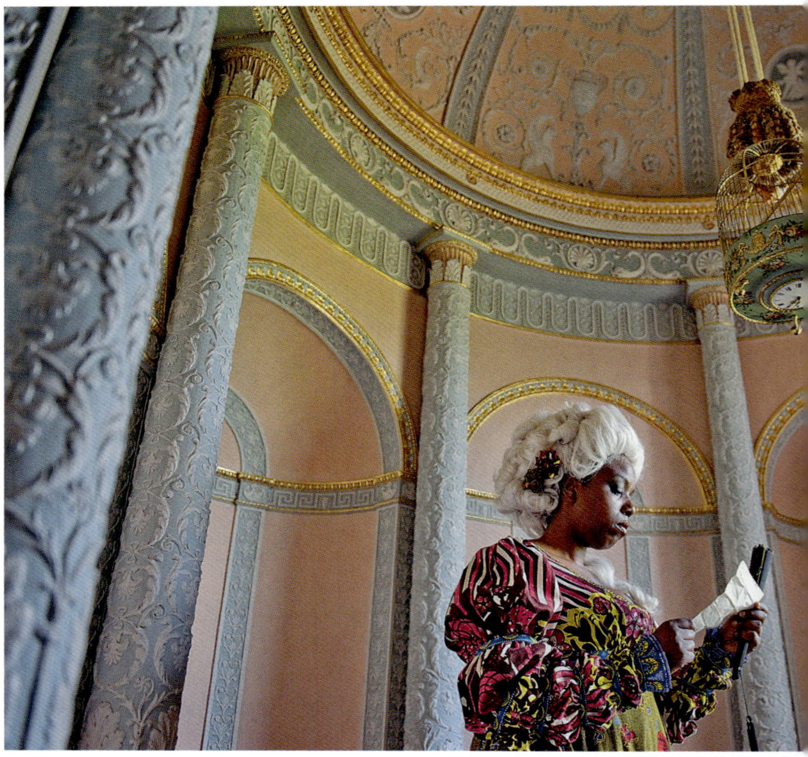

This and preceding spread:

Stills from **Addio del Passato**, 2011

Digital video, color, sound, 16:52 min., ed. of 6

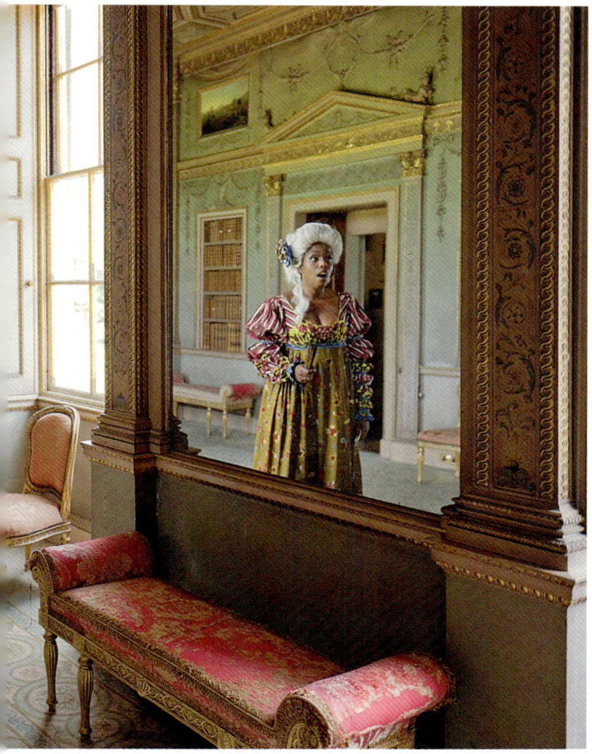

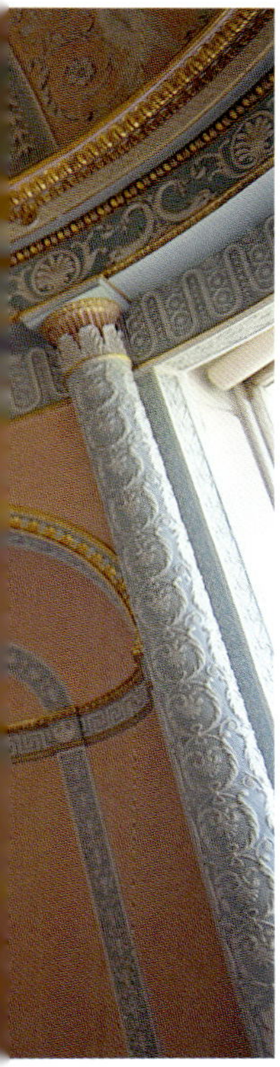

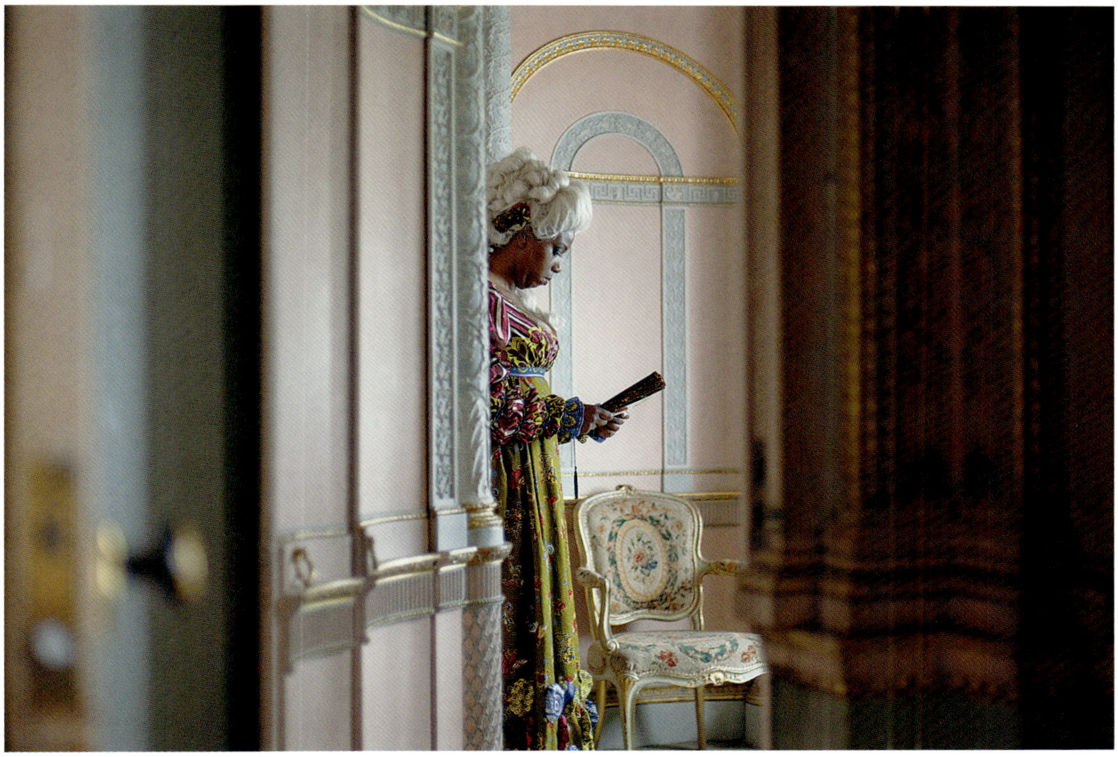

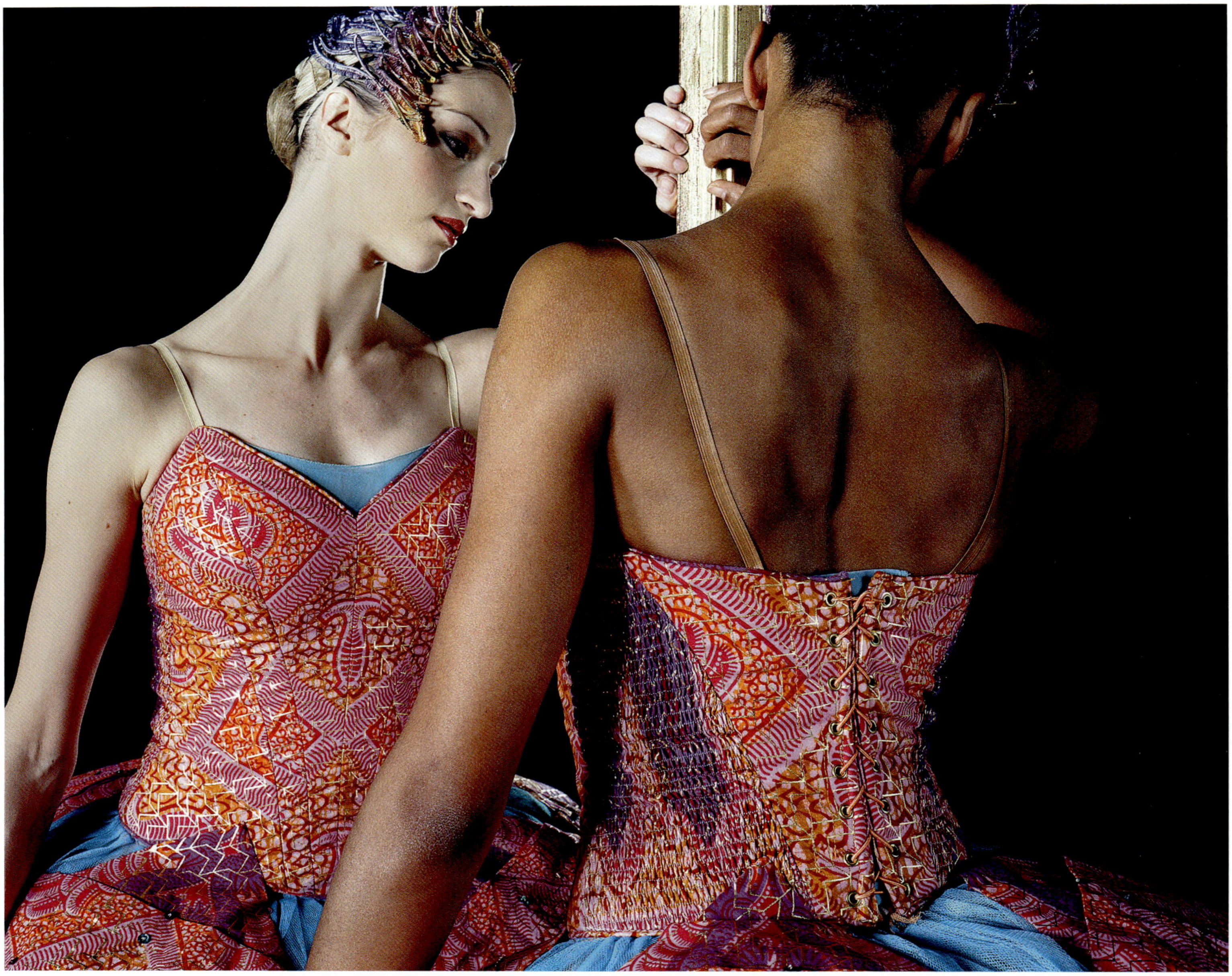

Stills from **Odile and Odette**, 2005

Digital video, color, sound, 14:28 min., ed. of 6

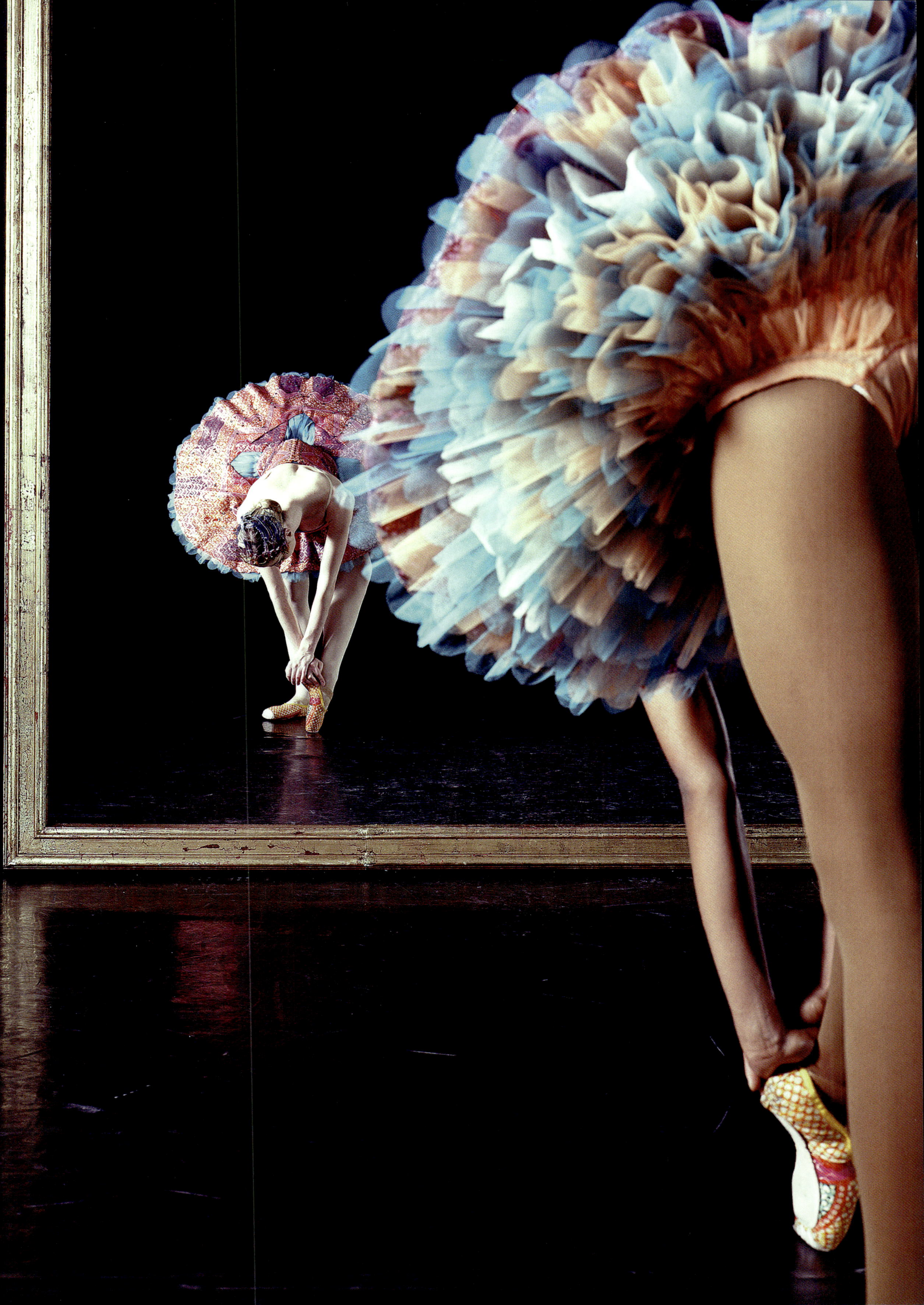

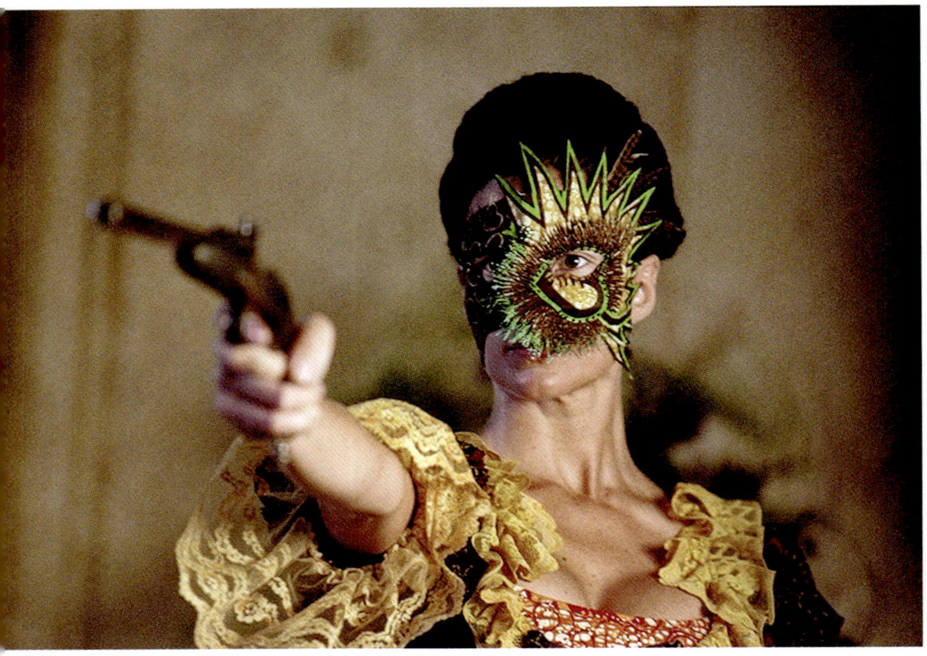

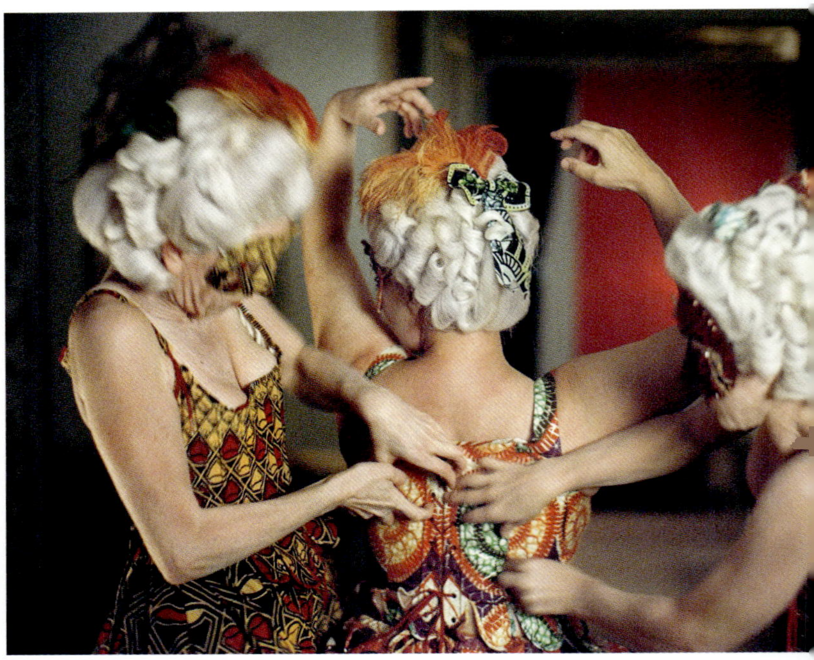

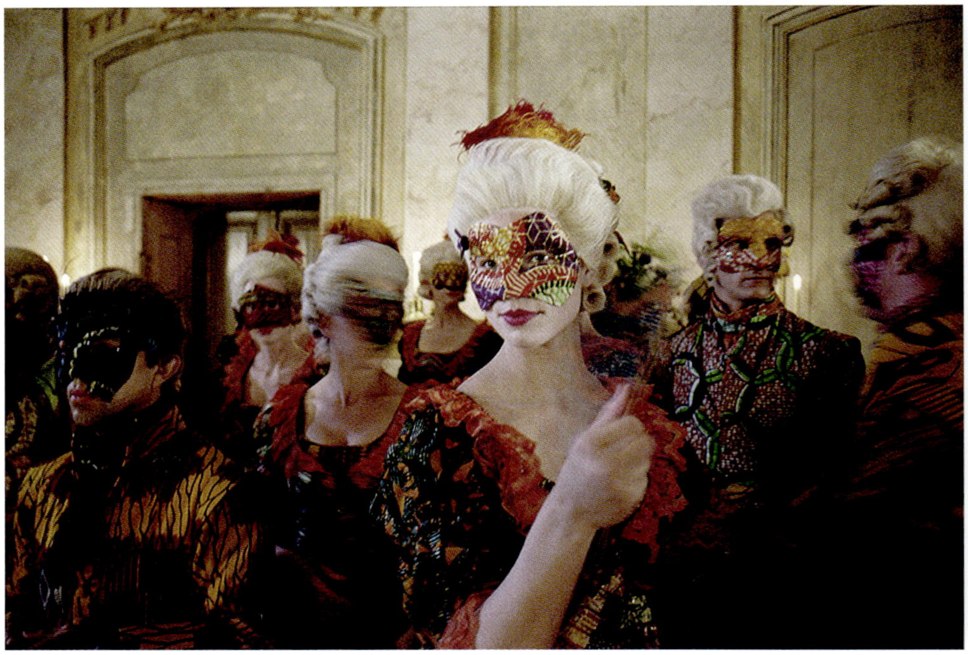

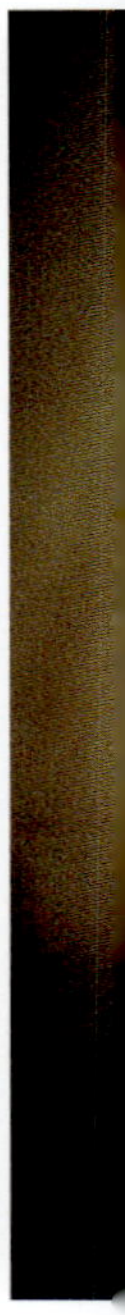

Stills from **Un Ballo in Maschera (A Masked Ball)**, 2004
Digital video, color, sound, 32 min., ed. of 6

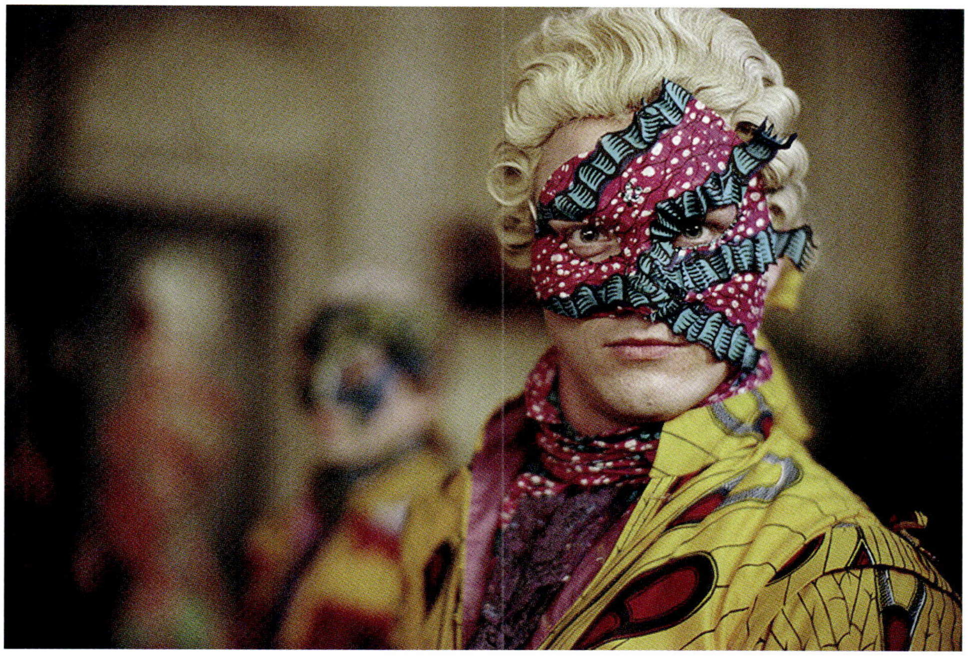
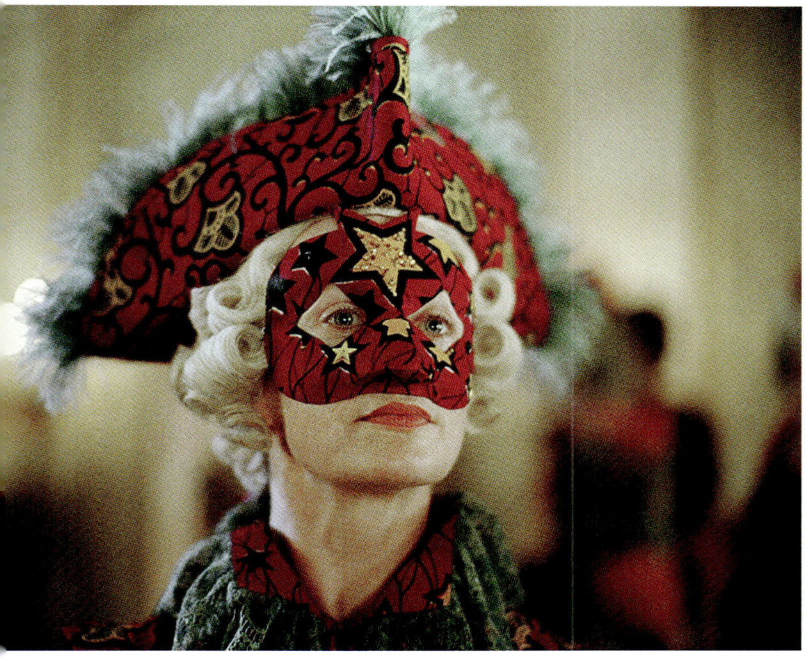
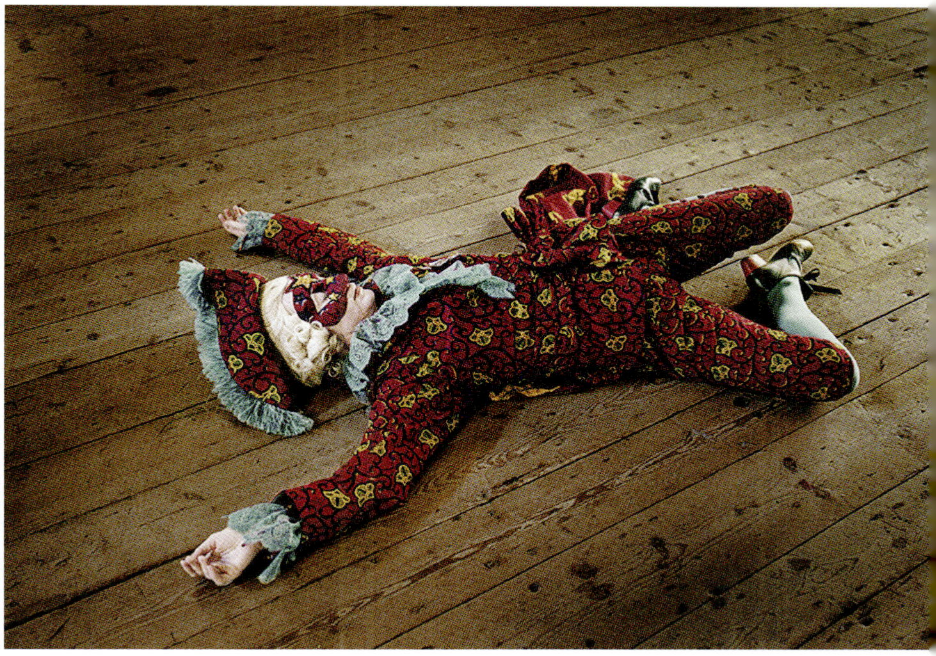

Institutional Acknowledgments

The Museum of Contemporary Art Australia would like to express sincere gratitude to the artist Yinka Shonibare MBE for his enthusiasm, support, and commitment to this exhibition and its monograph. We thank the artist's representatives, Stephen Friedman Gallery, London, and James Cohan Gallery, New York/Shanghai, for their assistance in bringing the project to fruition.

The MCA would like to acknowledge the pivotal role played by public and private lenders to this important exhibition of works by Shonibare. Without their support and generosity, the project could not go ahead.

The MCA is very pleased to work closely with its touring partners, the Brooklyn Museum, New York, and the National Museum of African Art, Smithsonian Institution, Washington, DC, on the presentation of Shonibare's exhibition to American audiences, and we thank them for their commitment and support. An edited presentation of Shonibare's exhibition was shown at the Auckland Art Gallery, New Zealand, and we thank the gallery for its dedication and support of this important artist's work.

Prestel Publishing has collaborated closely with the MCA on the realization of this monograph, and we thank the Prestel teams in New York and Munich for their support and enthusiasm. We thank essayists Robert Hobbs and Anthony Downey for their important contributions.

Curator's Acknowledgments

Rachel Kent would like to express deep appreciation to the artist Yinka Shonibare MBE for his patience and support at all stages in the realization of this exhibition and its publication. His involvement has been vital, as has that of studio staff past and present, including Ann Marie Peña, Mary Charlton, Anthony Bennett, Rachel Assaf, and Emily Lennox.

The artist's representative galleries and their staffs have been enormously helpful and supportive at all stages. They include Stephen Friedman, Joanna Stella-Sawicka, Angela Kunicky, Julia Jeuvell, and James Green of Stephen Friedman Gallery, London; and Jim and Jane Cohan, Jill Feldman, and Ginger Cofield of James Cohan Gallery, New York/Shanghai.

Institutional support has been generously provided by Charles Desmarais, Judy Kim, and Tumelo Mosaka at the Brooklyn Museum. At the National Museum of African Art, Smithsonian Institution, Washington, DC, the support of Johnetta Betsch Cole, Sharon F. Patton, Alan Knezevich, and Karen Millbourne is enormously appreciated. Sincere thanks are due to the team at Auckland Art Gallery, including Christopher Saines and Louise Pether.

The curator would especially like to thank Robert Hobbs and Anthony Downey, as well as Prestel's Chris Lyon and Anja Besserer for their guidance of the original exhibition catalogue, and Karen Levine and Friederike Schirge for their generous support and hard work on this revised and updated edition. Phil Kovacevich is to be thanked for the refreshed design of the new edition.

Rachel Kent is very grateful to all staff at the MCA Australia for their support and collegiality. She would like to acknowledge and thank curatorial assistants Naomi Evans and Joel Mu for their integral work across the exhibition and its monograph, as well as Karen Hall for her touring support at all stages; Claire Orrell for her elegant, thoughtful graphic design and Patrick Leong for his production coordination of the original catalogue; and the MCA's Registration and Installation staff for their close collaboration. She is also grateful to Margaret Farmer and Dr. Marian Kent for diligent reading and commentary.

Artist's Acknowledgments

Yinka Shonibare MBE would like to thank the following for their continued support and contributions: Kayode Shonibare Lewis, Sian Lewis, Maxa Zoller, Ann Marie Peña, Mary Charlton, Gaia Alessi, Anthony Bennett, Syl Devilly, Kari Furre, Debbie Gamble, Kevin Harlow, Anna Kesteven, Nina Leistner, Mandy Lock, Owen Moore, Barry Thewliss, Chris Wilson, Phil Allen, Cain McLaughlin, Robin Widdowson, Elaine Gerard, Karen Bennett, Lydia Bennett, Elizabeth Ann MacGregor, Rachel Kent, Suzanne Landau, Laurie Farrell, Okwui Enwezor, William Stover, and Hugo Glendinning.

A very special thank-you to staff at Stephen Friedman Gallery, London, and James Cohan Gallery, New York/Shanghai.

Index of Artworks

Unless otherwise indicated in parentheses, artworks are by Yinka Shonibare MBE. Page numbers in *italics* refer to illustrations.

Collection Credits

Captions throughout this book credit museum or private collections as appropriate. Unless otherwise specified in captions, all works by Yinka Shonibare MBE are courtesy the artist; Stephen Friedman Gallery, London; and James Cohan Gallery, New York/Shanghai. Artworks reproduced as fig. 2 and on pp. 84–85, 189, 190–91, and 192–93 are also courtesy Anna Schwartz Gallery, Sydney/Melbourne; artwork reproduced on pp. 181 and 182–83 is also courtesy Edward Tyler Nahem Fine Art, New York.

Photography Credits

Unless otherwise noted below, all Shonibare artworks © Yinka Shonibare MBE and provided courtesy the artist and his galleries as credited above.

Cover

Front: Jenni Carter, courtesy Museum of Contemporary Art Australia; back: Stephen White

Frontispieces

Pages 2–3, 4, 6, 26, 42, 51: Stephen White

Figures

Figures 1, 2, 10, 17: Stephen White; 3: © National Gallery, London / Art Resource, NY; 4: by kind permission of the Trustees of the Wallace Collection, London / Art Resource, NY; 5: Jenni Carter, courtesy Museum of Contemporary Art Australia; 6: by kind permission of National Galleries Scotland; 7: Patrick Gries for the Musée du quai Branly, Paris; 8: by kind permission of Punch Ltd., www.punch.co.uk; 9: NASA Harrison Schmitt; 11: John Webb, by kind permission of Sir John Soane's Museum, London; 12: Jason Mandella; 14: by kind permission of the National Gallery of Victoria, Melbourne; 15: David Westwood, courtesy the artist and National Maritime Museum, Greenwich; 16: courtesy Yorkshire Sculpture Park; 19: © VG-Bild-kunst, Bonn 2013; 20: courtesy the Library of Virginia

Plates

Pages 52–53, 59: Mark Blower; 54–55, 56–57, 80–81, 94–95, 204–5: Jonty Wilde; 60–61, 66, 67, 68, 69, 70–71, 72–73, 74, 75, 76, 77, 78–79, 84–85, 87, 88, 89, 90, 91, 96, 97, 98, 99, 116, 117, 118–19, 128, 129, 130–31, 132–33, 135, 136–37, 144–45, 146, 147, 152, 153, 154–55, 157, 166–67, 172, 173, 174, 175, 177, 178, 179, 184–85, 186, 187, 188, 189, 194, 195, 196–97, 198, 199, 200, 201, 202, 208, 209, 217: Stephen White; 64–65, 120, 143, 150–51, 156, 158–59, 160, 161, 162–63, 168, 170, 181, 182–83, 210–11: Jenni Carter, courtesy Museum of Contemporary Art Australia; 100–101, 103, 104–5, 106–7, 108–9, 110–11, 112–13: Brooklyn Museum photograph; 114–15: Ross Whitaker, courtesy Newark Museum; 82, 83, 121, 122, 123, 124–25, 127, 206, 207: Jason Mandella; 138–39, 140, 141: Patrick Gries for the Musée du quai Branly, Paris; 148, 149: Matt Flynn; 165: Peter Hauck; 166, 169: Ahlburg Keate Photography; 190–91, 192–93: courtesy Anna Schwartz Gallery; 203: Jean Vong

This edition is a revised and expanded version of a catalogue published in 2008 on the occasion of the exhibition *Yinka Shonibare MBE*, organized and toured by the Museum of Contemporary Art, Sydney (now the Museum of Contemporary Art Australia).

Published by Prestel,
a member of Verlagsgruppe Random House GmbH

Prestel Verlag
Neumarkter Strasse 28
81673 Munich
Tel.: +49 89 41 36 0
Fax: +49 89 41 36 23 35

Prestel Publishing Ltd.
14–17 Wells Street
London W1T 3PD
Tel.: +44 (0)20 7323 5004
Fax: +44 (0)20 7323 0271

Prestel Publishing
900 Broadway, Suite 603
New York, NY 10003
Tel.: +1 212 995 2720
Fax: +1 212 995 2733
E-mail: sales@prestel-usa.com

www.prestel.com

Editorial direction by Karen A. Levine
Design by Phil Kovacevich
Proofread by Dianne Woo
Production by Friederike Schirge
Separations by Repro Ludwig
Printed in China by C&C Joint Printing Co., Ltd.

FSC www.fsc.org MIX Paper from responsible sources FSC® C008047

Verlagsgruppe Random House FSC® N001967
Printed on FSC®-certified paper Chinese GS matt art

Library of Congress Cataloging-in-Publication Data
Yinka Shonibare MBE / edited by Rachel Kent. — Revised and updated edition.
pages cm
Summary: "Newly revised and updated, this authoritative book presents the exciting, ironic, and often subversive work of Yinka Shonibare MBE, one of the stars of the international art scene. Born in London and raised in Nigeria, Shonibare employs a diverse range of media—from sculpture, painting, and installation to photography and film—to probe matters of race, class, cultural identity, and history. He is perhaps best known for his signature use of a colorful 'African' batik fabric that actually originated in Indonesia and was introduced to Africa in the 19th century by British and Dutch colonizers. Incorporated into Victorian costumes, covering sculptures of extraterrestrials, or stretched like canvas for paintings, these vibrant textiles cleverly challenge issues of origin and authenticity. This book—the most comprehensive resource available on Shonibare—presents the best work of the London-based artist's career, including his high-profile project for the Fourth Plinth in London's Trafalgar Square and other innovative public sculptures. Whether lampooning Victorian propriety or commenting on what it means to be an 'alien,' Shonibare makes art that challenges straightforward interpretations"— Provided by publisher.
"This edition is a revised and expanded version of a catalogue published in 2008 on the occasion of the exhibition *Yinka Shonibare MBE*, organized and toured by the Museum of Contemporary Art, Sydney (now the Museum of Contemporary Art Australia)."
Includes bibliographical references.
ISBN 978-3-7913-4872-8 (hardback)
1. Shonibare, Yinka, 1962– Exhibitions. I. Kent, Rachel. Time and transformation in the art of Yinka Shonibare MBE. II. Hobbs, Robert Carleton, 1946– Politics of representation. III. Downey, Anthony. Setting the stage.
IV. Shonibare, Yinka, 1962– Works. Selections.
N6797.S53A4 2014
709.2—dc23

2013022332

Front cover: *Black Gold II* (detail), 2006. Acrylic on twenty-five Dutch wax printed cotton canvases, acrylic on wall; 330.2 x 673.1 cm. Private collection

Back cover: *Girl, Girl on Globe* (detail), 2009. Two life-size mannequins, Dutch wax printed cotton, globe; 98 x 109 x 50 cm, 50 x 115 x 33 cm (figures); 85 x 85 x 85 cm (globe). Private collection

Frontispiece (pp. 2–3): *Nelson's Ship in a Bottle*, 2010. Fiberglass, steel, brass, resin, UV ink on Dutch wax printed cotton, linen rigging, acrylic, wood; 290 x 525 x 235 cm. National Maritime Museum, Greenwich, London. Installation view, Fourth Plinth, Trafalgar Square, London, 2010

Frontispiece (p. 4): *Bling Painting* (detail), 2013. Emulsion and acrylic on twenty-seven Dutch wax printed cotton canvases, toys adorned with diamanté, acrylic on wall; 250 x 620 x 7 cm